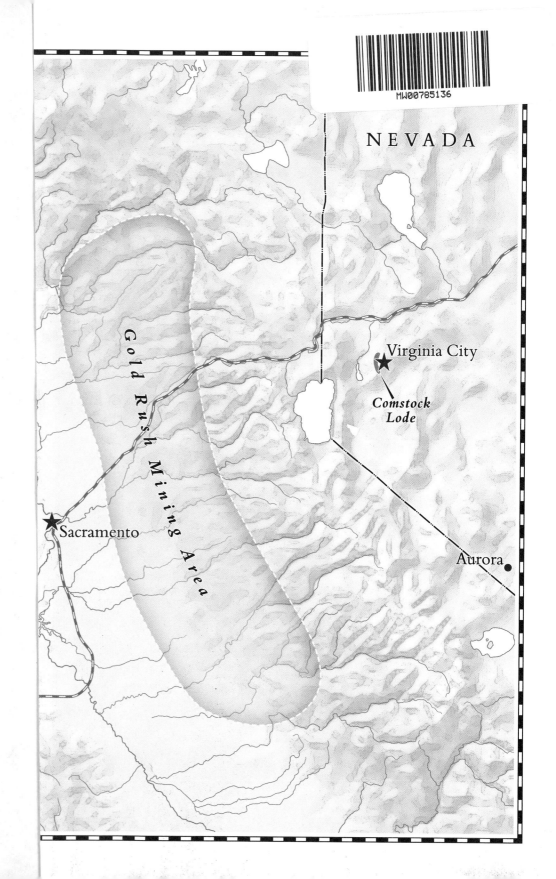

Trespassers

Golden G

Trespassers at the
Golden Gate

A True Account of Love,
Murder, and Madness in
Gilded-Age San Francisco

GARY KRIST

CROWN
NEW YORK

CROWN

An imprint of the Crown Publishing Group
A division of Penguin Random House LLC
1745 Broadway
New York, NY 10019
crownpublishing.com
penguinrandomhouse.com

Library of Congress Cataloging-in-Publication Data
Names: Krist, Gary, author.
Title: Trespassers at the Golden Gate: a true account of love, murder, and madness in Gilded-Age San Francisco / Gary Krist.
Identifiers: LCCN 2024022795 (print) | LCCN 2024022796 (ebook) |
    ISBN 9780593444214 (hardcover) | ISBN 9780593444221 (ebook)
Subjects: LCSH: Fair, Laura D., 1837-1919. | Crittenden, Alexander Parker, 1816-1870. |
    Murder—California—San Francisco—History—19th century. | San Francisco (Calif.)—
    History—19th century. | San Francisco (Calif.)—Social conditions—19th century.
Classification: LCC F869.S357 K743 2025 (print) | LCC F869.S357 (ebook) |
    DDC 979.461—dc23/eng/20240610
LC record available at https://lccn.loc.gov/2024022795
LC ebook record available at https://lccn.loc.gov/2024022796

Hardcover ISBN 978-0-593-44421-4
Ebook ISBN 978-0-593-44422-1

Printed in the United States of America on acid-free paper

Editor: Paul Whitlatch | Editorial assistant: Katie Berry | Production editor: Abby Oladipo |
Text designer: Aubrey Khan | Production managers: Philip Leung and Heather Williamson |
Copy editor: Rachelle Mandik | Proofreaders: Chuck Thompson and Robin Slutzky |
Indexer: Jane Farnol | Publicist: Dyana Messina | Marketer: Chantelle Walker

Ornate architectural detail on pages 1, 61, 133, and 193: Shutterstock.com/MaKars

9 8 7 6 5 4 3 2 1

First Edition

The authorized representative in the EU for product safety and compliance is
Penguin Random House Ireland, Morrison Chambers, 32 Nassau Street,
Dublin D02 YH68, Ireland, https://eu-contact.penguin.ie.

For Anna Chang-Yi

Of all the marvelous phases of the history of the Present, the growth of San Francisco is the one which will most tax the belief of the Future . . . Its parallel was never known, and shall never be beheld again.

—Bayard Taylor
El Dorado; or Adventures in the Path of Empire
1850

Contents

Part Two

Love and War

Part Three

Manufacturing Respectability

Part Four

A Woman in Name Only

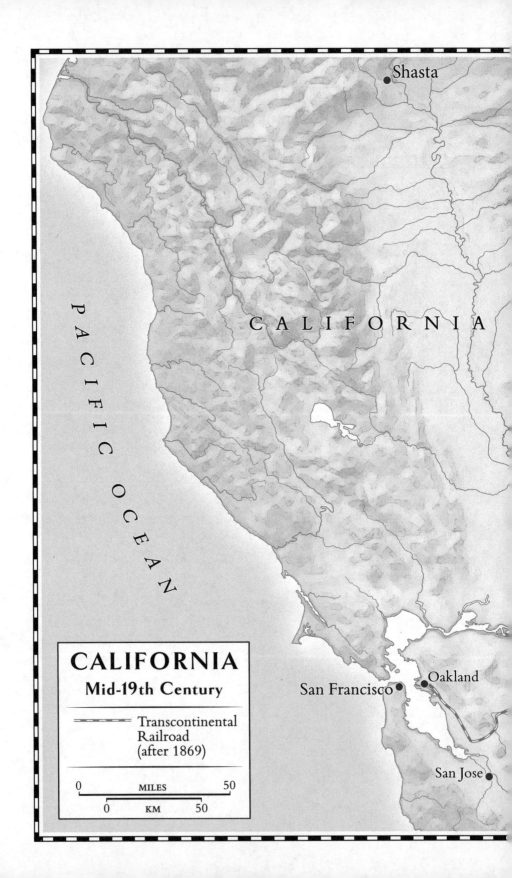

Shasta

CALIFORNIA

PACIFIC OCEAN

CALIFORNIA
Mid-19th Century

┅┅┅ Transcontinental
Railroad
(after 1869)

0   MILES   50

0   KM   50

San Francisco

Oakland

San Jose

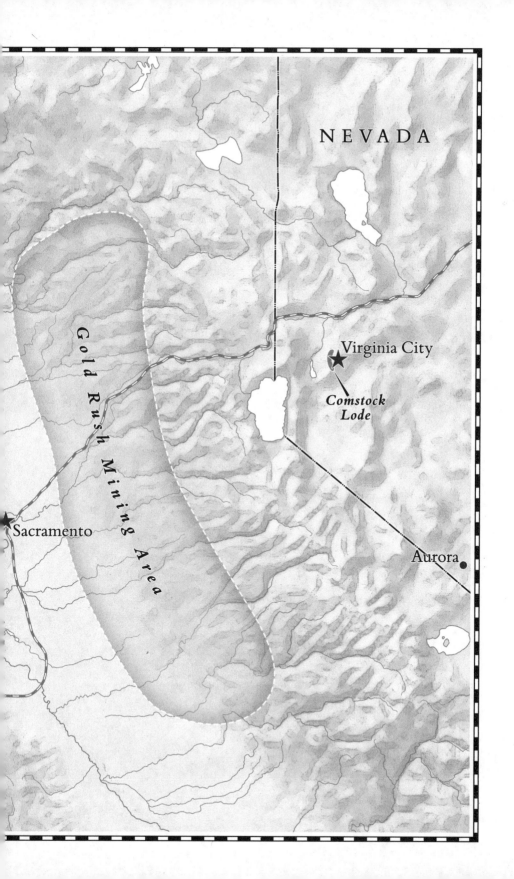

Author's Note

Trespassers at the Golden Gate is a work of nonfiction, adhering strictly to the historical record and incorporating no invented dialogue or other undocumented re-creations. Unless otherwise attributed, anything between quotation marks is either actual dialogue (as reported by a witness or in a newspaper) or else a citation from a court transcript, letter, memoir, or other document, as cited in the endnotes. Even in the subjectively narrated prologue, all interior thoughts and emotions are as reported in the individual's court testimony. In some quotations, I have, for clarity's sake, slightly edited the original spelling, syntax, word order, or punctuation. In the case of outdated and potentially offensive terms (for example, "prostitute"), I have tried to use more contemporary terms (like "sex worker"), except in direct quotations or when those terms would have seemed jarringly anachronistic or inconsistent with the narrative context.

Prologue

An Atrocious Act

(1870)

"I kiss no other."

Those were the words he'd said to her. They were a pledge—a solemn prom-ise he'd made just before going off to the ferry to meet that other woman. "I am sorry to see you doubt me that much," he'd said. "Have I not assured you that you are my only wife, and I kiss no other?"

That was at half past four—just a little over an hour ago. He could not have changed his mind in an hour.

"You know why I go," he'd said. "You have no reason to cry at all."

No reason? That other woman, Clara—Mrs. Crittenden in name, though in no other way—was returning to San Francisco, and he was going to meet her. Clara had been gone for almost six months; he had sent her away last spring, to live with her family in Virginia. Their separation was supposed to be per-manent, but now—against his wishes, he said—Clara was returning. But Mr. Crittenden insisted that there was no reason for worry, that it was she, Laura, who was his true wife in the eyes of God, if not yet in the eyes of the world. This was what he'd been telling her for seven years now—that he did not love his wife, that as soon as he could make enough money to pay his debts and leave Clara and the children reasonably secure, he would divorce her. He would make Laura the next Mrs. Crittenden, the only real Mrs. Crittenden.

And yet now Clara was coming back, and he was going on the ferry to meet her.

Laura had not slept in days. She had been ill. She had been crying. Her head had been aching all week.

"You know why I go; I go simply for the sake of the feelings of my children."

His children, her adversaries. They complicated the situation, as always. But Laura had a child too—a ten-year-old daughter, Lillian, whose unfortunate father had died when she was still an infant. Didn't Lillian, too, deserve security? Her prospects would be ruined unless Mr. Crittenden kept his promise to give her a respectable home. How many times over the past seven years had Laura reminded him of this?

But he was still going to meet that woman. He intended to take the ferry over to Oakland and rendezvous with Clara and the youngest Crittenden daughter on the wharf, where they would be waiting after disembarking from the Overland train. He would bring them back on the ferry to San Francisco, escort them in a cab to the Crittenden home on Ellis Street, and eat supper with them and the rest of the family—all for the sake of appearances. But then, that very night, he would return to Laura, to the only real wife he had on earth.

"I kiss no other."

He said he had to leave. Resigned now to his going, Laura told him that she would walk to the little German restaurant across the street for an early dinner and then wait for him to return. "You will be cheerful, and happy, and contented till I come back tonight, will you?" he asked. "Yes," she said, "I will try to be well and cheerful till you come." With that, he accompanied her down the lodging-house stairs and out onto Kearny Street. He bade her goodbye, and then she walked into the restaurant, watching him through the windows until he had turned away and found a cab to the ferry dock.

After a few moments, she left the restaurant. "I wanted to see how he met her," she would later explain. "I felt perfectly sure he would meet her without kissing her."

She followed him in a cab to the wharf. After watching him board the ferryboat El Capitan—*a large sidewheel steamer built expressly to meet the Central Pacific Railroad's new transcontinental trains—she embarked as well. She found a place at the back of the cabin where she could remain out of sight as they crossed the windy San Francisco Bay. Once the ferry arrived at the Oak-land wharf, she would quietly move to the forward upper deck. From that perch, she could look down at the area where passengers from the transcontinental train would be waiting to board the ferry for the ride back to San Francisco. She would be able to observe the Crittendens' reunion for herself.*

Shortly after five-thirty El Capitan *pulled up at the Oakland wharf. Laura hurried to her chosen spot and watched Mr. Crittenden as he disembarked with the other passengers from San Francisco. But somehow—amid the overwhelm-ing chaos of people getting off and people getting on, of fractious porters pushing handcarts full of steamer trunks and carpetbags, of train passengers and ferry riders shouting eager greetings to each other across the teeming quay—she lost sight of him. He was gone, vanished into that sea of bowlers and bonnets and parasols below her. Panicking, she hurried down to the lower deck, pushing through the crowds on the gangway. She searched for his familiar form, but it was no use. There were too many people. She couldn't find him. Frantic, she raced up and down the congested wharf until she lost track of time. A strange man suddenly grabbed her arm and brought her back to herself. The horn of the ferry was sounding. She had wandered far from the embarkation point, and now the ferry was leaving.*

She would later insist that she remembered little of what happened from that moment on. Somehow, she found herself aboard El Capitan *again, though she was uncertain how she got there. But as the ferry was pulling away from its berth, she heard a distinctive voice over the general murmur of the crowd. It was Clara Crittenden's voice, saying, "Hah, boys!" Laura thought it "a peculiar voice. It was disagreeable, the sound of it." She looked over to where the voice had come from. "I saw her and him together."*

Laura felt something cold and wet under her fingers. "I know I must have put my hand on some glass . . . I reached my hand out and I touched some-thing cold." She recalled thinking that she must have forgotten to put her gloves on.

The cold beneath her fingertips—was it glass or was it metal? There was a pistol in her purse. It was in her hands now. A confused idea came to her mind.

She saw herself in a large crowd, as in a church, and someone like a minister was up above the crowd. "I could not see the bodies at all, but just the heads . . . it seemed like a sea of them, and in the midst of that sea of heads was this man gesticulating."

These were the last details she claimed to remember—the man gesticulating, that woman's voice.

Seven years. "I kiss no other."

The next thing Laura was aware of—much, much later—was the cold of iron bars beneath her fingertips. Cold like the glass of the ferry window. Like the pistol in her purse. It was then she remembered: That man had been the ruin of Laura and her daughter. And now she was in a prison cell, and Mr. Crittenden was dead.

THE PEOPLE OF THE STATE OF CALIFORNIA

V. LAURA D. FAIR

DAY ONE

Monday, March 27, 1871

At ten minutes to ten o'clock, the Bailiff of the Court entered the door and flung wide both its leaves. A figure entered, dressed in black and thickly veiled, leaning upon the arm of Dr. Trask. It was Mrs. Fair, and behind her walked her mother and little daughter. When she had advanced a few paces into the room she threw back her upper veil, leaving over her face only a thin fall of black tulle, through which her features were plainly visible . . . Mrs. Fair has doubtless been a handsome woman, though anxiety and long sickness have left their indelible marks upon her face . . .

—*San Francisco Chronicle*

T HE TRIAL OF LAURA D. Fair for the murder of Alexander Parker Crittenden began on a brisk, cloudless spring morning at California's imposing Fifteenth District courtroom in San Francisco, the Honorable S. H. Dwinelle presiding. Because of the intense amount of publicity surrounding the case, Judge Dwinelle had insisted that three policemen be stationed at the entrance to the spectators' enclosure to prevent members of the public from entering. Only reporters, attorneys, and those directly involved in each day's hearing would be allowed to witness the proceedings. Always a stickler for decorum in his courtroom, Judge Dwinelle was determined to keep this trial as uneventful and by-the-book as possible.

The judge's hopes, however, were doomed from the start. Almost six months had passed since the fatal pistol shot was fired on the *El*

Capitan ferry, and the city's fascination with the murder had shown no signs of abating. During that time, the Fair-Crittenden case had dominated virtually all other subjects of conversation. Few could resist the lurid tale of the twice-divorced, twice-widowed young woman who had gunned down her longtime paramour—one of the most prominent figures of the city's legal community—right in front of the wife he refused to abandon for her. And now that the trial was finally starting, after weeks of legal maneuvers and pretrial motions, the public's obsession with the case was as consuming as ever. Far more people wanted to watch the spectacle than any California courtroom could hold. Three policemen at a doorway would prove no serious obstacle to those who really wanted to get in.

The man principally responsible for seeing that justice was done in this case was District Attorney Henry H. Byrne. A native of New York City, Byrne—like Judge Dwinelle and so many of the other principals involved in the case—had come to San Francisco some twenty years earlier, penniless and without reputation but eager to succeed in the wild new territory opened up by the discovery of gold. Like his colleagues, he had failed to attain fabulous wealth as a miner but instead had claimed a place for himself in the infrastructure of urban civilization that rapidly coalesced in Gold Rush San Francisco. Two years after his arrival, the neophyte lawyer had already risen to become the city's district attorney. Now nearing fifty, he was serving his fourth term in the office. And while he was physically unprepossessing—one contemporary remarked upon his short stature, stiff carriage, and "sharp, harsh, and screeching" voice—he compensated for these deficits with exalted eloquence. "Harry" Byrne, as he was usually called, was famous for peppering his courtroom speeches with high-toned literary allusions and, when necessary, a scathing invective that could wound both friend and foe alike.

The case he was about to argue would be the most important of Byrne's career so far, and he had good reason to be optimistic about its outcome—not least because he was satisfied with his jury. During the day and a half of voir-dire examinations to assemble the panel, nearly every potential juror had admitted that the defendant was probably guilty; the twelve men who had survived defense challenges were those who'd merely expressed a willingness to be persuaded otherwise by the evidence. The one member of the jury pool who'd claimed sympathy for the defendant and disdain for the victim ("I think any man who acts that way ought to be shot," he admitted) had been quietly excused.

So it was a sympathetic audience that Byrne approached on the afternoon of the prosecutor's opening statement. As expected, the courtroom was full to the rafters—all seats occupied, and with standing spectators jammed into every space available. It was all the three policemen could do to keep the aisles clear for the reporters and observing lawyers to come and go.

"Gentlemen of the jury," the DA began, one hand as ever in his waistcoat pocket in a classic lawyerly pose. "The defendant at the bar, Laura D. Fair, is charged with the commission of the crime of willful murder, alleged to have been committed on the third day of November last, on board a steamer called *El Capitan* . . ."

For this opening statement, Byrne chose to lay out the facts of the case as simply and straightforwardly as possible. No one, after all, doubted that it was Laura Fair who had fired the shot that killed A. P. Crittenden. The question was whether it was murder in the first degree, which required a demonstration of malice aforethought. So Byrne began by stating exactly how the prosecution would establish the necessary elements of premeditation and motive. Premeditation was self-evident: Mrs. Fair had made threats of violence several times in the past; she had acquired the murder weapon three days before the shooting; and she had thought to take a black veil aboard the ferry in order to hide her identity. There could be no doubt: "The defendant . . . took passage on that boat for the purpose of accomplishing what she did so successfully—the shooting of Mr. Crittenden."

As for motive, it was equally obvious: Crittenden had called his wife and family back to San Francisco in order to reconcile with them and end the seven-year affair with his mistress. Naturally, Laura Fair sought to avenge this rejection—by destroying the man she could not have for herself, in front of the woman who had kept him from her.

During the DA's recitation of these points, the defendant, looking pale and fatigued, sat in a rocking chair between her lawyers at the defense table, listening in grave silence. "Her expression is that of great sadness, weariness, and passive suffering," one newsman reported. Such a face, he felt, would likely be an aid to the defense in this case. What's more, Mrs. Fair's bright golden hair—worn today tied back in short curls—would also have a softening effect on the jury's sympathies, as would her blue eyes, well formed eyebrows, and appealing features.

But Harry Byrne, while fully aware of the defendant's potential to elicit an all-male jury's pity, was counting on there being no such effect with this particular group. These were practical businessmen who would understand the importance of the city's image in the mind of the general public. "That, gentlemen," the DA concluded, after a re-markably brief opening statement, "is substantially the case on the part of the people . . . So far as the definition of murder in the statute can fix it, this was a willful, deliberate murder, and in the name of the law we pronounce her guilty thereof, and ask at your hands a verdict of guilty." It was thus a straightforward case, open and shut—or that at least was what DA Byrne hoped for.

In truth, there was nothing straightforward about the trial that would unfold in that courtroom over the next four weeks. For this would not play out like the typical local murder case. The defendant was a woman, for one thing, and while female murderers were not unknown in Victorian-era California, Fair's gender was still enough of a novelty to cause a sensation on that score alone. But there were other, more fundamental, issues involved. At a time when reputable women were expected never to step beyond the private realm of home and family, Laura Fair had made a lifetime practice of invading the public sphere—as an actress, as a successful businessperson and investor, and as the unapologetic mistress of a prominent (and married) man. This brazen murderess, in other words, had posed a grave threat to the social order even before she ever pulled a trigger. Would a jury of respectable men feel sympathy for a woman like that?

Ultimately, the trial of Laura Fair would prove to be deeply controversial, provoking bitter debate nationwide and challenging long-held beliefs of a populace still searching for moral consensus after the shattering disruption of civil war. For many, even for those just looking on from the sidelines, the ethical stakes could hardly have been higher. By calling into question fundamental assumptions about the sanctity of the family, the value of reputation, and the range of acceptable expressions of femininity, the case would become profoundly divisive; it would cause rifts and arguments between husbands and wives, provide endless fodder for newspaper editorialists, and inspire paroxysms of indignation among sermonizing clergymen. Even such prominent national figures as Mark Twain, Horace Greeley, and Susan B. Anthony would be drawn into its orbit.

But while the spectacle of the trial would make front-page headlines from coast to coast, its outcome would be of particular importance to the city in which it unfolded—San Francisco, a still-adolescent metropolis in the early 1870s, hoping to shed its Gold Rush–era reputation as a raucous and untamed frontier town. For a city eagerly trying to establish its name as a mature, orderly, and law-abiding place, the kind of violence and depravity exemplified by Laura Fair's crime demanded the severest punishment. Only a death sentence would serve as a clear demonstration to the world (particularly to the East Coast capitalists whose investments the city needed in order to grow) that the rule of law had finally come to the former Wild West.

So for District Attorney Byrne and many of the other community elites of San Francisco, there could be only one acceptable outcome to what he called "the most important case that has been tried upon the Pacific coast"—a simple and straightforward verdict of guilty on the charge of murder in the first degree. But for those who knew of the events that had preceded the crime on the *El Capitan* ferry that November night, the matter of Laura Fair's guilt or innocence would be significantly more complex.

Part One

Converging Paths

(1816–1861)

Men had changed the whole face of nature. This inaccessible place
had been brought near to civilization . . . Yes, the Americans are a
great people! Great as discoverers, great as inventors—a moving, restless, unquiet people! A people whose special vocation it is to explore
and settle wildernesses, to lay out great cities and drive stakes where
mortal feet never had trod and never would tread again! A land-
robbing people. A Christian people who pave the way for the Gospel
and morality with whiskey, revolvers, Bowie knives, cards, and other
queer and inappropriate things. A people who carry vice to extremes
in order to display the beauties of virtue. An American scoundrel is
the greatest ruffian of the world.

—ALEXANDER PARKER CRITTENDEN,
Letter to his wife, Clara, April 8, 1851

1

A Restless Man

FEW MEMBERS OF THE LOCAL GENTRY in early nineteenth-century Kentucky would have denied that the Crittendens of Woodford County were one of the most distinguished and reputable families in the Bluegrass State. The family patriarch—John Crittenden, a major under George Washington during the American Revolution—had first come to Kentucky on a surveying expedition led by George Rogers Clark. Liking what he saw, he returned after the war to settle and start a family near Versailles, on a 2,814-acre land grant awarded him for his faithful service in the Continental Army. True, some skeptics might have questioned the Crittenden clan's extravagant genealogical claims tracing the family's roots back to William the Conqueror, Edward I of England, and a handful of Scottish kings. But certainly the more recent exemplars of the lineage were accomplished enough, the most prominent being John Sr.'s eldest son, John Jordon Crittenden, a lawyer who would go on to become governor of Kentucky, U.S. attorney general, and to serve terms in both houses of Congress. He would even be talked about as a potential candidate for president of the United States.

And yet there was something reckless about the Crittendens, something spendthrift and extravagant, at least about the Lexington-based branch into which Alexander Parker Crittenden was born on January 4, 1816. His father, Thomas T. Crittenden (younger brother of the more famous John J.), was a notable lawyer and politician in his own right, ultimately attaining the position of Kentucky's secretary of state. But he had a weakness for financial speculation, and when he died in 1832, at the age of forty-four, he left his widow and five surviving children with liabilities totaling some $30,000 to $40,000 (a breathtaking sum at the time). Young Parker, as the eldest son was called then, thus grew up in a state of genteel poverty, the family's pretensions to high living supported mainly by precarious amounts of debt. It was a condition that A. P. Crittenden would find himself in for much of the rest of his life.

As a boy, Parker led a rather nomadic life, cobbling together an education at various boarding schools in Ohio, Alabama, and Pennsylvania. He also carried on the family tradition of politics, though he showed early signs of a brash independence. Despite coming from a long line of Whigs, he campaigned in 1828 for Andrew Jackson, the quintessential Southern Democrat, who returned the favor by securing the precocious red-headed teenager a place at West Point a few years later. But even at the military academy, Crittenden showed more spirit than was good for him. Caught up in some rebellious undergraduate prank, he and several of his cohort were arrested and expelled. When even his well-connected uncle John J.—a U.S. senator at the time—couldn't get him reinstated, Parker took matters into his own hands. He went to see the president he had helped elect and pled his case. According to family lore, President Jackson listened to him politely and decided, "You are the kind of material we want in the army. You go back to West Point . . . There will be an order there to readmit you."

Crittenden managed to complete his military training without further incident, but army life proved to be incompatible with his independent nature. He resigned his commission as a second lieutenant less than three months after graduation in 1836, then worked briefly as an assistant railroad engineer before deciding to pursue the law. Now in his early twenties, he also decided that it was time to start looking for a wife. One of his close friends from West Point, Marlborough Churchill, wrote to him in January 1837 about a young niece of his named Clara Jones, Kentucky-born but now living with her parents and nine siblings in Charleston, Virginia. "I have spoken of you to her, [and] have sounded your praises so effectually . . . that she is dying of anxiety to see you, your red head . . . notwithstanding." Crittenden lost no time in traveling from Lexington to Charleston for a visit, and was instantly taken with the handsome, intelligent, and exuberantly talkative sixteen-year-old. By March he was sending her unabashed love letters. "Imagine all the affection you have ever felt for Father, Mother & relatives concentrated into one absorbing passion," he wrote, "and you would have some faint conception of the fervor of my attachment . . . You have so completely taken possession of my mind and feelings as to exclude all other objects."

Very soon he was pushing for an engagement, though Clara was hesitant at first. She claimed to be unsure whether she really loved him, or if her feelings might simply be esteem and respect. According to her uncle Marlborough, she also had misgivings about her suitor's rather unprepossessing looks (apparently Parker's red hair was an issue after all). But Crittenden was persistent. In his frequent letters to her, he spoke about his boredom with the social life of Kentucky and his intention to one day find someplace else where he could put down roots and become a rich and prominent man. Her "poor lovesick swain" also tried to amuse her with frequent jokes ("Knowing you are fond of mint juleps, I drank several for us"). And in an attempt to make her jealous, he would even drop hints that he was flirting with a certain attractive cousin of his—though he'd then hastily reassure her that "he never has and never will worship any but his own sweet Clara." Eventually the target of all of this playful wooing allowed herself to be won over. And so, despite the fact that Crittenden was still hopelessly far from paying off his late father's debts, the two got married in Virginia on April 24, 1838.

Not long after the wedding, Crittenden took leave of his new wife to scope out prospects in the newly independent republic of Texas. Having broken away from Mexico just two years earlier, this still-remote place was actively trying to attract population by offering land grants to all comers, and it was therefore being flooded by eager immigrants from all over the United States and Europe (especially Germany). For someone like Crittenden, Texas seemed to offer an ideal opportunity to get his career on track and start paying off his debts. "I want to become a great statesman, a great Financier," he confessed to a friend at this time. And so he decided to study law with his eldest sister's husband, Tod Robinson, who had moved to the Galveston area sometime before. By late 1839, Crittenden had already passed the Texas bar and was ready to summon his wife and brand-new daughter to join him there. Clara's mother vehemently opposed the young family's removal to such a rough and unformed place—"where there is neither law nor gospel"—and Clara herself likely had some trepidation, given the daily possibility of havoc from displaced Mexicans who still regarded the territory as theirs. But she dutifully followed her new husband south. The Crittendens settled in the town of Brazoria, just south of Houston, where A.P., as he was now known, attempted to establish himself as a lawyer. Meanwhile, Clara took on the task of making a home for what would eventually be fourteen children (though only eight would survive to adulthood).

It was not an easy life. Practicing law in the rugged new republic proved anything but lucrative, even for someone as well connected as John J. Crittenden's nephew. Despite getting help from some old family friends like Kentucky ex-congressman James Love, who tried to procure for him a diplomatic post in Austin, Crittenden struggled to support his rapidly growing family. "Money, you may recollect, was rather scarce when you left [here]," he wrote in late 1840 to his friend

Albert Sidney Johnston (later an important Confederate Army general) after the latter had moved away from Texas. "It is now more so. Business has not recommenced, nor will it for a year or two." Even so, the young lawyer tried to remain optimistic, playing chess by mail with Johnston and sending him amusing accounts of the vagaries of Texas politics.

The Crittendens went on in this manner for almost ten years. A.P. and Clara had their share of marital difficulties—by his own admission, he could be surly and impatient with her, while she was not above complaining ceaselessly about the discomforts of their frugal and spartan life on the prairie. Even so, the discord doesn't seem to have harmed their ability to produce offspring.

But then, early in 1849, news of the California gold strike finally reached Texas (by now a part of the United States). This was a time when many Americans were already on the move, emigrating west into the vast new territories just recently annexed to the United States after the Mexican War and the signing of the Oregon Treaty with England. The discovery of gold in the Sierra Nevada foothills, however, quickly turned that steady stream into a surging tidal wave, luring characters of all kinds to California with the promise of adventure and easy riches in the goldfields. These opportunists quickly became known as "forty-niners," after the year in which so many of them headed west.

Here was an opportunity that Crittenden simply could not pass up. Certain that this was the way to finally erase his numerous debts, A.P. gave up his languishing law practice and joined the tide of hopeful trailblazers. Like many of them, he knew he would be parted from family and friends for months or even years, but he promised to send for Clara and the children as soon as he was established. Along with Clara's brother Alexander Jones—a newly minted doctor who also had some debts to pay—he signed on with a group of several hundred emigrants making the journey to California by wagon via the southern route through Mexico. In early April, therefore, A.P. and Clara parted, unsure when—or if, given the dangers of the trip—they would ever meet again.

"Keep up your spirits, old lady," A.P. wrote her in his first letter from the road, "and do your duty, as I shall do mine. This absence is a painful one, but it is necessary and may prove a benefit to us in more ways than one." Alluding to their recent difficulties, he tried to make amends: "Everything like unkindness between us, Clara, is entirely forgotten by me, and I look for the same charity at your hands . . . I assure you that at no point since we first met have I felt as ardent and true love for you as I do now . . ." Then he closed the letter with a promise: "We shall meet again, Clara. Have no fear of that . . . Be cheerful and contented. God bless you."

Over the next six months, he wrote Clara from the trail whenever he could, always uncertain whether his letters would ever reach her. Official mail service was nonexistent in this thinly populated country, which was still uncrossed by road or rail. Letters usually had to be entrusted to the proprietor of some frontier outpost, who would then relay it (along with postage) to the next traveler passing in the other direction, who in turn might drop it at an actual post office on his route. Considering the obstacles to successful delivery—poor weather, dangerous terrain, lazy or unscrupulous go-betweens, bandit raids, and just plain bad luck—it was a marvel that any missives at all reached their destination. (One letter Crittenden wrote from Tucson took months to reach Clara, traveling first by wagon south to Puerto de Guaymas on the Gulf of California and then, according to its multitude of postmarks, by ship to San Blas, onward by land to Mexico City and Vera Cruz on the Gulf of Mexico, by ship again to New Orleans, and from there overland to Brazoria, where Clara had to pay various postages due to receive it.)

Crittenden's own journey was somewhat less circuitous, but it would still be months and months before he reached California. Even getting across southern Texas involved weeks of arduous travel: "The heat has been trying," he wrote from Presidio del Norte, on the Texas-Mexico border, "and we have suffered at times for want of water, having twice been obliged to travel 60 miles without it." One man they were traveling with was killed by the accidental discharge of his own pistol, and one of their horses was bitten by a rattlesnake (though the horse survived). Other migrants they met on the trail, however, had worse luck. One group had lost eight members to cholera, while two men traveling by themselves had run out of provisions and been forced to eat their mules.

Even so, Crittenden tried to maintain a spirit of high optimism. Some of the scenery he was passing through seemed surprisingly familiar, recalling the Kentucky of his youth. He wrote to Clara that she would be delighted by the terrain: "It would remind you of old times and old scenes. A rolling country of mixed woodland and prairie— rocky hills and clean streams running over gravel and occasionally taking a plunge down the rocks."

But other parts were distinctly more exotic. "We are now in the region of strange vegetation," he wrote several months later. "The hills here are covered with tall, fluted, column-like cactus and the still taller cactus gigantias [sic] with its four or five arms. And the flowers! If you could only see the gorgeous crown of crimson wax-like flowers that covers one species of cactus here."

Knowing that Clara would be somewhat melancholy taking care of the household in his absence, he tried to cheer her up with light-hearted accounts of his attempts at cooking over a campfire, and with other droll observations and anecdotes from the road. "We traveled for a day or two with some New York folks," he wrote Clara early in the trip, "and were not a little amused at their strange language, notions, and ways." But even the strangeness of New Yorkers paled—at least in the eyes of a nineteenth-century white southerner—in comparison with some of the Native peoples he met along the way. "The Comanches are the beauties," he told his wife. "Their dress is peculiar and somewhat immodest. Some were naked down to the waist and others naked up to the thigh. They were decked off in every possible manner with beads, feathers, gold, and silver ornaments."

But at times, in quiet moments on the trail, Crittenden would grow reflective and morose, looking back on the ten years of their marriage with many regrets: "The greatest source of misery to me—the cause of unceasing annoyance—has been the want of means to render you all comfortable . . . If I'd been wealthy—or at least unembarrassed [that is, not deeply in debt]—I should have been a very different character. Could I have done for you all what I desired to, I should, I am sure, have been as kind and gentle as I have been at times the reverse." Thus: California. If A.P. could make a quick fortune in the gold country, he would pay off his debts, build up some savings, and reunite with Clara for another, better start to their lives together. "It would be my pride to surround you all with ease, comfort, and luxury," he told her. The troubles of the past would then be nothing to them.

The low point of the long journey came in July, while crossing Mexico en route to the Arizona Territory. Crittenden had been walking for much of the way, his original mount having proved too troublesome to ride. "There was no alternative for me but to trudge on—which I did day after day under the burning sun, frequently in a cloud of dust and suffering from thirst." When they reached Chihuahua, moreover, they heard rumors that the tales of abundant gold in California had been much exaggerated, and that many early migrants were already returning in frustration. "But no [such] report can now stop me," he wrote Clara. "I must see for myself. I must go on, if it be only to return." Either way—gold or no gold—he was now disgusted with the whole endeavor. "Whether I remain there and make a fortune or return sooner than I want, my opinion will still be the same: I have played the fool in this adventure. I should have stayed at home. No money will ever pay me for a year's absence from you all."

And the remainder of the journey was no easier. Just after leaving Chihuahua, Clara's brother Alex had gotten into an argument with one of their fellow travelers, who ended up attacking him with a Bowie knife. In the "desperate fight" that ensued, Alex was injured but managed to kill his adversary. All witnesses swore that Alex had acted in self-defense, and his knife wound was not life-threatening. But still he had to be taken back to Chihuahua, where a surgeon decided that he should not travel for at least two weeks. A.P., running out of money and endurance, was forced to go on without him, leaving his brother-in-law in the care of friends until his wound healed.

Despite this setback and further trouble along the route—including encounters with unfriendly Indians, brutal heat, and a turbulent crossing of the Colorado River that swept one of his travel companions away, never to be seen again—Crittenden stumbled into the tiny California town called Pueblo de los Angeles in early October, feeling almost triumphant. "I am in most excellent health—never was in better health in my life and have fattened until you would hardly know me," he reported back to Clara after recovering from the journey. Best of all, he was brimming with optimism again: "I am satisfied with the prospect here fully. Gold is as abundant as was reported—money as plentiful as dirt. Everything promising. I tell you, old woman, I shall make a fortune here."

These high hopes notwithstanding, Crittenden was out of money, and he was forced to set out on the last leg of his journey—some four hundred miles to San Francisco—on foot. But on the road a few miles north of Los Angeles, he encountered an old West Point friend named Coutts, who lived nearby. Coutts took pity on his penniless friend, brought him home, and lent him enough money to put him back on his feet. Staying with Coutts in Los Angeles—still little more than a sleepy, dust-blown settlement of some 1,500 souls—also gave Crittenden an idea: California's very first general election was coming up in November, in anticipation of the region's becoming an official state of the union in 1850. Crittenden reckoned that winning a seat in the new state legislature might be an easy way to ensure that he arrived in bustling San Francisco—"where a person with no claim to attention was liable to be utterly lost and unnoticed"—as a dignitary of some importance. As he later explained it to Clara: "The instant I heard [about the election], I announced myself a candidate for the Assembly. It required no time or reflection to show me that to fail was nothing, [but] to succeed was to place myself in a position where I could be known."

Crittenden quickly got his name onto the ballot and, after a few short weeks of campaigning, managed to clinch the seat. This achievement was perhaps not as remarkable as it may seem, given the paucity of viable candidates, and the fact that Crittenden, while a rank newcomer to the territory, had at least some legal credentials to his name. The day of the vote, moreover, was derailed by torrential rain, depressing turnout at the polls, so it took him a mere 258 votes to win. Be that as it may, as one of two newly elected California assemblymen for the District of Los Angeles, he would be able to finish his delayed journey north in high style and at government expense.

In late November, Crittenden boarded a seventy-five-passenger schooner out of San Pedro, bound for San Francisco Bay. After the rigors of his recent overland trek, the quick sea journey up the coast must have seemed downright tame. But nothing he'd encountered in his previous travels could have prepared him for what he saw as he passed through the Golden Gate: On December 6, 1849, from the deck of the crowded schooner, Alexander Parker Crittenden got his first glimpse of the remarkable phenomenon of San Francisco at the height of the Gold Rush.

2

A Town of Mud
and Gold

THE CITY THAT CONFRONTED THE thirty-four-year-old
Crittenden on that December day was about as raw and anarchic
as a settlement of its size could be. This was hardly surprising, given that
the town of some twenty-five thousand souls—many of them just stopping en route to the mining districts—had been a place of any consequence for only a few years. Even as recently as early 1848, just before
the fateful discovery of gold nearby, it was a hamlet consisting of some
850 merchants and tradesmen, most of them living in tents or crudely
constructed shanties. The twenty months of explosive growth that followed had resulted in, as one of its early residents put it, "an odd place:
unlike any other place in creation . . . for it [was] not created in the
ordinary way, but hatched like chickens by artificial heat."

True, Spain had officially established a mission here as far back as
1776, creating a permanent settlement on land that assorted communities of Ohlone people had already been occupying for thousands of
years. In this temperate and bountiful place—a mix of hilly grasslands,
scattered woodlands, sand dunes, and abundant bulrush marshes—the
hunting and gathering Ohlone had thrived, eventually spreading over
the entire coastal region around San Francisco Bay. But despite this
prime location on the shores of the finest harbor on the coast, Spain

did little to exploit the area's advantages. The Spanish settlement here, consisting of the Mission of San Francisco of Assisi (aka Mission Dolores) and a small military garrison (the Presidio), had remained a sparsely populated outpost for many decades, serving mainly as a place-holder to keep Russia and Britain from extending their influence into Spain's New World empire. The local population of Presidio soldiers, along with the Franciscan friars and the Native populations they were "civilizing" (that is, enslaving and indoctrinating), were forbidden from trading with outsiders, and so the tiny settlement remained isolated and undeveloped. When the British explorer George Vancouver visited in November 1792, he was keenly disappointed: "Instead of finding a country tolerably well inhabited and far advanced in cultivation," Vancouver wrote, "there is not an object to indicate the most remote connection with any European or other civilized nation." So neglected was the outpost by its distant overseers in Mexico City that when one visiting ship gave a cannon salute on entering the bay, a representative of the poorly supplied Presidio had to row out in a borrowed boat and beg for enough gunpowder to return the courtesy.

After the end of the Mexican Revolution of 1820, when Alta California came under the flag of an independent Mexico, the region opened up somewhat more to the outside world. Mission Dolores, like the other California missions, was secularized; its vast properties were confiscated from the Franciscans (who had remained loyal to Spain during the revolution) and granted to a small number of so-called rancheros, private individuals who raised livestock and were allowed to trade leather, tallow, and wool with whatever ships ventured into these remote waters. But even under Mexican rule, the place remained largely underdeveloped. Traders from Britain, Russia, France, and the United States frequently expressed regret that its fertile lands sat uncultivated and its abundant natural resources lay all but untapped. As New Englander Richard Henry Dana Jr. wrote in *Two Years Before the Mast*, his classic account of a voyage to California in the mid-1830s, "What a country this would be in the hands of an enterprising people!"

There were in fact plenty of "enterprising people" just waiting to pick up the slack left by the Mexican government and exploit this promising territory for themselves. The first to arrive was a British sea-man named William Richardson, who in 1822 jumped ship from a whaler and decided to put down roots. A decade later, he had already taken Mexican citizenship and set up a small trading establishment in a tent on Yerba Buena Cove, near what is now downtown. By that time, Mission Dolores had closed as a church and was being used as a tavern and dance hall, while the Presidio lay more or less abandoned, its gar-rison sent on to a livelier posting in Benicia, across the bay. Over the following years, Richardson was joined by a few other venturesome tradesmen and entrepreneurs, mainly from the United States and Brit-ain, thus establishing the town of Yerba Buena, a tiny Mexican pueblo with a distinctly Anglo—and decidedly mercantile—flavor.

But as one visiting English naval officer had predicted as far back as 1826, Mexico would either use California or lose it: "The country will fall into other hands," wrote Frederick William Beechey, after stopping at Yerba Buena Cove as part of a Pacific survey. "It is of too much importance to be permitted to remain long in its present neglected state." And within two decades, Beechey's prediction had come true. In 1846, the U.S. government, operating under the dubious pretense of a "manifest destiny" to extend its borders to the full breadth of the North American continent, decided to take by force the territory it had been coveting for decades. War was declared against Mexico, and although U.S. military forces faced some fierce resistance in Southern California, the area around Yerba Buena was taken with barely a fight. On July 6, 1846, Capt. John B. Montgomery of the USS *Portsmouth* sailed into San Francisco Bay and raised an American flag over the undefended town's customhouse—to the delight of many of its resi-dent Anglo-American merchants.

At the time of the American takeover, the town still consisted of only some fifty houses and a population of several hundred. But its days as a geographic afterthought were numbered. Thanks to the imminent discovery of gold at Sutter's Mill in the Sierra foothills to the east, Yerba Buena—soon to be renamed San Francisco, after the great bay it commanded—would become the focus of the world's attention virtually overnight. As the most likely place for passengers and cargo to transfer from seaworthy ships to the smaller craft that would take them to the vicinity of the goldfields, San Francisco was the natural entrepôt of the region—the supply center and jumping-off point for every would-be miner coming in to claim a share of the bonanza.

And come they did, in haste and in huge numbers. By the time Crittenden arrived in late 1849, the little village had exploded into an instant city—"grown out of the Mexican pueblo," as one observer re-marked, "like a mighty oak out of an acorn." Crittenden himself was amazed by what he saw. "I can hardly give you any description of the region which would carry any idea of it," he wrote Clara after his first few days in San Francisco. "From morning till late at night, [the streets] are thronged with crowds, and present the appearance of business 100 times too great for a place of its size. There is hardly a shelter for the head of the inhabitants, though the hills around are whitened with tents . . ."

Although there were a few adobes still standing from pre-rush times—including the old customhouse on the main plaza, topped by its decorative Spanish-tile roof—the vast majority of buildings stretch-ing back from the waterfront were crude canvas stalls and makeshift shacks hammered together from old packing crates, most of them sub-divided into tiny compartments to accommodate the hordes of new-comers. But even with these improvised shelters and the multitude of tents speckling the cattle-grazed hills around the center, there were still too few places to sleep, and some brave souls spent the night on the hard ground of the plaza wrapped in blankets.

Meanwhile, the whole frenzied town was littered with enormous amounts of detritus, as if a twenty-four-hour street market had set up shop in a garbage dump. The beach, which was patrolled by rats of legendary size, was strewn with bales of cloth and clothing, barrels of tar and brandy, impressive piles of empty whiskey bottles, and the hulking forms of partially assembled gold-washers, sluices, and other mining machines. And the streets were hardly more orderly. "Goods of every kind are piled up in the streets, exposed to the weather," Crittenden marveled in his letter to Clara, "and wherever a shelter of five feet square can be found, there is an establishment for selling something. The sidewalks are blocked up with stalls. You can buy anything you ever saw anywhere, provided you have money enough. It is a perfectly bewildering scene . . ."

Things became even more chaotic when it rained. Although some sidewalks and a few streets were planked, most thoroughfares remained pure dirt because of the acute shortage of lumber and the utter dearth of cobblestones or other hard paving rock—meaning that they quickly turned to mud whenever there was a downpour. Loads of chaparral limbs would be cut from the hills around town and thrown into the viscous mud, which sometimes could be two or even three feet deep, and people would have to balance on the branches to make it across intersections. Meanwhile, the stories were legion of horses drowning and coaches sinking to the windows in the muck of the new town's streets.

But perhaps the most remarkable aspect of this remarkable place was the variety of people milling through those ragged streets. According to one early arrival, the new city teemed with "Yankees of every possible variety, native Californians in sarapes and sombreros, Chileans, Sonorans, Kanakas from Hawaii, Chinese with long tails, Malays armed with their everlasting creeses [knives], and others in whose embrowned and bearded visages it was impossible to recognize any especial nationality." It was, in other words, one of the most diverse urban populations on the planet—a fact that was not lost on the newcomer from Texas. "It is the wonder of the age, a perfect Babel," Crittenden wrote of the city. "The port is crowded with shipping from every quarter of the world and people of all nations and tongues are streaming through the streets of the city in a tumultuous and never-ceasing tide." Only gender seemed to be an exception to this general abundance of diversity: Very few women besides those engaged in prostitution came to San Francisco in these very early years.

In such a dynamic and chaotic environment, where virtually everyone was a transient new arrival from parts unknown, individuals could easily remake themselves as anyone or anything they liked. Regrettable pasts could be erased or edited; failed marriages, bankruptcies, and old unpunished felonies could be conveniently forgotten; identities could be recast; and the boundaries of race, class, and gender could be subtly crossed by people whose stated backgrounds were all but impossible to verify. Since San Francisco was still utterly isolated, with no rapid mail, telegraph, or railroad connections to the rest of the country, all that was required to start over again as a new and different person was a plausible story. Typical of early San Francisco was the tale of Talbot Green, a pioneer who had come overland to California in 1841; only when the popular and respected Green was campaigning for mayor some ten years later did the facts about his life emerge—namely, that his real name was Paul Geddes and that he had abandoned a wife and child in Philadelphia after embezzling a fortune from the bank he worked for. (Unsurprisingly, Green withdrew from the race and promptly left town, to the sorrow of his many friends.)

Another emblematic character of early San Francisco was William Alexander Leidesdorff, a native of the Danish West Indies, who first came to California as master of a trading ship, the *Julia Ann*. In 1843, after several years making regular trading runs between San Francisco Bay and Honolulu, he joined the small but growing cadre of foreign traders at Yerba Buena by purchasing a lot on California Street for an import-export establishment of his own. Like William Richardson, he also became a naturalized citizen of Mexico. This distinction made him eligible to receive a 35,000-acre rancho as a land grant from the Mexican government, which at the time was still trying its best to increase population in the area. And within a few years, Leidesdorff was one of the most prominent men in the region, proprietor of the town's first hotel, owner of the first steamship to operate on San Francisco Bay, and at various times the local U.S. vice-consul to Mexico, city treasurer, and an alderman on Yerba Buena's town council. After American troops raised the Stars and Stripes over the customhouse in 1846, it was on the veranda of Leidesdorff's spacious home that the ensuing celebration took place.

Just how many people knew about Leidesdorff's background—that he'd been born out of wedlock to a Danish Jewish father and a mixed-race Caribbean-born mother—is not entirely clear. Surely the well-educated polyglot entrepreneur, though often described as "swarthy," passed as white among many casual acquaintances. Others almost certainly knew his racial heritage and didn't seem to care. Such was life in a place where everyone was more interested in making money than minding other people's business. In these freewheeling early days of the city's history, enforcing traditional social boundaries was not a high priority, so individuals of various classes, races, and ethnicities were often able to achieve a level of success and acceptance that would have been impossible in more settled places.

Indeed, for some of the city's early African American residents, passing was no requirement for success. Mifflin Wistar Gibbs, a Black abolitionist who had made speaking tours with Frederick Douglass in New York State, came west in 1849, arriving in San Francisco a few months before Crittenden did. In a memoir, he described arriving with 60 cents in his pocket, of which he spent 50 getting his trunk hauled ashore and the last 10 on a cigar. Fortunately, he was able to find temporary work on a construction site using a set of borrowed tools. His salary was $9 per day, lower than his white coworkers', but high by the standards of the day in any other town. Eventually he got a job as a clerk in a shoe store owned by another Black man named Peter Lester. And once Gibbs had saved enough money to come into the business as a partner, Lester & Gibbs became one of the most successful footwear importers in town.

Even a number of enslaved persons were able to take advantage of the opportunities afforded by the Gold Rush, earning enough money to pay their way out of servitude and go on to succeed as freedmen. George Washington Dennis, like Gibbs, came to California as a forty-niner, but unlike Gibbs he came as the property of a white man—his own father, Green Dennis. The senior Dennis put his son to work as a porter in the El Dorado gambling hall, which Green and his partners established the day they arrived in the boomtown. Between a salary of $250 per month and the scavenged sweepings of gold dust left by careless gamblers, young George was ultimately able to save the $1,000 his father stipulated for his manumission. By 1890, according to one report, George Washington Dennis was a businessman with a net worth of over $50,000.

Another enslaved person who managed to make good was Alvin Coffey, who was put to work prospecting on two separate trips to the California goldfields starting in the spring of 1849. After seven or eight years of effort—working the placers for himself on the side during his off hours and washing the clothes of other miners for pay—he eventually earned the several thousand dollars required to release himself and his wife and children from servitude. Coffey, who eventually started a ranch in Shasta County where he raised turkeys and horses, went on to become the only African American member of the Society of California Pioneers, an exclusive cultural organization whose membership was confined to those who had arrived in California before 1850.

None of this is to say that the new state was in any way a model of racial harmony in the early 1850s. Conditions had in fact been far better during the Mexican period, when persons of color could achieve virtually any position in California society. Mexico had abolished Black slavery upon its independence from Spain in the 1820s and had subsequently granted full rights to members of all races. (Indeed, the last Mexican governor of Alta California was a man of African descent named Pio Pico.) But once California had become part of the United States, insidious American attitudes about race began to establish themselves, both in social behavior and in law. As Mifflin Gibbs himself observed of this period, "With thrift and a wise circumspection financially, their opportunities [that is, those of African Americans] were good; [but] from every other point of view they were ostracized, assaulted without redress, disenfranchised, and denied their oath in a court of justice."

Discrimination had in fact been baked into the California constitution from the beginning, despite the fact that eight of the forty-eight delegates to the 1849 Constitutional Convention had been Mexicans of various racial backgrounds who had accepted American citizenship after the takeover. True, the constitution written by those delegates had outlawed slavery, but as George Dennis and Alvin Coffey could attest, many southerners had little problem bringing their enslaved workers into the state. And although an effort to have even free people of color banned from California never succeeded, a number of other discriminatory laws did pass. Worst among them was a law denying the vote to "Indians, Africans, and their descendants" and a ban on Black court testimony in cases involving white people (this ban would be extended to the Chinese in 1854). Mifflin Gibbs personally felt the indignity of the testimony ban when, after his partner Lester was brutally beaten by a white customer over a misunderstanding about a pair of boots, neither Gibbs nor Lester was allowed to testify against the assailant, allowing him to go unpunished.

Still, the sheer diversity of the population and the chaotic, improvisational nature of life in these early years ensured a certain amount of both toleration and opportunity for African Americans, especially in San Francisco. In December 1849, a group of thirty-seven Black residents organized a Mutual Benefit and Relief Society to aid newcomers and encourage more Blacks to come west. They even sent a letter to the Boston-based abolitionist weekly *The Liberator,* assuring would-be migrants that opportunities existed here: "This will inform you that there *are* colored people in San Francisco," the letter began, "[and] that we are doing something for ourselves towards our future welfare." As proof, they cited the fact that every one of the letter-writers was earning from $100 to $300 per month. And such efforts to recruit new Black migrants bore fruit. By 1852 there were about 2,000 African Americans in California, out of a total population of about 300,000, with a community of some 464 in San Francisco alone—ample refutation of the enduring myth of the whiteness of the early American West.

. . .

A. P. Crittenden was no stranger to this general air of economic optimism in the city. "Money here is nothing," he wrote to Clara on Christmas Day, 1849. "I am more than satisfied with what I find here. I will inevitably accumulate a fortune here in a few months." Claiming that he could make more in a week in California than in a year in Texas, he was convinced that he could soon return to his family debt-free and with a nest egg large enough to lift them all out of the relative poverty they'd been living in. But he wasn't at all sure yet of his long-range plans. He knew that, after serving his term in the state assembly in nearby San Jose (Sacramento would not become the state capital for several years), he would make San Francisco his residence and practice law there until his fortune was made. But after that, who knew? "It would not at all surprise me," he wrote, "if I were finally to make this country my home." The assumption, of course, was that Clara and the children would eventually join him wherever he ended up. But in the meantime, he sent her enough money so that they could spend next summer with Clara's family in Virginia, after which he himself would come east to accompany her and the children to California. From there they could decide "what quarter of the world we shall all select for a home—Texas, California, the Sandwich Islands [Hawaii], or China." But whatever they decided, "your troubles are now over, wife. Henceforth I intend your life to be one of ease and comfort."

And in an act of characteristic bravado, he collected all of the letters Clara had sent him since they'd parted—letters "filled merely with details of want and distress" and "nothing pleasant or cheerful"— and tore them up into small fragments. "I think the destruction of these records of misery will be a good omen," he wrote. "Forget the past year. Forget its privations. Forget its struggles . . . Look now for bright days."

3

Setbacks

BRIGHT DAYS—THAT WAS WHAT ALL the newly arrived migrants were hoping for, whatever their race, ethnicity, or social class. But opportunities were already changing in the fast-evolving town. By mid-1850, the extreme chaos that had prevailed in the two years following the discovery of gold had settled down significantly. Gone were the days when the cost of everything from houses to toothpicks oscillated wildly, depending on extremes of supply and demand—when the price of a shovel could rise from $1 to $6 to $50 over the course of weeks; or when a repurposed bedpan might sell for $96 to an argonaut desperate to start panning for gold. No longer could an arriving journalist sell the East Coast newspapers lining his steamer trunk, as Bayard Taylor had, for an instant 4,000 percent profit. The cost of goods and services, although still extraordinarily high by normal standards, had stabilized, and while there was still easy money to be made for the luckiest miners (and for those smart enough to "mine the miners," as the saying went), many people were finding nothing but hardship and disappointment in El Dorado: "When the sufferings of the emigrants . . . [are] known at home," one disillusioned forty-niner wrote, "our people will begin to see California stripped of her gaudy robes, her paint and outward adornments . . . and will be content to stay at home . . . The greatness of California! Faugh! Great for what and for whom?"

Even so, the tendency for most people was to endure present hardships philosophically, since, like Crittenden, they were still convinced that an immense fortune lay just around the corner. Many therefore acted as if they'd already made it big, despite their current circumstances, meaning that there was still plenty of wildness left in this Wild West town. "In the course of a month, or a year, in San Francisco," observed the visiting Englishman John David Borthwick, "there was more hard work done, more speculative schemes were conceived and executed, more money was made and lost, there was more buying and selling, more sudden changes of fortune, more eating and drinking, more smoking, swearing, gambling, and tobacco-chewing, more crime and profligacy . . . than could be shown in an equal space of time by any community of the same size on the face of the earth."

All of this fast living made for a rowdy environment likely to meet with the disapproval of clergymen and puritanical moralists. "The town seemed running wild after amusement," one early resident recalled, "and the lower the tastes to which any of them pandered, the better it was sustained." Because of the rampant licentiousness, Crittenden was having second thoughts about bringing his wife and family into this lion's den of a town. "It is a noisy, drinking, gambling place," he wrote Clara after a few more months' residence, "where everybody is allowed the largest liberty . . . There is little female society and I imagine no sociability amongst the few ladies who are here. A lady is forced to stay at home. The streets of San Francisco are not a proper place for her to be seen."

Not that staying at home would have been all that comfortable for a respectable lady and her family. Although new houses and infrastructure were being built at breakneck speed (whenever the supply of wood and other building materials would allow it), living conditions were still quite primitive. What few wells and potable springs existed in town were already overtaxed, and without even a basic water distribution system in place (underground pipes would not be laid until 1858), water was still being sold door-to-door by the barrel or the bucketful; needless to say, bathing and laundry days for many households were few and far between. Meanwhile, sewage and garbage disposal were lingering problems. Demand for outhouses outstripped supply by a substantial margin, while trash and food waste were usually just left out on the streets for the rats, the vultures, and the seagulls to take care of.

As for seeing to a family's spiritual health, although several Protestant and Catholic congregations had already been established (with two Jewish congregations soon to follow), services still had to be held in makeshift quarters—in tents, in shacks, in the town's one schoolhouse (built on the plaza in 1848), or in one of the still-scarce brick buildings going up around the central plaza. Attendance was generally spotty in these early years, with so many transient people too busy making money to think about church, so preachers often took to the streets to save souls, with varying success. As one early resident matter-of-factly observed, "We are not burdened with religion here in California."

But it was the prevalence of gambling and other vices that made the prospect of family life in San Francisco most problematic, especially if the family included young boys who might easily be led astray. The city was, according to one early French consul, "the promised land of gamblers. The moment that a house is offered to let, the gamblers take possession of it . . . There are more than a hundred of these houses now in this city, where a multitude of vagabonds and adventurers from the Sandwich Islands, Malay-dom, China, and the rest of the world crowd and elbow each other every night. All the nations of the earth have poured their scum into this sewer of humanity."

Crittenden was less harsh, but he still regarded the phenomenon as something of a deal-breaker for bringing his family out. Gambling, he told Clara, was not just tolerated in San Francisco but was even authorized by law. "Here it is carried on openly and with some style. On the public square the finest buildings are the gambling houses. Night and day a dozen elegant saloons are open for any sort of game. Faro, monte, roulette, and other tables everywhere display their tempting piles of gold and silver."

And the prevalence of prostitution was, to his mind, just as bad. "The most degraded of all created things is an American prostitute," he opined. "Women excel us [men] in virtue, but far far more they excel us in vice when once their course is turned in that direction." Realizing that this last pronouncement might raise some jealous suspicions, he rushed to reassure his wife: "You may ask me how I know. My answer is evident: In California it is impossible not to know. The vast majority of women in this country . . . clearly do not fall within the class of respectable, and they are to be encountered everywhere, on the streets, in all public houses, saloons, shows, theaters. It is only of late that ladies, real veritable ladies, are becoming at all common."

His conclusion: "In no respect can San Francisco claim to be a moral place." And therefore, if he *were* to bring his family to California—and that was still a big if—he would likely choose someplace more decent to live, like San Jose or Sonoma.

Meanwhile, as a state assemblyman, Crittenden was doing his part in bringing regulation and respectability to his adopted home by establishing its new legal code. The first session of the state legislature ran from December 1849 to April 1850. This was before the official granting of statehood by Congress on September 9, but Californians were not going to wait for Washington, D.C.'s, imprimatur to get their legislative house in order. As chairman of the assembly's judiciary committee, Crittenden was instrumental in establishing the state's basic legal and governmental framework, introducing English common law as the basis for California statutes and court decisions. Unfortunately, the former Texan also authored the notorious statute (AB 60) banning court testimony by persons of African or Native American descent in cases involving a white defendant. Such were the types of laws that—to some minds, at least—served as the foundation of a respectable social order.

But whatever Crittenden's estimation of California as a fit place to bring his family, moving them west was still a financial impossibility for him. He was just not making the progress he'd hoped for in erasing his heavy debts. The main reason for this was the fact that—despite his disapproving tone about gambling—he was making his own share of risky wagers, albeit not in the casinos. As journalist Bayard Taylor noted, emigrants coming to California during the Gold Rush had a tendency to experience an increase in "reckless and daring spirit," and this was certainly true for Crittenden, who already suffered from the family weakness for rash speculation. Since coming west, he had in fact spent money as fast he could earn it, making bets on real estate and other investments that hadn't worked out as planned.

"Every sort of accident has conspired to defeat my hopes," he wrote Clara on October 15, 1850. "Two months ago I had not a doubt that I should be able to leave this country for a time [that is, to retrieve Clara and bring her and the children back with him] . . . Now it cannot be. That day is postponed indefinitely."

A month later, he worked up the courage to tell his wife of "a whole series of blunders by which I have thrown away a fair chance of fortune, and at this moment am placed in hardly a better position than when I landed here one year ago." He had made, according to his own reckoning, five big mistakes. First, he had invested in a farming venture with an old friend from West Point, but the experiment proved to be an expensive failure. The same was true for an ill-advised purchase of a one-sixth interest in the *San Francisco Herald* newspaper. ("It was always in difficulty and proved to be a source of constant annoyance," he admitted.) A bigger mistake was trying to bail out one of his banker clients by personally serving as security for loans needed to fend off a run on the bank; the client was still in difficulty, so now there was "a nice liability hanging over me of $20,000."

And finally, he had made two unfortunate career mistakes. One was deciding to run for the office of California attorney general after the completion of his first term in the state assembly, an election for which he ended up receiving only 36 votes, as compared with 10,405 for the winner. The other mistake was starting a law partnership with an attorney named Edmund Randolph—"a man of fine talents, whom personally I like very much, but indolent and of manners not calculated generally to please." By Crittenden's calculation, the two lawyers together had made less money than he himself would have made in a solo practice.

In fairness, his manifold setbacks had not all been of his own making; some of his misfortunes had been unavoidable twists of fate. In a roughly eighteen-month period starting in December 1849, a series of devastating fires had swept through the mostly wood-and-canvas city, collectively causing the kind of damage that would not be seen again until the great 1906 earthquake and fire. Crittenden's fortunes were hurt by several of these. In May 1850, just when he had finally found something resembling decent living quarters, one of the earliest fires had destroyed his brand-new home: "It did not last more than three or four hours," he wrote Clara, "but in that time it did a deal of mischief. The building we were in disappeared in [a] short time." Luckily, he had been able to save his books and most of his furniture before the fire totally consumed the place, as he showed in a melancholy illustration that he included in the letter, intended for his children.

The very next month brought another fire: "Well, I have been burnt out again," he wrote Clara on June 30. "No, not burnt out this time, but drowned out. I had just got back to my former quarters when a second fire came and did far more damage to the city than the first. Between the fire and water, though my rooms were saved in rather a singed condition, my books and furniture were destroyed, ruined, or stolen."

But the most dramatic and personally horrifying conflagration would come in May 1851. "It was a terrible affair," he wrote Clara a few days after it happened. He was in bed when he heard the alarm: "At the first sound of the bell, a presentiment came over me that a serious struggle was at hand."

His instincts proved correct. When he walked outside, Crittenden realized that the entire business portion of the city was at risk of going up in flames. He went about saving what he could, running to the law office he shared with Edmund Randolph and rescuing their business papers, along with a daguerreotype of Randolph's newly deceased baby daughter. While carrying these items out of the fire's path, Crittenden witnessed a gruesome scene: "A man was running down the street, seeking to escape, when the flames poured out of a house, completely enveloping him. He fell, but rose at once—all on fire—ran a few steps and fell again and was consumed."

Returning to his residence near the plaza, Crittenden realized that he and his fellow tenants were going to have to defend their home themselves. Water was still a scarce resource in the young town, but the tenants managed to gather together about twenty buckets full. Then they took all of the blankets in the house, soaked them in the buckets, and nailed them over all of the windows.

But very soon the fire was directly upon them: "It seized the opposite buildings and completely surrounded us. We were enveloped in flame. It was a perfect sea of fire roaring and rushing around us." Unable to escape, they were soon gasping for breath, overcome by the smoke, the heat, and exhaustion. At one point, a young lawyer from the same building panicked, crying out that all of them were going to die. But Crittenden talked him down. " 'No,' I told him, 'we shall not lose our lives unless through our own rashness . . . Keep cool and I'll answer for the life of every man here.' "

Fortunately, they managed to save their own building, which was constructed largely of bricks. But the rest of the city had not been so lucky. "It was a desolate-looking site next morning—that vast blackened and smoking expanse—dotted over with tottering walls and the few buildings which had escaped . . . The plaza was crowded with furniture and homeless people, watching it and looking upon the ruin."

That May 1851 conflagration proved to be the very worst of the series of fires of the early '50s, destroying about a quarter of the city.

But as one visiting Frenchman wrote in admiration in his diary, "Even while his house is burning, an American will think only of how to rebuild it." So after this fire, as after the others, San Francisco built itself back again with unprecedented speed. And this time, it did so largely in brick and mortar. (In fact, the city would soon ban all tents and wooden buildings in the central district.) As a result, the raw and makeshift settlement turned suddenly into a mature-looking metropolis. "Like so many other emigrants," the French diarist noted after the fires, "I had thought to find on my arrival here only the beginnings of a town, a cluster of tents and rude shacks, where I should scarcely obtain shelter from bad weather. But I was greatly surprised to see, instead, large and fine streets, well laid-out, and wooden and brick houses, all in regular order."

For Crittenden, the fires and his many losses had a chastening effect. More than anything else, they prompted him to resist the temptation of future get-rich-quick schemes and other speculations. "I shall do nothing but attend to my [law] practice," he promised Clara. "At that I can make money, and every dollar I make will be my own." And he was confident that his luck would improve in this "country of sudden changes," where "what is impossible now may in a month be perfectly easy of accomplishment." He even put himself on a strict timetable. By October 1851, he vowed, he would have several thousand dollars to his name, so that he could afford to come east and retrieve his family. "I am content to live anywhere, do anything, sacrifice myself and my own feelings in any way, to accomplish the one object for which I live—to meet you once more and to meet you in prosperity."

．．．

The physical changes brought about by the great fires of 1850 and 1851 had occurred with dizzying speed, supplanting the makeshift wood-and-canvas town with an instant city of bricks and mortar. But the changes to the city's moral tone that Crittenden was hoping for were somewhat slower to arrive. Crime statistics for the city at this time were typically exaggerated, often by politicians seeking office, with fanciful accounts citing the murder rate, for instance, as one or even two per day; more recent scholarship puts it at about one or two per *month*. But rates of disorderly behavior, assault, and especially burglary and robbery were high—as indeed was to be expected in a rapidly growing urban area with a transient and heterogeneous population of mostly young males. (To emphasize how young the city's population was in these early days, when a merchant named Nathan Spear died of heart disease at the age of forty-seven, the *Daily Alta California* reported the news under the headline: "Death of the Oldest Inhabitant of San Francisco.") And in the wake of that last fire in the spring of 1851, the city suffered a crime wave so intense that extraordinary measures proved necessary to maintain law and order.

Crime and corruption had in fact been endemic in San Francisco ever since the discovery of gold and the chaos it created. The *Alta* baldly stated the problem as far back as February 1849: San Francisco, the paper claimed, was "perhaps the worst governed community in existence . . . She is without law, without proper executive officers, and without the means of confining and punishing offenders, and were it not that gold is so abundant, no man could calculate how long before the assassin's knife would be at his throat." While a minimal level of municipal government may have sufficed for the small town of pre–Gold Rush days, the San Francisco of the 1850s required something less makeshift. A much more sophisticated infrastructure of police, courts, and civic administration was now needed to protect lives and private property. This point was made—rather bluntly—later in 1849, when the town's new mayor admitted in his inaugural address that the city he was supposed to govern was "without a single requisite necessary for the promotion of prosperity, for the protection of property, or for the maintenance of order."

The situation had improved dramatically in the two years since then. A jail had finally been constructed—before that, offenders had to be kept prisoner offshore on a highly insecure brig called the *Euphemia*—and a thirty-man police force had been established. But it still often took extralegal efforts to maintain order in town. After the fires of 1851, which some attributed to arson by a group of miscreants known as the Sydney Ducks (so-called because many of them were Australian ex-convicts), crime took a turn for the worse once more. In June 1851, a group of prominent citizens—frustrated that so few defendants were actually punished by the town's inept and corrupt justice system—formed a so-called Committee of Vigilance and started apprehending and trying suspects themselves. Municipal authorities objected, but the committee ended up holding sway for several weeks, once even taking up arms to storm the new jail and hijack several prisoners they felt were likely to escape punishment; the vigilantes ended up hanging the prisoners in the middle of Portsmouth Square. By September, having brought down the crime rate at least temporarily, the committee officially suspended its activities. But it was neither the first nor the last time that city residents would resort to vigilante justice to maintain order.

Clearly then, by the autumn of 1851—when, true to his word, Crittenden was finally in financial shape to bring his family west—his concerns about San Francisco's fitness as a place for women and children were not allayed. But he felt it would now at least be possible for them to live in some semblance of comfort there. Despite the high rate of crime, the city was already starting to offer the kind of amenities characteristic of a true metropolis, with new stores and restaurants opening every day. The first omnibus line had opened, running on the plank road between downtown and the old Mission. A regular steamship connection with Oakland across the bay was soon to be inaugurated. Meanwhile, the sand hills that ringed the downtown (and that made residents' lives miserable whenever the winds were strong enough to blow loose grains through the city streets) were actively being scraped away by state-of-the-art imported steam shovels; the sand was then carried to Yerba Buena Cove and dumped into the spaces between recently built wharves, creating new land that allowed the downtown district to grow eastward into the bay.

And so, after arranging for some of his law associates to look after his affairs for a few months, Crittenden took the so-called Panama route to the East, sailing from California to Panama, crossing the isthmus by land, and then continuing on a different ship to New Orleans and New York. This was a far faster and more comfortable trip than his original overland trek from Texas, but it was also far more expensive. So Crittenden tried to make good use of the trip. He took care of various bits of business in New York and Philadelphia before heading to Richmond, where Clara and their six children had been staying with her family. After what seems to have been an amiable reunion— their separation had lasted for a total of two and a half years—he helped the family pack up and accompanied them back to New York and then on to California via the Panama route in reverse.

On January 10, 1852, the Crittenden family finally steamed into San Francisco Bay. For Clara, with her husband at her side again, the life ahead must have seemed an exciting if somewhat frightening prospect, promising the comfort and support of marital companionship after a time of loneliness and hardship. For A.P. on the other hand, the future might have seemed almost the opposite, as he moved from an unfettered bachelor existence, full of travel, adventure, and risk-taking, back to the restrictive life of a lawyer and family man. Of course, we can't know for sure how either of them truly felt as they looked out at the city from the deck of the steamer *Golden Gate*—no letters survive from that precise period of their lives. But one thing we can be sure of is this: Neither one of them, husband nor wife, was destined to be happy with their new lives in hard-charging California.

4

No Place for a Lady

A MONTH AFTER BRINGING HIS FAMILY to California, A. P. Crittenden was still reassuring his now thirty-two-year-old wife that her troubles would soon be behind her. "The great difficulty is over," he told her. "You are here. That is a consolation for anything." He was fully cognizant of the hard life he had made for his wife so far in their marriage. Bad enough that he had dragged her as a teenage bride away from her comfortable family home to the rough backwater of frontier Texas. But then, after subjecting her to a decade of continual pregnancy on the prairie, he had essentially abandoned her for several years, with little money and six young children to raise, before finally arranging to have them all join him. "You have endured with me poverty and humiliation," he admitted. "You have earned the right now to wealth and honors."

Clara's reward, however, would have to wait for a little bit longer. Although Crittenden had installed his family in a small house in San Jose, a less hectic town some fifty miles south of the lingering sinfulness of San Francisco, it was as yet sparsely furnished and by no means comfortable. What's more, Clara, who was pregnant again, was forced to endure yet another period of grass widowhood. A.P. had won a second term as state assemblyman, this time representing Santa Clara

County. Since San Jose was then serving as the capital of both Santa Clara County and the state of California, his initial hope had been that he could serve in the assembly and still walk home every night to his wife and children. But then the state capital was reassigned—first to the tiny town of Vallejo and then to Sacramento, over a hundred miles distant from San Jose. Crittenden did try to find his family a house in Sacramento for the five-month-long legislative session, but he could find nothing suitable—or so he claimed.

Clara, understandably, was not pleased, and did not hesitate to complain about her situation, to her husband's frustration. "I have just received your letter of the 17th and am much distressed at the contents," A.P. wrote to her from Sacramento in late February. "[I am] distressed to perceive how dissatisfied you are, when I have done for you the best I could . . . I am not forgetful of your wants. I know that a great many things are essential for your comfort . . . and I hope in short time to [provide] all that you require and more." In the meantime, however, he was powerless to do anything further for her. "I have spent my last dollar in San Francisco to purchase you a few articles of furniture. Before many days, I shall send you more. Within a month you will probably be comfortably fixed."

But like so many of her husband's promises, this one proved overly optimistic. Months later, she was still feeling forgotten and abandoned. Even after the legislative session ended in May, A.P. still had to spend a good deal of time in San Francisco and Los Angeles on business. He was, in fact, in L.A. when their ninth child, Mary, was born in August 1852. Little wonder that Clara was "entertaining gloomy feelings" and writing him that she wished she had never left Virginia to come west. But A.P. was adamant. "I am fixed [and] expect to live and die in California," he wrote her in June. "If you are not content to share my fate, good or bad, say so, and if it cost me my life you shall return [to Virginia]."

Still, he did what he could to make life better for his wife, sending her furniture and a servant or two, neither of which he could really afford. He even mailed her some seeds to start a garden. But eventually he realized that the fundamental problem was her sense of isolation. Without a husband or any semblance of a social life in San Jose, the former Richmond debutante was miserable, just as she had been miserable during their residence on the Texas frontier. As he admitted to her, "Society I care nothing for. I should like to live out of the world, if it were possible. But your disposition is different and such a sacrifice I would not ask of you."

The solution, he decided, was to move everyone to San Francisco, where he could practice law and Clara could find whatever society the ever-growing city had to offer. He still had doubts that the boomtown was any place for a real lady, but at this point he felt he had no choice. And the town *was* improving, in his eyes. Even two years earlier, before Clara had arrived, he had started to notice a change: "Now there is rising a distinction between what is reputable and what is disreputable," he'd written her, "and in the course of a few years there will be as much outward morality here as in any older state." Had the San Francisco of 1853 become a place with enough "outward morality" to make a comfortable and respectable family life possible? The Crittendens would find out. Early in that year, they packed up their household yet again and moved into a house on Pacific Avenue between Powell and Mason, in the heart of what is now Chinatown.

•   •   •

Certainly the instant city of San Francisco had continued to grow and develop in the early 1850s, so that it now bore at least the appearance of a mature and important metropolis. This striking change impressed everyone who'd known the place back in the 1840s—including a future Civil War general named William Tecumseh Sherman, who moved to San Francisco right about when the Crittendens took the house on Pacific. Sherman had first come to California as a soldier during the Mexican War, and although he'd never seen any actual fighting, he *had* played a surprisingly notable role in the region's early history. As assistant adjutant general to California's military governor in Monterey, Sherman was present in the governor's office when the first specimens of gold from Sutter's Mill were brought in for official inspection—and indeed was the very person who tasted the metal and flattened the specimens with a hatchet to positively identify them as gold. Several weeks later, he led a party of soldiers out to the goldfields to verify the richness of the strike. During that excursion, he'd passed through San Francisco and found it nothing but "a poor contemptible village." Even by the time he left California in early 1850 ("having passed through a war without smelling gunpowder," as he lamented to his wife, Ellen), he was still unimpressed with the town, despite the fact that by then it had already started growing explosively. The climate was awful, he complained, and after rain the unpaved streets were so muddy that "I have seen mules stumble and drown in the liquid mud!"

But what a difference three years had made. Now, in 1853, Sherman was returning to San Francisco while on a temporary leave from the army, in order to open up a West Coast branch of a St. Louis bank called Lucas, Turner & Company. His employer, Henry S. Turner, was supremely optimistic about San Francisco's prospects, claiming that the young metropolis would become one of the great commercial cities of the world. Sherman, clinging to his earlier opinion of the town, was at first skeptical. But once he saw what the "poor contemptible village" had become, he was an instant convert: "San Francisco was on the top wave of speculation," he later wrote in his memoirs. "Everybody seemed to be making money fast." In fact, the town he had scorned just three years earlier was now, by his lights, "the most extraordinary place on earth." Convinced that he could finally make enough money as a banker there to adequately support his growing family, Sherman turned his military leave of absence into an outright resignation and brought his wife and children west. But Ellen Sherman, less impressed by the place than her husband, was unhappy from the moment she arrived, deeming San Francisco "forlorn" and "thoroughly wicked." Like

Clara Crittenden, she soon learned that a place replete with fine buildings and even finer commercial prospects did not necessarily conform
to her notions of civilized society, and, like Clara, she also began making noises about heading back home.

· · ·

As relatively prosperous married white women, Clara Crittenden and
Ellen Sherman could at least partially insulate themselves from what
they saw as the great wickedness of the overwhelmingly male city. But
other women arriving in San Francisco in these years faced greater
challenges. Some, in fact, were forced to become part of that very
world of vice that so appalled the others.

One of these was a young Chinese immigrant known as Ah Toy (or
Atoy), who came to San Francisco just months after the discovery of
gold (allegedly she was only the second Chinese woman in town). As
with many figures who, because of their race, class, or gender, are underrepresented in the historical record, it is difficult to separate the
truth of Ah Toy's life from the various legends that have grown up
around her. But according to one story, Ah Toy, just nineteen years
old, arrived in California as a brand-new widow; her husband—a
would-be miner attracted by the stories of "Gold Mountain"—had
died en route from Hong Kong, leaving her all but penniless. With few
other options available to her in a strange city far from home, she resorted to sex work. (Other accounts have her arriving as an unmarried
prostitute, but the fact that she had bound feet would seem to indicate
an upper-class background.)

After some months operating as a solo practitioner out of a glorified
shack in an alley off Clay Street, an area rapidly filling with such establishments, Ah Toy quickly improved her lot. She was apparently very
popular among her mostly white clientele, and there are stories, perhaps apocryphal, of frequent lines of customers in front of her establishment long enough to wind around the block. By 1850 she had

hired two other Chinese women to work for her, and two years later had become the madam of a pair of sizable "boardinghouses" (brothels) on Pike Street. There is evidence that she might even have expanded her operations to the towns of Sacramento and Stockton.

One possible reason for Ah Toy's success was the mostly positive view of the city's Asian population in these early years of the Gold Rush. Migrants from China, eager to escape the famine, high taxes, and civil unrest that followed the first Opium War of the mid-1840s, had only started arriving in San Francisco right around the time of the discovery of gold. And until 1852 or so, there were still too few of them in town to pose serious competition for white labor. The Chinese were thus regarded by many white residents with a kind of benign condescension, and by some with real admiration. "Search the city through and you will not find an idle Chinaman," the *Pacific News* wrote in late 1849; two years later the *Alta California* was even more complimentary, if paternal: "They are among the most industrious, quiet, patient people among us," the paper claimed. "They seem to live under our laws as if born and bred under them." In August 1850, the city sponsored a ceremony in Portsmouth Square honoring the Chinese population, and also invited "the China Boys" (the patronizing local nickname for the community) to participate in public celebrations of Independence Day and California statehood, as well as a mock funeral procession for the late President Zachary Taylor. As an early arrival, Ah Toy likely benefited from this atmosphere of relative tolerance.

But the young woman's fierce insistence on her rights was another driver of her early success. At a time when few in San Francisco's Chinese community made use of the courts, Ah Toy came frequently before judges as a plaintiff in actions against those who had wronged her, often appearing in flamboyant clothing that caused as much comment in the newspapers as her complaints. ("Atoy came into court," the *Alta California* reported of one of her appearances, "blooming with youth, beauty, and rouge, and bedecked in a decidedly 'gallus' [bold or daring] bonnet and orange-colored shawl.") Once, in 1849, she sued several customers who, she claimed, had paid for her services with brass shavings instead of gold dust; another time she filed charges against some men for stealing a $300 diamond brooch. She didn't always win these cases, but the fact that she brought them at all is testimony to her determination to be treated fairly.

Her success as an individual entrepreneur, however, soon brought her into conflict with the nascent Chinese tongs—secret societies or brotherhoods that wanted to control prostitution and other vice in the community. An alleged tong leader named Yuen Sheng (though better known by his American name, Norman Ah-Sing) allegedly tried to take over her operations in early 1851. When she successfully fought off these efforts, he resorted to subtler tactics, forging a letter from Ah Toy's "husband" in Hong Kong demanding her return to China. Taking to the courts again, Ah Toy denied the existence of this husband and accused Norman Ah-Sing of attempting to force her out of the country against her will. Here again, she succeeded. Norman Ah-Sing, who seems to have been prominent in both criminal and legitimate business worlds in the Chinese community, was arrested and held on a $2,000 bond.

But the situation for the city's Chinese changed rapidly as, drawn by the prospects of California's booming gold-fueled economy, their numbers grew precipitously over the early 1850s. Soon they were being seen as dangerous competition to members of the city's largely Irish working class, who themselves had arrived in great numbers to escape the continuing potato famine at home. And although one can't draw definitive conclusions from the opinions of two individuals, speeches by two successive California governors in 1852 were emblematic of this transformation. In January of that year, the outgoing governor, John McDougal, addressing the state legislature, endorsed the continued free immigration of Chinese to California, deeming them "one of the most worthy classes of our newly adopted citizens."

In April, however—by which time the Chinese population of California had jumped significantly—McDougal's successor, John Bigler, had a different perspective. Pointing out that more than two thousand Chinese immigrants had arrived in San Francisco in just the past few weeks, with an alleged five thousand more en route, he sounded an alarm: "In order to enhance the prosperity and to preserve the tranquility of the State, measures must be adopted to check this tide of Asiatic immigration." Outlining the ways in which he felt that the Chinese lacked the same family and cultural values as middle-class Americans, he called on lawmakers at both the state and federal level to curb immigration, especially of the poorly paid contract laborers known as "Coolies." He also urged legislatures to deny them American citizenship, to impose on them special taxes, and to restrict their access to the courts. (Interestingly, this address was publicly denounced by none other than Norman Ah-Sing in an open letter to the governor published in the *Daily Alta California* ten days later; the alleged tong leader gently pointed out that the Chinese were "not the degraded race you would make us," and had in fact "exercised most of the arts and virtues of civilized life" when the United States was yet a wilderness and Europe was still barbarous.)

Lawmakers and justices responded to the governor's call. Legislation implementing a heavy immigration tax on Chinese arrivals was passed, and a foreign miners' tax that had been declared unconstitutional in 1851 was reinstated, though as a foreign miners' *license* tax. And in 1854, the California Supreme Court ruled definitively that the Chinese be included in the law barring Black and Native Americans from testifying against whites in court.

This last act affected Ah Toy directly. During the brief reign of the 1851 Vigilance Committee, she had become the mistress of a white man named John A. Clark—ironically, the man in charge of the vigilantes' investigation of brothels. In 1852 Ah Toy took him to court on a charge of domestic abuse. The case was ultimately dismissed by the judge as a personal matter, and when she tried to bring charges against him again in 1854, she couldn't even get a hearing, since by that time the state supreme court had made its ruling about non-white testimony.

Changing attitudes toward the Chinese ended up drastically altering Ah Toy's entire relationship with the justice system. Whereas in the early 1850s she appeared mostly as a plaintiff or witness, by the middle of the decade she was appearing more often as a defendant. The city passed an ordinance banning brothels, and, predictably, it was more strictly enforced against Chinese and Mexican houses. Thus she soon found herself arrested and fined for "disorderly housekeeping" and other similar offenses. Her early success soon crumbled, especially after the local economy slumped and the tongs moved more aggressively to monopolize vice establishments. By 1855, on the brink of ruin, she reportedly attempted suicide. Finally, in 1857—financially squeezed and facing ever-increasing hostility from the tongs and harassment from white officials—she sold her businesses and returned to China, though her absence from the city would prove to be temporary. Despite the deteriorating outlook for Chinese women in particular, Ah Toy would find the lure of San Francisco difficult to resist.

*   *   *

"My dear Clara, I send you Laura's letter and the thingamabob you wrote for," A. P. Crittenden told his wife in a chatty letter sent in November 1853. For once it was Clara who was off traveling (probably visiting one of her siblings, several of whom had also migrated to California), while A.P. remained at home with the children. "Everything is getting along just as usual," he continued. "Howard had a fever on Saturday but has been perfectly well since. I think it was in consequence of going into the water. I found it impossible to do anything with the boys last week and had to let them be as wild as they chose. This week they will be confined at school part of each day at least."

It was a rare moment of domesticity for the peripatetic Crittenden. Although he had quit the state assembly for good after his second term, he was still traveling frequently to argue cases before the state supreme court in Sacramento, leaving Clara (who was pregnant yet again) alone with the children at the house on Pacific Avenue. And although their financial situation had eased at least somewhat since the move—and Clara had been able to find some social life in a "Southern set" of women and their husbands that had by now grown up in San Francisco—she was still discontent with things as they stood. The children could provide her only limited solace. Aside from baby Mary, there were two girls—Laura, age sixteen, and Ann, or "Nannie," age twelve—who could be willful and moody at times; but the real trouble, as Crittenden indicated in his letter, came from the four boys— Churchill (thirteen), James (twelve), Howard (nine), and Parker (four). Trying to raise an undersupervised quartet of young boys would be a challenge in any place; doing so in a town that still catered so openly to the tastes and desires of unattached males was enough to dishearten anyone. (When the founders of the College of California—the future Berkeley—had to decide where to build the school in the mid-1850s, they chose an East Bay location in order to protect students from what they called San Francisco's "brutalizing vulgarity.")

And Clara was to face a series of losses in 1854 that would merely deepen the depression she so often complained of to her husband. On July 27 of that year, the baby she was carrying, Edmund Randolph Crittenden, would die of an unspecified illness at the age of four months. The very next month, she would learn of her beloved mother's death back in Virginia, followed closely (and perhaps most agonizingly) by the death of little Mary Crittenden just weeks before her second birthday. Clara had barely a few months to mourn these losses, which must have tested her deep religious faith, before she was again pregnant—the eleventh time she would carry a child to term in their seventeen-year marriage.

"If I find a wrinkle or any appearance of care about you," A.P. had once written her teasingly, back when she was still in Virginia and he was still giddy with the prospects of success in California, "I'll get a divorce. Ugliness, ill temper, insanity, and poverty are all good grounds [for] divorce here. So you had better laugh and grow fat and banish crossness and learn to be smiling and cheerful. If you will supply good looks and good humor for two, I will supply the money."

But now, after several years in California, it seemed that neither one of them was living up to their side of this bargain.

5

Assorted Insurrections

B Y THE MID-1850S, as the situation for Chinese immigrants in California deteriorated, the leaders of San Francisco's small but relatively prosperous Black community were determined to avoid a similar fate. They thus began organizing to fight some of the state's discriminatory laws that targeted African Americans in particular. The most urgent task was to make sure that California lived up to its name as a free state. Uncertainty remained about the status of enslaved people brought from out of state, and while there was no formal system in place to uphold the alleged property rights of slave-owning southerners in California, neither was there any real attempt to enforce the state's antislavery provisions. As a result, southerners had been able to keep enslaved people in this allegedly free state without much fear of repercussions, and a significant number of them did just that. Tod Robinson, for instance—the brother-in-law with whom Crittenden had studied law in Texas—apparently brought at least two enslaved Black servants with him when he himself migrated to California in 1850. Some slaveholders were so confident of their property rights in California that they would even advertise in the newspapers when they had a cook or maid they wanted to sell.

One of the earliest attempts to address this situation had occurred in 1851, when a young enslaved man named Frank—brought into the state from Missouri by a certain John F. Calloway—disappeared from the goldfields one winter day. After a two-month search, Calloway finally located Frank in San Francisco, at which time he recaptured the eighteen-year-old and locked him up at the Whitehall Building on Long Wharf, apparently intending to take him out of the state by ship. But Frank had made some influential friends in the city's Black community during his time as a free man; these friends hired white attorney Samuel W. Holladay to bring Frank's case before Judge Morrison of the county court. The trial, which played out in a courtroom filled with a contingent of prominent Black San Franciscans, lasted just two days. Calloway's lawyers argued that the federal Fugitive Slave Law of 1850 required that all officials of free states cooperate in the restoration of fugitives to their purported owners. Holladay countered that the federal law did not apply here, since Frank had crossed no state lines in his escape. Judge Morrison was sympathetic to this latter argument, adding that Calloway's lawyers had not even established that Frank was an enslaved person belonging to their client. When the lawyers pointed out that Frank himself had admitted as much in his own testimony, the judge noted that, thanks to the state law banning Black testimony in a court case involving white persons, this evidence was not admissible. The irony of this situation, which not only enabled Frank to go free but also exposed Calloway to a potential charge of kidnapping, was lost on no one in the courtroom. As the *San Francisco Herald* reported the next day, "Mr. Frank went his way, rejoicing amid unbounded applause of his colored brethren."

It was the first victory in a campaign that would continue until the last enslaved Black person in the state was liberated. "The wealthy California Negroes have become especially talented at such abductions," one German visitor observed after one such liberation. "They exhibit a great deal of energy and intelligence in saving their brothers." Unfortunately, however, not all jurists proved to be as supportive as Judge Morrison, and similar efforts were soon complicated by the legislature's passage of a *California* Fugitive Slave Law, closing the federal law's border-crossing loophole and giving white people arbitrary powers to reclaim alleged property on the basis of affidavits and other flimsy evidence. Still, the city's Black population persisted in their efforts, providing financial and moral support to the growing number of African Americans—both free and enslaved—entering the state.

One of the key figures in this core group of prominent Black San Franciscans was a remarkable woman named Mary Ellen Pleasant, who arrived in 1852. As with Ah Toy, it's difficult to penetrate the cloud of mythology and folklore surrounding Pleasant's life and get to the facts, especially since she herself made contradictory claims about her background at different times in her life. Even the basic circumstances of her birth are contested. Some sources claim that she was born into slavery in Georgia, the daughter of a white Virginia planter and a Caribbean "voodoo priestess." But Pleasant herself, in a short, unfinished memoir written a few years before her death, claimed that she was born Mary Ellen Williams in Philadelphia in 1814 to free parents. Her father, "a native Kanaka" (Hawaiian), was a well-educated businessman who imported silks from India; she knew less about her mother, specifying only that she was "a full-blooded Louisiana negress."

When Mary Ellen was six (or seven or fourteen, depending on the source), she was sent to Nantucket to live with a white Quaker woman named Hussey, presumably because the island had a free Black population large enough to support a "colored school." However, if an agreement existed between Mary Ellen's parents and Mrs. Hussey about the girl's education, it was not honored, and she was instead put to work in the old woman's general store. But while Pleasant would always blame Mrs. Hussey for denying her a formal education, she ended up thinking that it was perhaps for the best. "I have run across a good many highly educated people who knew a whole lot about books and nothing about the world or the people in it," Pleasant would later write. "I have let books alone, and studied men and women a good deal." These "human nature studies," as she called them, taught her everything she needed to know in life, and more.

In 1842, the twenty-seven-year-old left Nantucket and eventually moved to Boston—"to better my condition," as she later remarked, perhaps implying that she was in search of a husband. If so, she soon succeeded. While working as a clerk in a shoe or clothing shop, she took note of one customer in particular—James W. Smith, a wealthy, well-dressed Cuban businessman of ambiguous racial heritage—and went out of her way to speak with him. Learning that he attended the nearby St. Mary's Catholic Church, she quickly became a member, reasoning that "one church was the same as another to me." She even joined the church choir, where, she thought, Smith would be sure to notice the tall and attractive young woman he had met at the shop. He did. After persuading the priest to make a formal introduction, Smith asked to walk Mary Ellen home after Mass that day, and a courtship ensued. "We were married inside of a month," she would later report.

One of the few things known with some certainty about Smith was that he was an ardent abolitionist. According to some sources, he even entertained the likes of William Lloyd Garrison and Wendell Phillips at his home in Boston. He apparently also owned a plantation near what is now Charles Town, West Virginia, where, according to Pleasant, "my husband frequently demonstrated his feeling for the colored race by purchasing slaves and freeing them." It's unclear whether this was where Pleasant developed her own commitment to emancipation, or whether it was already well established from her childhood in abolitionist Nantucket. But shortly before Smith died, less than two years into their marriage, he asked her to devote some of the substantial legacy he was leaving her to the cause of freeing enslaved persons. "I promise with a full heart," she said.

About Mary Ellen's second husband—John James Pleasants (the *s* was later dropped), another staunch abolitionist—just as little is known. The two apparently met and married in Nantucket, after the young widow returned there to live with the granddaughter of the original

Mrs. Hussey. Not long after their wedding, news of the gold strike in California reached the island, and John James decided to join the westward exodus. Mary Ellen remained in New England for a few more years—perhaps to care for their newborn child, Lizzie—before coming west independently in 1852, leaving Lizzie with a caretaker in Boston.

When Mary Ellen herself arrived in San Francisco aboard the steamship *Oregon* in April 1852, she came, unlike many new arrivals, with some capital behind her. The remaining bequest from her deceased first husband allegedly amounted to about $15,000 in gold coins. This she very shrewdly invested under the auspices of several businessmen she knew from the East, as well as through a scrappy new business called Wells, Fargo & Co. As she later recalled: "They put out the money for me at 10 percent interest [per month—not an unusual rate of interest for loans in the booming young city]. I [also] did an exchange business with Panama, sending down $1000 in gold and having it exchanged for silver. I had many bank books."

Even in a place as unconventional as California, however, the spectacle of an independently wealthy Black woman was liable to attract unwanted attention. It didn't help her case that she and John James were often apart for extended periods, especially after he became a cook on a Panama–to–San Francisco steamer—a very lucrative position, though one that kept him away from home for months at a time. So Pleasant also took pains to present herself, under a pseudonym at first, in a role less threatening to traditional ideas, hiring herself out as a cook and housekeeper to some of the young city's most prominent businessmen. Aside from providing herself with some cover, this ploy also had the advantage of allowing her access to wealthy and influential people, from whom she received valuable information about real estate deals and promising new ventures to invest in. Among these ventures was a laundry she opened at the corner of Jessie Street and Ecker Place, south of Market Street, where real estate prices were still relatively low. Laundry was at this time a stunningly lucrative business, with so many gold-flush young men willing to pay outrageous prices to have their clothes washed. Pleasant's laundry was so successful that she was soon able to open several more.

At the same time, she also became active with San Francisco's Black community, which now numbered several hundred people, mostly men. Always ready to put her wealth to work, she helped found the Atheneum Institute, a Black social club and cultural institution with a saloon and library, to which she contributed funds and other assistance. Together with the likes of Mifflin Gibbs and George Dennis, both of whom were likewise doing well for themselves as entrepreneurs, she supported campaigns to overturn California's bans on Black suffrage and court testimony, and assisted escapees from involuntary servitude, now a much harder prospect since the implementation of the state's new Fugitive Slave Law.

But while she was by now well known among the city's Black residents, Pleasant still maintained a relatively low profile in the larger community. Her activism was as yet mainly behind the scenes, with most official records of the various organizations she supported—the Atheneum Institute, the Franchise League, the Executive Committee of the so-called Colored Conventions of the 1850s—mentioning only their male members. However, the anecdotal evidence of her involvement is substantial. Her kitchen, in fact, was already becoming known as San Francisco's "Black City Hall." And Pleasant's days of relative anonymity would not last forever. It wouldn't be long before her activities started to make the local newspapers—not to mention the transcripts of various highly visible court cases—and the wider city would discover that they had in their midst a determined, if unconventional, advocate for change.

•　•　•

For Alexander Parker Crittenden, meanwhile, the mid-1850s was a time of hard work and growing discontent as he struggled to climb out of debt while at the same time maintaining a middle-class lifestyle in a still-pricey city. The frustrations of his home life—trying to juggle a houseful of unmanageable children and a depressed wife—were prompting him to absent himself from the San Francisco hearth with increasing frequency, typically in pursuit of one moneymaking opportunity or another. Restless as ever, he even involved himself in the affairs of the notorious William Walker, a fellow southerner who led several freelance invasions of Mexico, Nicaragua, and Honduras in the 1850s. These so-called filibuster expeditions—unauthorized military actions undertaken by private individuals—were intended to foment revolution and overthrow local governments, turning independent nations into puppet colonies that could accommodate the spread of slavery to new areas of the continent. Crittenden never took up arms himself, but acted as Walker's recruitment agent in San Francisco, provisioning him with enough soldiers, weaponry, and supplies to topple small and unstable regimes south of the border. For Walker's 1856 filibuster of Nicaragua, during which Walker himself usurped the role of president for a few heady months, Crittenden traveled down to Central America to handle some dubious legal maneuvers required by the new regime. And while Walker's efforts ultimately amounted to very little (he was eventually deposed and executed in 1860), being part of his exploits gave Crittenden a chance to engage in matters more exciting and consequential than real estate squabbles and mining-claim disputes.

But Crittenden managed to find some excitement closer to home as well, as San Francisco in the summer of 1856 faced a kind of insurrection of its own. In the five years since the brief emergence of the citizen-led Vigilance Committee, crime rates had again started climbing, while the local justice system seemed too slow, too corrupt, or simply too dysfunctional to punish the transgressors. As in 1851, the reported number of homicides was likely exaggerated, but two high-profile murders in early 1856—one of a U.S. marshal by a notorious gambler, the other of a reform-minded newspaper editor by the political hack he'd exposed in print—proved to be the precipitating factors for a revival of outright vigilantism. Unsatisfied with the official court proceedings against both men, the old 1851 committee revived itself and immediately began recruiting volunteers for a quasimilitary force to take matters into their own hands. Again armed vigilantes seized the prisoners from the jail by force. Again they marched them before an unofficial "jury" and, after the briefest of trials, hanged the guilty parties before a large crowd, this time from a platform on the second floor of the committee's headquarters on Sacramento Street.

But this was only the beginning. After these two miscreants were punished, the committee turned to other crimes and other criminals—most notably the "ballot-stuffers" responsible for keeping the city's allegedly corrupt political machine in power. (In fact, this political cleansing may have been the real motivation for the revival of the Vigilance Committee.) Over the next several weeks, the standoff between the two governments—the official and the de facto—grew ever more tense. By late June, when a California Supreme Court justice was seized for stabbing an officer of the Vigilance Committee, the city stood on the brink of an all-out war between the well-armed vigilantes and the California militia, serving under the command of William Tecumseh Sherman, called away from his banking duties to lead the struggle against what he regarded as an irresponsible mob.

Crittenden naturally got caught up in the episode, acting as an intermediary between the Vigilance Committee and supporters of the militia in order to release the supreme court justice (an old friend and fellow southerner named David S. Terry). But although A.P. was playing go-between, it was clear which side had his sympathy. As a lawyer and former state assemblyman, he was a great believer in the authority of legitimate government, and he found the extralegal methods of the vigilantes unconscionable. In fact, when Sherman decided to resign as head of the militia, he recommended that Crittenden, his fellow West Point graduate, serve as his replacement. It's uncertain whether Crittenden would have accepted the job, but it was never officially offered to him, and the feared violent confrontation never happened in any case. On August 11, 1856, the Vigilance Committee peacefully ceded control of the city back to its elected officials. But although the group's interregnum of hasty executions and forced deportations did again bring some semblance of order to the streets, it did so at a cost to the city's reputation as a civilized and orderly place. Crittenden expressed that cost in a letter to his uncle John in Washington, D.C.: "I am utterly heartsick at what I have seen here . . . My faith in republican institutions and in man's capacity for self-government is shaken."

These sporadic episodes of drama aside, however, Crittenden's life in these years was characterized mainly by long days of mundane legal work intended to keep his growing clan on an upward path to ease and material prosperity. And yet the restlessness that he had manifested ever since childhood would not allow him to settle comfortably into the quiet and stable family life that his wife, at least, desired for them. Now forty years old, A.P. was again chafing at the uneventful existence of a white-shoe lawyer, still looking for some kind of grand adventure to shake up his life. And though he had no idea of it at the time, an adventure of a most disruptive kind was just about to come his way. More than two thousand miles to the east, the young woman who would someday become his mistress—and his murderer—was starting out on the path that would eventually cross his own.

THE PEOPLE OF THE STATE OF CALIFORNIA

V. LAURA D. FAIR

DAY EIGHT

Tuesday, April 4, 1871

As it was announced that Mrs. Fair was to take the stand, there was a general commotion in the Courtroom; many rose from their seats and gathered around the Clerk's desk in groups. All eyes were bent upon her as she took the arm of Judge Quint, one of her counsel, and was led to the stand . . .

—*DAILY ALTA CALIFORNIA*

THERE WAS NO QUESTION WHY the spectators came, day after day, to fill the gallery and every other available space in the Fifteenth District Courtroom: They wanted to see the woman who had pulled the trigger. The other witnesses—the defendant's doctors, the dead man's children, even the dead man's wife—were only the spectacle's opening acts. The person they were really waiting to hear from was the notorious murderess. They wanted to hear what Laura D. Fair had to say for herself.

But so far, a week of the trial had gone by and they hadn't gotten what they wanted. True, the defendant had been called twice to the stand—creating a small upheaval among the spectators each time—but both appearances had been brief and inconsequential. The first time, on the fifth day of the trial, she had been called just to establish the authenticity of some letters written by Crittenden, so that they could be tagged as evidence. The second time, on the sixth day, she had merely been called on to corroborate the dates of one of her marriages.

Not that Mrs. Fair hadn't provided at least some entertaining theater from the sidelines. Throughout the first week of the trial, the former southern belle had often erupted in fits of moaning and weeping at the defendant's table, and more than once her attending doctor had been forced to administer a "stimulant" (that is, a shot of whiskey) from a flask to steady her nerves. One day the defense lawyers had even brought in an ornate lounge chair in which their client could repose, her mother cooling her brow with a fan whenever she was more than usually overwhelmed by her emotions.

Now, finally, she was being called to the stand by one of her own lawyers—Elisha Cook—to testify at length. On the arm of her other lawyer, Leander Quint, Mrs. Fair advanced slowly to the witness box, dressed as ever in black, but seeming far calmer and more composed than in days past. For virtually the first time since the trial began, utter silence reigned in the courtroom.

Cook began gently once the witness was sworn in: "What is your age, Mrs. Fair?"

"Thirty-three."

"How long since you first made the acquaintance of the deceased?"

"I made his acquaintance in 1863—in September."

"Where?"

"Virginia City."

"Did you at that time know him to be a married man?"

The answer was firm: "I did not, sir."

"How long before you ascertained that he was?"

"It was about a year before I ascertained that he had a wife."

A wave of disturbance ran through the courtroom—sounds of disbelief, sympathy, scorn. How could this woman possibly not know that her paramour had a wife and young children tucked away somewhere? How could this man keep such a secret from his intimate live-in companion for a full year? What kind of man would tell such a brazen lie? What kind of woman would believe it?

After a time, Cook continued, determined now to elicit the response that his entire defense would rest upon. He wanted the jury members to hear the firm belief held by the defendant that, however delusional, would explain—and conceivably excuse—the violent, involuntary impulse to which she had succumbed on the ferry *El Capitan*.

"And what," Cook asked, "what, if any, relation or understanding was there between you and Crittenden at that time, prior to your learning this fact?"

The defendant answered simply: "I was engaged to be married to him."

6

An Ungovernable Woman

EVEN AS A LITTLE GIRL, she was trouble. Born June 22, 1837, in Holly Springs, Mississippi—a newly established town of some four thousand migrants from the East, built on land recently vacated by the Chickasaw under Andrew Jackson's Indian Removal Act—Laura Ann Hunt showed early signs of being a stubborn and unruly child. Intelligent but willful, she was apparently not at all shy about making her wishes known to all who would listen. By the time she had reached her teens, she was already displaying the kind of "unfeminine" behavior—spending money that wasn't hers, consorting unsupervised with friends of the opposite sex—that was frowned upon in nineteenth-century America, particularly in the antebellum South.

The Hunts were a small family by the standards of the time, consisting of just Laura, her parents, a sister named Mary Jane, and a brother known as O.D. They moved frequently during Laura's childhood, living in several different places in the South before ultimately settling in New Orleans. Here, shortly after Laura's sixteenth birthday, she became engaged to a man named William H. Stone, an apparently wealthy liquor dealer several decades her senior. Laura would later claim that she married Stone at the request of her dying father—alleged evidence of a becoming filial obedience on her part. But she probably also saw some advantage in the match. With her father soon to be dead, attaching herself to an affluent older man would be crucial to her and her family's financial well-being.

This would be only the first of many marital miscalculations in her life. Stone proved to be a disastrous husband—"a dissipated man," according to Laura, who "would not quit drinking." Stone made her life miserable, forbidding her from seeing her friends and threatening to kill her if she disobeyed him. He, meanwhile, accused his young wife of carrying on an illicit affair with another man. Within a year of their wedding, the couple had already separated. To avoid the scandal of a divorce, Stone offered her $3,000 to leave New Orleans and never return. Laura took the money but never left the city, forcing Stone to go ahead with divorce proceedings. Before they concluded, however, Stone died—of cholera complicated by alcoholism, though some found the circumstances suspicious. He left his estranged wife a large but unprofitable property in Texas and little else.

Still a teenager, Laura moved to Mobile, Alabama. Presenting herself as the grieving widow of a happy marriage, she enrolled in the academy of the Roman Catholic Convent of the Visitation to be trained as a teacher, so as "to support myself and my mother, if ever need be." But like her future lover Crittenden, she was restless and mercurial, and this reclusive life soon proved intolerably dull. After just six months, she left the institution to be wed again—this time to Thomas Grayson, another substantially older man, who just so happened to be the person accused by the late William Stone of being his wife's lover. After a brief honeymoon in Vicksburg, the newlyweds came back to New Orleans to live with Grayson's mother.

Again, however, the match quickly became a nightmare. To Laura's horror, Grayson turned out to be another abusive alcoholic (or so she claimed). When particularly intoxicated, he would fire his pistol over her head while she lay in bed "to show what a good marksman he was." Other times he would take aim at the chickens in his mother's yard, shooting "fifty at a time, one after another." After six months of

this (a period of time that seemed to mark the limit of Laura's endurance), she left him, citing concern for her physical safety. When she
found that she couldn't afford to initiate divorce proceedings herself,
she encouraged Grayson to do so—on grounds of desertion, which she
agreed not to contest. Her only stipulation was that he bring no false
charges against her that might harm her reputation.

Grayson obliged and started a legal action, but Laura's hopes of
getting through the divorce with her reputation intact proved futile.
According to the mores of the day, a wife was duty-bound to honor
her marriage vows no matter what. "To suffer and to be silent under
suffering," according to *Godey's Lady's Book,* a popular magazine of
the time, was "the great command a woman has to obey." In the eyes
of the antebellum South, Tom Grayson's abusive behavior was insufficient cause for giving up on the marriage, and so the blame for its
failure lay as much with her as with him. In fact, a woman's seeking
divorce under any circumstances was regarded as deeply subversive of
the foundational principles underpinning society. By thus refusing to
be a loyal and obedient wife—not just once but twice—Laura Stone
Grayson (née Hunt) had already moved far beyond the pale of Victorian morality.

It was an untenable situation for a nineteen-year-old woman still
trying to get a start in life. Sometime in late 1856 or early 1857, she
decided to leave New Orleans and head west, bringing along her
mother (now known as Mary Lane, having herself acquired and then
lost a second husband by this time) and her brother O.D. In San Francisco, the three of them—like so many others drawn to the burgeoning
western metropolis—hoped to leave their problematic past behind and
begin again with a clean slate.

• • •

The San Francisco that greeted Laura Grayson on her arrival in California was a very different city from the one A. P. Crittenden had

encountered just seven years earlier. For one thing, the city had more than doubled in size. The population had now grown to over fifty thousand—a milestone that had taken New York 190 years, Philadelphia 120 years, and Boston 200 years to reach. And the great fires that had forced the town to rebuild in brick and mortar had given a semblance of social and spatial order to the formerly chaotic metropolis. There were now distinct residential, commercial, and entertainment districts, while the population had begun to sort itself into quiet middle-class neighborhoods, congested working-class districts, and leafy suburbs for the affluent.

By this time many upper- and middle-class white families had joined the population, meaning that the openness and social fluidity of the town's early years was no longer considered desirable. As the *Pacific* newspaper observed in 1855, if the city wanted to have any chance to grow and mature, it had to become "morally inviting" to respectable people. This meant that casual contact between white elites, especially women, and their alleged social inferiors of other races and classes had to be minimized. Among unequals, only necessary interactions—as between mistress and servant, employer and employee, merchant and customer—would be deemed acceptable. San Francisco, in other words, had to start remaking its image to better resemble the older, more established cities of the East—a development that would directly affect the fortunes of people like Mary Ellen Pleasant and Ah Toy, who would find their prospects hampered in a city where access to status and means was increasingly tied to race. Even Mexicans—initially offered at least partial integration into the new Anglo-American social order by the provisions of the 1848 peace treaty—were now implicated in this racialization process. Manuel Domínguez, a wealthy landowner who had actually served as a delegate at the California Constitutional Convention of 1849, found his status so diminished by 1857 that his testimony was rejected in a San Francisco court case because of his perceived non-whiteness.

Laura Grayson and her mother were white, but their class credentials, compared to those of a family like the Crittendens, were rather suspect, especially given Laura's marital history. As a result, their prospects for social success in San Francisco were not as good as they might have been just a few years earlier. (This is one reason why she and Clara Crittenden would not meet for years, despite the relative shortage of women in town.) Doubtless Laura tried to represent herself as wealthier and more respectable than she was—indeed, for their first few weeks in town, she, Mrs. Lane, and O.D. stayed at Rassette House, at the time one of the biggest and most prestigious hotels in the West. But this expensive pretense could not be sustained indefinitely, and soon they had to move to cheaper quarters.

To support herself, Laura tried at first to get by as a music teacher, but those earnings alone proved insufficient to live on. Having heard that many women made their way in this city of unattached men by "keeping house"—that is, running a lodging or boardinghouse—she found an affordable place to lease on Clay Street, perched on a steep hill just west of the neighborhood rapidly developing as "Little China" (the term "Chinatown" was not yet in use). But well-off lodgers did not appear in droves. Aside from one man who had been an old friend of Laura's family, her only tenants were two young sisters who also happened to be her music students. After six months of struggling to meet the rent, Laura and her mother moved to another house and tried again, but with no greater success. Finally, they had to cut their expenses by giving up the idea of keeping house and moving into a small set of rooms at the back of a commercial building near the plaza.

Part of the problem facing Laura in her quest for some kind of respectable prosperity was the fact that San Francisco, after its explosive initial growth spurt, had entered a bust cycle. The easy money of the early '50s had already been made, and now, by 1857, the amount of gold coming out of the Sierra Nevada—and the number of would-be miners going in—had tapered off. With the ebbing of the tide of new arrivals in town, buildings erected during the boom years were remaining empty, and real estate values plummeted. Many businesses,

too, were failing. Lucas & Turner, the bank for which William Tecumseh Sherman served as local representative, decided to close its San
Francisco branch in 1857, just four years after opening. That meant
that the future Union general and his family had to move out, joining
a significant backwash of people heading home after their fling out
west. By now he was reluctant to leave—San Francisco having grown
on him in recent years—but he ultimately decided that it was the wise
move, given that he was offered a job as head of Lucas & Turner's New
York City branch. When he returned to San Francisco briefly in January 1858 to clean up some of the bank's affairs, conditions in the city
had become even worse, exacerbated by the effects of the financial
panic that had swept the world in late 1857. "The whole town is for
sale," he wrote in a letter home, "and there are no buyers."

A. P. Crittenden, as a lawyer dealing largely with real estate title
disputes, was somewhat more insulated than most from the economic
downturn. In fact, his affairs had prospered enough that, by 1857, he
had almost climbed clear of the mountain of debt that had loomed
over him for years. He even managed to buy a nicer house for Clara
and the children on Taylor Street in Nob Hill—not as luxurious a
neighborhood as it would later become in the cable-car era, but certainly a few steps up, both in prestige and in altitude, from their former
home on Pacific. Even so, the city's slumping fortunes had taken a toll
on his finances, and he never quite emerged from debt before sinking
back into "embarrassment" by the end of the decade.

Nor had his political career prospered. After his two terms in the
assembly, Crittenden had run for state attorney general and state supreme court justice but was unsuccessful both times. In January 1857,
he even made a half-hearted attempt for the office of U.S. senator from
California. As he wrote to Clara a few days before the election: "I
think the prospect of my success very remote indeed as I cannot and
will not resort to the customary means to ensure it [that is, buying and
selling favors]." And he wasn't wrong about his chances. Despite receiving support from the state's other U.S. senator, David Broderick,

he failed to get past even the first round of voting in the legislature. (Senators at this time were not popularly elected but rather chosen by state legislatures.) However, Crittenden did remain a force in state Democratic politics, playing a role in the various inter- and intra-party conflicts that were becoming increasingly stark as the country inched toward civil war.

Laura Grayson, on the other hand, was too concerned with her own economic survival to worry much about politics. With prospects dim in San Francisco during the slump, she and her mother decided to try their luck in a smaller place—Shasta, a mining town located about two hundred miles north of San Francisco—where the now-twenty-two-year-old Laura took a lease on another lodging house. Here she attracted the eye of one of her short-term tenants: County Sheriff William D. Fair, introduced to her as a lawyer, former army colonel, and West Point graduate from Virginia (who just happened to have served with A. P. Crittenden in the first California state legislature a decade earlier, though there is no evidence that they had kept up the acquaintance). After a whirlwind courtship, during which time William Fair allegedly made sure that his fiancée's divorce from her previous husband had been finalized, Laura Grayson and William D. Fair married in February 1859. According to the presiding minister at the wedding in Shasta, the ceremony was attended "by nearly all the first ladies and gentlemen of the place." The clergyman also insisted that the new Mrs. Fair "was regarded and esteemed by all a lady, demanding the first consideration of society." For a time, then, it looked as if Laura's goal of comfort and respectability might actually be achieved.

But it was the husband, not the wife, whose past proved problematic in this marriage. For William Fair, true to the pattern of many early migrants to California, turned out to have invented many key aspects of his ostensible life story. His commission as an army colonel proved to be fictitious, as did his degree from West Point. And while he was in fact a lawyer, he had none of the family wealth or bright professional prospects he had pretended to during their courtship. Bitterly disappointed, his new wife tried to keep up the outward appearance of prosperity and connubial bliss, even after the Fairs left Shasta and moved farther north to the smaller mining town of Yreka, a move for which William had to borrow $200 from his friends. But times would remain tough for the newlyweds, and the birth in August 1860 of a daughter—Lillian, or Lillias, though nicknamed "Baby" for most of her childhood—only increased the financial pressures on them.

Then, just when it seemed as if all of the mines in California had been exhausted, rumors of another major mineral strike began spreading all over the state. The discovery had been made on the eastern slope of the Sierra Nevada, just over the border in Washoe (in an area of the Utah Territory that would soon split off to become the Nevada Territory). Eventually to be world-famous as "the Comstock Lode," the Washoe's enormous silver vein—judging by early reports—was destined to dwarf in wealth production even the original gold discovery in the western Sierra. This was just the kind of news the depressed Pacific coast needed to hear at that moment. If the rumors proved to be true, the prospects of the Fairs, the Crittendens, and the city of San Francisco were about to improve dramatically.

7

Blue, Gray, and Silver

O N   T H E   A F T E R N O O N   O F   November 14, 1860, a sweat-soaked rider for the new overland mail service known as the Pony Express galloped up to the relay station in Carson City, a small town in the still-desolate but soon-to-be-bustling Washoe mining country. In the rider's pack was a collection of letters and dispatches from the East, most of them bound for San Francisco and other towns in California. But while this physical mail would still require another five days of hard riding to reach the Pacific coast, some important tidings that the rider brought could be delivered almost instantaneously. Thanks to a recently completed telegraph line crossing the rugged Sierra Nevada, San Francisco would hear the news before nightfall—namely, that the 1860 presidential election had been won by . . . Abraham Lincoln, the Republican.

Lincoln's unexpected victory would have deep and wide-ranging repercussions for the people of what was now the fourteenth-largest city in the nation. San Francisco—along with the rest of California—may have been physically far removed from the goings-on in the country at large, but both city and state were being roiled by the same internecine conflicts that were tearing the rest of the country apart. California's surprisingly large contingent of pro-slavery Southern Democrats, the so-called Chivalry faction of the party (aka the "Chivs"), were a minority statewide, but they wielded disproportionate sway in politics. Chivs in the state legislature, for instance, had actually managed to pass a bill in 1858 to split California into two separate states—the northern one free, the southern one slave—though the U.S. Congress had fortunately stopped that plan from ever coming to fruition. Meanwhile, since the new Republican Party had been slow to gain power in California, opposition to the Chivs came mainly from their fellow Democrats belonging to the northern-leaning, anti-slavery faction of the party.

These local North-South tensions had in fact played out violently in the year leading up to the national election, culminating in a high-profile duel, often regarded as the last notable duel fought in the United States. The antagonists were two of the state's leading politicians. U.S. senator David Broderick, a former stonecutter, bouncer, and fireman who had learned Tammany-style politics in his native New York City, was the head of California's free-soil Democrats. David S. Terry, former chief justice of the California Supreme Court and originally from Kentucky, was a prominent Chiv who had been trying for years to amend the state constitution to allow slavery. The genial Broderick and the fiery Terry had been friendly, if often adversarial, colleagues for most of their careers. Broderick, like Crittenden, had even interceded on Terry's behalf when the latter was threatened with execution by the second Vigilance Committee in 1856. But their starkly opposed positions on slavery had soured the friendship in recent years. And when a dyspeptic Terry accused Broderick of being "Frederick Douglass's pawn," the senator responded with invective, calling the judge an "ungrateful wretch" whom he never should have saved from the vigilantes' noose. One insult led to another until finally, on the morning of September 13, 1859, the two men and their seconds met behind a barn at the Lake House Ranch, just beyond the San Francisco city limits. In a duel witnessed by seventy-three spectators, Broderick ended up taking a bullet in the breast while his own premature shot went harmlessly into the dirt a few feet in front of him. Mortally wounded, the senator died three days later, an instant martyr to the cause of abolition.

For Alexander Parker Crittenden, the results of the duel had both personal and political consequences. He and Broderick had been cordial ever since the two served together in the first state legislature in 1850, and he served as one of the pallbearers at the elder man's funeral. But as a Chiv, Crittenden was much more closely aligned politically with his fellow Kentuckian Terry, whom he had known in Texas even before he came to California. For this reason, he was particularly chagrined when the wave of sympathy for the slain Broderick ended up further polarizing the state's Democrats. Northern-leaning newspapers started portraying the affair as a cunningly planned political assassination, fanning the flames of intra-party hostility and hurting both factions politically. In Crittenden's opinion, the duel was a personal matter, pure and simple. "There was nothing political in the quarrel between Terry and Broderick," he wrote his uncle John a week after the duel, "and the idea of any conspiracy is absurd as well as monstrous."

And his worries that the duel would hurt Democrats of all types proved warranted. The rancor created by Broderick's death ended up splitting the Democratic vote in the 1860 elections and allowing the Republican Lincoln to carry the state, just as a divided Democratic vote in the nation at large allowed him to win the overall election. Even so, the numbers in California's race were breathtakingly close. With only 7 of 55 newspapers supporting him, Lincoln won the state's four Electoral College votes by fewer than a thousand ballots.

For Crittenden, Lincoln's victory was very bad news. Granted, the Kentucky-born lawyer's politics were not always predictably aligned with that of other Southern Democrats. In fact, he confessed in a letter to his son Churchill that for a time he'd considered voting for northern Democrat Stephen Douglas for president rather than John Cabell Breckinridge (James Buchanan's vice president, who ran as the Southern pro-slavery Democrat). But after studying the slavery question "as I would study any question of law," the inveterate attorney confessed,

"I came to the conclusion that the doctrine of Mr. Douglas was utterly untenable—that it was the right of the people of the South to carry their slavery into any territory of the United States . . . I then voted for Breckinridge." Either way, the one outcome he definitely did *not* want was victory for Lincoln, the man his brother-in-law Alex Jones scorned as "that old abolitionist fool and humbug." And when the alleged humbug eked out a victory, the future looked to Crittenden very bleak indeed. "I hope there will be no secession," he told his son, "[but] if it does come, and collision should occur, . . . the South would have my hearty sympathy and probably my active aid."

Exemplifying the extreme divisiveness of this time, there were even members of A.P.'s own Kentucky family who found themselves on opposite sides of the major question of the day. His uncle John, for instance, though no fan of Lincoln, would remain loyal to the Union, having joined with other conservative former Whigs to create a short-lived third party—the Constitutional Union Party—that distanced itself from both the Republicans and the two factions of the Democratic Party. And there were other Crittendens, including Uncle John's own sons, who would go on to serve as officers on opposing sides of the coming conflict. Clara's relatives in Virginia were somewhat more united in their loyalty to the South, but even the Jones family had its renegades. Clara's father—Alexander Jones Sr., a well-known clergyman in Richmond—eventually chose to remain true to the Union, causing acute embarrassment to every one of his children, Clara included. Facing disapproval and downright hostility from his Virginia neighbors, the Reverend Jones was forced to leave family and congregation behind and move north to New Jersey.

What's more, even some of A.P. and Clara's own children were showing disturbing signs of disagreement with their parents. In April 1858, Churchill (now almost eighteen) had gone east to enroll at Hanover College in Indiana; James (just nineteen months younger) had followed him the next year, to attend prep school at Phillips Exeter Academy in New Hampshire. A.P. and Clara had urged their sons to go to school in the South, but neither boy took their advice. "Don't worry," Churchill wrote to his mother, "I won't change loyalties from south to north. There's little difference between them anyway." He also attempted to reassure her about his younger brother: "James will always be a Southerner, but he may change his mind about slavery, which is a curse." This last sentence prompted an angry letter from his father: "You speak of slavery as a curse," A.P. wrote back in July 1859. "From this I can only infer that you entertain opinions on that subject which I would regret that any son of mine should have. If I thought that James too would abandon the sentiments of his family, I would recall him without delay."

Meanwhile, the Crittenden children who remained at home were creating worries of their own. The two oldest girls, nineteen-year-old Laura and fifteen-year-old Nannie, were no trouble; both were on the cusp of adulthood and already on a fast track to be married. But the younger children were a constant source of anxiety. In December 1858, two-year-old Tommy seriously burned his cheek on a hot poker, while three-year-old Carrie's hair caught fire from an open candle-flame; both "suffered severely," according to their father. Then, on New Year's Day, fourteen-year-old Howard was accidentally shot in the back while hunting with a friend, receiving a wound that would cause him to limp for the rest of his life. But the most serious mishap came in February of 1859, when the accident-prone Tommy, after being put to bed with a candle in his room, got up for some reason, spilled a bottle of cologne onto his nightshirt, and somehow managed to set himself ablaze. The boy was scorched so badly that he lost part of his left hand, and for weeks afterward he had to take chloroform for the excruciating pain he suffered whenever anyone changed the dressings on his burns. Little wonder that Crittenden's own health seemed to be deteriorating, as he complained ever more frequently of insomnia, intense rheumatism, and chronic pains in his throat and chest.

At least his material prospects had begun to improve again. At the outset of the 1860s, San Francisco's economy was finally coming out of its extended slump, thanks to that much-talked-about mineral strike in the Washoe country. The rumors of a massive silver discovery had proven accurate, and so the dwindling gold profits from the western Sierra were soon replaced by even greater silver profits from the eastern side of the mountains. Over the next five years, in fact, there would be six major bonanzas at the Comstock Lode, bringing enough wealth back to San Francisco to lift its economy to new heights. Naturally, Crittenden found his own financial boat lifted as well, as legal disputes over mining rights multiplied. For just one of his cases alone, settled in August 1860, his personal fee was $18,000 (the equivalent of well over half a million dollars today).

Suddenly San Francisco was growing again. "The whole city has improved immensely," Crittenden wrote Churchill in late 1859. "A great many houses have been built this year—far more than ever before in a single year, and yet a decent house cannot be found that is vacant. I think the population of the city at the next census will be 100,000."

Crittenden was exaggerating a bit; after the slowdown of the late 1850s, the tide of migration had required some time to reverse itself, so the city's 1860 population was actually just under fifty-seven thousand. But much of the excitement and optimism of the early Gold Rush years had returned. The pace of physical improvements to the town—there was now a steam-powered street railroad on Market Street, for instance—had picked up again, and the city had begun to take on the appearance of a true major metropolis. Lick House and Russ House, the city's first two really palatial hotels, were just nearing completion on downtown sites within a few minutes' walk of each other, while the so-called Montgomery Block, one of the finest commercial buildings in the country, stood four massive stories tall a few blocks north. One Frenchman visiting at this time, engineer Louis Laurent Simonin, found parts of the city comparable even to Paris— "well built, magnificently laid out, gas lighted, and crisscrossed with beautiful streets, some of which are quite grandiose, like Montgomery Street, which reminds one of the Rue de la Paix." And Simonin found the attire of the people on these grandiose streets just as impressive.

Admitting that he had come expecting to see inhabitants decked out in sombreros, red woolen shirts, enormous boots, and belts bristling with knives and revolvers, he was quickly disabused of this outdated notion. "Imagine my astonishment upon disembarking in San Francisco to find all the fashions of Europe!"

And those fashionable San Franciscans had begun to surround themselves with the other trappings of sophisticated urban living. On that same Montgomery Street, there now stood Platt's Hall, a theatrical venue with seating for more than two thousand. Platt's and its competitor Maguire's Opera House, an equally grand theater on Washington Street, were now attracting some of the most prestigious visiting musical and theatrical productions in the country. Smaller theaters and music venues were cropping up everywhere, while cultural institutions like the Mercantile Library Association and the Mechanics Institute provided educational opportunities to compare with those on the East Coast. The city itself was growing geographically, too, as the street grid was enlarged with a new Western Addition of some hundreds of square blocks west of Larkin Street—a virtual Louisiana Purchase to make room for a burgeoning population. All of this growth was being financed by the first freshets of wealth flowing from the Washoe silver mines. And those freshets would become a mighty river in the years to come, assuring San Francisco's future growth no matter what happened in the rest of the country in the wake of the ongoing political crisis.

This silver-fueled economic renaissance also attracted the beginnings of a literary community to the rapidly maturing city. It would still be a few more years until Mark Twain made his appearance on the scene, but his soon-to-be friend and rival, Bret Harte, arrived in town in the spring of 1860. A shy, retiring twenty-three-year-old, Harte had had a rough time realizing his early ambition to be a writer. As a boy growing up in New York State, he'd tried writing poetry, and in fact had seen his first poem published in a local newspaper when he was just eleven years old. But his family had discouraged him. Harte's late father, a schoolteacher, had apparently also suffered from literary inclinations, and had left the family destitute when he died. So when the boy brought home his first published verse—a satirical piece titled "Autumn Musings"—his family greeted the accomplishment with ridicule rather than the praise he'd been expecting. "It was a terrible experience," he would later recall. "I sometimes wonder that I ever wrote another line of verse."

Harte had first come west to California as a teenager in 1854, following his widowed mother to Oakland, where she had married again to a lawyer who would eventually become the town's mayor. Young "Frank," as Harte was called then, had no marketable skills to speak of, having left school at the age of thirteen. But he'd done a fine job of educating himself in his father's library; by his own report, he had started reading Shakespeare by the age of six, Dickens by seven, and Montaigne by eight. He continued this self-education project in California, spending most of his time reading alone in the garret of his stepfather's Oakland home. But eventually he realized that it was time to make his own way. He left the family home and for several years wandered aimlessly around the state, working odd jobs as a druggist's assistant, a tutor to a wealthy rancher's children, and an agent and messenger for Wells, Fargo. He even did a short, unsuccessful gig as a miner in the gold country. But finally, on New Year's Eve of 1857, he made a resolution to do everything he could to become a writer—since, as he confided to his diary, "I was fit for nothing else."

He ultimately found a job as a printer's apprentice on a new publication called the *Northern Californian,* published in Arcata on Humboldt Bay, several hundred miles north of San Francisco. The newspaper was a small operation, and Harte was occasionally allowed to write short pieces to fill an extra column inch here or there. He also began to publish pieces in other newspapers around the state, and even placed a poem—"Dolores," about a nun who abandons the convent for a life of passion—back east in the well-regarded New York *Knickerbocker* literary magazine. "Dolores," like most of his early work, was somewhat awkward and stilted ("Turn that pensive glance on high / Seest thou the floods in yon blessed sky," etc., etc.), but it was a start. And the editor

of the *Northern Californian,* a Colonel S. G. Whipple, apparently decided that the neophyte was competent enough to take on more responsibility. The next time Whipple traveled out of town, therefore, he
entrusted the running of the newspaper to his young apprentice. It
would prove to be both the immediate breaking and the ultimate making of Harte's literary career.

During Whipple's absence in late February 1860, a brutal massacre
of the native Wiyot population occurred in several villages around
Humboldt Bay. The episode was anything but uncommon; since the
American takeover of California, the state's Indigenous populations
had been the target of what can only be called a systematic attempt at
genocide by whites—not just by private settlers but also by state mili-
tiamen and U.S. Army soldiers acting under explicit orders of their
superiors. By one historian's estimate, between nine thousand and sixteen thousand members of California tribes were killed by non-Natives
in the three decades after the start of the Mexican War in 1846. This
"war of extermination," as California's first American governor called
it, was ostensibly waged to protect white settlers and punish Indigenous crimes. But the fundamental reason for the slaughter was simply
that California's Native populations stood in the way of "an enterprising people" seeking to own and use the land for themselves.

Even by these standards, the so-called Humboldt Bay Massacres of
1860 were particularly horrifying—"a scene of atrocity and horror
unparalleled not only in our own Country, but even in history," according to an official military account. In four separate villages in and
around Humboldt Bay, a total of 188 mostly Wiyot people were sadis-
tically murdered by white "volunteers," apparently without any specific provocation. Appalled, the temporary editor of the *Northern
Californian* took up his pen. "Neither age or sex had been spared,"
Harte wrote in an editorial a few days afterward. "Little children and
old women were mercilessly stabbed and their skulls crushed with
axes . . . A more shocking and revolting spectacle never was exhibited
to the eyes of a Christian and civilized people." So impassioned was his

editorial, which blamed the "barbarity" entirely on its white perpetrators, that the young author was forced to flee town or else risk being
lynched by an angry mob.

"The event," according to one of his early biographers, "ended his
life as a wanderer." Harte took refuge back in San Francisco, where,
fortunately, jobs had again become plentiful because of the nascent
silver boom. He quickly secured a place as a typesetter at a popular
newspaper called the *Golden Era,* which had published a few of his
pieces in the past. Soon, when not setting other authors' work in type,
he was allowed to write a few things himself, often composing right at
the type case, without bothering to put pen to paper. At this time, the
Golden Era was trying to expand the audience for its eclectic mix of
pulp fiction, satire, and farming columns, which so far had attracted a
mostly rural readership. Editor Joe Lawrence wanted to appeal to
wealthier, more urban (and urbane) readers, like the ones now building
luxurious residences in fashionable San Francisco neighborhoods like
South Park and Rincon Hill. The twenty-three-year-old Harte proved
to be just the kind of sophisticated writer Lawrence was looking for.
Within a month of starting at the paper, Harte already had his own
weekly column called "Town and Table Talk," which he wrote under
the pseudonym "the Bohemian." And somehow, perhaps because he
was forced to cover local people and events, his prose soon lost many
of its East Coast pretensions and adopted a looser, more informal tone
better suited to the city's temperament.

Harte's work in these early *Golden Era* years, according to his future
friend Twain, stood head and shoulders above the awkward scribblings
that until then had passed as California letters. It struck "a new and
fresh and spirited note that rose above that orchestra's mumbling con-
fusion and was recognizable as music."

In fact, Harte's tenure there—first as marquis contributor and then
as the publication's editor—would sow the seeds for a flowering of
literary talent on the Pacific coast that would transform the character
of American letters, producing a kind of literature entirely different

from the stuffy perorations of New Englanders like Hawthorne, Long-
fellow, and John Greenleaf Whittier. "The literary West," as one critic
would later put it, "may be said to have founded itself upon the imagination of Bret Harte." The transplanted New Yorker was thus San
Francisco's first and founding literary light. There would be others—
one even brighter—emerging in the years to come.

.   .   .

As the turbulent year 1860 drew to a close, an eruption over Lincoln's
election and the issue of slavery seemed all but inevitable. Would
southern states secede from the Union before the new president even
took office? This possibility put California in a precarious position.
Given that Lincoln had won, however narrowly, a plurality of votes in
what was still a free-soil state, many people assumed that it would remain loyal to the Union. But this was by no means certain. The state
legislature and California's contingent in the U.S. Congress were both
dominated by South-leaning Democrats. Governor John G. Downey,
though he had supported northern Democrat Stephen Douglas in the
election, was not a guaranteed Union loyalist either. Perhaps most
troubling of all, the military leaders in control of the arsenals and forts
in the state were mostly southerners as well; the commander of the
army's Department of the Pacific—the general in charge of all U.S.
soldiers west of the Rockies—was none other than Albert Sidney
Johnston, A. P. Crittenden's old friend from Texas, who was not only
a supporter of slavery but a slave owner himself.

What's more, some of these Democrats were unabashedly preach-
ing secession for California, either to join the anticipated confederacy
of southern states or else to declare independence from both sides and
set up as a separate entity called the Pacific Republic. And many in
California seemed ready to fight for this cause. At one meeting of the
state legislature in January, an assemblyman from El Dorado County
announced that there were at least thirty thousand men in the state

willing to take up arms against the new president and his supporters, should the situation in the East deteriorate. For months, California waited in acute anticipation for reports from Washington, D.C., which still took weeks to arrive at the West Coast, despite the fast new Pony Express service across the western wilderness.

In a last, desperate attempt to stave off the looming secession crisis, Crittenden's uncle John, now a U.S. senator from Kentucky, proposed a sweeping series of six constitutional amendments and four congressional resolutions designed to reconcile North and South and avert the crisis. But many northerners felt that the so-called Crittenden Compromise would permanently preserve slavery, making it unconstitutional for the federal government ever to abolish the institution in the southern states. And so the proposal was doomed to fail in the deeply divided U.S. Congress. Five days before Christmas, South Carolina seceded from the Union, followed in close succession by Mississippi, Florida, Alabama, and the rest of what would soon become known as the Confederate States of America.

On April 24, 1861, a report reached San Francisco about the attack on Fort Sumter that had occurred twelve days earlier. Newspaper offices were instantly besieged by people of all political stripes, while the downtown districts, according to the *Alta California,* "were in a fever of excitement," resounding with the cries of newsboys and the "deep-muttered oaths" of Yankees cursing rebels and rebels cursing Yankees. Twelve days delayed it may have been, but news of civil war had finally reached the streets of San Francisco. And it was news that would have momentous consequences for two California-based southern sympathizers in particular—Laura Fair and Alexander Parker Crittenden.

"Madness rules the hour," proclaimed the editor of the *Herald* in the next day's edition. "The first blow has been struck in an internecine war, the end whereof no man knoweth or can judge."

Part Two

Love and War

(1861–1865)

We have so many inhabitants in this country who were brought up in the South . . . Though most of the citizens in this city profess to be loyal Union people, yet when probed to the quick, they hoist the Confederate flag.

—JAMES V. MANSFIELD
Letter to his wife, Mary, sent from
San Francisco during the Civil War

8

The Fortunes of War

THIS WAR WAS TURNING Alexander Parker Crittenden into a hypocrite. Of course, he had no one to blame but himself. It was A.P., after all, who'd decided that the Crittenden family would remain in California, even after it became clear that the state was not going to secede from the Union. True, a small group of determined southerners—calling themselves the Committee of 30—had for a time planned to launch a coup d'état, seizing local armories and taking California out of the Union by force of arms. But the plot had never gotten off the ground, and the committee eventually voted to dissolve itself. And while the lawyer in Crittenden would almost certainly have disapproved of any such extralegal attempt to compel the state into the Confederacy, his sympathies were still very much with his native South. Hence the hypocrisy. The Crittendens, as California residents, were now forced to pretend a fundamental loyalty to Lincoln and the Union, no matter what their private feelings. Anything else would have been treason.

Other friends and family had made different choices. Two of Clara's brothers, for instance—Alex and William Marlborough Jones—had immediately joined the Confederate Army once war was declared. Crittenden's former law partner Edmund Randolph (who had been a member of the thirty-person committee behind the aborted coup) had done likewise. Even Albert Sidney Johnston had joined the exodus of southerners, resigning his commission as U.S. Army commander of the Pacific Division in April and then decamping to Los Angeles, after which he managed to make his way out of the state before he could be detained by authorities. By the end of summer, he was a full general in the Confederate States Army with a position similar to his previous one, in command of that army's Western Military Department.

But the debt-ridden Crittenden, with a large family to support and the prospect of much lucrative legal work involving the new Washoe mines, felt that he couldn't afford to follow suit. And so he remained out west, becoming a member of California's Breckenridge (Chiv) Democratic State Committee. As a member of this "loyal opposition," he could advocate for an immediate negotiated end to the war while still paying lip service to a baseline support for the Union. Meanwhile, his true feelings were revealed only to his closest friends and family. For instance, when sons Churchill and James—apparently succumbing to the patriotic mood at their schools in the East—proposed joining the Union army to put down "the rebellion" and punish "the traitors," their father was incensed. "I am utterly amazed at the ideas both James and yourself have expressed on the subject," he wrote in a letter to Churchill. "You wish to enlist in the cause of the North against your own people! Well, in the ranks of those whom you call traitors, and whom you would meet in the field as enemies, you will encounter your own father and at least one of your brothers. Come home at once!"

Churchill, the more obedient son, repented immediately and complied with his father's wish, returning to San Francisco and apologizing to his family for even temporarily forsaking his heritage. But his younger brother James was less compliant. Visiting Clara's family in Richmond in May, the callow nineteen-year-old made no secret of the fact that he intended to go to Washington to present himself to Abraham Lincoln as a Union army volunteer. He even wrote to his uncle

John, soliciting the senator's influence to procure an appointment to West Point—"to save our noble country." The young man's professions of support for the Union became so strident that one of his Richmond uncles eventually arranged for him to be put in jail for a while, lest he be attacked on the streets of what was soon to become the capital city of the Confederacy.

James's parents and siblings back in California, of course, had to be more circumspect about their loyalties, as wartime San Francisco rapidly became a center of staunch pro-Union sentiment. Part of this was a natural development; a country's entrance into war always tends to erase all ambivalence from the minds of the bulk of its citizens, sweeping away any mixed feelings in a flood of unambiguous patriotism. But this arousal of nationalistic feeling had been substantially aided by the efforts of a firebrand Unitarian minister named Thomas Starr King, who had come west from Boston just before the war and quickly turned his substantial skills as an orator to the cause of Lincoln and national reconciliation. Though little known outside California today, Starr King was at one time considered a towering figure in the state's history, regarded by many (Abraham Lincoln included) as the man who kept California in the Union.

The diminutive and sickly clergyman did not look the part. Five feet tall and only 120 pounds, the Reverend Starr King had been lured to California to take the reins of San Francisco's First Unitarian Church, which had run through five unsatisfactory pastors in the past decade and now found itself in debt. Hoping to bring new life to the congregation, the church had sought out the young New Englander, who had an excellent reputation but whose lack of Harvard credentials apparently limited his prospects back east. And while the sight of the unprepossessing clergyman had at first distressed his new parishioners, all doubts ended once they heard the man speak. Starr King's debut sermon—a rousing paean to the moral potential of the Pacific Slope as a force to reconcile North and South—inspired passionate enthusiasm in nearly everyone who heard it. Word about the rousing new orator

spread quickly, and soon Starr King was flooded with lecture and sermon requests from all over Northern California.

Once the war started, however, Starr King's message became more
pointed and overtly political. He began speaking at huge, unapolo-
getically pro-Union rallies in places like Platt's Hall in San Francisco
and in the city's open plaza later renamed Union Square, in honor of
these very gatherings. Starr King made no concessions to southern
sensibilities in these orations, and his rhetoric could be biting: "The
old Declaration of Independence will live," he declared at one rally, but
"the new one [that is, that of the seceding states] will not. The old was
drawn by patriots, the new by traitors." No wonder he began receiving
hate mail from the remaining Confederate sympathizers in the state,
along with threats of physical violence and even assassination. But California's Union loyalists were electrified. "He is a torrent of eloquence,"
one witness exclaimed, "so heartfelt, so convincing, so powerful, that
he excites the multitude into a whirlwind of applause." James V. Mansfield, a visiting spiritualist from New England, was so smitten that he
admitted (in a letter to his wife!), "I am so fond of King I don't know
but I would marry him, were he a Lady . . ."

Starr King's rallies began to have an effect. Buoyed by this tide of
patriotic rhetoric, Republicans triumphed in the state elections of
September 1861, setting off another exodus of southerners and deci-
mating the ranks of the state's Chivalry Democrats. With Republicans
now in control of both houses of the state legislature, and with the
reform-minded party stalwart Leland Stanford in the governor's chair,
fears that California might somehow turn against the Union disappeared entirely. A. P. Crittenden and other like-minded Breckenridge
Democrats could only stew in silence.

· · ·

The rise of anti-slavery Republicans in statewide politics proved to be
good news for Black Californians, as the state soon began lifting some

of the restrictions on African Americans that Mary Ellen Pleasant and her associates had been contesting for years. The state legislature's repeal of the ban on Black court testimony in March 1863 was particularly welcome. With that egregious law gone and the state and federal Fugitive Slave Laws obviated by the start of the war, members of San Francisco's Black activist community could turn their attention to other concerns, like voting rights and segregation in schools and public transit—issues that could now be pursued in the courts unhampered by any testimony ban. And pursued they would be, by no one more avidly than Mrs. Pleasant herself.

Mary Ellen and husband, John James, had in fact only recently returned to San Francisco, after spending an eventful few years in Canada and the eastern United States. It's difficult to corroborate details about their activities during this time, but the couple seem to have left the city in 1858, just after playing a role in the final fugitive slave case to be tried in California. The whole incident had been a dramatic one, involving the last-minute rescue of a young man named Archy Lee just as his enslaver was attempting to spirit him away on a steamship bound for the South. According to the reminiscences of at least one witness, Pleasant, while probably not involved in Lee's physical liberation, had helped finance both the rescue and the subsequent legal case in the district court. She had then hidden Lee in her home after the judge freed him, lest he be kidnapped again before his relocation to Canada could be arranged.

It's unclear whether their own journey to Canada had something to do with helping Archy Lee escape, but sometime shortly after the resolution of his case, the Pleasants traveled via New York to the town of Chatham in what is now Ontario, where there was a sizable population of free Blacks. Chatham had become a center of abolitionist activity in the late 1850s—a place where fugitives from slavery could find refuge, and where rescue missions of various kinds could be organized safely beyond the reach of U.S. laws. Records indicate that the Pleasants bought property in town, apparently to house freedom-seekers from below the border. They also joined a local committee of thirty-four Black and twelve white abolitionists that in May 1858 met with white agitator John Brown to plan and finance his ill-fated raid on Harpers Ferry. According to Pleasant, she personally donated $30,000 to the cause—an implausibly large sum, though some of the money may have been collected from other members of San Francisco's Black community. In an interview conducted some years later, two of Brown's children did confirm that their father "went to Chatham in '58 and met a colored woman who advanced him considerable money," so it may indeed have been true.

What is more probably apocryphal, however, is the story Pleasant told about making a tour of the plantations on the Roanoke River in Virginia, disguised as a jockey and traveling with a man and a string of horses in order to spread the word of the coming rebellion among local enslaved people. "We arranged that when Brown made a stand at Harpers Ferry," she told a journalist late in life, "the negroes were to rise [in revolt] in every direction." But Brown apparently acted too soon, launching the raid "before the time was ripe," and so she was forced to quickly return north. According to Pleasant's account, when Brown was arrested after his unsuccessful raid, he was carrying a letter from her—signed "M.E.P."—stating: "The axe is laid at the root of the tree. When the first blow is struck, there will be more money and help." But this incriminating document was luckily never tied back to her, thanks to her sloppy penmanship. As she told the journalist: "I read in the papers that the detectives were on the track of W.E.P. who wrote the letter, and I had a quiet laugh when I saw that my poor handwriting had given them a false trail."

The Pleasants' return to San Francisco at the start of the Civil War came at a propitious time, given the more tolerant tone of state politics and the recent revival of the local economy. John Pleasant seems to have returned to his job as a cook on the Panama steamers, while Mary Ellen quickly secured a position as housekeeper in the extensive household of Selim Woodworth, one of the wealthiest merchants in the city.

It's possible that she took the job simply because the John Brown debacle had exhausted her substantial supply of capital; but working for
Woodworth also put her again in close proximity to one of the city's
movers and shakers—a situation whose manifold benefits she had
learned to appreciate back in her housekeeping days in the early 1850s.
("Black or white," as one journalist would later marvel, "no other
woman in this state ever had the confidence of so many of its prominent men.") In any case, whatever financial setback she may have suffered seems to have been overcome in the booming war years, as she
worked for and learned from the well-connected Woodworth and his
wife, Lisette, with whom she became intimate friends.

Once settled into her new post, she immediately turned the focus
of her activism back to local issues. By now the Black community in
San Francisco was well established, boasting three churches, four Ma-
sonic lodges, numerous businesses (liveries, real estate agencies, laun-
dries), and even a weekly newspaper, the *Pacific Appeal*. But much
remained to be done. In particular, the segregation issue in San Francisco had reached a critical juncture, as the city's attempts to emulate
the racial landscape of more mature American cities—where contacts
between white and Black were carefully controlled—were stepped up
in the war years.

The first important battleground was the streetcar system. The introduction of cable cars on the city's hills was still a few years in the
future, but by the early 1860s San Francisco was already interlaced by
a number of street railways, most powered by horses or mules but at
least one by steam. For city residents, this was a welcome new sign of
urban development, but it came with a price for some. At around
7 P.M. on the evening of April 17, 1863, an African American woman
named Charlotte Brown boarded a streetcar of the Omnibus Rail
Road on Powell Street near Filbert, en route to a doctor's appointment
across town. After she had taken a seat, she was approached by the
conductor, who declined her ticket and flatly informed her that "colored people were not allowed to ride." When she refused to get off,

noting that she had been riding on that very horsecar line ever since service began the previous March, the conductor took hold of her arm and forcibly removed her. Thanks to the recent repeal of the testimony ban, she was able to sue the company and act as her own witness. And while she ultimately won her case, the amount of damages awarded dwindled over the course of various appeals from $25 to a mere 5 cents—the cost of her ticket.

The ruling was considered a victory for Black Americans—at least by the white-owned *Alta California* and *The Call,* which declared it the end of the "war between the negroes and the Railroad Company"— but others knew better. The court's final ruling applied only to Brown as an individual, leaving ambiguous the status of other Black San Franciscans on this and other lines.

Writing to the *Pacific Appeal* after the trial, one Black reader insisted that, whatever the white press might like to believe, "the war . . . has just commenced." And indeed, a few months later, Charlotte Brown and her father, James, co-founder of the first Black newspaper in the Bay Area, the *Mirror of the Times* (predecessor of the *Pacific Appeal*), were ejected from another Omnibus car, prompting a second lawsuit that she again won, receiving $500 damages, one-tenth of what she initially asked for. But even this more definitive ruling led to little actual change in the policies of the horsecar lines. Clearly, winning this fight was going to require significantly more tenacity, patience, and money—resources that the Browns' friend and ally Mary Ellen Pleasant fortunately possessed in abundance.

*   *   *

The improving wartime economy may have been helping other Californians recover from the hard times of the late '50s, but so far it was having few benefits for the luckless Fair family of Yreka. Located in the extreme northern part of the state, Yreka was far from the booming silver mines of the Washoe, and William Fair struggled to make any kind of respectable living as a lawyer there, a fact that just put more pressure on his already troubled marriage. Hoping for better luck in their old haunts, he and Laura decided to move again to San Francisco, which had snapped back so smartly from the slump that it now qualified as the city with the highest per capita income in the country. Laura and baby Lillian moved first, taking up residence in November 1861 in a Bush Street house rented from a certain Dr. Hitchcock. William Fair, after closing down the Yreka law office, followed a few weeks later. However, he did not move into the house with his wife and daughter; he instead began sleeping on a cot in the office of his old friend Dr. S. N. Murphy, causing some comment among those who knew the lawyer from his previous time in the city. Laura would later deny it, but it seemed clear that the couple had separated.

One night toward Christmas—already behind on the rent of the rooms she had moved into less than two months before—Laura went to see her husband at Dr. Murphy's office to tell him that she badly needed money. Unable or unwilling to help, Fair sent Laura away empty-handed. Several days later, her landlord, Dr. Hitchcock, went to Murphy's office to see Fair, perhaps to demand the rent his wife owed. When no one answered his knock, he tried to enter the office but found the door blocked by something heavy. He forced the door open only to find the body of William Fair, killed by a gunshot to the head.

When Hitchcock brought news of the death to his tenant, Laura rushed over to Dr. Murphy's office to see her husband's body. "Crazed and frantic with grief," she brashly accused Murphy of shooting William Fair, since the two had allegedly had a confrontation earlier about some disputed property deeds. But after making this charge, as Laura later told the story, "I was immediately surrounded by a number of gentlemen (none of whom I know) who urged me to be silent and not make any such accusation, frightening me with the idea that it would get me into inextricable trouble." Laura's insinuations aside, virtually everyone familiar with the situation was convinced that the depressed

and destitute William Fair had committed suicide—a verdict confirmed by the subsequent coroner's inquest. And although the likely
cause was despair over his dire financial condition, at least one local
newspaper implied that "domestic troubles" lay at the root of the matter. There was even some suggestion that Fair's young and attractive
wife may have given him reason to be jealous.

A widow now for a second time, and with a sixteen-month-old
baby to support, Laura Fair was in desperate straits. Abandoning her
rented rooms, she took refuge with her mother, who had returned to
San Francisco sometime before the Fairs had, and joined her in man-
aging a lodging house on Mission Street. But here again, she fell behind on the payments for rent and furniture. Since her late husband
had been a Mason, she tried applying for aid from the fraternal organization's local Board of Relief. Three investigators were sent to her
house to interview her, but they were apparently unmoved by the
widow's plight. "I am surprised, Madam," one of them remarked, "that
so handsome a woman as you should find it necessary to apply to the
Masons for assistance." His implication was clear. For a woman trying
to achieve respectability for herself and her child, this was the worst
kind of insult. "My indignation rendered me speechless," she later recalled, "and I merely showed them the door."

Meanwhile the unpaid bills kept accumulating. Her old landlord
from Bush Street, Dr. Hitchcock, filed suit against her to recover $100
in back rent—a sum Laura could not hope to pay. Then, a particularly
aggressive creditor (the merchant who provided wood and coal for the
lodging house) tried to force his way into her rooms to demand payment of his bill. Struggling to keep him from pushing the door open,
she struck out at him with a pair of scissors, cutting a long slash in his
coat. Outraged, the merchant took her to the police court, displaying
the torn coat as evidence. Judge Cowles was sympathetic and released
her immediately. Even so, she again felt humiliated. "God and my own
soul alone know what I have suffered in my struggles with poverty," she
later said.

•   •   •

But while 1862 may have marked the low point in Laura Fair's troubled life so far, San Francisco as a whole saw only brighter days ahead, despite the bitter conflict taking place thousands of miles to the east. On July 4 that year, the traditional celebration of Independence Day—always a big event in San Francisco—was sweetened by two pieces of good news for the city's future. The first was the completion of the Spring Valley aqueduct, bringing free-flowing fresh water to the city for the first time and ensuring an adequate supply to allow local industries to grow. But the more important news came via the newly completed long-distance telegraph line from Washington, D.C. Just a few days earlier, President Abraham Lincoln had signed the Pacific Railway Act, commencing a project that would connect Northern California directly to the rail network of the East, and thus to cities, suppliers, and markets all over the country. It would still take several years to build the transcontinental railroad line, but San Francisco's time of isolation would soon be ending.

9

The Silver Magnet

IRONICALLY, IT WAS LAURA FAIR'S new notoriety, rather than any of the solid respectability she yearned for, that finally enabled her to extract herself from these dire financial straits. In the months after William Fair's death, gossip about his young widow had circulated among the self-styled gentry of Northern California—not just in San Francisco, but in Sacramento, Shasta, and other places where the lawyer and former state legislator had been known. People whispered that it was Mrs. Fair's imperfect fidelity and constant demands for money that had driven her poor husband to suicide. Meanwhile, Laura's reputation as an "ungovernable woman" had only worsened after the slashing incident with the bill collector, which had been reported widely (and snidely) in the newspapers.

But Laura discovered that her dubious celebrity had some advantages: She became an actress. "Debut of Mrs. W.D. Fair," ran the advertisement in all of the San Francisco newspapers on March 13, 1863. "She will appear this evening as Lady Teazle in Sheridan's beautiful comedy of *The School for Scandal*." That this role was uniquely appropriate for her (Lady Teazle is an ungovernable young wife who torments her husband with her imperfect fidelity and constant demands for money) was a fact lost on no one, least of all the play's producers.

In their advertisements for the show, they ran Mrs. Fair's name even larger than that of her eminent costar—Junius Brutus Booth Jr., brother of the man who would assassinate the current president two years later. How better to fill the house, they reasoned, than to feature the now-infamous Laura Fair in the play's juiciest role?

This ingenious reinvention had originated with an actor named McKean Buchanan, one of Laura's tenants at her new lodging house in Sacramento. After her swift acquittal in the bill collector's assault case in 1862, she had decided it might be best to leave San Francisco for a while, so she and her mother had moved to the state capital for yet another attempt to "keep house." And while the new venture was not an immediate success, Laura and Mrs. Lane do seem to have attracted a somewhat higher class of tenant this time, including several state legislators as well as the forty-year-old Buchanan—a "world-renowned tragedian," according to Mark Twain—who had made a celebrated debut as Hamlet a generation earlier. Aware that his much-talked-about landlady was still struggling to pay her bills, Buchanan suggested that she might earn enough to satisfy her harassing creditors with just a few appearances on the stage. Laura objected initially, but at this point—having pawned most of her jewelry and with both Baby and Mrs. Lane seriously ill in bed—she was desperate enough to give it a try. She agreed to allow her tenant to organize a benefit performance of "Sheridan's beautiful comedy" in Sacramento, as long as he would help her prepare for the role.

To Buchanan's delight, Laura proved to be a natural actress. And when the Sacramento benefit attracted an enthusiastic paying audience, he contacted a producer, Charles Tibbett, to arrange for several other performances, most notably the one at Tibbett's Metropolitan Theatre in San Francisco. Junius Booth and some of the other actors reportedly chafed at having to share the stage with a rank amateur like the widow Fair. If so, their disgruntlement likely deepened once the reviews came out, since she ended up getting more praise than they did. According to the *Daily Alta*'s critic, Laura's "excellent conception and rendition of her part put to blush many of the professionals who were associated with her." Booth, by contrast, came in for particular criticism, being described as "ill at ease and imperfect as Sir Peter Teazle." Laura's critical triumph must have been pleasing to her, but perhaps even more satisfying was the fact that she earned enough money from her portion of ticket revenues (she also starred in at least one other production in the mining town of Marysville, playing the heartless seductress in Charles Selby's romantic fantasy *The Marble Heart*) to erase all of her debts and then some, and all in the space of a few short weeks.

Having finally earned a modicum of capital, Laura began to think about how she might best achieve her heart's desire—namely, some kind of financial stability and a measure of social respectability for herself and her child. Her brief career as an actress had been lucrative, but this was an age when acting was still considered a disreputable profession, especially for women; the class of society that Mrs. Fair aspired to did not readily welcome even the most famous of actresses, since their profession put them conspicuously in the public sphere, where respectable women did not belong. Besides, as naturally talented as Laura may have been, her box-office appeal as a scandalous novelty would probably not have lasted very long.

So Laura Fair had a decision to make. Over the brief twenty-six years of her existence, she had made three attempts to achieve prosperity and mainstream respectability by marrying older, socially well-placed men; all three tries had failed miserably. Clearly, she would have to make her way by herself from now on, without a man to rely on, preferably in an untried new place where money was abundant and moral standards were less severe. And in the 1860s' West, the place that fit this bill best was the region's newest wellspring of affluence and excitement: the Comstock Lode.

· · ·

In 1863 the silver mines of the Comstock, centered on a brand-new boomtown called Virginia City—located some 250 rough, mountainous miles northeast of San Francisco—were just approaching their first peak of productivity. More than a decade had passed since prospectors first began trying their luck in this area, not long after the discovery of gold at Sutter's Mill on the other side of the Sierra Nevada. Would-be miners reasoned that the same gold veins that eroded into the streams and rivers on the west side of the mountains probably also eroded into those on the east side. But this reasoning was flawed, and most of the gold finds in what would eventually become the Nevada Territory had proved meager. One problem was that the gold ore unearthed here was typically mixed in with a kind of "annoying blue stuff," as one miner called it—a hard blue-black mud that made extracting any meaningful amount of gold difficult. But in June 1859, a rancher named Harrison took a sample of the nuisance "waste" rock to an assessor in Placerville for analysis, and received some excellent news: There may not have been much gold in the samples, but there *was* an extraordinarily high concentration of silver. And with that report, a second major mineral boom was born.

Unlike the early gold finds in the western Sierra foothills, the Nevada silver strikes were not conducive to the kind of easy surface mining that allowed individuals to work claims with little more than a tin pan, a pick, and a shovel. On the contrary, the Comstock ore required heavy-duty milling of large amounts of rock in order to be profitable; in other words, major capital investment was needed to reap significant returns here, meaning that corporate entities moved in on the Comstock Lode much quicker than they had in the California goldfields. Hastily organized mining companies were soon buying up any and all promising claims on offer, raising capital to dig mines and mill ore by selling shares of stock on a brand-new stock market—the San Francisco Stock and Exchange Board, created in September 1862. Before long, a relatively small number of capitalists controlled almost all of the mining activity in the Washoe, making themselves very, very rich in the process.

Probably the most influential capitalist riding the early waves of the Comstock boom—and a figure who would play an important role in the lives of both A. P. Crittenden and Laura D. Fair—was William Chapman Ralston, a native-born Ohioan who would make it his life-long project to build San Francisco into a world city. Having settled in California in 1854 as a twenty-eight-year-old agent for one of Cornelius Vanderbilt's steamship lines, he had almost immediately lost his job when the mercurial Commodore abruptly decided to sell his Pacific-based steamships. Recovering quickly, the ever-resourceful Ralston insinuated himself into the businesses of some of the older and more established entrepreneurs of the city, becoming a junior partner in a new bank established by former San Francisco mayor Cornelius K. Garrison. But here again, Ralston's timing proved unfortunate; the bank opened just as the city was entering its late-1850s economic slump, and after just a year and a half, Garrison and one of the other senior partners decided to cut their losses and close up shop. By this time, however, Ralston had become a true believer in the potential of San Francisco. And so, four days after the demise of the old bank in July of 1857, he and another partner, Ralph Fretz, opened a new bank of their own—with a meager $50,000 in capital.

Ralston's business ventures would not remain small for long. Once news of the Comstock strike reached San Francisco, he and his bank moved quickly. In April 1860, the Ophir Mining Company was incorporated, capitalized at $5 million and boasting as principals important San Francisco figures like business titan and future U.S. senator George Hearst. This new fountainhead of wealth, aside from making its major investors rich, was also fueling a second wave of development in San Francisco, as Ralston and others plowed mining profits into plans for new urban projects like railroad lines, luxurious hotels, insurance and utility companies, and updated port facilities. And once the war started, the Ophir and other Nevada mines proved to be an important source of funding for the entire Union war effort—especially important at a time when revenues from the Gold Rush mines were tapping out.

Meanwhile, the excitement in the Washoe was drawing people to this remote area in droves, creating a sudden population explosion in Virginia City not unlike the one in San Francisco a decade earlier. Among the newcomers was one Samuel Clemens, a twenty-five-year-old Missourian hoping to sit out the Civil War far from the actual gunfire. Coming west from Missouri with his older brother Orion, whose work for Lincoln's election campaign had earned him the position of secretary of the Nevada Territory, Sam arrived in Carson City on August 14, 1861, eager to find his fortune in the West. And although the ostensible plan had been for him to be Orion's unofficial assistant (a sort of secretary-to-the-secretary), Sam had very quickly succumbed to the mining fever that was sweeping the entire territory and decided to try his hand at prospecting.

Unfortunately, freelance mining proved to be much harder work than Sam expected. "My back is sore and my hands blistered with handling [a pick and shovel] to-day," he wrote his brother from the mining district around Aurora. "But something must come, you know." Alas, something never came, and after several disappointing months as a miner, he decided he might have better luck doing something he was good at—that is, telling stories. Sometime in September 1862—sporting a slouch hat, a dust-caked miner's shirt, and a beard halfway to his waist—he walked into the Virginia City office of the *Territorial Enterprise* newspaper. Clemens had sent the paper a few unsolicited satiric sketches over the past months, which the editor, Joe Goodman, had liked well enough to publish, though not well enough to pay for. But now, seeing that his young contributor looked "as if he had been living on alkali water and wang leather," Goodman took pity on him and offered him a real job as a staff reporter. The pay was $25 a week—not the mining fortune Clemens was hoping for, but a livable salary even for an expensive mining boomtown.

The job turned out to be a good fit for both writer and editor. The

Territorial Enterprise had already earned a reputation as a lively, irreverent, and not altogether trustworthy observer of life in the Nevada Territory, and the young Missourian soon proved that he could serve up hokum and balderdash with the best of them. He spiced even the most conventional local news items with enough exaggerations, jokes, and outright lies to keep his readers well entertained, if not well informed. As one of his biographers puts it, "Rather than focus on the facts that any fool could observe and report, Sam reported facts that would have occurred in a better and more interesting world."

Just about a month after being hired, he convinced Joe Goodman to send him down the valley to Carson City to cover the six-week session of the new territorial legislature, and where he could board quite inexpensively at the home of brother Orion and his wife, Mollie. Sam knew very little about legislative procedure, but that was also true of the legislators themselves, so they all learned together on the job. Meanwhile, he enlivened his dispatches to the *Enterprise* by trumping up a mock feud between himself and the Carson City correspondent from a competing newspaper, the Virginia City *Union*. According to Sam's reports, his more experienced rival, whose real name was Clement T. Rice but whom Clemens referred to as "The Unreliable," was an incompetent and dissolute sybarite who got all of his facts wrong and had an infuriating habit of borrowing Sam's clothing and possessions without permission. Rice, of course, returned the abuse in his own reports—to the delight of readers of both newspapers, who found this particular conflict a welcome respite from the more serious one going on between North and South. Soon Sam's feud pieces, which did contain *some* real news, were being reprinted in newspapers all over the territory. And while it was clearly all done in good fun (the two reporters were actually close drinking buddies), these early *Enterprise* stories offer a glimpse at the birth of a fresh new voice in western letters. Like the literary style that Bret Harte was experimenting with in the *Golden Era* in San Francisco, Sam's prose was colloquial and facetious in tone; but it was its own thing entirely—offhandedly outrageous, full of slang, exaggeration, and a kind of cantankerous rebellion against orthodoxy and decorum. It was a unique style that would very soon become inextricably associated with the pseudonym with which Clemens signed the first of these Carson City reports, printed in the January 3, 1863, edition of the *Territorial Enterprise:* Mark Twain.

.   .   .

Also drawn to the silver magnet of Nevada at this time was the ever-restless Alexander Parker Crittenden. The forty-seven-year-old lawyer had been feeling his age in recent years, between his chronic rheumatism and various other ailments, and the political situation in California had only gotten more uncomfortable for him as the war continued. The Breckenridge Democratic Convention, for which Crittenden himself served as chairman, had put up a full slate of antiwar Chiv candidates in the September 1862 state elections; virtually all of them had suffered crushing defeats. Meanwhile, Thomas Starr King had continued to whip up anti-Confederacy sentiment all over the state, making life distinctly unpleasant for Clara Crittenden, who complained bitterly about living in "a hateful Yankee community." Starr King was on a barnstorming tour to raise funds for the U.S. Sanitary Commission, a precursor of the Red Cross, created to aid sick and wounded Union soldiers. The fiery orator was so successful at rousing pro-northern emotions during this campaign that California, whose entire population was still just half that of New York City alone, ended up contributing over 25 percent of the funds donated to the commission—far more than any other state. For Crittenden, who was surreptitiously raising funds for the southern equivalent of the Sanitary Commission, this must have been particularly galling.

Perhaps as a consequence, A.P. had grown rather philosophical and rueful about the path his life had taken in its first five decades. In a chiding letter written to his profligate son, Churchill, Crittenden had reflected on some of his own faults: "It perhaps hardly lies in my mouth to say anything to you about carelessness in money matters," he admitted, "for I am free to confess that extravagance is one of my own vices . . . [But] let my fate be a warning to you. Recklessness about money made me and has kept me unhappy all my life." The price paid for his spendthrift ways was steep. "[With] the best part of my life past, [I] find myself still doomed to incessant toil and the prospect of leaving at my death a helpless family unprovided for."

In a letter to Clara two weeks later, he was equally remorseful. "You have been to me a true and loving wife—a far better one than I have deserved," he admitted. "When I look back upon our married life, I find very much in my own conduct to condemn. I am free to say that I have not done my duty by you as you have deserved . . . I think, however, that you do me the justice to believe . . . that I love you beyond all things in this earth."

Such professions of undying love notwithstanding, the contrite husband was soon to abandon his wife for yet another extended period. In September 1862, Crittenden had to leave San Francisco to pursue a legal case in the booming new mining town of Aurora (where Sam Clemens had made his short-lived attempt at prospecting). Aurora had the unique distinction at this time of being claimed by both California and Nevada, since the border between state and territory was still disputed. And because the town was such a "rough, struggling place," A.P. insisted that his wife and the younger children remain in San Francisco, where they could live in the more civilized environment of a city now well stocked with creature comforts. This was hardly Clara's preference. Letters between the older Crittenden children indicate that their mother was distraught at being left alone yet again, and she pleaded with A.P. to be allowed to join him. After all, she insisted, their eldest daughter, Laura, and her husband, Ramon Sanchez, were living in Aurora, however rough and struggling it might be; even the Crittendens' eighteen-year-old son Howard had moved there to take a bookkeeping job. But A.P. was adamant. He claimed that there was no house available in Aurora suitable for a respectable matron and her brood of young children (the three youngest were now four, six, and seven years old). So Clara would have to remain on Taylor Street in San Francisco, at least for the time being.

And now she didn't even have her oldest sons nearby to give her comfort and support. Churchill and James (the latter having finally been persuaded to come home after his misadventure in the Richmond jail) had convinced their parents that they should pursue their education in Europe while the war raged on in the United States. Clara and A.P. had been opposed to the plan, but the boys, now twenty-three and twenty-two, respectively, decided to chart their own course. In early 1862, the two had boarded a steamer and headed out on the long trip to England by the Panama route. By late March, they were supposed to have been well on the way to Europe, but then Clara received a letter from James postmarked Havana, Cuba. "Dearest mother," he began. "Knowing our destination to have been Europe, the heading of this letter must greatly surprise you . . ."

In this and subsequent letters to his parents, James described how he and Churchill had decided that, rather than go off to school in Europe, they would do their duty as southerners to "save [our] native land from being enslaved by its invaders." Their erstwhile pro-Union feelings, it seems, had been entirely eradicated by an overwhelming rush of new loyalty to their ancestral heritage. Early in April, therefore, the boys had jumped ship in Havana with the aim of joining whatever Confederate Army regiment would have them. Each had made his way separately to southern territory, with both experiencing the thrill of being shot at by "the Enemy" en route. But after several weeks of separation, they reunited in Richmond. By mid-1862 they'd both become bona fide soldiers. Churchill had joined a regiment of anti-Union Marylanders, while James had already seen some action in Virginia and received a flesh wound in his upper arm. "Have I not been fortunate in coming so near being killed and escaping?" James asked in a letter to Clara. But the onetime Lincoln loyalist insisted that, the perils of soldiering notwithstanding, "we must do our duty and trust God for the rest. If it is his will that we should die in battling for southern freedom, we should humbly bow to his decree . . ."

This, of course, is not exactly the kind of talk a forlorn and worried mother wants to hear from her beloved sons, and Clara's anxieties were probably only deepened by the fact that she had no husband beside her to share them with. She couldn't confide in her neighbors, many of whom would likely have shunned the mother of two rebel soldiers actively participating in the ongoing conflict. And so she suffered in silence, her misery relieved only by occasional visits from her ever-traveling husband. In April 1863, A.P. came down to San Francisco to celebrate their silver wedding anniversary on the twenty-fourth. He arranged for a party on the day, complete with dinner and dancing and as many of the older children attending as could make it. It must have warmed Clara's mood for at least a night, but a few days later, he left her again to return to Aurora. She worried aloud to her children that he might have a lady friend somewhere who was drawing him away. Making light of Clara's concerns, Howard wrote her back in early May: "It is nothing strange for Pa to take a fancy to any pretty young girl he saw, is it?" he teased. This did nothing to reassure her.

More likely the reason for Crittenden's haste is simply that he was making too much money up in Aurora—both with his legal work and with his mining stock investments. "If I am fortunate in my specula-tions," he wrote his daughter Nannie, "I shall have paid every dollar I owed . . . and shall have money enough on hand to last for months." His stock maneuvers, however, required him to be near the mines, where he could be privy to information about promising new strikes. Even when yet another of their young children died—four-year-old Henry, who succumbed to a fever on May 16—A.P. did not come down to San Francisco and would not even allow the grieving mother to come up to see him in the mountains. "Pa thought that you would be uncomfortable in Aurora," Howard explained to her in June. "He feels very badly about you; he is going to build you a house on Nan-nie's lot and will then come for you . . . Cheer up, my dear Ma, and then you will be with all your children once more and be comfortably fixed."

But even this reunion plan eventually fell through. At about this time, the Republican-dominated California legislature passed a series of new laws designed to crack down on Confederate sympathizers. One law in particular required all lawyers practicing in the state to sign an oath of loyalty to the Union. Specifically, it forced attorneys to promise not to "knowingly . . . aid, encourage . . . or assist the so-called Confederate States." Since Crittenden was doing precisely that, and since there was still disagreement about whether or not Aurora was located in the state of California, A.P. thought it best to move on and take advantage of the even richer opportunities afforded by the Nevada Territory's Comstock Lode. "Pa says he has had some very handsome offers to go to Virginia [City] to live," their daughter Laura wrote Clara in late May. "He says if he goes he can make a hundred thousand a year without any troubles."

Sometime in the summer of 1863, A. P. Crittenden pulled up stakes in Aurora and headed to Virginia City. "I can no longer practice law in California," he wrote Clara on August 1, so "I must either try it in Virginia [City] or engage in some other business." Of course, he assured Clara, she and the children would join him there . . . eventually, once he found a suitable residence for them.

In the meantime he needed a place to stay for himself, and even that was not an easy prospect in Virginia City in the summer of 1863. The town's population had grown from four thousand to fifteen thousand over just the past year, and while buildings were going up at a furious pace, there was still a serious housing shortage facing the incoming hordes (one reason why Sam Clemens spent his first weeks in town sleeping in the offices of the *Territorial Enterprise*). But one of Crittenden's old friends from his days in the state assembly—Charles Snowden Fairfax, the heir of an ancient Scottish title of nobility—had a lead for him. Charley Fairfax, as the potential 10th Baron Fairfax of Cameron was now known, lived in a place called Tahoe House—a brand-new lodging house and hotel on C Street run by the very charming woman who had been his landlady in Sacramento the previous year. In fact, this woman was the widow of another colleague from their early days in the legislature. Her name? Mrs. Laura D. Fair.

Crittenden, eager to get settled and start making money, inquired at Tahoe House and discovered that Mrs. Fair—a tall, very attractive, auburn-blond woman of twenty-six, and a fellow southerner to boot—did indeed have rooms available. The suite on offer—two rooms on the second floor, just across the hall from her own suite—was not cheap at $100 a month. But Tahoe House was quite comfortable and convenient, being centrally located right on the main commercial street of the burgeoning town. And it didn't hurt that his potential landlady was so easy on the eyes. So yes, he told Mrs. Fair, the suite would be quite satisfactory. It would be a perfect living situation for an (*ahem*) unattached widower like himself.

In a letter dated September 25, 1863, this "unattached widower" wrote to his wife back in San Francisco. "I have made up my mind to settle here," he informed her. "I am satisfied that in one or two years I can make all the money we shall need and that afterwards we can live where we please." In the meantime, with Clara and the younger children safely in San Francisco, a thirty-hour coach ride away, his life at Tahoe House could be very interesting indeed.

10

Love in Bloom

UNLIKE HER EARLY ATTEMPTS AT keeping a lodging house in San Francisco, Laura Fair's new venture turned out to be perfectly timed. In 1863 Virginia City was still riding high on the first wave of the Comstock boom, and there were any number of big-spending and furiously busy solo males flooding into town in need of low-maintenance accommodations. Tahoe House proved ideal for her purposes: a newly built, three-story brick structure with space for retail stores on the ground level and a variety of residential rooms and suites on the floors above. Her lease on the two upper floors didn't come cheap—to meet the initial payment to the landlord, Laura had to supplement her Lady Teazle earnings by pawning an expensive ring given to her by her late husband—but it proved to be a worthwhile investment. Laura found that she had no trouble filling the thirty-seven rooms of the place, and she was soon clearing about $1,000 a month after expenses. With her mother and her brother O.D. helping her run the place, Tahoe House quickly became one of the most popular addresses in town for both long-term tenants and short-term guests in need of a bed for a night or two. There were times, Laura would later insist, when she'd have to turn away fifteen or twenty would-be guests a night.

One tenant in particular caught her eye: her neighbor across the hall. Her romantic affair with Crittenden began very soon after his move into Tahoe House. True, Mrs. Fair's new tenant was twenty-one years her senior, but that kind of age difference was nothing new for her. And Crittenden still cut a reasonably smart and presentable figure by the standards of the day. Besides, he was a respectable professional man of good breeding and comfortable income, with a heart apparently unspoken for. It was therefore only natural that, given their daily proximity, an intimacy developed between these two like-minded supporters of the Confederacy. In fact, as Laura would later tell the story in court, the two soon became engaged to be married, though A.P. was reluctant to set a specific wedding date just yet.

For Crittenden, maintaining this deception involved keeping Clara as far away from Virginia City as possible. In late October—giving in finally to his wife's constant entreaties and complaints of loneliness—he had arranged to sell the San Francisco house on Taylor Street and move Clara and the children temporarily to Aurora. There, a safe hundred miles south of Virginia City, they would live with the second-oldest Crittenden daughter, Nannie—who had recently set up house there with her husband, Sidney Van Wyck, a mining assayer—while A.P. looked for a house to rent, buy, or build in Virginia City. Naturally, he was not optimistic. "It will be almost impossible to get a house for you for months," he wrote to Clara. "The place [Virginia City] is rugged beyond imagination. I have looked around and do not see anywhere a spot which is desirable for a residence."

To satisfy his wife's curiosity, however, Crittenden did offer some details about his new accommodations—and made what seems in retrospect a rather dangerous little joke about his landlady. "I have rooms, two of them, at the Tahoe House kept by Mrs. Fair, of whom you may have heard," he wrote Clara in late November. This Mrs. Fair was "the one whose husband, W.D. Fair, a lawyer in San Francisco, killed himself—but don't be alarmed. I am not her husband and shall not kill myself." True, he was not Laura Fair's husband, but apparently he *was* her fiancé.

As for Laura's being in the dark about his marital status, she may or may not have been truly deceived. She would always insist that she knew nothing about her lover's wife until months later. ("He courted me as a single man, went with me as a single man, and engaged himself to me as a single man," she testified in court. "How could I think, then, that he was a married man?") But it's possible that she had some inkling and chose to ignore it. This was particularly likely after Howard Crittenden came to visit his father in January 1864, shortly before sailing to Europe to attend college. Now nineteen, Howard stayed at Tahoe House for two weeks and got to know Mrs. Fair quite well. But although she understood that Howard was her lover's son, this did not mean that the young man's mother was still alive. "I supposed he [A.P.] was a widower," she insisted. "I knew he had children, but I did not think he was a married man." Even so, it would have been strange indeed if Howard had not once mentioned his living mother over the course of his two-week stay under Laura's roof—unless, of course, he had been coached by his father not to do so.

It's difficult to know how brazenly Laura and A.P. lived together as a couple, even when Howard was not around to bear witness. Laura would later say that they went about together quite openly on the streets of Virginia City, but since many of the Crittendens' San Francisco acquaintances had moved to Nevada to share in the Comstock bounty, A.P. presumably hoped to keep his relationship as discreet as possible. But discretion may have been wishful thinking with a woman like Laura Fair. Already somewhat notorious from her marital misadventures, she had a knack for attracting attention to herself, as she had done shortly before Christmas of 1863, near the beginning of their affair, when an incident at Tahoe House brought her name into the papers once more. Another tenant—a man named Dale, who ran a toy store on the street level—had erected a series of Christmas trees above his store windows. The trees, which stood on a balcony that technically belonged to the second-floor lodging house, were patriotically adorned with large American flags. Outraged by this presumption ("I paid five hundred dollars a month for my portion of the house," Laura would later say, "and [Dale] had no right to my portion of the house at all"), she confronted the man and insisted he take them down. Dale refused, and the two of them argued noisily about it on the street, attracting a crowd, until she fetched her brother O.D. to cut the flags down with a knife. Laura would later insist that she had them cut down because they blocked the view from her windows, but the story spread around town was that the hot-blooded southern belle just couldn't stand the sight of the Stars and Stripes on her balcony. And while that sentiment must have endeared her to her new paramour, the public scrutiny it brought to Tahoe House may have been most unwelcome to him.

Discretion became even more difficult once Crittenden found a rental house he deemed suitable for his wife and family (or perhaps he just felt that he could not put off the inevitable any longer). On February 4, 1864, Clara and the young children finally came up to Virginia City, along with daughter Nannie, now pregnant, and her husband, Sidney, all of whom took up residence in a small house at 184 South B Street. Given that this new Crittenden family hearth was essentially a five-minute walk from the cozy Crittenden love nest at Tahoe House, A.P. had some difficult logistics ahead of him. But he succeeded in keeping wife and mistress ignorant of each other, at least for the first few days. Did the always-busy lawyer make excuses to Clara for spending some nights away, working at his "office," and offer similar excuses to Laura for being absent the other nights? What's known for sure is that, after a few days of what must have been a stressful juggling act, A.P. decamped to San Francisco, allegedly on business, while wife and mistress remained in Nevada. He managed to delay his return until early March. This would at least have given him some breathing time to figure things out.

The deception, however, could not last forever. Sometime after A.P.'s San Francisco trip, Laura overheard someone mention in casual conversation that Mr. Crittenden was a married man. This, she would later claim, was the first she'd known of a living wife. She confronted him that evening: "I asked him if he was divorced," she recounted. "He said he was not, but he expected to be within six months." Crittenden went on to explain how unhappy his marriage had been for years, and how he had hoped to keep Laura ignorant of it until the divorce could be finalized. "[He] begged of me not to give him up, and to wait."

After this revelation, Laura was, she claimed, "very miserable . . . I told him he was placing me in a very bad position in regard to the world." Certainly, being known as the mistress of a married man would do great harm to her hopes of attaining any kind of middle-class respectability for herself and her daughter. But Crittenden promised that he would make it all up to her once he was divorced and they could be married. "He said it would be an evidence of my love if I would bear it and wait," she said, "which, after a while, I consented to do."

As for Clara, she always swore that she did not become aware of her husband's affair until much later. But she must at least have had her suspicions. After all, Virginia City, though bustling, was still not a large city, and people do notice things and talk, however circumspect A.P. and his colorful landlady may have been. Whatever the case, Clara decided in late June—after just a few months in her new home—to go back to San Francisco and take up residence with the youngest Crittenden children at the new Occidental Hotel. Had she discovered the existence of her husband's mistress and gone away in anger and mortification? Or did she merely prefer living in the comforts of a large city, as A.P. implied in his letters? It's impossible to know. (Unfortunately, when Clara would try to explain her reasons during the trial, she was interrupted midsentence and never ended up returning to the topic.)

With Clara gone, A.P. and Laura could worry a little less about traveling under society's radar—a good thing, since the notorious

Mrs. Fair got involved in another high-profile brouhaha with toy-store-owner Dale just days after the departure of her fiancé's wife. On the Fourth of July, the stubborn merchant again put up the Stars and Stripes on "her" balcony, but this time it was Laura, not O.D., who took scissors to the offending flags, slashing Dale's palm in the process. (Scissors seemed to be a formidable weapon in her hands.) Dale took her to court, decrying the disloyal and unladylike behavior of the "Se-cesh She-Devil"—an overblown show of outrage that earned him and his defenders some high-spirited ridicule in the local newspapers. Crittenden, making light of the whole episode, sent Clara a clipping of one of these articles with his next letter. Apparently a number of local lawyers had sprung to Mrs. Fair's defense (he didn't say whether he was one of them) and managed to get her off scot-free. "You will see that she came out with flying colors," he wrote, "but she has been very sick ever since." One wonders, of course, why Crittenden would go out of his way to draw his wife's attention to the doings of his mistress. But at this point he seemed almost to enjoy treading on dangerous territory, dropping hints about his secret life that must have caused Clara no end of anguish.

• • •

Laura Fair's "unladylike" conduct on Independence Day, while a source of amusement in a rough new mining town like Virginia City, would likely have caused more genuine indignation in rapidly matur-ing San Francisco. By the mid-1860s, a growing class of reform-minded improvers and "respectable" women in the city, where the female-to-male ratio had risen from one in seven to almost one in two over the course of just ten years, was actively trying to get the city's house in order—morally and socially. With more nuclear families in town, more children attending local schools, more married, middle-class women trying to uphold Victorian ideals of hearth and home, pressures to "clean up the town" were mounting, and the spectacle of a brazen young woman grappling on the street with her neighbor would not have suited the environment that reformers were hoping to create. A flurry of legislative activity in 1863 (referred to as a "good morals and decency" program) had resulted in the passage of a bevy of new city ordinances, including laws against immoral performances, lewd acts, indecent exposure, public nudity, and cross-dressing. Efforts were also made to confine vice and prostitution to certain specific areas, like Chinatown and the so-called Barbary Coast, a rough and crime-ridden entertainment district around Pacific and Kearny Streets.

Meanwhile, barriers between races and classes were likewise being reinforced—as with the increasing efforts to segregate public conveyances like the horsecars. Even brothels were subject to racial segregation pressures. A Chinese madam like Ah Toy, who had returned to San Francisco in 1859 after just two years away in China, was now being doubly condemned by local politicians—not only for posing an alleged threat to the health of white men but also for taking away work from white women. And the city's theaters were another prime venue for attempts to enforce racial boundaries. In an 1863 letter to his wife, James Mansfield (the visiting spiritualist who had expressed a desire to marry Thomas Starr King) took note of the hypocrisy on racial issues that had arisen in town during the war years. Describing how the instructor from the city's "colored" grammar school was expelled from an all-white ceremony at Platt's Hall, Mansfield scoffed: "This city boasts of its loyalty to abolition sentiments . . . yet [the instructor] was waited upon by a committee of 'abolitionists' . . . [and] ejected in the sight of all the people in the hall. My heart bled for that man."

An important function of these new ordinances was to increase the legibility of bodies on the street, so that unwanted contacts between respectable and disrespectable could be avoided. Laws intended to police sexuality and gender expression—concepts that were typically conflated for most of the nineteenth century—seem particularly harsh when looked at with modern eyes. Sodomy, which had been illegal throughout the state since the 1850s, was punishable by up to fourteen years in jail. But even San Francisco's new cross-dressing ordinance—prohibiting a person from appearing in public "in a dress not belonging to his or her sex"—carried a maximum fine of $500 and six months in jail. This was a clear sign that the "European cult of middle-class respectability," as one California historian has called it, was making deep inroads among the city's establishment elites.

Anxiety over gender uncertainty had in fact been an issue in California ever since the Spanish era. Catholic missionaries traveling with the first conquistadors were dismayed at the number of gender-nonconforming individuals—called berdache or mujerado by the Europeans but two-spirits by the Ohlone—living among the Indigenous peoples of the Bay Area. Regarded as belonging to a third gender, these individuals, who were thought to possess special spiritual gifts, often lived with partners considered heterosexual; occasionally a tribal chief would take a two-spirit person as a second spouse, since it was believed that they would work harder than the female first wife. The scandalized missionaries tried to stop this practice, separating couples and insisting that each partner marry a spouse deemed more appropriate, but the attempts at coercion seldom worked. According to one report from the 1770s, when a previously discouraged couple at Mission San Antonio de Padua was discovered living together again—and indeed actively having sex—they expressed bewilderment at the padre's energetic disapproval, insisting that they were now married and therefore not committing a sin.

Disapproval of homosexuality and nonconforming gender expression continued into the Mexican and American periods. Here again, however, the early Gold Rush years proved atypically tolerant in San Francisco and nearby mining towns. In these overwhelmingly male places, men would often wear dresses for purposes of couples dancing and amateur theatrics. Some police records from this era do indicate arrests of cross-dressing males acting as sex workers on the waterfront, but as one historian of sexuality has pointed out, a man providing such services to another man was not unexpected in this kind of all-male environment: "Whether for money or love or lack of female 'compan-ionship,' [it] would not have been perceived as a 'perversion.'"

These activities, however—like so many other behaviors that con-flicted with Victorian notions of decency—met with much more dis-approval and legal discouragement as the city matured in the 1860s. "A tremendous sensation was created about nightfall last evening by the appearance of a female dressed in black doeskin pants, men's boots, riding jacket, hat, etc.," began a report in the *Daily Alta California* in May 1866. The female in question, an advocate of women's dress re-form named Mrs. Eliza DeWolf, had been promenading down Mont-gomery Street on the arm of a man (or "what appeared to be a man, although it might have been a woman," the paper quipped), trailed by a mob of hooting boys. Despite the disturbance, police did not arrest Mrs. DeWolf until the next day, after a barrage of outraged protests from the press and various members of the community. "As the police arrest every man caught on the street in woman's clothes," the *Alta* insisted, "we see no reason why the rule should not be applied to the other sex as well." City officials evidently agreed. Indeed, in the three decades after passage of the ordinance, San Francisco police would make more than a hundred arrests for cross-dressing—more than for lewd acts, indecent exhibitions, or sodomy. And while enforcement of the cross-dressing law was sporadic through the 1860s, the even-more-straitlaced 1870s would see such violations more consistently and harshly punished.

One person in particular—Jeanne Bonnet, a French-born frog-catcher for local restaurants—would be arrested no fewer than twenty times for cross-dressing throughout the early 1870s, before being mur-dered under mysterious circumstances while cohabiting a hotel room with a female companion. Unlike DeWolf, whose adoption of tradi-tionally male attire was motivated by feminist principle more than gender identification, Bonnet may have been what we would now recognize as nonbinary or transgender: "You may send me to jail as often as you please," the repeat offender swore after one arrest, "but you can never make me wear women's clothes again." Unfortunately for Bonnet, however, gender legibility had become an important priority in the new Victorian city. This was clearly evident in the *San Francisco Chronicle*'s response to the frog catcher's murder in September 1876. "Her career and fate furnish an illustration of the difficulties under which women labor when they undertake to disregard the conventional rules," the editors opined, essentially blaming the victim for the murder. "She seems to have been an eccentric girl of an independent turn of mind, who was disposed to live her own life without regard to conventional laws. She thus made herself a social outlaw."

* * *

One visiting cross-dresser who seems to have been given a free pass on San Francisco's new ordinance was Adah Isaacs Menken, a celebrated actress who made a specialty of playing male and androgynous roles on the stage. Menken came to town in August 1863 to play the part of a Tartar prince in the hippodrama *Mazeppa,* based on a poem by Byron, and was an instant sensation. Apparently, the main draw was the evening's climax, when the boyish Menken was stripped of her clothing (down to a pair of "flesh-colored tights" suggestive of total nakedness) and tied to the back of a live mustang, which proceeded to canter off the stage with Menken writhing on its back. Maguire's Opera House was filled to capacity every night of the run, and Menken's profoundly physical performance, which one critic characterized as creating an "idealized duality of sex," seems to have especially impressed the city's literati. Bret Harte's protégé Charles Warren Stoddard, a poet and memoirist regarded as San Francisco's first identifiably gay author, greatly admired Menken's "half-feminine masculinity" and confessed in his journal that he fantasized about occupying a woman's body, so that his physique could be "made whole."

Somewhat less impressed was the city's newest literary figure— Samuel Clemens, now writing as Mark Twain and making frequent trips to San Francisco as a correspondent for the *Territorial Enterprise*. Twain found that the city could talk of little else than Adah Isaacs Menken. "Here every tongue sings the praises of her matchless grace, her supple gestures, her charming attitudes," he wrote in his first dispatch back to the Nevada paper. But once he saw the show for himself, he was disappointed. He found her performance to be less graceful and athletic than lunatic, with her wild hand gestures and supine gyrations that reminded him of a "pack-mule after his burden is removed." One suspects that if Menken *had* been arrested under the cross-dressing ordinance, the always-cantankerous reporter might have approved.

Until coming to San Francisco, Twain had been deeply unenthusiastic about California—"How I hate everything that looks, or tastes, or smells like California," he'd written in a letter home in early 1863. But upon seeing the state's thriving major metropolis, he changed his outlook: "After the sage brush and alkali deserts of Washoe," he admitted, "San Francisco was Paradise to me." Reluctant to return to Virginia City after each of his three visits in 1863, he came down for a much longer sojourn in 1864, when a series of misbegotten hoaxes he'd written for the *Territorial Enterprise* backfired and he was forced to leave Nevada to avoid being arrested or thrashed on the street. Arriving in town in May, he decided to apply for a job at the *San Francisco Call* and promptly got it. And although this gig was hardly inspiring ("If there were no fires to report, we started some," he would later claim), Twain would very quickly become a fixture in the city's rapidly coalescing literary golden age—a phenomenon that arguably began in earnest on the cool summer day in 1864 when Twain's boss at the *San Francisco Call* introduced him to a fellow writer by the name of Bret Harte.

11

Provocateurs

W HEN BRET HARTE AND MARK TWAIN first met in the summer of 1864, Harte was still working a day job at the U.S. Mint on Commercial Street, while editing and writing during his off hours. In the four years since arriving in San Francisco, the twenty-eight-year-old former New Yorker had come to be regarded as the most promising new literary talent on the Pacific Slope. He had in fact attracted the attention and energetic support of some very influential people in town—premier among them being Jesse Benton Frémont, daughter of powerful Missouri senator Thomas Hart Benton and wife of the famous explorer, military commander, and politician John C. Frémont. A redoubtable figure who presided over the cultural and social life of the city like a proto–Gertrude Stein hosting her expat protégés in 1920s Paris, Frémont had been impressed by Harte's pieces in the *Golden Era* and had summoned the young man to her Gothic cottage at Black Point, high atop a steep hill overlooking the city's northern waterfront. Here she introduced him to that other local eminence, the pro-Union firebrand preacher Thomas Starr King, and the two of them together decided to help put Harte on the literary map. Starr King began promoting the young man's work among his publisher friends in New England, while Frémont used her many political connections to procure him a series of governmental sinecures, like the job at the U.S. Mint, that would allow him to earn a regular salary with a minimum of responsibility. And although Harte had yet to produce anything of any true literary importance—"On this coast," Starr King admitted in a letter to a friend back east, "we raise bigger trees and squashes than literati"—the *Atlantic Monthly* had, on Starr King's recommendation, been persuaded to publish the young man's first short story. It appeared in the October 1863 issue, alongside an essay by no less a figure than Henry David Thoreau.

The city's literary culture took a significant step forward a few months later, when Harte and an author named Charles Henry Webb managed to raise enough money to start a new publication—*The Californian,* a large-format monthly with high production values and artistic aspirations to match. The journal's purpose was, as one literary historian has put it, "to wage an all-out war against mediocrity, materialism, and the middle-brow," qualities they deemed all too characteristic of the city's ethos to date. But its founders' main goal was to be noticed. Gathering together the work of the best local "Bohemians" that they'd been cultivating at the *Golden Era*—including Charles Warren Stoddard and the poet Ina Coolbrith, who together with Harte would soon become known as the "Golden State Trinity"—*The Californian* would serve as San Francisco's new calling card for western writers hoping to attract the attention of readers, reviewers, and editors nationwide. While still getting off the ground, however, this "Bohemian's Protective Union," as Webb called the new publication, would be forced to pay Bohemian rates: "Any author expecting pay for anything which he contributes is to be kicked down the stairs in an ignominious manner."

And now an important new name was to be added to that calling card. When Mark Twain was ushered into Bret Harte's office on Montgomery Street by *Call* editor George Barnes, Harte was immediately impressed: "His head was striking," Harte later recalled. "He had curly hair, the aquiline nose, and even the aquiline eye—an eye so eagle-like that a second lid would not have surprised me—of an unusual and dominant nature." Dominant, perhaps, but Twain had yet to make the mark on even the local literary world that Harte had—something that Twain was both keenly aware of and hoping to change.

Though the two almost exact contemporaries would eventually become rivals and competitors, they struck up an immediate friendship. Certainly they were polar opposites in many ways: Harte was something of a dandy, always impeccably dressed and groomed ("He was distinctly pretty," Twain would later grudgingly admit). Twain, on the other hand, cultivated dishevelment and slovenliness as a matter of principle. But maybe the fact that both had come to San Francisco fleeing the wrath of outraged readers—Harte for his scathing condemnation of the Humboldt Bay Massacres, Twain for his offensive fabrications at the *Territorial Enterprise*—gave them something in common. And Twain certainly felt he had something to learn from his slightly more experienced friend. According to Twain, Harte "trimmed & trained & schooled me patiently, until he changed me from an utterer of coarse grotesquenesses to a writer of paragraphs & chapters that have found a certain favor." In any case, Harte soon gave his new friend a monthly column in *The Californian,* for which (Webb's quip notwithstanding) the writer was even paid.

This new gig came at an especially trying time for Twain. He'd been looking for a more rewarding outlet for his talents than the drudgery of daily reporting at the *Call,* where he had to put in brutal hours covering drunk-and-disorderly cases at the police court. And as it happened, he soon lost even that dreary job. One day while out on the streets, he'd witnessed the unprovoked beating of a Chinese man by a group of young hooligans—while two city policemen looked on and did nothing. Twain wrote up a scathing report on the incident, which the *Call*'s editors promptly killed for fear of offending the newspaper's largely Irish readership. Angry and demoralized, not to mention discouraged by having missed out on a mining stock speculation that would have made him rich, Twain let the quality of his work suffer until he finally had to be discharged.

At about the same time, he found himself once again in the position of having to skip town ahead of the authorities. One night in November 1864, his friend and roommate Steve Gillis was arrested for assaulting a Howard Street bartender with a glass pitcher; Twain gallantly stepped up to underwrite his friend's $500 bail bond. But then, when Gillis decided it might be best to make himself scarce before his case went to trial, Twain found himself responsible to pay a bond he could in no way afford, and so he was forced to disappear as well. He ended up hiding out for two months in a mining camp called Jackass Hill, some hundred miles distant from San Francisco, where he apparently became so depressed that he contemplated suicide. But then he had the good fortune, while at a hotel bar in nearby Angels Camp, to hear someone tell an anecdote about a jumping frog and a $50 wager that went bad. Twain wrote up a story based on what he'd heard, and when he was finally able to return to San Francisco in February 1865, after laboring over it for weeks, he sent it off to a newspaper in New York. The tall tale later immortalized as "The Celebrated Jumping Frog of Calaveras County" was published by the *New York Saturday Press* to immense and immediate acclaim. Reprinted in newspapers across the country (including *The Californian*), the story gave Twain his first national recognition; in the process, it also made "frontier humor" the newest literary fashion.

Twain and Harte, then, were quickly becoming complementary forces in the shaping of a new western literary sensibility. As one critic has put it, "Harte strove to be the Pacific coast's conscience, Twain took great pleasure being its provocateur." Together, the two young writers were pulling the center of gravity in American letters—gradually but inexorably—from New York and New England toward the West Coast.

•   •   •

But then, in early 1864, San Francisco's budding literary establishment suffered a heartbreaking loss: "This morning the only man I ever worshiped, Thos Starr King, breathed his last," wrote James Mansfield to his wife on the morning of March 4. "Never did this city feel such a shock from the death of any one citizen since San Francisco was a city. A great light has been extinguished and I doubt if the man lives [who] can make his place good."

The death of the powerhouse Unitarian minister—of diphtheria, or "putrid throat," at the age of thirty-nine—was a tragedy mourned by multitudes, not just in San Francisco but by Union supporters all across the remaining United States. For months, friends and followers had noted that the man they called the "Yankee Poodle" (for his fighting energy and lanky hair) had been stretching himself too thin. In addition to his ongoing rallies for the Sanitary Commission and the Union war effort (after one of which, at Platt's Hall, Bret Harte found him collapsed backstage), he had been fundraising to build a new Unitarian Church for San Francisco. On top of this, he was also working to ensure the election of the Union Party candidate for governor, Frederick Low, in the California state elections of 1863. "I am worn out," he admitted early in the campaign, "and yet on the treadmill." By the time the election was finished, with Low winning in a landslide, Starr King was dangerously exhausted, but felt he still had work to do. "As soon as [the new church] is paid for," he wrote his sister, "I shall think my mission is accomplished in California, and shall be ready to surrender the driver's seat, the reins, the horses, and the carriage to a new and stronger arm . . . When all is done, I shall be ready to drop into my grave."

For a full three days after Starr King's death, the California state legislature closed its doors, so that members could travel to San Francisco for the funeral. State and municipal courts did likewise. In all, twenty thousand people swarmed the ceremony at the newly completed Unitarian church. Bret Harte wrote three separate poems for the occasion; the other two members of the Golden State Trinity,

Stoddard and Coolbrith, also published tributes. Jesse Benton Frémont, now living in St. Louis as her husband helped fight the Civil
War, sent the bouquet of violets that sat on the dead man's chest. And
although Starr King had requested that no tombstone be erected in his
honor ("Let the church, free of debt, be my monument," he insisted on
his deathbed), schools, churches, streets, and other public places all
over the country were subsequently named in his honor. A giant se-
quoia in the Calaveras Grove was eventually given his name, as was a
mountain in his beloved Yosemite.

The untimely demise of Thomas Starr King was, of course, less
devastating to those who supported the other side in the ongoing conflict, the Crittendens and Laura D. Fair among them. Indeed, for
members of the southern diaspora, the Yankee orator's death was practically the only recent piece of good news they'd received. After a
promising start for Confederate troops in 1861 with their unexpected
victory at the Battle of First Manassas (aka Bull Run), things had
started to sour for the South in 1862, though there would, of course,
be ups and downs for both sides over the course of the war. Two developments had been particularly disheartening for A.P. and Laura—
the death of Crittenden's dear friend Albert Sydney Johnston at Shiloh
in early April 1862, and the Union capture of Laura's beloved New
Orleans just a few weeks later. The following year had brought more
disappointments, most notably the almost simultaneous Confederate
losses at Vicksburg and Gettysburg in mid-1863. The Crittendens' son
Churchill had actually been in the thick of the latter conflict, though
Clara had since received a much-delayed letter from him, reassuring
them that he was safe. Churchill's numerous close calls included once
even having a toothbrush in his breast pocket shattered by a Union
bullet. "I have had three horses killed and four wounded while in front
of the enimy [sic]," he wrote. "Often coming out of a fight I have
looked and wondered to find that I was not touched." These, of course,
were details that probably did not ease his mother's fears much.

But while the war news in 1864 had scarcely been better—most recently, W. T. Sherman's capture of Atlanta had held a personal sting for A.P. since he and Sherman had been friends during the latter's career as a San Francisco banker ten years earlier—the Crittendens and Laura Fair had less to complain about financially. War or no war, the Comstock Lode just kept producing silver, and those lucky and/or daring enough to weather the inevitable fluctuations of bonanza and borasca were making plenty of money. A.P.'s new law firm of Critten-den & Sutherland had been picking up large contracts for legal work involving the mines—$30,000 from the U.S. government, $10,000 from the Savage Mine Company—and the lawyer had been using those monies to invest in the mines themselves (which were sold in "feet" rather than shares): "Have been dipping deep into Baltic stock," he wrote Clara, "holding now 132 feet. Think I shall do well with it." A week later, he added: "Yesterday or two days ago I bought some stock in 'Golden Swan'—Is not that a pretty name? I paid $14-½ and $15 for it and in three or four hours it rose to eighteen. I think it will soon be at $50, when I mean to dispose of it." After so many years of struggle, Crittenden seemed finally to be making the serious money—on paper, at least—that he'd come west for.

Laura, too, was getting into this game. Like her new tenant/lover, she suddenly found herself with some money to invest, and was soon playing the market as boldly as any man, buying and selling shares via telegraph on the San Francisco Stock and Bond Exchange. She was not alone. California was one of the few states whose constitution gave married women the right to own property of their own, independent of their husbands, and many—like Mary Ellen Pleasant—were taking advantage of the opportunity by investing in mining and other stocks, sometimes with great success. There even was a local slang term for the female speculators who haunted the streets of San Francisco's financial district—"mud hens"—and they were generally disapproved of by so-ciety types.

Like A.P., Laura was often using borrowed money to make these purchases—a risky but often lucrative bet in a virtually unregulated market where price manipulation was a regular occurrence—and the money was coming from none other than banker and inveterate city booster William Chapman Ralston. In the summer of 1864, Ralston had founded yet another new bank—this one called the Bank of California—with $2 million in capital. Now Ralston and his new bank were doing everything possible to keep injecting capital into the booming market, lending money out at below-market rates of interest. "In all I have borrowed from $9,000 to $10,000 at 1-½ percent per month," A.P. told his wife. "Ralston has been very kind to me indeed." Soon, Ralston sent a trusted lieutenant, William Sharon, to open a branch bank right in Virginia City, where he, too, began making loans at very low rates. Just how "kind" this practice would be to investors over the long term, however, remained to be seen.

．　　．　　．

And so the many loved ones of Alexander Parker Crittenden lived out the remaining war years scattered widely over the globe. Sons Churchill and James—the former still a private, the latter now a first lieutenant on the staff of Gen. Simon Bolivar Buckner—were fighting for the Confederacy in Virginia and Tennessee, respectively. Their younger brother Howard had by now gone to study in Saxony, crossing paths with the likes of Empress Eugénie of France and Alexandre Dumas père, both of whom he saw one night at the opera on his way through Paris. Clara and the younger Crittenden children were ensconced in a suite at the Occidental Hotel in San Francisco, where she could enjoy the society and comforts of a real city. And A.P. himself was in Virginia City, trying to keep his affair with his landlady secret from his two adult daughters, Laura and Nannie, both of whom were now living locally with their husbands and children. All in all, it was an effortful existence for the ailing family patriarch, and in low moments he was not above complaining bitterly about it to his much-neglected wife. "True, it is a wretched life," he wrote to Clara in July, after scolding her for her extravagant spending in the city. He pointed out how hard he must now work just to pay off his remaining debts, let alone to support his far-flung and free-spending family, all the while battling his chronic rheumatism. "I am growing very gloomy and hopeless. My future is brief and promises to be the most cloudy and miserable part of my whole life. Well, let it be so. My life has been but a series of errors and any misfortune now is but a deserved punishment."

And yet none of this doom and gloom seemed to prevent his going out on the town with his young and presumably expensive mistress. The two lovers were no longer attempting much discretion about their relationship, and with communications between Virginia City and the coast steadily improving, Crittenden found that rumors of his dalliance with Laura Fair were reaching the offices and parlors of San Francisco, where such behavior could no longer be dismissed with a smirk and a wink. Hoping to stanch the rumors before they reached his wife, he came up with an audacious plan: On his next trip to the metropolis, he would bring Laura with him and put her up at the same hotel where he would be staying with Clara and their daughter Carrie. He would even arrange for all of them to eat together in the hotel restaurant, in front of hundreds of witnesses. Surely that would dispel any notions that he and his landlady had some kind of inappropriate relationship. After all, would any man actually put his wife and his mistress together in the same public dining room?

Of course, pulling off this plan would require some fancy explaining to both women. To Clara, A.P. depicted the proposed meeting as an act of charity. Mrs. Fair, he wrote his wife, was being unfairly maligned by gossips as a disreputable woman, because of the three husbands, the stage appearances, the run-ins with the toy-store proprietor, and so on. Being seen publicly with a woman of Clara's unimpeachable respectability would do her much good in the eyes of the world. Would Clara therefore do him the favor of enduring Mrs. Fair's company for a few days and showing her some kind attention?

Whether Clara actually believed this ruse or not, she finally agreed, though she certainly wasn't happy about it. Laura also needed some convincing. She later claimed that she knew nothing of the planned rendezvous with Clara until after their departure for the coast from Virginia City. She had thought that their excursion was just to be a pleasure trip and relished the thought of being seen in San Francisco with the eminently respectable man she eventually would marry. But on the last leg of the journey—as they traveled on the steamer heading from Sacramento to San Francisco Bay—Crittenden pulled her aside and told her that "he wished to ask a sacrifice" of Laura. He then revealed his plan to introduce the two women at the Occidental. According to Laura's later testimony, Crittenden claimed that it was the only way to dispel the rumors. "He said that if I did that, and she would be introduced to me and be friendly to me, the world would not believe anything that would be said then. He did not wish me to be talked about."

Again Laura balked at making this kind of humiliating gesture, but again she relented—"as an evidence of my love for him." Crittenden, clearly pleased, assured her that "it would all be right when I was his wife; that he would make it right, and show the world the respect he had for me."

And so, on a brisk day in September or October 1864, Crittenden and his mistress of almost a year stepped off the steamer at the San Francisco wharf. Once downtown, he would install the young woman in a room at the Occidental Hotel, directly above the rooms that he would be occupying with his wife and youngest daughter. And then the four of them would dine together. In public.

In a life that had involved more than the usual share of risk-taking, Alexander Parker Crittenden was taking his biggest gamble yet.

DAY FOURTEEN

Tuesday, April 11, 1871

The Assassin of the late Hon. A. P. Crittenden on Trial

≈

Testimony in Rebuttal for the Prosecution

≈

MRS. FAIR INSULTS MRS CRITTENDEN
WHILE ON THE STAND

≈

JUDGE DWINELLE ORDERS HER TO PAY
A FINE OF $250 FOR CONTEMPT

≈

The Chastity of the Accused Attacked

—*Daily Alta California*

FIREWORKS OF SOME KIND HAD been expected for days. Over the past few court sessions, the two women had been taking turns on the witness stand, testifying about what seemed like two different men, telling two different narratives about him, depicting two different realities. There was Clara, the dutiful wife of the one Mr. Crittenden—that solid family man—describing how she'd condescended, at great risk to her own dignity, to be charitable to her kindhearted husband's infamous and scandal-ridden landlady. And there was Laura, soul mate of the other Mr. Crittenden—that ardent lover and fiancé—explaining the sacrifice she'd made by agreeing to meet with the unloved and unpleasant dowager whose days as his current

wife were running out. For each woman, listening to the other's account of events must have been infuriating. A boiling point seemed
almost inevitable.

It came, finally, a little over halfway through the trial. On the morning of the fourteenth day of the proceedings, prosecutor Alexander
Campbell recalled Clara Crittenden to the stand as a rebuttal witness.
He wanted to question her further about the circumstances under
which Mrs. Crittenden had first met her husband's murderer. But this
proved difficult to accomplish, since defense attorney Elisha Cook—as
he had done repeatedly throughout the trial—kept interrupting Clara's
testimony with objections, insisting that nearly everything she said was
either hearsay or irrelevant:

MR. CAMPBELL: What I asked is, where you first met
[Mrs. Fair], at the Occidental Hotel?

MRS. CRITTENDEN: I first met her at the Occidental Hotel;
yes, sir.

MR. CAMPBELL: I ask you how you made her acquaintance.

MRS. CRITTENDEN: I made her acquaintance because I told
my husband to introduce me to her—

MR. COOK: [interrupting] I object to her stating the reason of
making her acquaintance. Let her state the facts.

JUDGE DWINELLE [to the witness]: State just the facts only.

MRS. CRITTENDEN: Judge Dwinelle, I cannot state how I
came to be introduced, without stating how I came to ask that.

JUDGE DWINELLE: I suppose somebody introduced you. Just
state that, and not why you were introduced. That has not
been asked.

It went on like this for some time. Clara, clearly frustrated, seemed determined to get her version of the meeting on the record and before the jury, even if that meant straying beyond the narrow bounds of the questions being posed. She wanted the court to know how she, a respectable woman, felt about meeting this notorious lodging-house operator. But Cook, aware of how this could damage the image of his client that he wanted to project, interrupted every time the witness overstepped, and Judge Dwinelle had no choice but to sustain his objections:

> Mr. Campbell: Now, will you state what conversations you had with her on that occasion at the hotel?
>
> Mrs. Crittenden: Well, I first went with her to dinner, and, of course, the ordeal was a very severe one to me . . .
>
> Mr. Cook: I ask that that be stricken out!
>
> Judge Dwinelle: Strike it out.
>
> Mrs. Crittenden: I was taken sick at the dinner table. I became sick from the effects of this thing—going to the table, with her, before four hundred people.
>
> Mr. Cook: I ask that that be stricken out!
>
> Judge Dwinelle: Strike it out.
>
> Mrs. Crittenden [to the judge]: Well, I do not see why!
>
> Judge Dwinelle: Strike it out!

But then, Cook finally stopped objecting long enough for her to tell at least a part of her story without interruption:

> Mr. Campbell: Well, what became of her?

MRS. CRITTENDEN: I left the table and went to my room. After dinner, Mrs. Fair came into my room, and she found that I was sick; whether she knew the reason or not, of course, I cannot say . . .

There was no objection from Cook, and so she went on.

MRS. CRITTENDEN: . . . but she came to the lounge where I was lying, and she knelt on her knees before me, and took my hand, and begged to be allowed to kiss it . . .

MRS. FAIR: That's a lie!

[Tumult in the courtroom]

JUDGE DWINELLE: Order! Mr. Cook, you will speak to your client!

For several minutes, there was too much commotion in the court-room for the examination of Clara Crittenden to continue. To publicly accuse a respectable Victorian woman of being a liar was an insult of major proportions—the kind of affront that, had the parties been male, might have precipitated a formal duel or at least a thrashing on the street. But Laura was riled beyond endurance. According to the re-porter for the *Chronicle,* "Mrs. Fair's eyes blazed with fury, and her whole face lighted up. Even when, at the earnest solicitation of her counsel, . . . she calmed herself to some extent, the vicious glitter re-mained in her eyes, and her barely restrained fury showed itself in nervous twitchings of the mouth."

Clara Crittenden merely ignored the defendant's outburst, offensive as it was. When she resumed her testimony, picking up right where she left off, it was calmly and without emotion. "She said to me with tears in her eyes, 'Mrs. Crittenden, you are the first woman that has shown me kindness for ten years,' and then she said, 'There is nothing on earth that I would not do for you.'"

We can only guess how many doses of whiskey from her doctor's flask were required to dampen the defendant's agitation as she listened to this. It does appear, though, that Mrs. Fair settled down sufficiently for Clara Crittenden to complete the rest of her testimony without interruption (except from the ever-persistent Elisha Cook). Only when the older woman stepped down from the witness stand and exited the courtroom did the judge address the matter.

> JUDGE DWINELLE: There has been an occurrence here, which
> it becomes the duty of the Court to notice. A gross insult has
> been put upon a witness, which is a contempt of Court. It is
> useless to consign the party guilty of that contempt to prison,
> because she must be consigned there [in any case] at the
> adjournment of the Court to-night. But in order that the
> proceedings may be properly conducted hereafter, and no
> witness insulted, I impose a fine upon Mrs. Fair of two
> hundred and fifty dollars, for contempt of Court. Let
> execution issue forthwith.

But it was uncertain whether Judge Dwinelle's fine would prevent future outbursts from the defendant. For Mrs. Fair, according to the reporter for the *Daily Alta California,* "did not seem to realize the effect of the Judge's remarks." There were still many more days of testimony ahead of them, and many more opportunities for disruption.

12

Living Dangerously

O N AN OTHERWISE UNREMARKABLE FALL evening in 1864, diners at San Francisco's elegant, three-year-old Occidental Hotel were treated to a spectacle that probably drew the stares of virtually every person present: one of the West's most prominent attorneys entering the dining room arm in arm with his forty-four-year-old wife, his nine-year-old daughter, and his twenty-seven-year-old mistress. Seated together at a prominent table in the vast, high-ceilinged space, which had quickly become the choice meeting place for the city's business and social elites, the unlikely foursome proceeded to indulge in one of those rich, multicourse banquets for which the era was known. After starting with oysters and Champagne, they moved on to fish, fowl, and meat courses before finishing off with ices and coffee. Perhaps they even enjoyed the eponymous cocktail newly invented by the Occidental's mixologist—the Martinez, later known as a martini.

All three adults at the table must have been intensely self-conscious about the attention they were attracting among their starchy fellow diners. In a place where, just fifteen years earlier, dusty denim trousers and open-necked flannel shirts had been the costume of choice, these people wore impeccable Victorian ensembles of crinoline-skirted gowns and woolen tailcoats, and sported attitudes to match. In any case, conversation at the Crittenden table, if there was much of it, was probably strained and awkward, perhaps sustained chiefly by the prattling of little Carrie. But at a certain point before the last course, Clara Crittenden rose from her chair and, complaining of an indisposition, excused herself from the table. Her husband also stood and then gallantly accompanied her to their rooms upstairs, leaving Laura and Carrie behind to finish their dessert.

After the meal, Laura and the girl followed the elder Crittendens upstairs to the suite that Carrie and her mother had been occupying for some weeks. Laura was staying right next door—an arrangement that had been an issue in itself. At first, when A.P. and Laura had arrived the evening before, the hotel had put her into a suite on the floor directly above the Crittendens. But Laura had declared this unacceptable. Her lover had made a solemn promise to her that he would not sleep with his wife while at the hotel—he said he would merely pretend to reside with Clara and Carrie for appearances' sake, but would quietly move to another room in the hotel every night after bedtime. Laura wanted to make sure he kept that promise, so she'd had the hotel move her to a suite on the same floor as Clara's. This way, Laura could keep an eye on what went on after hours next door.

Clara was reclining on a lounge in her parlor when Laura and Carrie arrived. The older woman apologized for not getting up, but asked her guest to take a seat near her, while Carrie retreated to the piano and A.P., claiming urgent business downtown, quickly disappeared. For a while, the two women listened to Carrie play. Then Laura, the former music teacher, took a turn at the keyboard, singing to her own accompaniment. Whether at any point before or after this Laura knelt at Clara's feet—thanking her tearfully for her kindness in seeing her—is a matter of dispute. Clara claimed it happened; Laura denied it. "I sang one or two songs," she later testified, "and then I got up and bade them good night, and left the room. This is everything that occurred that night."

All in all, it seems doubtful that this rashly concocted demonstration of feminine solidarity achieved Crittenden's twin goals—that is, convincing Clara and the rest of San Francisco society that the relationship with his attractive landlady was totally innocent, and convincing Laura Fair that his attentions to his wife were merely pro forma. The whole masquerade ended rather abruptly, in any case. Clearly upset by the situation, Laura decided to return to Nevada the next day, even though her visit was supposed to last two weeks. A.P. accompanied her to the 4 P.M. Sacramento steamer to see her off but remained in San Francisco for another week to move Clara and Carrie into even more luxurious accommodations at the newly built Cosmopolitan Hotel. Even so, both women would later insist that they were convinced. Clara testified that she didn't know for sure about her husband's infidelity until two years later, while Laura claimed to believe him when he told her that he and Clara did not sleep together in their hotel suite. Members of San Francisco's gossiping classes, on the other hand, were probably less gullible.

Also less gullible was Mary Lane, Laura's mother, in whose care they had left both Tahoe House and baby Lillian while on their excursion to the metropolis. Having become aware of Mr. Crittenden's status as the husband of a still-living wife, Mrs. Lane felt that his continued courtship of her daughter would do irreparable harm to Laura's reputation, regardless of any promises to marry her in the future. Once Crittenden had returned to Virginia City, therefore, Mrs. Lane, speaking as co-proprietor of the lodging house, delivered an ultimatum: Unless and until Mr. Crittenden divorced his wife and took Laura to the altar, he could not spend another night under her roof.

Apparently irritated at being lectured on morals by a woman he considered his social inferior, Crittenden called her bluff. Fine, he told Mrs. Lane, he would move out immediately—but he would take her daughter and baby Lillian with him. Laura, after all, had sworn to stand by her lover until his divorce, which he again promised would occur within six months. Defying her mother, Laura agreed to go with him, professing her certainty that she and Crittenden were engaged in God's eyes.

Fortunately, an investment property that Laura had bought on nearby A Street was available for their use. It was much smaller than Tahoe House but still had a few extra bedrooms that she could rent out to single gentlemen in need of accommodations. So the three of them came to an understanding whereby Mrs. Lane and brother O.D. would take over the running of Tahoe House by themselves; A.P., Laura, and Lillian, meanwhile, would leave the premises and move into the house on A Street. It was a less convenient and more expensive arrangement for everyone involved, and some excuse for the change of address would have to be concocted for Clara, but no one, it seems, was going to tell A. P. Crittenden how to live his life.

. . .

On October 31, 1864—just eight days before the presidential election—Nevada was admitted to the Union as the thirty-sixth of the still-disunited states. This rush to statehood had an ulterior motive. Nevada still lacked the sixty thousand residents usually required for a territory to become a state, but the ten thousand who lived there were overwhelmingly pro-Union, and Republicans wanted every vote they could get in the upcoming election; in fact, Lincoln supporters had telegraphed the entire proposed state constitution to Washington, D.C., in order to get it approved in time for Election Day—purportedly the longest and most expensive telegram in history to that date. As it turned out, however, the incumbent president didn't need Nevada's three Electoral College votes to win a second term, as Lincoln beat former general George B. McClellan in a landslide. For Crittenden, who still remained active in Democratic politics after his move to Nevada, this was just another bitter pill to swallow, chased down with the bile of Republican or "National Unity Party" victories in the new state's gubernatorial and congressional elections.

But there was worse news still to come. Ever since their two eldest sons had enlisted in the Confederate Army, the Crittendens had received only sporadic communications from them, usually in the form of hastily composed letters smuggled north and then either hand-carried or else mailed discreetly from a northern address to one parent or the other. As a high-profile Copperhead (anti-war Democrat), A.P. had to be especially careful that these letters didn't fall into unfriendly hands, since they would almost certainly be considered treasonous. ("When you have read these letters burn them," he advised Clara in a July 14 letter in which he forwarded two missives from their sons.) Usually, the arrival of these letters would be a huge relief. Even if months old, they reassured the parents that their sons had been alive and well at least until the date the letter was written. But then, in late November, a long note from James arrived with tragic news: "My own dear father and mother," the boy wrote from Richmond, Virginia, "I know not how to write to you [of] our common calamity, our irreparable loss . . . My dearly beloved brother Churchill, your peerless son, is dead . . ."

It was the first of three letters James wrote describing the circumstances under which the twenty-four-year-old Churchill was killed in the line of duty, each letter sent by a different route so that at least one was sure to get through. (All three did.) Churchill, James explained, had been fighting for months in northern Virginia with Company C of the 1st Maryland Cavalry Battalion. This was toward the end of the Shenandoah Valley campaigns of 1864, when the forces of Union general Philip Sheridan and Confederate general Jubal Early were battling over possession of this agriculturally rich and strategically important region. By this point in the war, both sides were profoundly weary of the struggle and staggered by the massive loss of life it had exacted. But although the momentum of battle seemed to be in the Union's favor, a northern victory was still by no means certain, and it was quite possible that, without a decisive victory to lift the commander-in-chief's image, Lincoln might lose his bid for reelection in November. The stakes in the Shenandoah Valley were therefore very high for both sides, and the fighting was fierce.

According to James's report, sometime in early October, Churchill and about a dozen other members of his company found themselves cut off from the rest of their unit while on patrol near Luray, Virginia. Forced to fend for themselves behind Union lines for several days, they were soon running low on provisions. Their senior officer, Lieutenant Waters, asked for volunteers to sneak out from their hiding place in the woods to a nearby farmhouse, where a sympathetic local named Brubaker would be willing to provide them with food and water. According to James, who later interviewed witnesses to the scene, Churchill valiantly offered to take on this dangerous task, while the other men drew straws to see who would accompany him. A man named Hardigan drew the short straw, and the two of them set out. While engaged on this errand, however, the pair was spotted by a party of some twenty-five Union troops, who set off in hot pursuit. As James reported it, the cowardly Hardigan surrendered almost immediately, but Churchill put up a fierce fight, killing several of the Yankees as he desperately tried to escape. But finally, wounded in his side and having exhausted all of his ammunition, he fell into their hands and was taken prisoner.

Churchill and Hardigan were marched north through the Shenandoah Valley to the Union camp a little north of Luray. As they were passing through that town, Churchill was allowed to stop at a house to write a short note to his uncle George in Richmond, reporting his capture. The hand-scrawled note, which is still extant, is dated October 4, 1864, and reads, "My dear Uncle, I am slightly wounded. C. Crittenden. I am a prisoner." (On the reverse side of the note, someone—either A.P. or Clara—later wrote: "The last words of my son.")

After spending a night under guard at the camp, Churchill and Hardigan were brought before Col. William H. Powell, commanding officer of the Union army's 2nd Division of Cavalry. Powell questioned them briefly and then ordered that they be taken out and shot. According to James, Hardigan begged for his life to be spared, but Churchill "received Col. Powell's cowardly and brutal order with the utmost composure." The two prisoners were then marched to a nearby wooded ravine by a firing squad, where they were told to make a run for it. Hardigan, "unworthy of the privilege of dying with so brave a man as Brother," bolted for the woods but was shot down as he fled. Churchill, however, refused to run. "If you intend to murder me," he said, "you can do it." Then he sat down on a rock, folded his arms, and waited for the bullet to the head that killed him instantly.

The two Confederate soldiers were promptly buried where they fell in the ravine. Some days later, however, after the Union troops had moved on, members of Churchill's company located the gravesite, disinterred the bodies, and placed them in boxes to await a more dignified burial. James, who was also in Virginia at the time, traveled to Luray once he heard of his brother's death and brought the body back to Clara's family in Richmond. Churchill was buried with all due ceremony in the city cemetery, where his mother's loved ones could visit the grave. "Thus died the noblest, most disinterested and generous of your sons, my own dear lion-hearted brother," James wrote. "The reflection that he died as I have always hoped to die—fearlessly, bravely, and gloriously—has brought me some little comfort, while the hope of vengeance has nerved my soul."

If James's tale was somewhat embellished in the retelling, he can perhaps be excused. He understood that Churchill's death would be devastating to his parents, and this reassurance that their son had faced his execution bravely would at least lessen the pain somewhat. As it happened, however, unconfirmed rumors of the death had reached A.P. in early November, before the arrival of James's letters. At that time, he had traveled down to San Francisco—both to be with Clara and to pursue inquiries in a place better connected than Virginia City with sources of information in the East. But while they did receive confirmation of their son's demise, it apparently wasn't until A.P. had returned to Virginia City, leaving Clara and the younger children to mourn alone in the metropolis, that details about the episode reached him. "It is something to know that our boy sleeps in our country," he wrote to Clara once he had heard of the proper funeral in Richmond, "and that he is honored and loved as he should have been." Even so, he admitted that his heart was "full of bitterness & curses." "I have never been so depressed and wretched in my life, nor so indifferent about life and all its concerns. I must endure this alone and overcome it."

Of course, he *wasn't* enduring it alone; presumably he was finding at least some consolation in the arms of his young mistress, which may be why he kept insisting that Clara stay in San Francisco. ("I really think it best for you to remain in San Francisco till Spring," he wrote her in December, "till I can make some suitable arrangements here for the comfort of you all.") But at this point, hypocrisy seemed to be second nature to Crittenden, even as he grieved: "Last night I did not close my eyes till 6 o'clock in the morning . . . I thought I should have gone mad. If it had been possible for me to leave my business without harm to others, I should have started this morning for California."

As for Clara, the death of her eldest son was only the latest blow she had endured in recent years, and she was suffering keenly. Most of the very few letters of hers that survive are from this period, and they are full of pathos. "Oh, this life is nothing but battle, battle all the time," she wrote her daughter Nannie in December. "I almost wish I could lie down & rest from the constant struggle." She was haunted by images of Churchill's ordeal: "In the midst of anything I may be doing, my Son's cruel murder & the scene rises up before me. Oh, why was it allowed for him, my brave Son, to be shot in that way? My heart can never forget this bitter cup of agony."

Living in a hotel in enemy territory, as it were, made her trials that much harder to endure. She complained of having to sit cheerfully among Yankees in the Cosmopolitan Hotel's dining room: "Every day we live in this corrupt land among these wicked people, my Son's murderers," she wrote Nannie a few days later. "Great God, when will you have mercy on my native land & avenge the blood of the cruel murders & fiendish outrages committed on my people?"

Clara, a devout Christian, had another intense worry—that Churchill had died without a heartfelt devotion to his religion, and that her husband would also die an unbeliever. This had been a source of much concern among her other children as well. "Should God call me hence, my last thoughts will be of home," James had written her when he first joined the Confederate Army, "and the last mental pains I shall ever suffer will be caused by the reflection that my dear father and brothers are not Christ followers and I may not meet them in the world to come." Even Howard was troubled by this. As he had written his mother the previous year: "I would be perfectly happy (that is, as happy as 'I' could be), if Pa would only rely and put his trust in our Almighty and everlasting Father."

But Crittenden was at least claiming to look for some kind of religion to believe in: "Seeing how much strength and consolation you and Nannie derive from your faith," he wrote Clara in the midst of their shared tribulations, "it is natural I should desire to possess the same faith. [But] you do not know [to] what an extent I am a disbeliever in everything like revealed religion and even in the immortality of the soul." Clara tried sending her husband some religious tracts, but he couldn't bring himself to read them. "Essays on the subject of religion and exhortations to embrace it are all wasted on me. What I need is to be satisfied that there is a God and a hereafter." To that purpose, he insisted, there was one book he *would* read, though it is remarkable that he would even mention it to his wife, given the title and his current situation: "It is Nelson on Infidelity," he told her. "I have heard Dr Nelson's work often spoken of as a convincing argument, and should like to read it." (The book in question—*The Cause and Cure of Infidelity: Including a Notice of the Author's Unbelief, and the Means of His Rescue,* published in 1841 by the Reverend David Nelson—is about infidelity to God, not to one's spouse.)

Of course, this shared tragedy—losing their eldest son at the peak of his youth and vigor—could have been the thing that brought the Crittendens back together again. The wayward husband would have been wholeheartedly welcomed home by his wife, not to mention by respectable society, which would have forgiven him for his transgressions far more readily than it would his wayward mistress. Instead, however, the reckless adventurer in A. P. Crittenden kept the upper hand in his character. Despite his professed desire for self-improvement, he was not about to mend his ways, and more tragedy was to come.

Clara may have had an intuition about this. On Christmas Eve that year—which she spent in San Francisco, without her husband—she wrote Nannie a letter telling her that she intended to take flowers out to the gravesite of the four young children—Mary, Edmund, Florence, and Henry—she'd lost since coming to California. "It is the [only] Christmas present I can make them, & even that I must trust to other hands for my son [that is, Churchill, buried in Virginia] . . .

"May the next Christmas be a more happy one than this," she concluded, "but every [new] year I now dread, for it seems to take one of us with it."

13

The War After the War

NEWS OF THE END OF the Civil War reached California much more promptly than news of its beginning had. Thanks to the transcontinental telegraph line, which had been completed just a few months after the attack on Fort Sumter in 1861, the *Daily Alta California* was already printing the terms of surrender on its front page within hours of Robert E. Lee's capitulation at Appomattox Court-house in April 1865. Reaction on the streets of San Francisco was jubilant. "The batteries around the harbor [poured] forth their thunders in exaltation over the glorious news," the *Alta*'s editor effused, barely able to contain his glee: "Civilization has trampled medievalism under foot on this continent . . . The National Government has triumphed. The rebellion is dead!"

News of Lincoln's assassination arrived just as promptly a week later, to a markedly different response: Shops all over the city closed down, church bells tolled in mourning, and roving gangs smashed windows and set fire to the offices of "certain obnoxious publications" perceived as too sympathetic to the rebel cause. Even the *Alta California* had to bar its doors against rioters—not because of anything they'd published (the newspaper's sentiments were emphatically pro-Union) but because they shared quarters with a French-language weekly called the *Echo du Pacifique,* whose Copperhead leanings inspired the mob to try burning the whole building down.

In Virginia City—a place always more concerned about money than politics—the reaction to the end of the war was emphatic enough to grate on the nerves of the resident southerners. "The whole town was wild yesterday with excitement and drink," A. P. Crittenden wrote to his wife on April 11. "The bells were ringing, church bells and all, steam engines whistling, music sounding, and cannon firing all day. I need not tell you how I feel at this destruction of all hope. The dreadful sacrifices that have been made have been in vain."

Crittenden's personal life was also in something of a shambles. Clara was becoming ever more critical of his "friendship" with his landlady, whether or not she believed the gossip about her. After the debacle of the women's first meeting the previous fall, A.P. had actively tried to avoid any more contact between them. When Clara had made noises in January about leaving the children in San Francisco and coming to Virginia City to visit him, he energetically discouraged the idea. "The only reasons I have for not wishing [you] to take the trip across the mountains are that it will make you sick and that I have been doubtful about your making any suitable arrangements for the care of the children," he wrote her on New Year's Day. "The roads, according to accounts, are terrible. [One] man who came last night told me that no lady could stand the journey."

Concerns about the hardships of the trip were not unfounded. The crossing of the Sierra Nevada was never to be taken lightly, especially in winter, when sudden snowstorms could strand the stagecoach for days at a time. And this area of the West was still untamed enough for other dangers to pose a threat. When Clara and the children had returned to San Francisco the previous summer, for instance, they had just missed being held up by a gang of genuine Wild West outlaws lying in wait on the road. "So you came near to having an adventure," A.P. had mused ironically in his next letter to her. "What a pity you all missed it! If you had only been an hour or two later you would have been robbed and badly scared. Nannie would have taken it very quietly. Carrie would have been frightened and taken a big cry. Tommy would have looked on in amazement, and you would have got mad and called on Ned Eyre [an acquaintance traveling down on the same coach] to shoot some of the rascals, wouldn't you?"

Despite the real peril in making the trip, Clara was determined to come. She also insisted that she stay in her husband's new rooms in Mrs. Fair's A Street house when she got there. Of course, this seemed like a recipe for another disaster, but Crittenden had to relent. Despite the fact that Clara would not travel on a Sunday and apparently refused to come over the mountains "in charge of a Yankee," she did manage to get to Virginia City by the end of January. Laura Fair, none too pleased, was forced to welcome her rival into her own home and pretend again that there was nothing between her tenant and herself beyond a platonic friendship.

Clara ended up staying about ten days. Trying to keep up the innocent appearance of their living arrangement, A.P. and Laura put on quite a show while Clara was there. In the evenings, Mr. Crittenden would invite Mrs. Fair into "his" parlor to drink a toddy with him and his wife. "Come in, Madame," he would say. "We are two old people and would like your company." After a quiet evening, Mrs. Fair would return to her own quarters, allowing Mr. and Mrs. Crittenden to retire for the night, at which time, according to Clara's later court testimony, the wife made sure that her loving husband stayed put all night in the marital bed.

After a week of this charade, however, Laura could stand it no longer. "It was worrying my life out," she later testified, and she told Crittenden "that I would either have to leave my own house, or she must leave, and that night. If she did not leave, I must tell her everything, and give him up and go away." Crittenden warned her that if she did that, he would be desperate enough to kill both Laura and himself.

But she didn't believe this melodramatic threat. That night Laura heard husband and wife talking in their parlor and resolutely knocked on the door to request a glass of apple toddy, a bowl of which Crittenden kept on his sideboard every evening. Then she told Mrs. Crittenden that she wished to speak to her in her dining room. A.P. followed them in, but then Clara turned to him and said, "It is me she wished to see and not you. I wish you to go out of the room a little while." She clearly wanted to hear what Mrs. Fair had to say to her in private.

According to Laura, A.P. complied, but just as he was leaving—as he stood in the doorway where Laura could see him but Clara could not—he took out his derringer and flourished it at her. Rattled by this, Laura lost her nerve. "It frightened me," she confessed, "so that I did not dare to tell her as I was going to do." Instead, she ended up inventing a tearful story about a young man having broken an engagement with her because of fallacious rumors about her relationship with Mr. Crittenden.

After assuring Mrs. Fair that she herself gave no credence to such gossip, Clara insisted that there was an easy solution to the problem. "I talked with her," Clara later explained, "and reasoned with her, as I would have done with my own sister." She told the younger woman that the one way to stop the world from talking about Laura and Mr. Crittenden would be for her to send him away. "For his sake, do not let him stay here. Tell him to go away from here, and then the thing will die out, and people will not believe it."

How this conversation ended was never revealed, but after this close call Crittenden began insisting that Clara return to San Francisco immediately. She wanted to stay on, but he would not take no for an answer, maintaining that the children needed her back home and that at any point a snowstorm in the mountains could make her return to the coast impossible for weeks. Less than thirty-six hours later, Clara was on the stagecoach heading back to California. Displeased, she apparently made her feelings known to her adult daughter Laura, who responded with an outburst of proto-feminist frustration: "Pa thought that he had a good reason for insisting upon her return," she wrote in a letter to sister Nannie, "and you must know too well, how often we *poor women* are compelled to give up to some men just because they say so, and *of course* they *always* know what is best for us as well as for themselves . . ."

But Clara was no fool. She understood now that her family life and her standing in society were both being threatened, and she knew exactly who the enemy was. Clara's letters to A.P. have not survived, but his responses to them speak volumes: "My dear Clara, I have a bad headache today and feel almost too unwell to write," he moaned in a letter to her dated February 16, beginning with a familiar complaint about his poor health, "but your letters of the 13th and 14th are so unkind and unjust that I do not feel inclined to leave them unanswered for a day. They have very much surprised and, I must say, very deeply hurt and offended me . . ."

He pointed out that he had troubles enough in life—"working desperately, almost hopelessly," to pay off his debts and support his spendthrift family—without his wife adding to his woes with complaints and suspicions. Then he proceeded to lie to her flagrantly: "The meaning of all this is, I suppose, that you have come to the conclusion that, 'gay youngster' as I am, Mrs. Fair has won my heart from you. I told you of the story I had heard, which was calculated to do great injury to Mrs. F, to myself, [and] to you and to our children. I told you of it in the belief that, like a true woman and wife, you would show the world your disbelief in it. In that I suppose I am doomed to disappointment. Apparently you give faith to the first idle rumor of the world, for it seems you do believe what it says. For myself, I have nothing to say . . . If I cannot have the confidence and love of my family, if my very wife and children turn against me, I have one consolation left . . . You know well that life has lost all charm to me and I would willingly lie down and go to sleep forever. And you know that, in my opinion, death is but a sleep . . ."

Apparently this thinly veiled suicide threat had an effect; in his next missive Crittenden noted that Clara's most recent letter "is more like yourself. It is kind in tone." But she clearly wasn't giving up on the subject of her husband's landlady. "Your letter . . . is full of Mrs. Fair and nothing else," he wrote her soon thereafter. "I beg you to dismiss that subject from your thoughts." Ten days later, he wrote her again, apologizing for his recent silence: "I am not dead and have not run off, nor been carried off by Mrs. F or any other woman." Clara was obviously still making insinuations about the affair, urging him to come to his senses and remember his duty to his family. Laura, meanwhile, insisted that he go through with the promised divorce and make a respectable woman of her. The American Civil War might have been over by the spring of 1865, but the war between Clara Crittenden and Laura Fair was just beginning.

● ● ●

Clara launched her next major offensive that summer. She and A.P. had been arguing by letter for several months. Clara wanted him to allow her to return to Virginia City, or at least to have some kind of assurance from him that he still cared for her and that they were not just together for the sake of the children. This annoyed him. You seem, he wrote to her, to be "asking me to write a love letter. You have known me for twenty-six years and certainly you do know that if there is anything of which I am incapable, it is growing sentimental or romantic." Instead, he insisted, "you may believe in a man's feelings when his actions show what they are." And certainly his own actions should suffice, as he had been at the office until 2 A.M. every night, working himself half to death in order to lift himself out of debt and keep his wife and family alive and well. As for her coming up again to Virginia City, it would be totally impractical. Contrary to what a friend of hers had been saying, there were few good residences available in town at reasonable prices. "It is not impossible that on A Street near Union there may be some cheap houses—[but] most of the houses there are very indifferent and it is a bad neighborhood—I would not live there if anyone would give me a house free of cost." Meanwhile, his stubbornness on this issue was again causing bitter rumblings among his children. "I am going to write to Pa . . . & tell him what I think of the way he is treating Ma," Laura Sanchez wrote her sister Nannie that spring. "He ought to be ashamed."

Perhaps because of this added pressure on him, or because their daughter Nannie was now pregnant in Virginia City, A.P. finally relented—to an extent. He agreed to have Clara come up to help Nannie through her confinement, but with the understanding that Clara would live with Nannie and her husband out at their house in Gold Hill, a "suburb" of Virginia City; he, on the other hand, would continue to live in his rooms at Mrs. Fair's A Street house, which were close to his office, where he spent most of his time anyway. He also stipulated that Clara must not come to the A Street house to see Mrs. Fair when he was not present. Clearly, he wanted to avoid any confrontation that might bring the whole truth out in the open.

In this last matter, however, Clara defied her husband. Shortly after her arrival, she went to see Mrs. Fair on A Street when A.P. was at his office. Unfortunately, the historical record is silent on what exactly was said and done on this and a subsequent visit, though Clara did testify that she felt perfectly justified in making the visits since she and Mrs. Fair had been friendly during her stay in January. Was the conversation tense, even barbed? Clara certainly was trying to pressure Laura into ending her association with A.P., but did the two women openly acknowledge the true nature of that association, or did they maintain the pretense that Mr. Crittenden and his landlady were merely victims of malicious gossip? Either way, Clara left the A Street house both times without having accomplished her goal.

But then Clara scored something of a coup. She seems to have made a bargain with her husband: She told him she wanted to stay with him again at the A Street house—but this time without Mrs. Fair on the premises. Crittenden, knowing that Laura would not be happy about this, approached her cautiously. "He begged of me to allow it," Laura later testified. "He said otherwise she might make a great deal of fuss, and cause a great deal of talk and difficulty, and he [claimed he] never would come near her at night." A.P. proposed that Laura and Lillian could leave Virginia City for a while to visit Mrs. Lane, who was now living in San Francisco. Crittenden promised her that this would give him the opportunity to finally have it out with Clara and convince her to agree to a divorce; meanwhile, he planned to take a room at Mitchell's on Sutton Street, where he would secretly spend his nights.

Reluctantly, Laura agreed—perhaps because A.P. sweetened the deal by offering to buy her a $600 Steinway piano. She and Lillian thus left Virginia City in early July for a small vacation, allowing Clara to move into the A Street house, ostensibly cohabiting with her husband. For Clara, it may have been a way to save face, to show the world that she still held a claim on her lawful husband's affections and fidelity. But Laura hated the idea of her lover's wife living even temporarily in *her* house, in *her* place. "I didn't believe it possible to live away from you," she wrote to A.P. after arriving in San Francisco. "*Indeed, I did* almost die in the stage after bidding you good-bye. Just think that I dared not let my grief be seen, when my very heart seemed breaking—*my* husband, too; mine, *my* own, are you not, darling?"

Over the next few weeks, Laura wrote A.P. every day, claiming to be sick, bored of all social engagements in the city, thinking only of him. "Darling, remember all your promises to me," she wrote, "for on those depend *my future*." Her letters became increasingly resentful and despairing, especially after hearing that Crittenden was not sleeping at Mitchell's every night. And yet *he* was the one doubting *her*, expressing jealousy in his letters over the male visitors she was entertaining at the hotel suite she was sharing with her mother. "I have never, since my arrival, set my foot out the door of my room in company with a gentleman," she insisted to him. "I've never been to any place of amusement—I've never taken even a walk with a gentleman—have received no attention from anyone—and when a visitor calls in the evening (I receive none in the day), it is understood between Ma and myself that she remain in the room, so that I have never been alone with one. God knows, this ought to satisfy you, who are sleeping, or, if not sleeping, lying by the side of a woman every night."

Laura's indignation escalated when she heard that Clara was selling the furniture from her husband's A Street rooms, since it apparently did not suit her taste. Granted, the furniture belonged to A.P., but Laura could not bear the impertinence of the woman she now referred to as "the Madam." "I promised myself not to reproach you for my banishment and her presence with you," Laura wrote, "[but] you must know the bitter, bitter, galling feeling it brings to my heart." She began to complain of being unable to eat or sleep at night, and of an incessant pain in her chest. "I think I am going to die," she wrote, "but, darling, one of us—either she or I—ought to die. We—at least I—cannot live this way."

A few days later, complaining about the climate in this "wretched city," Laura left San Francisco for San Jose, now just a two-hour train ride south, thanks to the recent completion of the San Francisco and San Jose Railroad. She then moved on to Fremont, just north of the former state capital, and took up residence at the Warm Springs spa. In early August, while taking the cure at this fashionable lake resort, she received a letter from A.P. informing her that Clara—at long last—had returned to San Francisco. He thus was free to ask Laura to come back "to our home," and doubtless expected her to jump at the chance. But Laura was not to be won back so easily. She had a few conditions he had to meet before she would return to him—namely that he totally refurbish the rooms that Clara had "redecorated" in her rival's absence. ("I can't help dreading to see any of her goods in my house," she wrote him.) Laura also insisted that A.P. promise to stay with her every night he spent in Virginia City, and that he have no other abode in town besides the one with her. "Our future depends *entirely* upon you," she wrote. "This is the last letter I shall write to you, darling. So, goodbye, till we meet, nevermore to part—unless forever."

Whether Crittenden agreed to all of these stipulations is not entirely clear, but he did ultimately persuade her to come back to their newly spruced-up love nest on A Street before the end of summer. Their reunion was by all indications a joyous one, perhaps marred only by a panic in mining stocks that took a toll on the lovers' by now significant portfolios. Stockholders had become worried that the Comstock Lode would soon be tapping out; meanwhile, recent mineral finds in the Owyhee Valley of Idaho were drawing so many miners north that the newspapers feared that Nevada might lose what little population it had. This was not the first time that optimism about the future prospects of the Comstock Lode had dimmed temporarily; as in the past, odds were still good that a new strike would turn the bust back into a boom, and so Crittenden was not particularly pessimistic. He did, however, perceive that most of the big lawsuits concerning mining rights in the region were near settlement. Thus he warned Laura that, once his remaining legal cases in Nevada were wrapped up, he should probably return to San Francisco again. With the war over now, there were no loyalty oaths to worry about, so he could practice in the city again without any fear of reprisal. Of course, he hoped that Laura would follow him eventually, once she disposed of her business interests in Virginia City. It was still very much his intention, he claimed, to divorce his wife and marry Laura as soon as practicable. In the meantime, he would still come back to Virginia City periodically on business, so it was not as if he were really leaving her.

They had several months together before A.P. left, though privacy was becoming ever scarcer in Virginia City as more and more Crittendens arrived in town. This time it was young James, who by now had returned west from the battlefields of Virginia and was staying for a time at Tahoe House. Back in 1863, when James's brother Howard had been staying at Tahoe House, the young man had been so enchanted by Mrs. Fair that he was still thinking about her months later in Germany ("If my landlady was as young, handsome, and as interesting as Mrs. Fair," he wrote his father from Freiberg in Saxony, "I can assure you that I would overcome all obstacles in the German tongue . . ."). Now James also began succumbing to the lady's ample charms. He even made the awkward mistake of writing Clara about her rival's hospitality. "[I] take my meals with Father," James wrote in an October letter, "sometimes at the restaurant, other times at Mrs. Fair's, who has been kind enough to invite me to take my meals at her house."

Less enamored of her father's landlady was the Crittendens' daughter Laura, who with her husband, Ramon Sanchez, had also come to live in Virginia City that October. In her letters to Clara, she refused even to mention Mrs. Fair's name. Discussing A.P.'s proposed return to San Francisco, Laura Sanchez wrote, "As for that woman, if she chooses to follow him, she will do so." She commiserated with her long-suffering mother, noting that if only gossips would keep quiet about what was not their business, "the world would be a happier place." Clara undoubtedly agreed.

Virginia City was clearly getting a bit uncomfortable for A. P. Crittenden, whose principal Comstock cases were now in any case all but wrapped up. In December 1865, he finally made up his mind to end his two-year residency in Virginia City and move back to San Francisco. He did so with the explicit understanding that his relationship with Laura Fair would not only continue but would eventually culminate in their marriage, once she followed him back from Nevada. What Crittenden did not fully realize, however, was that the city he would be returning to was not the same one he had left just a few years earlier. San Francisco was growing up—and buttoning up. An adulterous affair between a fifty-year old man and a much younger woman—something that could pass in wartime Virginia City with little more than a bit of snickering gossip—would have greater trouble surviving in the more straitlaced environment of postwar San Francisco. The long arm of American Victorianism had by now reached as far as the Pacific coast.

Part Three

Manufacturing Respectability

(1865–1870)

I read the signs of the times, and I, that am no prophet, behold the things that are in store for you. Over slumbering California is stealing the dawn of a radiant future! . . . Has any other State so brilliant a future? Has any other city a future like San Francisco?

—MARK TWAIN
Farewell Address
December 10, 1866

14

A City on the Move

"IN AFFAIRS OF PUBLIC MORALS and education and religion, there is much activity in San Francisco, and a healthy progress in the right direction is visibly constant." So wrote journalist Samuel Bowles in *Across the Continent,* his bestselling account of a cross-country journey he made just after the end of the Civil War. Bowles, publisher of the nationally influential *Springfield Republican* newspaper, attributed the city's improvement to the fact that its civic life was now clearly dominated by his fellow New Englanders, who infused it with "their best qualities of decency, of order, of justice, of constant progress upward in morality and virtue." Those new vice ordinances passed during the war years had apparently had an effect, and Bowles was robustly approving of the results: In recent times, he observed, "there has been a steady, though struggling and sometimes hesitating, improvement in the character of all life of City and Coast."

For the growing cadre of social and business elites in this "improved" city of some hundred thousand inhabitants, these words were especially welcome—not just as a boost to their civic pride but also for practical economic reasons. Bowles, after all, had a wide readership among the eastern titans of industry and government whose capital and political backing would be crucial to the city's plans for the future.

In particular, eastern support would be needed to fulfill the late Abraham Lincoln's dream of a transcontinental railroad, for which everyone on the coast was waiting "with hunger and prayer and hope." Good reports about the city's ongoing transformation into a stable and investment-worthy place were thus especially important right now, when the nation was turning back to business after the disruptions caused by the Civil War. At that very moment, in fact, the influential politician and publisher William Bross (who had been on the same fact-finding trip to California with Bowles and Vice President Schuyler Colfax) was back on the East Coast, addressing the New York Chamber of Commerce about the rich possibilities out west. Bross was especially optimistic about the potential for further western mining profits to fuel the entire country's growth into a global power. "The production of so vast an amount of the precious metals," he told his receptive audience of businessmen, "will give to this nation a power to control the commerce and civilization of the world—far beyond all that the wildest imagination ever dared to picture."

Even in advance of this coming boom, however, San Francisco had been making strides toward reinventing itself as a world capital. As Bowles happily noted, the city was already "full-armed in the elements of civilization, wanton with the luxuries of the senses, rich in the social amenities, supplied with churches and schools and libraries, even affecting high art." And the postwar building boom was actively adding even more urban polish to the town. Down on California and Sansome Streets, William Ralston was constructing the first Bank of California building—"the most opulent edifice in the West"—part of his long-range plan to pull the city's financial district farther south toward Market Street (where, conveniently, he had bought up much of the real estate). Out to the city's west, in an area still known as the "Outside Lands," plans were being developed for a huge Golden Gate Park—shaped just like New York's Central Park, but 20 percent larger. And shortly before Bowles's arrival in town, entrepreneur Robert B. Woodward had opened his lavish "respectable resort" on the old Frémont estate on the Mission Road, complete with beer garden and amusement park, and soon to host the nation's first aquarium.

Given all of this progress, did San Francisco now qualify as "the Paris of the Pacific," as some were calling it? Local boosters like Ralston had higher aspirations. "I would prefer that Paris be known as 'The San Francisco of the East,'" the banker insisted.

Even so, there were still parts of town where a kind of frontier roughness persisted beneath the patina of sophistication and gentility. And although a degree of informal geographical sorting had been achieved—with vice and prostitution largely confined to certain districts, well away from wealthy residential neighborhoods—unwanted interactions between women of different types were still perceived as a danger. As historian Roger Lotchin has put it: "A trip to the dentist, the doctor, the milliner, the husband's office, and even to the church kept the situation explosive by renewing the contact between housewives and harlots."

Meanwhile, the mixing of races and ethnicities in the urban environment also remained an affront to Victorian sensibilities. For many white San Franciscans, sharing public space with Chinese, African, Native, and Latin Americans became increasingly undesirable. According to another city historian, Barbara Berglund, conforming to nationwide attitudes about class, gender, ethnicity, and race played a crucial role in "making the recently acquired, heavily immigrant city into a recognizably American place." Maintaining this version of white supremacy typically involved subjecting groups like the city's now-substantial Chinese population to a kind of "othering" process. Thus, for example, while San Franciscans ate at Chinese restaurants as a matter of course in the early 1850s ("The best eating houses in the town are those kept by Celestials, and conducted Chinese fashion," one forty-niner remembered), by the 1860s the emphasis was on the deplorable strangeness and foreignness of such establishments, and of all things Chinese. ("Nobody was so low, so miserable," the ubiquitous Samuel Bowles observed, "that he did not despise the Chinaman.")

Even brothels were subjected to this race-based discrimination. An edict called an "Order to Remove Chinese Women of Ill-Fame from Certain Limits in the City" was passed by the San Francisco Board of Supervisors in 1865. The state legislature followed suit the next year by passing the equally self-explanatory "Act for the Suppression of Chinese Houses of Ill Fame," which was answered in brisk fashion by another municipal ordinance known as the "Hawes Anti-Chinese Prostitution Law." Ah Toy, for whom life had become increasingly difficult since her return from China, was arrested under the state law in 1866. Tried in the police court, the woman described as beautiful in the white press in the early 1850s was now denigrated by the *San Francisco Call* with the most degrading and offensive language imaginable. Perhaps even more revealing, an Englishman who appeared as a witness for the defendant—and who admitted to being on intimate terms with her, eating at her table and otherwise "treating her as his wife"— was regarded by both judge and prosecutor as so depraved that he was subsequently arrested himself on a charge of vagrancy, a crime flexible enough to serve the purpose of punishing him.

The city's Black residents—although buoyed by the outcome of the war and the rise of Republican politicians at the state level—were not immune to this insidious dehumanization process. In the early Gold Rush years, for instance, San Francisco's white press would typically praise every sign of "race advancement" in town, from the building of Black churches to the establishment of Black institutions like the Atheneum. But the situation was changing ten years later. As Bret Harte noted in a July 1866 letter to the *Springfield Republican,* Blacks had been excluded from that year's Independence Day celebrations, apparently "to spare the sensitive prejudices of our Irish and Southern fellow citizens." Harte declared the ban a disgrace to the city and predicted that it would be a onetime display of civic moral weakness. However, given that the city's Chinese population had already been excluded from the July 4 celebration for several years running, after also being welcomed in the early '50s, his optimism seemed somewhat misplaced.

San Francisco's streetcar lines continued to be a common venue for this insistence on racial boundary lines. Even though, in the wake of the 1863 Charlotte Brown suit, a judge had declared segregation on public transportation illegal, the practice continued on the city streets. Streetcar drivers would typically speed away (in a "sudden fit of negrophobia," as the *Pacific Appeal* put it) whenever a Black person attempted to board his car. The company's rationale, often stated explicitly, was that they were "protecting white women from social contact with Black people." Here was an injustice ripe for a challenge from one of the city's most determined Black activists.

On the afternoon of September 27, 1866, Mary Ellen Pleasant stood—"proud and erect," as was her wont—at a streetcar stop on Folsom Street, waiting for the arrival of a No. 21 car of the North Beach and Mission Railroad Company (NBMRR). By prior arrangement, a white woman—Lizette Woodworth, Pleasant's friend and former employer—was already seated on the car scheduled to arrive next. When it approached the Folsom Street stop, Pleasant hailed it, but the driver refused to pick her up. "Stop this car," Woodworth said to the conductor. "There is a woman who wants to get in." The conductor took no notice of her, until she insisted again that the car be stopped, at which point he replied, "We don't take colored people in the cars."

These words provided the basis of a suit against the NBMRR that would last two years and end up reaching the California Supreme Court. Represented by a prominent lawyer named George W. Tyler, Mrs. Pleasant (having shrewdly ensured that her testimony would be corroborated by a white witness from the upper echelons of local society) claimed that she had suffered great physical and mental harm by being denied service. The lower court agreed. Finding that the plaintiff was "willfully and purposely deprived . . . of the exercise of a plain legal right," the court ruled in her favor and awarded damages in the amount of $500. But the NBMRR was persistent. The railroad filed a motion for a new trial, insisting that the damages were far out of line with the magnitude of the offense. When this motion was denied, the company appealed to the state supreme court, which proceeded to reverse the lower court's decision. "The damages were excessive," the court ruled. "There was no proof of special damage, nor of any malice, or ill will, or wanton or violent conduct on the part of the defendant, and it was [therefore] not a case for exemplary damages."

Not until 1893 would the California legislature pass effective statutes prohibiting racial discrimination in public accommodations. But although Pleasant's suit ultimately failed, it was not lost on white San Franciscans that more and more Black Americans—women in particular—were forcefully insisting on the equal protection granted by the 1866 federal Civil Rights Act. And in Pleasant's case, detractors had a sly way of dealing with the irritant. At some point in her testimony during the trial, Lizette Woodworth had mentioned that when Pleasant worked for her, she would sometimes call the older woman "Mamma." This detail—redolent of the comfortably familiar relationship between white mistress and Black maid—was picked up by the local press, which soon began to refer to the plaintiff as "Mammy Pleasant." It was, of course, a way of marginalizing her, of trivializing the figure of an affluent and intellectually formidable Black woman—one who could be friendly with her white former employer on terms of equality—by casting her in the unthreatening role of loyal family retainer. Pleasant, as might be expected, hated the nickname, but it was as "Mammy Pleasant" that she would henceforth be known to white San Franciscans, even as her wealth and influence continued to grow in the years ahead.

. . .

It was to this ever-less-tolerant city that A. P. Crittenden returned after his wartime sojourn in Nevada. Moving into the rooms that his wife and younger children shared in the Cosmopolitan Hotel, he set about reestablishing a legal practice in town. What he told Clara about the state of his relationship with Laura Fair is something we can only guess at, but the surviving correspondence between the lovers (which was now being conducted via the address of a friend, N. D. Anderson, presumably to keep Clara from knowing about it) indicates that their affair was by no means finished. "Oh, the desolation—the misery in my soul since you left," Laura wrote him from Virginia City shortly after his move. "I tell you, Darling, you have become my life—my all. Oh, the sin upon your soul if you should forsake me!" He responded with reassurances of his devotion to her, but she was not satisfied. "I do not feel secure," she wrote. "How can I? You are living with another woman, separated from me."

Nor were these feelings one-sided. "My God! Why will you not get out of my mind and heart?" A.P. wrote her a few months into their separation. "Do you know that I am perpetually uneasy, anticipating from day to day that I will hear something which will part us forever?" He confessed to feeling intensely jealous, worried that she might be entertaining other men in the A Street house—"desecrating our happy home," as he put it—to the point of making himself ill. He even had reason to be jealous of his own son. James had moved back to San Francisco with his father in late 1865, but he hadn't forgotten "the charming Mrs. F," as he called her in a letter to his sister Nannie. Awkwardly, the twenty-four-year-old went so far as to write Mrs. Fair a letter so baldly flirtatious that she felt it necessary to show it to the young man's father. ("It is perhaps well for me to have left Virginia City as soon as I did," James wrote. "I begin to fear that a lady so beautiful and so attractive might in time succeed in conquering a heart which has thus far escaped from the many dangers which have assailed it.") A.P. told her not to answer the letter, but whether he then gave James a stern talking-to is unclear. In any case, the fact that Laura had smitten one of his own sons did nothing to ease Crittenden's bouts of jealousy.

Laura responded to her lover's green-eyed protestations quite reasonably. If he was so miserable without her, she asked, why did he not send for her to join him in San Francisco? "Why don't you let me come?" she wrote. "I am not only willing but very anxious to leave this life of gaiety and pleasure, which exists only in your imagination." His professions of misery notwithstanding, A.P. extended her no concrete invitation. Instead, he merely turned up the volume of his prose: "Oh, how I do want you!" he wrote her back. "Every hour or two I take your likeness out of my drawer, and look at it . . . I cannot live without you, and I won't." Not since his courtship of a teenaged Clara Jones some thirty years earlier had A.P. waxed so ardent in his declarations of love.

But while Crittenden's personal life may have been something of a mess at this point, his professional life was prospering. The recent drop in mining stocks had hurt his investment portfolio, but if anything it was increasing the amount of legal work coming his way, and he soon found himself traveling frequently back to Nevada to argue financial and real estate cases before the new state's supreme court in Carson City. "We have long regarded this gentleman as at the head of our bar," one newspaper said of Crittenden after he gave a masterful argument in one case, "but on this occasion he surpassed not only his eloquent and able associates but transcended all [of his own] former efforts." The law partnership he had started with another prominent lawyer named Samuel M. Wilson (Wilson & Crittenden) quickly became one of the premier firms in San Francisco. Soon Crittenden was doing well enough to move the family to a house in the newly fashionable South Park neighborhood, about a half mile southeast of Market Street, which was rapidly becoming the center of society for the local gentry. Unfortunately, however, this put his personal life under greater scrutiny, and his relationship with Laura Fair, which at this point had become an open secret among Crittenden's friends and associates, was beginning to tarnish his good name. At least one important connection refused to do business with him because of it, and several of his closest friends—Solomon Heydenfeldt, a fellow lawyer and judge, and Lloyd Tevis, a banker and future president of Wells, Fargo & Co.— urged him to end the affair immediately. The irony of the situation was hard to overlook: The town that Crittenden had once deemed too louche and immoral to be a home for his wife had become a place too tight-laced and sanctimonious to tolerate his mistress.

But Crittenden's passion had by now rendered him impervious to all sensible advice. And when in late summer he and Laura had one of their frequent long-distance squabbles, he reacted with very un-lawyerlike recklessness. Laura's mother had apparently been scolding her again about her compromised position as mistress to a married man, and for once Laura found herself in agreement. In a pet, she wrote A.P. that, as devastating as it would be for her to stop loving him, she would call it quits unless he truly went through with his divorce from Clara.

The very idea of a breakup sent Crittenden into a panic. "Why, oh why, do you write to me in such a way? Would you drive me mad?" he wrote her. "Instantly—*instantly*—upon receipt of this, *without the loss of one single second,* telegraph me 'Yes' or 'No,' if you would not have my life upon your soul; if 'Yes,' it will mean that we are parted forever; if 'No,' that you did not mean what you have said; that you do and will always love me; that you are mine, forever."

Her answering cable is lost to history, but her response to these rather confusing directions was apparently "No"—meaning, in other words, that she would not give him up, that she would always be his, forever. But this close call, if indeed Laura's threat had been serious, was apparently enough to get A.P. to change his mind about Laura's remaining in Nevada. He relented, and within a few weeks, she was making arrangements to sell or rent the Virginia City lodging house and all of its furniture and join her lover in San Francisco—permanently.

A. P. Crittenden's already tangled love life, it seems, was about to become more complicated than ever.

15

Broken Promises

I T DIDN'T TAKE LONG FOR the new high-minded tone of San Francisco to create difficulties for the still-notorious Mrs. Fair. Her new life started off promisingly enough: Upon returning to the city she had twice abandoned in desperate poverty (first after her unsuccessful attempt to make a living during the mid-1850s slump, and again in 1861, following the suicide of William Fair), Laura now found herself in a position to live there in some style. She leased a suite of rooms for herself and Lillian at Russ House, a newly opened residential hotel on Montgomery Street that was now, along with the Occidental and the Cosmopolitan Hotels, one of the most prestigious addresses on the Pacific coast. Unfortunately, however, Laura was soon to discover that being able to afford such a respectable abode in postwar San Francisco did not necessarily mean that she would be welcome there.

The trouble began not long after her arrival. A.P. had been coming to her rooms regularly, making the mile-long trip over from South Park every evening after dutifully having dinner with Clara and the children. What he told his wife about these nightly disappearances is unclear. As an endlessly busy lawyer, he could always claim that he was retreating to his office on Pine Street to burn the midnight oil; or perhaps he no longer cared at this point what Clara did and did not suspect. But these frequent calls on his mistress did not go unnoticed at Russ House. One day another guest at the hotel—a man named Searles—was bold enough to make a few acerbic comments about Mrs. Fair's reputation within her hearing. Appalled, Laura mentioned the episode to Crittenden, and he, outraged by this insult, proceeded to confront Searles in one of the hotel's public rooms. Crittenden all but strong-armed the offending gentleman up to Laura's apartment and demanded that he apologize to her. Searles reluctantly complied, but later complained about his rough treatment to H. H. Pearson, the hotel's owner. Pearson in turn "had words" about the incident with his attractive but problematic new guest. This kind of impropriety, he apparently told her, could not be tolerated at a place like Russ House. Mrs. Fair would have to leave at once.

Until she could become A. P. Crittenden's wife, apparently, A. P. Crittenden's mistress would require a more discreet living arrangement. The lawyer quickly found furnished rooms for her and Lillian—*and* a servant—in a private house on Rincon Hill, a newly fashionable neighborhood just a short walk from the Crittenden home in South Park. Laura would later insist that she paid the rent herself—after all, her stock portfolio was by now substantial, and she still had monthly income from her Virginia City lodging house. But the lovers' correspondence indicates that Crittenden was helping her with at least some expenses, since he felt it would be foolish for her to sell any of her mining stocks while their prices were temporarily depressed. Not that Crittenden himself could really afford these extravagances. But as Clara's brother William had once remarked to her, making money was rarely difficult for "Mr. C"; the problem was *keeping* the money he made. And so Crittenden characteristically took on an extra load of monthly overhead to provide comfortable households for both a family and a mistress, in a city where the cost of living had always been high and was soaring ever higher.

This expensive arrangement, however, would merely be temporary, or so Crittenden claimed. He assured Laura that he was now making plans to take her east to Indiana, where famously lenient divorce laws would allow him to part from Clara with a minimum of fuss. But Crittenden was clearly exaggerating the ease with which divorces were obtained, even in Indiana. Granted, divorce laws all over the country were becoming more relaxed than they had been in the early nineteenth century, when in most states an act of the legislature was required to end a marriage. But even in 1866, the separation of man and wife was widely discouraged, the institution of marriage being regarded as the basic building block of a stable and moral society. In some states, including New York, divorced persons were not allowed to remarry; in South Carolina, divorce was forbidden for any reason whatsoever. The so-called divorce mill of Indiana was different. Judges were given the discretion to grant divorces for any reason they deemed proper, including one spouse's adultery, habitual drunkenness, or cruel treatment of the other. But even in Indiana at this time, one had to reside in the state for a year before applying for divorce, and it's not at all clear that lawyer Crittenden had fully explained this fact to his would-be second wife.

Indeed, Crittenden insisted that the wait would be a matter of only a few months. He was confident that by the end of the year 1866, he would have enough money from his current business dealings to pay off his more pressing debts and still have enough left over to leave his current wife comfortably fixed. Then he would be free to put an end to their long three-year wait and finally make Laura his legal wife, as she was already his "spiritual" one.

Laura was naturally elated by this development. Once she became Mrs. Crittenden, her future—and that of her now six-year-old daughter, Lillian—would be assured. True, there would be those who would never accept her, who would never invite her into their parlors or acknowledge her in restaurants or at the theater. And yet she would be safely, if just barely, within the pale of Victorian respectability. More important, Lillian would have a father, a protector, and a name that she would never have to be ashamed of.

But alas, Crittenden would renege on this promise. Regardless of whether he ever actually intended to follow through, when December came around, he claimed that his financial affairs were not in order yet, and that essential business required his continued presence on the West Coast. But he promised her that in six months or so—by summer 1867—he'd be free to go. In what was to become a recurring theme in their relationship over the next few years, A.P. insisted that Laura would just have to be patient.

* * *

Laura Fair's return to the great western metropolis happened to coincide with that of another local celebrity—Mark Twain, who had spent the last half year in the Sandwich (that is, Hawaiian) Islands, writing regular dispatches for the *Sacramento Union*. This opportunity to report on a place of intense interest to Americans had come at an excellent time for the now thirty-year-old writer. Despite the recognition and remuneration brought by his jumping-frog story the year before, he found that he still had to scramble to support his heavy spending habits. Like Crittenden, Twain seemed to stay just one or two steps ahead of ruinous debt, mainly by taking on Herculean amounts of work. Along with his various pieces for Bret Harte's *Californian* and regular theater reviews for the *Dramatic Chronicle* (a paper founded in 1865 that would eventually become the *San Francisco Chronicle*), Twain was also writing several items per week for the *Territorial Enterprise* back in Virginia City. All of this work paid decently enough, and yet Twain's outgo still seemed to exceed his income, a predicament that depressed him deeply. "If I do not get out of debt in three months," he wrote his brother Orion, "[give me] pistols or poison for one—exit *me*."

It didn't help that he was succumbing to a few of the city's less salubrious pleasures in his off hours. Twain had become a habitué of the dives of the Barbary Coast neighborhood, and apparently partook willingly of the hashish that was just then becoming a vogue among literary types about town. "It appears that a 'Hasheesh' mania has broken out among our Bohemians," the *Chronicle* observed one day in September 1865. "Yesterday, Mark Twain and the 'Mouse-Trap' man [another columnist for the *Californian*] were seen walking up Clay street under the influence of the drug, followed by a 'star' [a patrolman], who was evidently laboring under a misapprehension as to what was the matter with them." The police were apparently keeping a close eye on Twain at this time, as many of his dispatches to the *Territorial Enterprise* complained bitterly about the brutality and corruption endemic in the police department. These pieces brought the young journalist a certain amount of harassment from the city's law enforcement officers—including at least one night in jail for alleged drunkenness.

So when, in early 1866, the California Steam Navigation Company offered Twain a free passage on its new ultrafast steamship service from San Francisco to Honolulu, he accepted with alacrity. Here, he reasoned, was an opportunity to make some extra freelance money and at the same time find colorful new subject matter for his satiric and journalistic skills. He ended up discovering a wider variety of material than even he (or the steamship company) had hoped for. Over the course of his four-month stay in the islands, he toured temples and tropical rain forests, watched a volcano erupt, and tried, unsuccessfully, to learn surfing. He even got the chance to interview survivors of a major maritime disaster who—having spent weeks in a lifeboat after their clipper, the *Horton,* burned at sea—washed up on the shore of the Big Island. He reported on all of these adventures for a very grateful editor at the *Sacramento Union*. The story of the *Horton* disaster he also wrote up at greater length (and, wisely, in a style more sober and factual than was his wont) and sold it to *Harper's Monthly,* where it caused a bit of a sensation and again brought the name of Mark Twain to the notice of readers back east.

Twain's plans to turn his recent travel experiences into much-needed cash did not stop there. Having witnessed the success of an 1863 lecture tour by the comic writer Charles Farrar Browne—who, under the nom de plume "Artemus Ward," had been one of President Lincoln's favorite writers—Twain decided to adapt his Hawaiian pieces as a stage performance that he could give at various rented theaters throughout California and Nevada. The ever-persnickety Bret Harte warned his friend that he would be debasing himself to engage in such a low practice, but Twain went ahead and booked one of the biggest theaters in San Francisco, Maguire's Academy of Music. And Twain's instincts proved correct: The lecture premiered on October 2, 1866, to a packed house and enthusiastic reviews. "One of the most interesting and amusing lectures ever given in this city," the *San Francisco Evening Bulletin* raved. The *Examiner* was also impressed by the clever raconteur: "The most delightful discovery made was, we think, this: he speaks as he writes. The same unexpected jokes—the same inevitable drollery—the same strong sense embodied in quaint phraseology." Even Harte had to admit that the evening was a triumph, which he gracefully conceded in his own review for the *Springfield Republican.* The Sandwich Island lecture, which Twain went on to perform to great acclaim in other western cities, set the pattern for travel classics like *The Innocents Abroad* and *Roughing It,* in which much of the Hawaiian material eventually appeared. And as Laura Fair had discovered a few years earlier, even a handful of appearances onstage could earn enough money to satisfy insistent creditors. There was even enough left over for him to finally realize his hopes of leaving California to travel the world.

On December 10, at the end of a reprise performance of his Hawaiian lecture at Congress Hall, Twain briefly stepped out of his ironic persona to speak to his audience from the heart: "My friends and fellow-citizens," he said. "I have been treated with extreme kindness and cordiality by San Francisco, and I wish to return my sincerest thanks and acknowledgments." Looking back on the miracle of the city's unprecedented flowering, and predicting an even greater future ahead, he announced that he was nonetheless departing. "I am bidding the old city and my old friends a kind, but not a sad, farewell, for I know that when I see this home again, the changes that will have been wrought upon it will suggest no sentiment of sadness; its estate will be brighter, happier, and prouder a hundredfold than it is today. This is its destiny, and in all sincerity I can say, So may it be!"

Five days later, after taking leave of his friend and mentor Harte, Twain boarded the steamship *America* (perhaps the very same ship that A. P. Crittenden and Laura Fair would have been on, had plans for their December trip worked out). In the writer's pocket was a contract to produce a series of weekly letters for the *Daily Alta California,* covering his proposed future travels to Europe, the Middle East, India, China, and Japan. "We feel confident [that] his letters to the ALTA," the paper announced, "will give him a world-wide reputation."

This prediction turned out to be prophetic. The pieces Twain wrote would make their thirty-one-year-old author a household name. The young man who had come west in 1861 as an unemployed fugitive from the Civil War was now heading east, just five years later, as the leading representative of a vigorous new school of American literature.

•   •   •

Early in 1867, San Francisco investors were feeling gleeful again, thanks to a smart recovery in mining share prices. A report issued by the California Geological Survey (and much promoted by William Ralston and other city boosters) provided a supremely optimistic outlook for the mines of the Washoe, suggesting that the silver discoveries made so far had barely scratched the surface of the Comstock Lode's potential output. This analysis, combined with some new ore strikes at the end of the relatively fallow year of 1866, lent new energy to the markets, whose promise of easy money soon turned many city residents into the nineteenth-century equivalent of day traders. "Every man you met was a president, every other one a trustee, and all [were] stockholders," Bret Harte wrote of this period. "Your washerwoman had 10 feet in the High Flyer [mine], your office boy held certificates for 50 shares of

Aladdin . . . Young couples, in corners, no longer quoted Byron and Moore, but [rather] the stock list, and exchanged, instead of rings and vows, certificates and transfers."

Nor were older couples immune to the excitement. "I have the mania upon me, and there is no resisting it," Laura Fair admitted in an April 1867 letter to her lover, who was temporarily back in Virginia City on business. "I expect if you don't return soon I shall speculate myself out of money, stock, house, and home." Earlier in the year, she had moved out of the Rincon Hill house and taken rooms in a fashionable lodging house on Kearny Street run by a Mrs. Hammersmith, and A.P. had taken a room there for himself. (He now had three residences in town—not even counting his law office—in order to accommodate his convoluted love life.) Both lovers were now doing well enough in the market to support a rather luxurious lifestyle. And Laura, whose portfolio was now worth a prodigious $40,000, was aiming even higher, buying stocks on margin and taking out loans to buy more, always on the advice of her well-situated paramour: "I am still of the opinion that you will be able to get $22,000 for [your Savage Mine shares]," Crittenden advised her in a letter written on March 27. "[But] you must sell at that price. It will not be safe to try for more."

A few days later, he wrote again, giving her a rundown on the prospects for Gould & Curry, Chollar-Potosi, and other mining stocks. "As to Savage, you may rest perfectly easy; you must make at least $18,000 clear out of your 10 feet." This was a significant amount of money for an unmarried woman to control at the time. But lest this new wealth give her any untoward notions of independence, Crittenden was sure to remind her that she owed her current and future prosperity entirely to him: "In all of these matters, my darling, only have implicit confidence in me, and do what I advise, and you will be entirely satisfied with the result."

When he'd gone back to Virginia City in February (Lloyd Tevis had sent him for several weeks of legal work involving ownership of the Savage Mine), Crittenden had grown nostalgic for the early years of his romance with his then-landlady. He'd apparently mended fences with Laura's mother, and she was allowing him to stay in their old rooms at Tahoe House. "I am in the big arm chair, which used to be in your dining-room," he wrote Laura, "and it is placed right in the corner of the room, upon the very spot where it first dawned upon us that we loved each other, and where the first kiss was given." He was clearly falling ever deeper under Laura Fair's spell, and when heavy snows in the Sierra Nevada delayed his return to San Francisco after the Savage case was settled, he grew positively melodramatic: "Man never loved woman as I do you . . . The separation has become insupportable . . . My God! I do so long to see you; and if another storm should come, I will cross the mountains on foot, but I will come to you. What do I care for hardship or exposure if every step I take brings me near to you—to the other and better half of my own soul." This passionate missive then concludes, characteristically, with some decidedly unromantic advice about switching the broker she used to buy and sell stocks.

Crittenden finally returned to San Francisco in late April—traveling by stagecoach and steamboat, since there was no longer any need to heroically traverse the snow-choked mountains on foot. Laura was grateful to have him back. She'd had a difficult few months. Beyond being deprived of her lover's company, both she and Lillian had been so sick in early April that Mrs. Lane had had to come down from Virginia City to nurse them, and the illness had left Laura disconcertingly thin. Meanwhile, her brother O.D. had gotten into some kind of scrape with the law that forced him to disappear; Mrs. Lane had managed to locate him in early April in San Jose, but he had been through "horrible trouble," she said, and apparently needed to remain in hiding. Through all of this, Laura had been so lonely without A.P. that she'd even started sleeping with her pet parrot. Polly, as the bird was rather unimaginatively named, could be relied on to provide at least some comfort, since she'd taught it to say the word "darling." But Polly had been a poor substitute for the other creature who was allowed to call Laura by that name.

Now that the two lovers were reunited, however, all was well. Again their talk turned to the promised trip east for the Indiana divorce from Clara and remarriage to Laura. The current plan was to leave sometime that summer. Since the transcontinental railroad was still two years from completion, they would go by steamer via the Panama route to New York—a faster journey than it had been in the early 1850s, thanks to swifter steamboats and a reliable railroad connection across the isthmus, but not nearly as fast as the future train route directly across the United States.

Whether Crittenden told his long-suffering wife about this imminent end to her twenty-nine-year marriage is doubtful; one wonders how serious he was about this alleged plan. But Laura—at least according to her later testimony—was convinced of his sincerity, and accordingly prepared for their departure. She was more than ready to spend some of her new wealth in the East, and to travel as a soon-to-be-married woman, with her respectable future husband at her side.

The last part of this dream, however, would have to be postponed again. As the date approached for their trip, Crittenden again insisted that he could not get away quite yet. In early June, he and several partners had incorporated their own mining company—Consolidated Virginia, capitalized at over $2 million—which proposed to merge several existing mining properties so that a new shaft might be sunk into a previously untapped level of the silver lode. While this merger was in the works, it was just not possible for Crittenden to absent himself.

This second disappointment, naturally, did not sit well with Laura, but there was little she could do about it. She refused to postpone her own trip again; she had even liquidated most of her mining stocks in order to pay for the extended journey. Crittenden reluctantly told Laura that she should just go ahead without him; he promised that he would meet up with her and Lillian somewhere in the East by September or

October at the latest, when they could start planning for the Indiana divorce. In July 1867, therefore, Laura took passage on the steamer *Sacramento,* headed for Panama en route to New York—a lady of means now, with a charming young daughter as a companion, but still lacking that essential element of Victorian respectability: a well-born and honorable husband to complete her family tableau.

16

Bicoastal Relationships

H E WASN'T COMING. When autumn arrived, A.P. wrote
Laura in New York to say that he still couldn't join her. Having
failed to realize the hoped-for gains on his mining shares, he still didn't
have enough money to pay off his debts and provide Clara with enough
of a nest egg to ensure the family's comfort without him. He was determined not to leave Clara until he could leave her well-off—that
much he felt he owed the mother of his children. But he was certain
that it would happen eventually. His shares were sure to recover soon.
In the meantime, he wanted Laura to come back to San Francisco,
since he couldn't concentrate or get anything done without her. He
even had the nerve to blame her for leaving him behind.

The would-be Mrs. Crittenden was understandably exasperated.
Laura was now living a fairly luxurious existence at the sophisticated
redbrick New York Hotel, located on Broadway between Washington
and Waverly Place (a site now occupied by NYU). The hotel was
popular at the time among Democratic politicians and southerners in
particular, so Laura was in her element, and she was apparently making
friends both male and female. But waiting for her lover was a frustrat-
ing business, and Laura couldn't conceal her irritation. "It is cruel to
write as you do," she wrote him in late September. "This separation is

not of my choosing, and it can never be final unless you make it so. [If not] for your promise of coming here and making me your wife, I had never left you—not though the scorn and slander of the world had crushed out my life, as it was doing. I would have died under your very eyes."

These numerous broken promises, she told him, were playing havoc with both her physical and her mental health. "Am I free to ruin forever the future of my child?" she asked. "You say you would have done thus and so, but what have you, being a man, with all the man's thousand privileges, done? Have you given up the world or society for me? Are you in the least injured by all the talk that has been? No, with a man it is so different. You could have let the whole world know [that is, of their relationship], and it would not have affected you either socially or pecuniarily. Where a woman is utterly ruined, a man is not injured. And the only thing which could have saved me and can save me, without injury to you, you now show by your letter you never intend doing, *viz:* to come and place yourself in a position to make our past right. I was a fool to even hope [for] such a thing."

This remarkably astute bit of sociological analysis (complete with the Latin abbreviation *viz*!) indicates that Laura was keenly aware of the gender disparities in the moral code of American Victorianism. An adulterous affair like theirs had very different consequences for the man and for the woman. Certainly the man's behavior would be frowned upon and disapproved of—some over-particular individuals might even shun the man's company, like the individual who had previously refused to do business with him on the basis of these rumors— but he would not typically be excluded from society. The woman, on the other hand, would be ruined, banished from the parlors and drawing rooms of any household aspiring to respectability. Laura realized that her only hope was for Crittenden to "make our past right"—in other words, to legitimize their relationship by marriage, which, of course, could occur only after a divorce from the existing wife: "You have not said it in so many words," Laura continued, "yet I know by what you have written that your choice has been made. You are willing to have me, but you are not willing to give *her* up, and both you cannot have."

And yet Laura continued to hold out hope, and after a few more days even rashly wired him that she would return to San Francisco and lay claim to him—Clara or no Clara—if he did not come soon. But by that time A.P. was angry with her; he said he'd heard a rumor about her and a certain Mr. H. (Indeed, given Laura's frustration, she was quite possibly and justifiably entertaining the attentions of the resident males in New York.) So Crittenden insisted that she not come back just then, sending her two separate ill-tempered letters—one by steamer and one by overland mail, to ensure that she received at least one of them. She wrote back in despair in October: "Your two letters . . . filled to overflowing my cup of bitterness . . . Alone in this bleak world, I had no hope but in you. Now, all my hope is dead, and today I have rolled the first gravestone upon our cherished past." Laura informed him that she had burned all of his recent letters and was now leaving the country. She and Lillian would be taking a steamer from New York to Havana to get some rest in warmer climes, traveling with a Mrs. Bowie, an acquaintance she'd met at the hotel. "If you love me, you will come," she added, offering him a last chance. "I have no life, no hope, no happiness, until I hear from you."

But when she did hear from him—he wired to say he couldn't come to Cuba, either, and that the divorce would again have to be postponed—her despair turned to wrath, and for the first time her tone turned downright threatening: "You will run me crazy," she wrote back while still in New York, awaiting her departure to Havana. "Your telegram this morning is dreadful . . . Mark my oath now, darling, I will return to San Francisco to be your wife, in the face of all the world. If you will not get a divorce I will make her [get one], or I will ruin *all; I alone* shall not be sacrificed."

The wildly vacillating tone of Laura's letters from this time— veering from anguish to ardor to anger—indicates how confused and frustrated she was by the mixed signals her alleged fiancé was sending her with each new communication. Crittenden was obviously torn by conflicting emotions, his genuine passion for Laura at odds with his feelings of obligation to Clara and his reluctance to jeopardize his standing in the community. His only surviving communications from this period reveal that he, too, was mercurial in his moods. He would beg her in one letter to come home to him and then turn around and cable her to stay away, alternating between abject requests for signs of her love and resentful jealousy about the other men he repeatedly accused her of seeing. "It nearly killed me when you said you were going to Havana," he wrote her just before her planned departure. "Why? With whom?" His first thought was that she was going with this Mr. H, and the idea had obsessed him. Meanwhile, the Sturm und Drang of their relationship had taken a physical toll on him, exacerbating the rheumatic condition that he was sure would kill him before he reached old age. "Mind and Body I am a wreck," he told her. "It is so hard to move and think." And then, rather melodramatically: "I have made my arrangements for death at any moment."

The postal time lags didn't help. Letters could still take weeks to go from coast to coast, and transcontinental telegrams, while much faster, were too expensive for all but the briefest and most urgent messages. This meant that the lovers' communications were often at cross-purposes. Apologies would arrive earlier than the news that needed to be apologized for; bitter reproaches would be received long after the offense in question had been put right. If only the transcontinental railroad were finished! Everything would be easier once the travel time between coasts was drastically shortened: Their letters—and thus their moods—would be in better sync, and A.P. might even be able to join her in the East, carving out enough time to travel without having to leave his business unattended for too long. As she had told him numerous times over the years, "I suffer so much more [apart] than if we were together, for so many weary hours must elapse before a harsh word or act can be rectified." If only he could be with her, she maintained, she could endure anything—poverty, social rejection, illness. But the completion date of the railroad, while racing ever closer, was still over a year away. In the meantime, Laura and A.P. would have to continue playing out their dramas in the same disjointed, unsynchronized manner, with weeks of delay and an entire continent between them.

· · ·

A. P. Crittenden and Laura Fair were hardly alone in yearning for the completion of the transcontinental railroad; many other Californians were also impatiently awaiting the date, hoping to reap benefits from the new bicoastal relationships that a rapid rail connection would make possible. San Francisco had already grown into a major port, acting as a shipping portal for produce and manufactures from the Pacific Slope to the markets of China, Japan, and the rest of Asia. With a more efficient overland pipeline of goods to and from the Midwest and the East Coast, it was hoped that the city would become *the* preeminent center for trade between the two continents. In a high-profile article called "What the Railroad Will Bring Us," political economist Henry George laid out these potential gains in tantalizing detail. George, still in his twenties at this point but eventually to become famous as author of the bestselling tract *Progress and Poverty,* predicted that the transcontinental would pull the center of power and population in the United States westward and herald "a new era of great material prosperity" on the Pacific Slope. This shift would benefit San Francisco in particular, which he estimated would grow to become the second largest (or even largest!) city on the North American continent. And the positive effects, George argued, would be more than just economic. Not only would the railroad spark a flowering of the city's cultural life—enriching it with more museums, theaters, libraries, universities, parks, and gardens—it would also be a boon to its social tranquility: "We shall have more home influences, a deeper religious sentiment, less of the unrest that is bred of an adventurous and reckless life." In other words,

San Francisco would become an even more "mature" city that would better conform to Victorian standards of rectitude and respectability.

The momentous final meeting of the tracks was slated to occur sometime in the spring or summer of 1869, at a location yet to be determined. But certain complications threatened to push the date back. In particular, a strike of Chinese workers on the Central Pacific in mid-1867 seemed destined to seriously disrupt the railroad's time-table. Given how much was depending on the timely completion of the project, the strike did nothing to improve the already-deteriorating reputation of the Chinese population among white Californians.

Back in 1863, the work of building the transcontinental had been contracted principally to two different railroads—the Central Pacific (CP), which was responsible for laying track from Sacramento east-ward over the Sierra Nevada, and the Union Pacific (UP), working westward from the existing end-of-tracks in Council Bluffs, Iowa. (A third railroad, the Western Pacific, was given the task of building the much shorter section of the line between Sacramento and the San Francisco Bay.) Former governor Leland Stanford, now one of the Big Four owners of the Central Pacific, had discovered early on that build-ing a railroad with Chinese rather than Irish labor had numerous ad-vantages; Chinese workers, he found, were cheaper to hire than their European counterparts, and less prone to grumbling about the long hours and grueling, sometimes hazardous working conditions in-volved in blasting a train line through the mountains. For that reason, labor recruiters aggressively arranged for thousands of laborers to em-igrate from Hong Kong to California; eventually the crews working on the CP line were almost 90 percent Chinese. This development, combined with a similar rise in the use of Chinese construction work-ers in urban areas, led to substantial labor strife in the late 1860s, usu-ally incited by the white immigrant laborers that the newcomers had allegedly supplanted.

By early 1867 anti-Asian sentiment in California had risen to a new level of bitterness. On February 12, Chinese workers at a con-

struction site near the South Beach wards of San Francisco were attacked by a group of whites who objected to the low wages the Chinese
were willing to accept for their work. After brutally beating the workers and setting fire to their barracks, the white mob (mostly Irish, according to the newspapers) roamed through the southern parts of the
city, wreaking similar havoc at other worksites, killing one Chinese
worker and wounding at least a dozen more. Ten white rioters were
arrested and convicted for the spree, but thanks to the intervention of
an organization called the Anti-Coolie Association, all ten were ultimately released.

Perhaps inevitably, the railroad strike erupted five months later.
Several thousand Chinese laborers at work on the CP's transcontinental line staged a mass walkout, demanding higher wages, shorter work-
days, and an end to beatings of recalcitrant workers by work-gang
overseers—apparently a not-uncommon practice. The strikers' complaints were entirely valid. The railroad had been paying the Chinese
far less than their white counterparts, even while subjecting them to
more difficult and dangerous working conditions. This despite the fact
that Charles Crocker, the project's construction supervisor, admitted
that Chinese workers exhibited "greater reliability and steadiness" and
more "aptitude and capacity for hard work."

On June 25, at the height of the construction season, some three
thousand of these allegedly quiescent Chinese workers walked off the
job, in a fully planned and coordinated action that qualified as one of
the largest strikes to date against a private employer in the United
States. Unfortunately, the strikers received no support from their white
fellow laborers, belying their claim that their anti-Chinese feelings
were prompted by the willingness of the Chinese to accept low wages.
This lack of support allowed the company to adopt a hard line against
the strikers. And since the CP's management was desperate not to fall
behind on their all-important timetable, they quickly resorted to ruth-
less tactics to end the walkout, even cutting off the strikers' food supply. As a result, the strike petered out after just a week, with the

workers winning few if any concessions (although there is evidence that the company quietly raised the pay of at least some Chinese laborers once construction resumed). Three weeks later, the company's legal counsel, Edwin Crocker (Charles's older brother), was able to report that construction was again "progressing rapidly," and that a visiting official from Washington was "highly pleased with the character of the work, & all he saw." The potential crisis had passed, in other words, and the project remained on schedule—at whatever cost to those who were building it.

· · ·

Even with no further delays, it remained to be seen whether the transcontinental line would be finished in time to save the romance of A. P. Crittenden and Laura Fair. Sometime in late October of 1867, accompanied by Lillian and their new friend Mrs. Bowie, Laura left New York as promised on a steamer bound for Havana, her future more uncertain than at any time since meeting her supposed fiancé some four years earlier. She would later claim that she was determined at this point to "give him up, if it was possible to forget him," but her letters suggest that she still hoped he would live up to his promises. In the meantime, while she may not have been able to provide her daughter with a father and a respectable family situation, she could at least afford to surround the child with the trappings of a prosperous upper-middle-class life.

Once established at their hotel in Havana, Laura and Mrs. Bowie apparently availed themselves of all that local society had to offer. Thanks to its prime location as a stopping-off point for the steamers from the East Coast to California via the Panama route, the Cuban capital had become quite a cosmopolitan metropolis, rife with luxury hotels, nightclubs, casinos, theaters, mineral spas, even an opera house. Here again, the milieu was heavy on southerners, many of whom came after the Civil War to oversee the sugar and coffee plantations surrounding Havana. And although Laura would later claim that she was sick almost the entire time she was in Cuba, it was clear that her illness was not keeping her confined to her hotel room with Lillian. In fact, she soon found herself being courted at various social events by an expatriate commission agent from Virginia named Sauers (Laura's taste in male company seemed to be confined to sons of the South). Mr. Sauers, she would later testify, was "the only gentleman I had ever seen since I made Mr. Crittenden's acquaintance that I could thoroughly respect." And when, after several weeks of acquaintance, Sauers proposed marriage to her, she did not immediately discourage him. "I thought that if Mr. Crittenden was entirely lost to me, and it was inevitable that I must give him up, I could, perhaps, make a future with Mr. Sauers, and perhaps be comparatively happy with my child."

In response to the marriage proposal, Laura told Mr. Sauers that she had some important matters to take care of back in the United States, but that she "would return in two months if my business was settled to suit me in San Francisco." Whether she admitted to him that this business involved her engagement to a certain prominent lawyer in that city is uncertain. But she did make sure to wire said prominent lawyer about this new ace in her pocket, and her telegram apparently had the desired effect. When she and Lillian got back to New York in December, after less than two months in Cuba, she found a pile of frantic communications from Crittenden waiting at their hotel. These letters and telegrams are lost, but all of them, according to Laura, demanded unequivocally that she abandon her wedding plans and return to California. "His letters and telegrams forced me back," she would later testify. "He said he would kill any man who married me, and kill me."

When Laura and her daughter arrived back in San Francisco on January 2, 1868, A.P. was at the dock to meet their steamer from Panama, all kindness and solicitude. Laura would not regret coming back to him, he said. He assured her that he would soon be free to take her to Indiana for the divorce, that she should trust him and have faith in him. Then he accompanied them back to the old rooms at

Mrs. Hammersmith's lodging house, which he had re-rented for her as soon as he heard she was returning.

But Laura wasn't quite ready to capitulate. Once settled into her rooms, she showed him letters from Sauers proving their engagement. She also declared that, although she didn't really love Sauers, and would probably never meet *anyone* she could love as much as she loved Crittenden, she would nonetheless marry the commission merchant "for the sake of my little child." A.P. dismissed this notion out of hand, again claiming that he would shoot Sauers if necessary to prevent it, and that he was certain that by August of that year he would be free to take her east for the divorce and remarriage. God had clearly intended Laura to be his wife, he said, and if she could just "bear with all this talk which the world was having about him and [her]," just for a little while longer, "he would make it right afterwards."

It's doubtful how sincere Crittenden was in making these promises of marriage. Granted, the few letters we have between A.P. and Clara at this time are somewhat chilly and businesslike, suggesting that their marriage was less than rock solid. Even so, no longer loving one's wife and divorcing her were two very different things, especially in Victorian times. But Laura, as ever, was seemingly persuaded: She broke off her engagement with Mr. Sauers (at Crittenden's advice not even answering the poor man's pleading and bewildered letters) and once again became her old lover's betrothed. And, as expected, there was soon a lot of talk around town, which Laura just had to "bear with." The world of San Francisco society, in fact, expressed its disapproval of their reunion loudly and vehemently—no one more loudly and vehemently than her fiancé's wife.

DAY SIXTEEN

Thursday, April 13, 1871

The regular attendance at the Fair trial yesterday was equal to that of any previous day. If anything, the interest seemed enhanced, and a larger crowd filled
the halls, lobbies, and were assembled within the bar. Mrs. Fair seemed to be
in average spirits, and was attended by Dr. Trask and her mother . . .

—*San Francisco Chronicle*

M RS. FAIR'S "AVERAGE SPIRITS" ON THAT April morning were destined to be spoiled. For the better part of the past
two sessions of her trial, Laura had been forced to endure the testimony of a parade of witnesses—more than twenty in all—brought to
the stand by the prosecution for essentially one reason: to attest to the
fact that the defendant was a notoriously unchaste woman. Her main
attorney, Elisha Cook, had tried valiantly to have this type of testimony
excluded before the fact. But despite Cook's long argument citing
authorities ranging from Samuel March Phillips on evidence to Francis
Wharton's *A Treatise on the Criminal Law of the United States,* Judge
Dwinelle had ruled the testimony admissible.

For the defendant, the litany of witnesses testifying to her bad
reputation must have been hard to listen to. ("I have always understood that her reputation was slack," one typical witness said, "what
we call a loose reputation.") Then, to add injury to insult, Laura had
to listen to a woman she had once helped—the late William Fair's

sister, Mrs. Sophy A. Abbott, whom Laura had once supplied with furniture and rent money when Abbott was in desperate need—testify that Mrs. Fair had once threatened to kill Mr. Crittenden if he didn't buy her an expensive diamond and emerald jewelry set. It was just the kind of unverifiable but damaging testimony that the prosecution hoped would sway any juror with lingering doubts about the defendant's guilt.

Finally, about midway through the sixteenth day of the trial, Cook recalled the defendant to the stand to rebut these and other witnesses. This she did calmly and effectively (disposing of Sophy Abbott's accusation with particular venom) before her lawyer moved on to ask her more about the testimony of her principal nemesis, Clara Crittenden. Cook wanted the jury to hear about the last conversation they'd ever had—the day Laura Fair and the obstacle to her happiness had finally taken off the gloves and confronted their rivalry head-on.

Mrs. Crittenden had described this episode in her own testimony two days earlier. The encounter had occurred in January 1868, Clara confirmed, just days after Laura's return to San Francisco from the East. More than four years had passed since the affair between her husband and his landlady had begun, but—according to Clara, at least—this was the first time she'd really acknowledged to herself that the rumors were more than just idle gossip. "I had reason to fear that this thing [that is, the adulterous affair] was true," she testified, and so she had gone over to Mrs. Fair's rooms on Kearny Street—"to entreat her, for the sake of my husband and his children, to go away from this country."

Now Laura was getting the chance to tell her version of the story.

MR. COOK: Do you remember the circumstances of
Mrs. Crittenden's coming to your rooms, when you had rooms
at Mrs. Hammersmith's?

MRS. FAIR: Yes, sir.

MR. COOK: Will you state the entire conversation that occurred there at that time?

MRS. FAIR: Mrs. Hammersmith knocked at the door, and said there was a lady who wished to see me, and Mrs. Crittenden was shown into my parlor. She threw back her veil . . . [and immediately] asked me why I had returned from Havana. I told her I came because Mr. Crittenden said he was dying, and could not live without me.

Laura paused on the stand and let this sink in. Now it was Clara Crittenden who would have to endure some testimony that would be difficult to hear. If there was any part of this whole long trial that would possibly give Laura Fair any satisfaction or even pleasure, this was going to be it.

17

Wife vs. Wife

C LARA CAME TO HER ON the Sunday after Laura's return to San Francisco—during the church hour, when few people with their prying eyes would be out on the streets. Late in the morning, Mrs. Hammersmith informed her tenant that there was a woman downstairs who wished to see her. Laura knew exactly who it must be; A.P. had warned her that Clara would be coming, and urged her to be honest. Tell her the truth, he'd said; there was no reason to maintain the charade any longer. So when Clara was shown inside and, without preamble, asked why Laura had come back to California, the younger woman held nothing back. Mr. Crittenden, she told Clara, was by his own admission dying without her. He'd said he couldn't concentrate or accomplish anything toward his goals while she was away. He'd written and even telegraphed her in New York to beg her to return.

Clara did not want to hear this. If only you had stayed away, she responded, it would have given her, his legal wife, an opportunity to win him back, to recall him to his sense of decency and loyalty to his family. This, of course, was hardly a line of argument that would persuade her rival to cede the field, so Clara began outright pleading with Laura to go away again. She insisted that it was Laura's duty— "as a woman, and as a mother, for the sake of her child, whom she was bringing to shame and ruin, and for her own name, and for the sake of *his* children, and for the sake of *his* honor, not to lead *him* to shame and ruin."

This lecture on her womanly duty apparently got Laura's much-celebrated dander up, and she grew more heated in her reply: "I told her that he loved me and I loved him, that he did not love her [Clara] . . . and that he was more my husband than he was hers."

When Clara pointed out that Laura was committing adultery, regardless of Mr. Crittenden's feelings, she shocked the older woman by saying that it was *Clara* who was the adulteress, for she was not truly his wife. "[This] of course startled me considerably," Clara later testified, "as I had been taught that when I vowed to love, honor, and obey, till death do us part, in sickness and in health, I thought that I was doing my duty."

But Laura was just getting started. She said that she would never leave Crittenden unless he himself told her to, that he had even made her promise never to go unless and until he specifically requested it. In other words, all Clara had to do was bring word from A.P. that he wanted Laura to go away and she would do so. Despite—or because of—her intense love for him, she would give him up and disappear forever from his life.

But of course Clara knew her husband and his weaknesses better than anyone. She understood that A.P. could never bring himself to say the word and let Laura go—"that, whether he wanted to or not, he could not say it." That's why Laura had to be the one to break it off.

But this Laura refused to do. And when she said that Clara should instead sue her husband for divorce, Clara became even more upset. "She went on to tell me that she would never give him a divorce," Laura testified, "and that he never should marry me while she lived, that she would rather see him die at her feet—those were her words exactly—that she would see him die at her feet before he should marry me." That's when Laura thrust her sharpest dagger to her rival's heart, contending that Clara's own words proved whose love for Crittenden was really genuine, for she, Laura, would gladly let him go if that was what would make him happy. This, Laura insisted, proved that *her* love was true love, and Clara's was not.

Mrs. Crittenden "did not care for that," Laura claimed, "and she got very excited, and told me . . . that she would fight his ever getting a divorce forever, [even] if both of them died. She said she did not care; she would rather see him there dead than to give him a divorce." And at this point, Clara, by her own admission, stormed out of the lodging house, uttering a solemn vow: "I will never sue for a divorce, so help me God!"

This would be the last time the two women ever spoke. Although they would occasionally see each other on the street over the next two years—and again, of course, aboard the Oakland ferry on that evening of November 3, 1870—each would refuse to address the other directly. There would be no further offerings of "sisterly advice."

· · ·

Clara Crittenden was hardly the only person in postwar San Francisco not speaking to Laura Fair. Indeed, to members of the local gentry—in particular, the wives of prominent movers and shakers, like Mrs. Susan Tevis—Laura and other conspicuous women of her type were anathema, no matter their wealth or pretensions to high culture. Mrs. Tevis, whose banker husband, Lloyd Tevis, was one of A. P. Crittenden's clients and closest friends, belonged to the elite few who controlled the guest lists of San Francisco's exclusive society gatherings, and a woman in Laura Fair's position would be regarded with frosty disdain, even by those who may have risen from similarly humble beginnings. Only by marrying A. P. Crittenden would she have even a chance of being accepted in such circles, and a slim chance at that.

Not that the husbands of this set were invariably paragons of virtue. William Ralston, for one, was hardly living an irreproachable life. Just the year before, while his wife, Lindsay, and their children were away on a trip to France, Ralston had taken on a mistress, and he had not given her up upon his family's return to California. The impropriety did not go unnoticed, and its blatant hypocrisy drew comment in the newspaper column of the city's newest literary import, the sharp-tongued journalist and short-story writer Ambrose Bierce. But ganders and geese played by different rules in this flock, and as long as Ralston kept his extramarital affair discreet (or at least somewhat more discreet than Crittenden kept his), no one would have dreamed of excluding him from the guest list.

Of course, Ralston the entrepreneur was happy to have cordial relations with someone like Mrs. Fair (and with her $40,000 investment portfolio), as long as the contact was in his business office and not in his drawing room. After all, the project of building his adopted town into a great metropolis was always his first priority. "Anything that is calculated to promote the interests of this coast," he once remarked, "is the thing that I am working for, and I will use all the powers at my command to accomplish this." If attaining his goals required investment capital from a socially notorious source, so be it.

There were few development plans that Ralston was unwilling to listen to and invest in. An immigrant Hungarian count named Agoston Haraszthy, for instance, had conceived the notion that Northern California could become a world-class winemaking region, growing Old World varietals in New World vineyards. Haraszthy first tried to grow grapes on the hills south of San Francisco, but found the weather too foggy to serve. Undeterred, he next tried the Sonoma Valley, northeast of the city. Here the climate proved more conducive to the purpose, and so Haraszthy came to Ralston with a project called the Buena Vista Vinicultural Society, hoping to finance vineyards and wineries throughout the region; Ralston helped him capitalize the corporation at $600,000 and even became one of its directors. Eventually a Buena Vista–grown sparkling wine called Eclipse, made by Haraszthy's son Arpad, was the fashionable quaff of choice in San Francisco. And thus was born the California wine industry.

But Ralston's latest project was a more personal one—building a mansion for himself in Belmont, twenty-two miles south of the city. The completion of the San Francisco–San Jose Railroad had made points south of the city much more easily accessible, so wealthy suburbs like Belmont were growing up among the scenic wooded hills overlooking the bay, just a one-hour train ride away from Market Street. Starting in the mid-1860s, Ralston began renovating and expanding the already lavish villa of a Count Leonetto Cipriani, the first Italian consul in San Francisco, to create an elaborate 55,000-square-foot showpiece loosely modeled on the palace of Versailles (though it was a Versailles with a bowling alley and a Turkish bath). Here Ralston would invite important visitors, often journalists or political and financial titans from the East, whom he wished to convince of the investment-worthiness of the city he envisioned for the 1870s and beyond. Belmont quickly became a required stop on every visiting dignitary's California itinerary.

Meanwhile, Ralston was tirelessly working to bring that aspirational San Francisco into being. Down in the neighborhood south of Market, he was building the Grand Hotel, conceived as the most luxurious in the city so far, and a vital part of his overall scheme to develop the city's more southerly neighborhoods. And in anticipation of California's imminent railroad connection with the East, which would facilitate bringing the world's finest musical and theatrical talents to San Francisco, he was also building a new Corinthian-style California Theater on Bush Street. He'd already commissioned Bret Harte to write a play that would premiere at the theater's gala opening in January 1869. Typically, however, Harte would end up taking Ralston's money but never delivering the play, forcing the theater to open, disappointingly, with Edward Bulwer-Lytton's thirty-year-old chestnut, *Money.*

Perhaps the problem was that Harte himself was busily working on another bright new ornament to the city's cultural life. Sometime in the late 1860s, a publisher named Anton Roman—who, like Ralston, was eager to promote "the material development of this Coast"—decided that what the city needed was a high-toned journal modeled on Boston's celebrated *Atlantic Monthly*. Convinced that the completion of the transcontinental railroad would make San Francisco "the center of the world," Roman felt it should have a literary showpiece commensurate with its new importance. His answer was the *Overland Monthly,* designed to be the signature publication of the world's youngest literary capital.

To edit this new journal, Roman seriously considered only one person: Bret Harte. The publisher did worry that Harte might "lean too much toward the purely literary" for the kind of wide audience he hoped to attract, but he knew that he needed the cachet that the now-thirty-two-year-old writer would bring to the *Overland Monthly*. As for Harte himself, he had doubts about the long-term viability of such a journal; an earlier project he'd done for Roman—an 1866 anthology of California poetry called *Outcroppings,* featuring poems by Coolbrith and Stoddard—had been a commercial and critical failure. But he did end up taking the *Overland* job on the condition that Roman give him total editorial control. "I am trying to build up a literary taste on the Pacific slope," he professed in a letter to a New York friend at this time. "We [that is, the *Overland Monthly*] may be short-lived, but I want to make a good fight while it lasts." And certainly Harte had high ambitions for the magazine. As one historian has put it: "For years [San Francisco's literary community] had watched the coast grow, and had grown along with it: from the *Golden Era* of its infancy to *The Californian* of its adolescence. Now came *The Overland Monthly* to usher in its adulthood, on the eve of the railroad that would complete California's coming-of-age."

Harte and Roman quickly got down to work. They spent the next three months cloistered at various mountain retreats far from the distractions of the city, hammering out a concept for *Overland Monthly* and editing an inaugural issue. That first number, which appeared in July 1868, proved not particularly groundbreaking. It featured poetry

contributions from Harte's by-now-usual suspects, Coolbrith and
Stoddard, along with a rather pedestrian travel piece by Twain.
("[France] is a pleasant land," the nodding author wrote. "No word
describes it as felicitously as that.") The journal began to hit its stride
in the second issue, in which Harte's short story "The Luck of Roaring Camp" first appeared. "The Luck" was a starkly original piece of
work in its way, and like Twain's "Celebrated Jumping Frog," it was a
story that would become something of a landmark in the development
of the literature of the West.

But "The Luck" was controversial at first. The story is a parody of
the Nativity narrative, set in a Sierra mining camp, in which a child
born to an unwed prostitute becomes a figure of devotion for the entire community. Amusing as it is, even the *Overland Monthly*'s own
printer regarded it as too sacrilegious to publish, but Harte persuaded
him to go ahead nonetheless. And sure enough, once the story appeared, it created an uproar. "The Luck" was energetically denounced
by several local religious publications, one of them even urging the
nascent journal's advertisers to boycott "this picture of Californian society that is not conducive to Eastern immigration" or "investment of
foreign capital."

But "The Luck" was an instant hit with the eastern press. So, too,
were the subsequent eight stories that Harte produced for the *Overland,* including what is perhaps his most famous work today, "The
Outcasts of Poker Flat." Granted, these stories, populated with a colorful cast of "miners, gunslingers, golden-hearted prostitutes, and wanderers," play into then-current eastern clichés about the West. But
Harte infused the tales with a heavy dose of irony that lifts them above
the familiar tropes they traffic in. Praised in reviews for their "Pacific
freshness" and "Far Western flavor," these stories (despite the fact that
many were first published without a byline) made Harte an instant
literary commodity. In fact, James Fields, an editor at the *Atlantic
Monthly,* the *Overland*'s paradigm, wrote a letter to Harte offering to
publish anything the story's anonymous author might choose to write,

under any terms he cared to name. Once his identity was revealed, Harte's new renown even crossed the Atlantic and reached no less a personage than Charles Dickens, who, shortly before his death, invited Harte to contribute to *All the Year Round,* the English novelist's own weekly literary magazine.

· · ·

So now San Francisco had two writers of international reputation to boast of. Twain, after abandoning California for residence in the East, returned for an extended stay of several months in 1868. One purpose of his visit was to renegotiate the publishing rights to the *Alta California* dispatches he'd written about his recent travels in Europe and the Holy Land. As the newspaper predicted, these pieces had proven enormously popular, and now the editors were eager to bring them out in book form. But since Twain wanted to do this himself (an arrangement that would be far more profitable to the author), and since neither letters nor telegrams had elicited any concessions from the newspaper, he'd decided to come back west to force them, face-to-face, to accept a compromise.

Fortunately, the representatives of the *Alta* turned out to be surprisingly compliant and waived their publishing rights in exchange for little more than a promise of acknowledgment in the published work. Impatient to get to work, Twain hunkered down in the Occidental Hotel (site of Laura Fair's ill-fated dinner with the Crittendens some years back) and spent the next weeks furiously adapting the original *Alta* pieces for hardcover publication—larding them, according to one of his biographers, with "undigested data culled from guidebooks and local histories, and passages from the travel books he aimed to lampoon." By mid-June he had the equivalent of a six-hundred-page draft of what would become *The Innocents Abroad.* Realizing that it was still hopelessly rough, however, he turned to his friend and now rival Bret

Kentucky-born lawyer Alexander Parker Crittenden was barely eking out a living on the 1840s Texas frontier when news of the gold strike in California became public, offering a possible solution to his perpetual money problems.

HO! FOR CALIFORNIA.

THE EMIGRATION TO EL DORADO.

In April of 1849, he left behind his wife, Clara, and their children to join the westward tide of migrants, promising to bring his family west once he had established himself in the new territory. (From left to right: James, Nannie, Churchill, Clara, and Laura Crittenden)

Before the discovery of gold in the nearby Sierra Nevada, San Francisco (seen at top ca. 1846) was a backwater town of a few hundred residents, mostly small traders dealing in leather, tallow, and wool. But its days as a tiny outpost were numbered. As satirized in the lithograph cartoon (bottom), the rush to California was momentous and chaotic as people found their way west by whatever means possible.

Among the other early arrivals in San Francisco were future Civil War general William Tecumseh Sherman (left), who first came as a soldier and later returned as a banker, and William Chapman Ralston (right), founder of the Bank of California, who would do more to promote the growth of the city than any other individual.

A series of five major fires swept through the burgeoning town over the space of eighteen months in 1851–1852; each time the city built back with greater care and expense. Quite soon, the former frontier outpost had become a modern-looking city.

Pleasants v. North Beach & Mission Railroad, 34 Cal. 586 (1868)

1868 · Supreme Court of California

34 Cal. 586

*

JOHN J. PLEASANTS,
and MARY E. PLEAS-
ANTS, His Wife

v.

THE NORTH BEACH
AND MISSION RAIL-
ROAD COMPANY

Gold Rush–era San Francisco attracted a number of African American migrants, including Mary Ellen Pleasant, a near-legendary figure who brought her formidable wealth and determination to bear on the struggle for civil rights. Among other causes, she and her husband filed suits against streetcar companies that refused to carry Black passengers.

The gold bonanza also brought a multitude of immigrants from many other nations, China in particular. Welcomed at first, the Chinese newcomers faced increasing hostility from whites as their numbers grew— especially from Irish immigrants, who saw them as competition for jobs.

San Francisco.—The Chinese Must Go.

In the fall of 1863, A. P. Crittenden moved to Virginia City, Nevada, where the silver-rich Comstock Lode was creating even greater opportunities for wealth than the Gold Rush a decade earlier. Here, while wife and family remained in San Francisco, Crittenden began an adulterous relationship with his landlady, Laura D. Fair, a widowed fellow Southerner with a somewhat scandalous past, including a short stint as an actress in (appropriately) The School for Scandal.

As the city of San Francisco matured during the Civil War, a distinctive literary culture developed under the stewardship of transplanted New Yorker Bret Harte (top left). Unitarian minister and orator Thomas Starr King (top right) enlisted Harte and other writers in his important efforts to drum up support for the Union in California. But the greatest figure in this new literary universe was Mark Twain (bottom), who spent just a short time in the city but left an indelible mark.

THE WAY LAWYER CRITTENDEN WAS MURDERED,

Back in San Francisco after the war, the longtime affair between A. P. Crittenden and Laura Fair turned stormy, as Crittenden continually vowed to divorce Clara and marry Laura, only to renege on his promises. Finally, the whole affair ended in tragedy on November 3, 1870, when a distraught Fair shot her lover on the El Capitan *ferry, right in front of Clara and two of the younger Crittenden children.*

1566. Railroad Ferry Steamer "El Capitan."

A WOMAN'S REVENGE.

Assassination of A. P. Crittenden, Esq., by the Noto-
rious Mrs. Fair.

HE AS SHOT ON THE OAKLAND BOAT
WHILE' SURROUNDED BY
HIS FAMILY.

The Career of the Assassin---The
Wicked Wiles of a Bold,
Bad Woman.

OFFICIAL REPORT

OF THE

TRIAL

OF

LAURA D. FAIR,

FOR THE MURDER OF

ALEX. P. CRITTENDEN,

INCLUDING THE TESTIMONY, THE ARGUMENTS OF COUNSEL, AND THE
CHARGE OF THE COURT, REPORTED VERBATIM, AND THE
ENTIRE CORRESPONDENCE OF THE PARTIES,

WITH PORTRAITS OF THE DEFENDANT AND THE DECEASED.

FROM THE SHORT-HAND NOTES OF

MARSH & OSBOURNE,

OFFICIAL REPORTERS OF THE COURTS.

*What followed was one of the most notorious court cases in American history,
spurring controversy and debate nationwide. The trial, a transcript of which was
published commercially, ultimately became a kind of referendum on the moral
fitness of the city of San Francisco (seen at bottom, ca. 1878), which by now had
grown, in just three short decades, into one of the great cities of the world.*

Harte to edit it. Busy as he was, Harte agreed, asking only that he be allowed to publish four of the chapters in *Overland Monthly* without payment. And apparently he earned this privilege. "Harte read all of the MS," Twain later told a friend, "& told me what passages, paragraphs, & chapters to leave out—& I followed orders strictly." *The Innocents Abroad* would appear in hardcover the next year to great acclaim and eventually become one of the bestselling travel books of all time.

But Twain had another purpose in returning to his old California stomping grounds. He was also hoping to duplicate the success of his 1866 Hawaii lectures by presenting a series of theatrical evenings on his more recent travels to the Middle East. This part of his agenda, however, proved to be a mixed success. Although Twain managed to pack Platt's Hall on two successive nights with eager and appreciative audiences (at $1 a head!), the performances were panned by the press of this ever more tight-laced community, which criticized their "sacrilegious allusions, impotent humor, and malignant distortions of history and the truth." Even the critic for the *Alta California,* which had published the original source material, was decidedly cool, calling the lecture ill-prepared and only sporadically eloquent. And the reaction of local churchgoers was hostile. As with Harte's faux Nativity story, Twain's irreverent reflections on the Holy Land provoked rage from conservative clergy wherever he traveled. In fact, while attending a service at a Baptist church in San Francisco one Sunday evening, Twain had the unique honor of hearing himself excoriated from the pulpit. The resident preacher, who had no idea that Twain was present, grew increasingly livid at the writer's effrontery, denouncing "the letters of this person, Mark Twain, who visits the Holy Land and ridicules sacred scenes." Special invective was reserved for the author's "puerile attempts at wit and miserable puns upon subjects that are dear to every Christian heart." Afterward, Twain introduced himself to the preacher and confessed, perhaps not quite earnestly, that "I feel that I deserve everything you have said about me, and I wish to heartily thank you."

Just before leaving to head east again, Twain arranged to give one more lecture in San Francisco, this one on the topic of Venice. Perhaps because he had learned his lesson with the Holy Land lecture, or maybe thanks to Harte's judicious editing, the Venetian evening met with near-universal acclaim. As one newspaper put it, the talk displayed "wit without vulgarity"—surely an improvement over the earlier performances. The evening proved to be a triumph more in line with his earlier Sandwich Island success, and it made for a happy envoi to the writer's short but formative adventure in the American West. Four days later—on July 6, 1868—Twain boarded the steamship *Montana*, bound for the usual Panama crossing to the East. He would never come to California again.

. . .

That *Montana* sailing in July was one that Laura Fair sorely wished she could have been on as well. A.P. had promised her a summer departure, and Laura's desire to leave San Francisco had only intensified in the months since her return from Havana and New York in January. Facing "scorn and slander" of all kinds—including what one trial witness would later describe as "casual remarks" on the street as to her character—the now-infamous mistress of one of San Francisco's most prominent jurists had come to deeply dislike the town, and could hardly wait to leave it behind.

However, the promised departure date came and went, as Crittenden once again claimed that his financial affairs were too unsettled to permit him to leave. This latest delay was infuriating enough, but Laura had also received some news in the meantime that promised to complicate her life considerably. Word had reached her from New Orleans that the lawyers who'd handled her divorce from Thomas Grayson (her trigger-happy second husband) had failed to properly register the papers that would finalize their divorce a decade ago. This was potentially disastrous news. Not only did it mean that her marriage

to William Fair may have been technically bigamous, but also that
Grayson, very much alive in New Orleans, could conceivably still
claim her as his wife.

Exactly when Laura had become aware of this problem is unclear;
prosecutors in her later trials would argue that she knew even before
marrying William Fair that her divorce from Grayson was not final,
but hoped she could conceal this fact because of California's isolation
in those days. But with the imminent completion of the railroad, bury-
ing inconvenient pasts would no longer be possible. The problem, in
other words, would have to be handled sooner rather than later. And
so Laura would again go east without her lover and just hope that he
would eventually follow. In any case, she did not tell Crittenden about
the divorce problem before she left, being frightened of his reaction
and hoping that she could have it fixed herself, without his help or
knowledge.

In mid-September, A.P. accompanied Laura and Lillian to the dock
on San Francisco Bay and saw them aboard the steamer *Sacramento,*
headed to Panama on the first leg of another trip that he should have
been taking with them. He again assured Laura that he would follow
her whenever his affairs would allow it. Whether or not she truly believed he would come this time, her frustration must have been extreme. It was as if they were making no progress at all—lovers for
almost five years already, and still no closer to their (or at least her) goal.
And now it appeared that they would have to end two marriages, not
just one, before she could realize her aspiration of becoming Mrs. Alexander Parker Crittenden.

18

A Splendid Ruin

IT ULTIMATELY TOOK EIGHT MORE MONTHS—and the long-awaited completion of the transcontinental railroad—for Crittenden to finally follow his lover east. Just two days before Leland Stanford drove the final golden spike at Promontory Summit in Utah, A.P. wrote to Laura in New Orleans with the news: "I am making my arrangements now to leave on the 17th, Monday week," he informed her in a letter dated May 8, 1869. "I shall go overland [by train] to St. Louis and from there by the most direct route to New Orleans . . . I will soon look into your eyes and tell you what you are to me, and then I will defy you to doubt me ever again."

Clearly, whatever the new rail connection might do for San Francisco's economic, moral, and cultural life over the next few years, it had already changed the lives of A. P. Crittenden and Laura Fair. An overland trek that in 1849 had taken A.P. six grueling months to accomplish—and that even in the mid-1860s still required several uncomfortable weeks on the fastest stagecoach line—was now an easy train trip of some three or four days. The town that had once seemed like the far end of the earth was now just another destination on the American rail network. And so, with the new speed and ease of cross-country travel, Crittenden was now able to keep at least one promise to his long-thwarted mistress. After so many delays and excuses, he was finally coming to join her, and leaving Clara behind.

Not that Laura hadn't had plenty of reasons to doubt him over the past eight months. She and Lillian had been on the road the whole time—spending the fall in New York and Baltimore, celebrating Christmas in Virginia, and then heading south to New Orleans—and so she had again received Crittenden's letters late and sometimes out of order, whenever they managed to catch up with her. As during her previous trip east, the two lovers had often been out of sync with each other—he ardent when she was acting cold, she affectionate when he was in a sullen pout. At times they almost seemed to take turns making jealous threats and resentful complaints about being ignored or insufficiently loved by the other.

A.P. had started playing the resentful lover even before her steamer reached New York: "My own Darling," he cooed in a letter dated October 4, "I have written you one letter to-night—a wild one, I fear, for I have been and am very wretched. It is so hard to be separated from you. To-morrow it will be three weeks since I had my arms around you and your dear lips pressed to mine. It seems to me an age." But despite knowing that she could not possibly have gotten off a letter to him yet, he was already scolding her in advance. "Don't fail, darling, to write to me very regularly and fully. You have never communicated with me as unreservedly and confidentially as you ought to have done. It would have saved us many a heartache if you had done so."

Buried amid this gentle chiding was another message, surely dismaying to Laura—inklings that he might have to postpone the divorce yet again, mainly because of his continuing inability to engineer the financial windfall he needed to leave Clara and the children. "My darling: I have had the blues dreadfully for the last three days," he wrote her in October, lamenting a $4,000 loss on Savage mining stock that week. The loss had been a blow to his finances *and* his spirits. But he assured her that he was obsessively doing everything he could to permit their plan to go forward—so obsessively, in fact, that he was beginning to disgust himself. "I am growing very sordid; and [am] possessed with a mania for accumulation. I study my bank account intently, and scheme and contrive incessantly how I may make the credit side of it grow . . . Before the end of this month I hope to have made a great stride toward fortune."

That stride, however, never seemed to come, despite the fact that his fixation was taking a heavy toll on his health. Even his children had noted this. "If Pa continues to work as he does now, he cannot last much longer," his daughter Laura Sanchez wrote Clara in early 1869. "If he would only put what spare money he has in real estate instead of stocks, he would soon get ahead and not be worried half to death all the time." But although her father did start buying some real estate, he could not resist dabbling in mining stocks, even if the anxiety it provoked was making him ill. "I find it hard to get any sleep," A.P. wrote his lover in one of many letters complaining about his high stress level and his chronic rheumatism, which could cripple him for days on end. "I must succeed quickly or the struggle will kill me."

Meanwhile, Laura was taking care of business on her end. Traveling to Virginia over Christmas, she had spent the holiday with William Fair's sister (a Mrs. Mitchell, not the sister—Sophy Abbott—who would later testify against Laura in court). Apparently, the two women had remained on very friendly terms since William's death seven years earlier, and Laura had enlisted the aid of Mrs. Mitchell's young son Robert, a lawyer like his late uncle, to come with her to New Orleans to settle the issue about her divorce from Thomas Grayson. Early in the new year, they traveled to the Crescent City by train—her first time back to her old hometown in a decade. Dreading an accidental meeting with Grayson, who still lived in town and would be just perverse enough to insist that she was still his wife, Laura kept a low profile at her hotel, while Robert Mitchell consulted the archives of the appropriate court. He discovered the clerical error that had prevented the decree from being finalized, but, as Laura later put it in court, the young man "was not lawyer enough" to know for sure how serious the matter was. That would have to be determined by a more experienced attorney—someone like A. P. Crittenden himself.

But then Crittenden suffered a major financial setback: "All I had been able to accumulate was invested in Yellow Jacket," he wrote Laura in April. "The mine was in splendid condition, was paying dividends of five dollars a share regularly, the stock was rising, and according to all human calculation, in a month more my projects would be accomplished." But then a fire had swept through the mine, killing some fifty miners and sending the stock price plummeting. Thus his plans again seemed smashed, for the same monetary reasons: "I am threatened with the loss of every dollar I have for immediate purposes," he told her. Add to this disappointment the fact that her recent letters to him had been cold and distant, and he was understandably desolate: "To-day if you were to put a pistol to my head and blow out my brains, I should smile lovingly in your face to the last moment . . ."

Reading this, Laura must have braced herself for yet another delay in his coming east to her. But then that letter of May 8 arrived, announcing a definite departure date for Saint Louis and, ultimately, New Orleans. Something seemed to have broken in Crittenden—some pride in his ability to provide for everyone near to him—and he seemed ready to give up the hope that he could leave his family well taken care of. "Loss after loss has fallen upon me in the last three weeks," he told her. "My health is wretched, and I have been very miserable . . . [I am] a ruined man for the present, so far as money is concerned." But despite all of that, he was coming. Finally. And he would ease her mind as to the problem with Grayson, which she finally had told him about when Robert Mitchell proved incapable of advising her. "We will soon talk it over face to face," A.P. assured her. "It shall be made all right."

But while Crittenden's decision to come east must have seemed to Laura a momentous development—the fulfillment of a long-postponed deliverance for herself and her child—to Clara and the rest of the Crittenden family it was regarded very differently. To them, A.P. had depicted this trip as merely a much-needed vacation, and an opportunity to see a few relatives, take care of some business, and take a ride on the new transcontinental railroad while he was at it. If anyone in the family suspected he was heading off to meet "that woman," their letters bear no trace of this concern. "I am sorry that Pa has lost again in 'stocks,'" daughter Laura Sanchez wrote Clara in April, "but do hope it will not be the cause of keeping him from making the contemplated visit East this year, for he does need a change so much and cannot live long if he keeps on working so hard. It is a duty he owes himself and all of us to go." Subsequent letters even hint that Clara was considering coming along on the trip, though this was an idea that her husband surely would have found a way to squelch. He clearly had not informed Clara that her marriage was ending—perhaps because he had no intention of ever going through with the Indiana divorce and marrying Laura Fair. A.P. was thus deceiving both of the women in his life, harboring an agenda all his own.

The trip certainly appeared innocuous enough from the outside. A.P. was traveling with a festive entourage that included three Crittenden cousins visiting from Kentucky (children of his late uncle John), a number of local San Francisco notables, and young Howard Crittenden, who was heading only as far as Elko, Nevada, for a new job as foreman of a Hearst mine in Treasure City. Since this was one of the very first scheduled transcontinental trains to leave the Pacific coast, a correspondent for the *Alta California* was also aboard. This reporter—identified only as "Podgers"—traveled with the Crittenden party and wrote a two-part article describing the trip in detail, which Clara must have been grateful to read in the June 1 and 2 issues of the paper. She also heard about the trip from Howard, in a letter from Nevada dated May 19: "The persons composing Pa's party are all pleasant and good travelers," her son assured her, but he did have one piece of bad news: The elaborate picnic basket she had packed for A.P., which included "ham and tongues and chicken and oysters" for the journey, had suffered a mishap: "The basket you packed was not opened except to take the bottles of whiskey out. They were all broken."

Notwithstanding this dearth of alcohol, the traveling party endured the inevitable delays and discomforts of the journey with good humor. The Central Pacific and Union Pacific transcontinental lines would very soon be equipped with luxurious coaches and sumptuous dining cars from end to end, but service, facilities, and scheduling were still somewhat improvised in these very early days. There were no first-class Pullman sleepers on the initial leg of Crittenden's journey, for instance, so he had to stretch out on two opposing seats on a day coach. At Promontory Point, where they missed their connecting train by several hours, they were forced out of their coach when a disgruntled group of about 150 recently discharged railroad laborers commandeered the car; the passengers retreated to the caboose, where the women and children could stretch out on long upholstered benches but the men were forced to sleep on the floor. Meanwhile, they also had to put up with construction delays and other stoppages. And all of this despite the premium prices charged for a ticket ($70, or the current equivalent of well over $1,000, for even a third-class passage from San Francisco to New York, and more than twice that for first class). As A.P. admitted in a letter to Clara: "There was much want of arrangement and management, and consequently much unnecessary delay . . . But matters will soon be better regulated."

Crittenden's party fortunately took all of these difficulties in stride. "We lived high, chatted and laughed, played cards, and occasionally had singing," A.P. later told Clara. And the level of comfort and organization did seem to improve the farther east they traveled. Ultimately, the only real disappointment, at least according to reporter Podgers, was that they faced no exciting and romantic dangers en route—no Indian attacks, no trampling herds of wild buffalo, not even a grizzly bear bent on having one of them for breakfast. And the journey was disconcertingly quick and easy. "Summing it up," Podgers concluded, "it is not a trick at all to come from Sacramento here [Omaha] in four days and a half, one [more] day to Chicago, and thirty-six hours to New York—total, seven days, running on easy time." The American

West, with its legendary remoteness from the law and order of civilization, would never be the same.

As for the jolly traveling party, they parted ways once they reached Chicago. Some went on to New York and other destinations, while A.P. accompanied his cousins Kitty and John back to the Crittenden family seat in Frankfort, Kentucky. He registered at a hotel under the name "P. Alexander" and then just showed up unannounced at the family home, where no one except the two cousins he'd traveled with had any idea who he was. A.P.'s mother had died just a few months earlier, and all of his siblings were either deceased or else living elsewhere, so the resident Crittendens were mostly first and second cousins who, after all, had not seen him in decades. "No one recognized me," he wrote Clara that evening. "We talked for a while and then I rose up and turning to cousin Kitty said, 'Well, Kitty—I told you so—none of them know me.' You never saw so astonished a crowd—they did not understand how a stranger would dare to address Kitty so familiar." Only when someone mentioned his name did everyone realize that this impertinent stranger was actually their long-absent relative Parker.

After this brief visit with his Kentucky family, A.P. traveled around for a few weeks, keeping his movements a bit vague in his letters to Clara, naturally, since he was actually heading to New Orleans to join Laura Fair. And in that city, sometime during the last week of May, the two lovers were finally reunited. This had been their longest separation in the six years they'd known each other, and despite the long-distance misunderstandings during their eight-month hiatus, the reunion, as Laura later depicted it, was congenial. First on their agenda, however, was taking care of her little legal problem. This proved straightforward enough. Crittenden apparently had the required papers filed with no difficulty, and the specter of Laura's being claimed as "Mrs. Grayson" (a name she shrank from in horror) receded into insignificance.

And now it was time to enjoy a bit of the upper-class life of leisure that Laura had always aspired to. Leaving New Orleans after a couple of weeks, A.P., Laura, and Lillian traveled together like any other happy and prosperous family, first proceeding to New York and then on to West Point for a week, where Crittenden revisited the scenes of his mischievous years as a cadet. From there they moved on to that most Victorian of vacation destinations—the hot springs spa at White Sulphur Springs in West Virginia. Just how Crittenden managed to find the money for this extravagance remains a mystery, assuming he truly was as insolvent as he claimed to be. Most likely he was simply plunging himself ever deeper into debt, recklessly allowing his expenses to exceed his income, as he had done for his entire life. In any case, the time they spent together at the hotel known as "Old White" (predecessor of today's Greenbrier) appears to have been happy and storm-free. Of course, the pair were still not married, and so would have checked into two separate rooms, especially since Lillian was with them. But what happened after hours is impossible to know. And any improprieties could always be justified (in Laura's mind, at least) by the prospect of the upcoming Indiana divorce and marriage, which A.P. promised would happen once business resumed in the fall.

It's unclear whether the famous hot springs were helping A.P.'s rheumatism; he claimed in a letter to Clara that his chronic ailment had miraculously left him once he got east of the Sierra Nevada. But the ever-restless lawyer could bear only so much idleness. Sometime in July, he told Laura that he had some business to take care of while he was in the East. Leaving her with Lillian at White Sulphur Springs, he headed first to Richmond, where he likely met with Clara's family and visited his son's grave. He then moved on to Washington, D.C., where, he told Laura, "there are some papers connected with the Churchill murder that I must see." Even with this somber duty occupying him, however, he still had time for their ongoing love dance. He sometimes wrote her several times a day, teasing her with petty jealousies about a certain "Mr. F.K." or some other suitor he'd heard rumors about. He was also not above some odd bits of self-pitying melodrama: "When I am with you, you do make me very wretched sometimes," he professed, "but that wretchedness is happiness itself compared with the hours of absence from you."

But then, while he was in Washington, some unspecified business cropped up that would call him back to San Francisco—or so he claimed to Laura. This "unexpected development," of course, had been expected by Clara and the rest of his family from the beginning, since to them Crittenden had always depicted his trip as a brief two-month vacation to rest from overwork. In fact, he had been blithely lying to Clara for weeks about the nature of his trip: "I am getting tired of hotel life in this city—it is too lonesome," he wrote from New York in June, while in the arms of his mistress. True, he was making the dutiful visits he told her about—to Clara's father in Perth Amboy, and to her siblings and cousins in Richmond—but there were other parts of the trip about which Clara heard nothing.

As for Laura, we can only infer her reaction to his sudden need to return to California, since her letters to him from White Sulphur Springs have not survived. But judging from A.P.'s half of the correspondence, she was responding icily. "Do you want me to come back to the White Sulphur before I leave for California," he asked in a letter dated July 16. "If yes, telegraph me to Baltimore, at the Barnum Hotel, the word 'Yes,' and I will understand it to mean come. If I don't get such a telegram I will be off, and I have an idea I shall not get it, and that you don't want me to come."

When he didn't hear back from her immediately, he assumed the worst. "I leave at 11 o'clock this morning for Washington, and go with the worst possible forebodings," he wrote to her on July 18. "It is the first step away from you, and I feel, now, as you did, that if we part we will never meet again." His angst only intensified when he reached the capital. "I am going to leave this afternoon for Baltimore, to get such letters as I may find there from you," he wrote her the very next day, having taken care of the Churchill business in a single day. "Much depends on them. I hope they will be good and kind. If otherwise, God help us."

But then—miracle of miracles—he learned the next day that her answer was "Yes" after all, although she sent it via letter rather than telegram. A.P. was elated. "You can make the world all brightness or gloom to me by a word," he wrote her back. "I think only of you and live only in your love." He returned for another blissful week in White Sulphur Springs, where they were joined by the perpetually traveling Howard Crittenden. (Howard admired Mrs. Fair as much as his father did, and could apparently be relied upon to keep a secret from his mother and sisters.) Finally, at the end of July, A.P. left her to return to California. Given the ease with which one could now travel by train across the continent, this was not as disruptive as it would have been just a year earlier. In fact, Crittenden promised that he would come back to her at the spa in a month, at which time they would proceed to Indiana for the errand that would fulfill all of her long-postponed aspirations.

It would prove to be just another of the lawyer's many lies. After leaving her in White Sulphur Springs, Crittenden just disappeared. Weeks passed without any telegram or letter from him. This silence (the nineteenth-century equivalent of ghosting, perhaps) did little to help his lover's emotional stability, fragile even at the best of times: "A month! Think of it—a month since you wrote me a line," Laura wrote in a desperate letter of September 6. "Good God! You seem to be trying to kill me! . . . For days I have been like one crazed—and where will it end? I'll tell you: in murder—in a madhouse—and in death."

Had she lost him to Clara after all? Something she'd heard from a San Francisco friend made her fear so: "A woman—curse her—wrote me that Mrs. C. had a baby, or was soon to have one. Is this true? God help you and me, if this is true! I will know the truth, so it is better for you to tell me—and at once." She signed off with a thinly veiled threat of suicide or worse: "Six years of life gone, and what have I for them? A splendid ruin—a wreck. Perhaps your letter brings death."

But no letter came. And so she had no choice: Laura and her child would have to go back to San Francisco, without telling him, and see for herself whether they had any kind of future there.

19

A Threat

E CONOMIC FORECASTING HAS NEVER BEEN an exact science, but rarely has it been as mistaken as it was in San Francisco in 1869. Notwithstanding the exuberant projections of Henry
George and other local economists, the opening of the transcontinental railroad, far from bringing an instant jolt of prosperity to the
city, actually contributed to a sudden, sharp recession that rattled the
entire business community of what was now the tenth-largest metropolis in the country. Greater connectedness proved to be a double-
edged sword. Yes, it gave local manufacturers easy access to a plethora
of potential new customers in the rest of the country. But it did
the same for more established manufacturers in the East and Midwest, who could often produce goods more cheaply and thus sell
them at lower prices in the newly accessible western markets. And
while this may have been a boon for consumers, who got some
welcome relief from the region's traditionally high prices, it was a
disaster for local industry. As one historian has noted, the first transcontinental train from the East brought a flood of eager traveling
salesmen (or "drummers," as they were known at the time), determined to undercut California's home-grown manufacturers with
bargain-basement goods: "The prices they quoted for hats, shoes,

blankets, shovels, furniture, and dozens of other commodities rang like the clang of doom."

Amplifying this clang was the fact that local entrepreneurs, in anticipation of the transcontinental's completion, had overbuilt dramatically, opening new factories, warehouses, regional railroads, and other infrastructure to meet the new waves of demand that didn't appear as instantly as promised. The worst offender here was William Ralston. He and his Bank of California were both highly overextended now, simultaneously bankrolling projects related to hydraulic and hard-rock mining, a real estate company, various new regional railroad lines, sugar refineries, woolen mills, the new California Theater, his ever-expanding Belmont estate, and even an investment in Alaskan seal fisheries. And after the closing of the Yellow Jacket mine (the event that hit Crittenden so hard as well), Ralston and his bank found themselves in deep trouble. One night in July 1869, lacking enough hard cash to meet the next day's anticipated demand from bank customers, Ralston and two accomplices spent the overnight hours surreptitiously exchanging nonnegotiable gold bars from the bank's vault for gold coins from the nearby U.S. Mint—a highly illegal escapade that nonetheless prevented a run on the bank and a possible region-wide financial panic.

The 1869 business slowdown also caused a jump in unemployment that hit the Asian population particularly hard. Many newly idled Chinese railroad workers came flooding back to San Francisco in search of work, just when the demand for labor was falling, exacerbating already-tense relations between white and Chinese workers. The slump reinvigorated the output of anti-Chinese regulations emanating from Sacramento. The California legislature began passing new laws with names like an "Act to Prevent Importation of Chinese Criminals and to Prevent the Establishment of Coolie Slavery" and an "Act to Prevent the Kidnapping and Importation of Mongolian, Chinese, and Japanese for Criminal or Demoralizing Purposes," deceptively titled measures designed to prevent Asian immigration of any kind. As one historian has noted, the assumption behind laws of this kind was that "all Asian females were prostitutes, all Asian children kidnapped, and all Asian males criminal or indentured."

Given this hostile atmosphere, it's surprising that more Chinese immigrants didn't decamp and head back across the Pacific. But even in a time of economic slowdown, California offered greater opportunities for moneymaking than did their home villages, and so even those who did go back sometimes returned. There was Ah Toy, for example, and Moy Jin Mun, a Chinese miner who had originally come to California in the 1850s from a modestly prosperous and educated family in Guangdong Province. Still a boy when he arrived with his older brother Jin Kee (their passage having been financed with a bag of gold dust sent by an uncle who preceded them), Jin Mun was left in the care of some cousins in San Francisco. Here he began to study English in school—a choice that distinguished him from a majority of Chinese immigrants at the time. Eventually, he had the good fortune to be taken on as a gardener for none other than Leland Stanford when the latter became governor in 1861. Perhaps because of his language skills, Jin Mun quickly became a favorite of the governor and especially of his wife, who even offered to adopt the bright teenager—though the offer was courteously refused on his behalf by older brother Jin Kee, who pointed out that the boy's parents were still very much alive back in their native Guangdong.

Eventually, however, Jin Mun succumbed to the lure of Gold Mountain, and in 1867 he decided to leave the Stanfords' employ and try his luck as a miner. His timing was not ideal. By the late '60s, most of the mining operations in the Sierra Nevada were industrialized, so individual prospectors like Moy had to resort to reworking old, abandoned claims—a practice that required little capital investment but that yielded correspondingly minor returns. Even so, in two years he had managed to make enough money to travel back to China and get married. And while he did return after a year or so, he chose not to bring his new wife back to California just yet. The San Francisco of the early

1870s, he realized, would not be receptive to the idea of a respectable Chinese husband and wife.

The position of Black Americans in the postwar city was only marginally better—a fact that made Mary Ellen Pleasant's continuing economic and social success upsetting to many in the white community. As Laura Fair had done, Pleasant was now amassing a fortune by using the proceeds from "keeping house" to fuel savvy investments. In 1867, after years of serving as a domestic in the houses of prominent men, Pleasant had begun opening a series of boardinghouses geared to the needs of the city's ever-growing cadre of business elites. Her most luxurious property was at 920 Washington Street, known, according to one latter-day historian, for its "fine food and wines and its mysterious, lavishly furnished upstairs rooms which were set up as combined private dining and bedrooms." Her guests were business titans and leading politicians, among them Newton Booth, a future governor and senator from California, as well as Charlie Fairfax, the Scottish nobleman manqué who had first introduced A. P. Crittenden to his landlady in 1863. It's possible that the amenities on offer at the Washington Street establishment included sexual assignations; at the very least, according to reports from members of the household staff, introductions were made between Pleasant's powerful male customers and a series of attractive young protégées. In any case, Pleasant soon found herself in possession of many potentially damaging secrets about men who were in a position to help her succeed in all kinds of endeavors. As one of her associates told an interviewer many years later, "Mammy had a way of finding out terrible things about everyone. Only a saint could have escaped her."

Whether or not blackmail was one of her business practices (and the evidence for it is purely hearsay), Pleasant reaped benefits from her proximity to the representatives of white male power in the city. Information, particularly in a boom-and-bust economy like California's, was a form of wealth that could bring substantial returns if deployed properly, and Pleasant knew this better than anyone. And she also knew which local players had the best information of all. "The officers of the Bank of California," according to the son of one of her employees, "often had dinners at Mammy Pleasant's Washington Street house . . . The men were too busy talking to notice her much, but she was always listening."

Even so, Pleasant was doing as much talking now as listening, having learned much from her lifelong devotion to "human nature studies." And there were many in San Francisco who thought it wise to pay heed. "I have always noticed that when I have something to say, people listen," she told a newspaper reporter late in life. "They never go to sleep on me." Indeed, it was at this point that Pleasant entered into an informal business partnership with one of those officers of the Bank of California who had patronized her Washington Street house. Thomas Bell, a Scottish-born financier, was a vice president of Ralston's bank. He and Pleasant had known each other for years, having arrived in California on the same ship—the steamship *Oregon*—in 1852. (Legend has it that on entering San Francisco Bay, young Bell noticed Pleasant shivering on deck and gallantly gave her a cloak, which she kept until her death.) Eight years her junior, Bell was by the late 1860s a successful banker, but apparently he could still learn something from the older woman. While the lore that Bell was merely a "front" for Pleasant's business dealings is likely an exaggeration, it seems clear that the two were partners with entwined investments and finances. And once Bell became the sole boarder in Pleasant's newest residence—an impressive mansion on Octavia Place purported to be worth $100,000—the rumors began to fly with a vengeance.

Of course, this kind of border-crossing relationship, which may have passed unremarked in the freewheeling city of just a generation earlier, was deemed highly inappropriate in the Victorian San Francisco of the postwar period. The ability of this middle-aged Black woman to attract power and money to herself—and now to enter into some kind of ambiguous relationship with one of the city's richest and most eligible bachelors—was a source of consternation to many. The press started supplementing the image of "Mammy"

Pleasant with another marginalizing caricature—as the sinister local "Queen of the Voodoos." Stories were published claiming that Pleasant had once studied Voodoo (or, more correctly, Vodou) and other occult matters with Marie Laveau in New Orleans. And while some circumstantial evidence exists that Pleasant may indeed have been a practitioner of the much-misunderstood folk religion, the rumors and newspaper stories were clearly intended to malign her, insinuating that her influence over important men like Bell had more to do with potions, herbs, and spells than with hardheaded business sense. How else to explain the fact that an alleged former slave was now one of the wealthiest women in the state of California? For many San Franciscans—white *and* Black—a dark, supernatural force was the only thing that could explain this anomaly.

. . .

As for that other disruptive woman accused of bewitching important men, Laura Fair—having made a mad dash across the country by rail—showed up unannounced one day in September 1869 at the law office of Wilson & Crittenden in San Francisco. According to Laura's later court testimony, A.P. was clearly taken by surprise, but tried to mollify his irate lover as best he could. "Why did you come?" he asked incredulously, ushering her inside. He claimed that he'd been planning to return to her in White Sulphur Springs in a matter of days. When she told him her fears about Clara, he assured her, first of all, that his wife was emphatically not pregnant. And no, he was not living with Clara and the children on Ellis Street. Admittedly, he took meals there for the sake of appearances, but he slept every night in the bachelor rooms he kept on Pine Street. His marriage, he reiterated, was pure pretense at this point, a charade maintained to spare Clara as much embarrassment and humiliation as possible.

Did Laura believe all of this? Perhaps, but she could sense that something was wrong, despite A.P.'s protestations that nothing had changed between them. And she was now desperate enough to risk everything to force his hand. Laura told him that she had no desire to hold him against his will. If he had tired of her—if he had decided to go back to Clara after all—she would cede the field and give him up. It would likely kill her, she said, but she would go away if he wished her to.

This was it, then—Crittenden's opportunity to extract himself from an affair that had been costing him his money, his reputation, and even his health for six years. But he just couldn't go through with it. Instead, he told her that she was being ridiculous. Of course he didn't want her to go away. The divorce *would* happen, and soon. In fact, A.P. rashly insisted that Laura not even unpack her travel clothing from her trunk. Within two weeks he'd be ready to take her east to Indiana as promised. The financial matter that had brought him back to San Francisco would be settled. It had been a foolish thing—a $7,000 debt that his son Parker, now a profligate twenty-year-old, had run up with his stockbroker. Since Parker was barely an adult, A.P. had felt responsible for the boy's debt, and so had wanted to make it good himself. But once that was paid, he'd be free to go on with the original plan.

For now, then, these assurances would have to suffice. And to give Crittenden his due, practically the only thing he never seemed to have lied about over the years—either to Laura *or* to Clara—was his various money problems. Never in his life had the man been unburdened by debt. It was likely, in fact, that at this point in their relationship—given Crittenden's recent setbacks—Laura Fair was in better financial condition than her supposed benefactor. Like Mary Ellen Pleasant, she faced constant incredulity from outside observers about the extent of her wealth. Surely she must be Crittenden's kept woman, for how else could a widow left penniless at her husband's death in 1861 be a wealthy woman of leisure just eight years later? (This was a line of argument that would eventually be pursued by prosecutors in her trial.) And while it does seem that Laura was not above accepting gifts from her lover (that piano, for one, not to mention the occasional bank draft for several hundred dollars), the money Crittenden had invested on her behalf was very much her own. In fact, she would later claim that she offered to give her entire fortune to Clara if only it would free A.P. to make Laura the second Mrs. Crittenden. He did not take her up on this offer.

And so Laura Fair and A. P. Crittenden resumed the affair that circumstances and geography had put on hiatus for a time, though the relationship seems to have entered a new and rockier stage. Laura took rooms with her mother and Lillian at a lodging house on Bush Street, directly across from William Ralston's new California Theater, and A.P. made the ten-minute walk there nearly every night to see her. But the lovers argued frequently. Both were in ill health, and suffering under pressures that were hardly conducive to amorous harmony.

Then, late one night in November, matters came to a head. A.P. had arrived at her rooms, as he often did during this period, to spend the latter part of the evening with her. But tonight, when she asked him to take off his overcoat and sit down, he told her that he wouldn't, that he wasn't feeling well and couldn't stay long in any case. According to Laura, this was often his way; Crittenden frequently insisted that he couldn't linger, but what he really wanted was for her to urge him not to go. And so she played along. She locked the door with a key and impishly said, "Well, now you will have to stay." He laughed, then shed his overcoat and threw himself on her lounge. "I am so fatigued," he said, "that if I get down here I shall not get up, and shall probably stay all night."

Laura saw her opportunity. Drawing a stool up to the lounge, she told him that she was quite eager for him to stay that evening, because she was "in a good deal of distress of mind" about his intentions. More than a month had passed since he'd told her not to unpack her trunk, because he'd be ready to go east with her within two weeks. She had been patient, but the promised time had come and gone and now her patience had run out. "I told him I wanted him to tell me that evening what I was to do—whether he was really going, or whether I should unpack my things, or what I should do," she later explained in court. "I wanted a decided answer that night, once for all."

A.P. insisted that he was too tired and sick to talk about this subject that night. But when she refused to relent, he became upset. "Anything like that excited him very much," Laura admitted, "because he did not like to be coerced at all." But since "the suspense was killing me," she wasn't going to give in. They argued back and forth; at one point, he even grabbed her by the shoulders and shook her in exasperation. Finally, she went into the bedroom to "get a powder, or some valerian," which she was in the habit of taking to calm her nerves. But while she was getting it from her nightstand, she heard the front door slam. She ran back into the parlor and found that A.P. had gone.

"I immediately threw on a cloak I had, and without any hat, I started after him," she later explained. "My mother tried to stop me as I was going downstairs, but I did not heed her, and I went on."

Once on the street, she saw Crittenden walking a little ways ahead, but he wasn't going down in the direction of his bachelor rooms on Pine Street; he was instead walking uphill on Bush Street, away from downtown. Suspicious now, she followed him at a distance for several blocks west and then south, until he arrived at the large home on Ellis Street where Clara lived with five of their children—and where, he claimed, he only took meals with them for the sake of appearances. Laura watched, hidden by the late-night fog, as he unlocked the door with a key and disappeared inside.

Accounts of what happened next would vary somewhat in the trial, depending on who was doing the telling. But what is certain is that Laura, confronted with this evidence that her lover was in fact spending at least some nights with his wife and children, resolved not to let things stand. She had to know which of the two of them—herself or Clara—he was going to choose, and she had to know now.

She ran up to the door and pulled the bell rope. When no one came to the door, she rang again and again, waking everyone in the house. Finally, Howard Crittenden, the now-twenty-five-year-old son she knew from Virginia City and White Sulphur Springs, walked onto the porch, arriving home from some evening engagement. Their relationship had always been cordial, so, as he let himself in the door with a key, Laura asked him to call his father. Howard agreed, but when he went inside to the foot of the stairs, A.P., standing at the top, said, "Don't let her into the house."

The scene turned uglier from there, with poor Howard in the middle of it, while Clara and the younger children listened from their doorways on the second floor. A.P. refused to see her; Laura refused to leave until he did. The volume of the standoff increased steadily. Finally, Crittenden told his son Parker to go and get a policeman. This infuriated Laura. She "threatened to do some injury" if they brought the police. But Crittenden insisted that Parker go. As the young man ran out of the house, Laura shouted, "Take care, Mr. Crittenden, there will be bloodshed here!"

All witnesses—even Laura—agreed on what Crittenden said next: "I am disgusted with you women! You have unsexed yourselves!"

Whether "you women" meant Laura and her mother or Laura and Clara is unclear. Certainly all three women had been pressuring him into acting according to their wishes, and he was now fed up. This was not the way good Victorian women were supposed to behave. By asserting themselves so forcibly in his life, attempting to exert their will over his prerogatives as a man, they were "unsexing" themselves—overstepping the boundaries of Victorian womanhood and trespassing on the male's terrain. Laura's "manly" threat of violence was, for Crittenden, the final stroke.

But whatever anger A.P. may have felt right then was nothing compared to Laura's. When she finally left—just moments before the return of young Parker with two policemen—she was nearly frenzied with rage. The threat she had uttered in the heat of the argument— "there will be bloodshed here"—may have seemed like overblown melodrama to the Crittenden family members who heard it that night, but it was a warning they should not have ignored.

20

The Restless Ghost

I T WAS AN UNEASY FEW weeks for everyone involved. In the days following the scene at the Ellis Street house, A.P., as mercurial as an adolescent, decided that he couldn't live without Laura after all, and came repeatedly to her rooms on Bush Street to apologize. But Laura refused to see him. She was still in a fury that he'd actually called the police to get rid of her—an act of disrespect that shattered any pretensions to dignity and social standing she'd ever entertained. When she would not answer his increasingly maudlin letters, he took to stalking her. "Last night I saw you and Baby at the window," he wrote in one of those letters. "It was an almost irresistible temptation to run up and give you and her a kiss . . . It is horrible, and I can't endure it. My thoughts wander to you all the time. It is ruining me in every way."

Finally, he could stand it no longer. On November 24, after being refused admittance at Bush Street three times in one day, he tried to force his way into the apartment past Mrs. Lane, who screamed as she tried to hold the door against him. Laura came to the door with a pistol in her hand. This sight apparently cowed A.P., and he retreated back into the dark stairway. Laura kept coming, pushed her mother aside, and fired a shot into the hallway. She later claimed that she was just trying to frighten him away and so had aimed well above his head.

But the morning light next day revealed that the bullet had lodged in the frame of the street door at the bottom of the stairs, "about four or five feet from the floor."

Crittenden, however, was too desperate to allow even this unsubtle hint to deter him. Later that same day, he wrote another note: "I am coming to see you tonight. Think, if you will, I am mad. I am so. I cannot endure this state of existence any longer . . . At 8 o'clock see me. Kill me then, or do anything you please with me. Death is better than this sham and miserable life."

This reckless attempt to see her was also rebuffed, and this time (perhaps fortunately for Crittenden's health) he didn't even get past the front door. Laura did, however, write to him to say that, before she would consent to see him in person, she wanted an apology—before witnesses—for the indignity he had subjected her to on the doorstep of his family's house. She would send a gentleman to him to accept the apology, which had to be made in front of Clara and any of the children who'd been present at the house that November night. Crittenden agreed and, to Clara's keen humiliation, met with a man sent over by Mrs. Fair and formally expressed his contrition: "I apologize," he said, while his family looked on, "for the manner in which I treated her on such a night." The gentleman, who was never identified, accepted the apology on Laura's behalf and promptly left to report back to her.

But there was still more humble pie to be eaten. Laura further stipulated that A.P. would now have to recite—again before witnesses—the promises he'd made to her about divorcing Clara. Again he agreed. Laura first asked William Ralston, of all people, to hear this recitation in his office, but the banker demurred, being at this time deeply immersed in his financial troubles. So Laura had to settle for her former landlady, Mrs. Hammersmith. Laura and A.P. agreed to meet at the old boardinghouse where they had taken rooms together two years earlier, when they needed a place to rendezvous without provoking comment. Here Mrs. H would witness his promises to Laura—first, that he would divorce his wife, and second, that he would not come to Laura's flat on Bush Street until he had, though she did concede that they could meet occasionally at Mrs. Hammersmith's to discuss matters.

It took some time, not to mention a lot of abject pleading on Crittenden's part, but Laura did eventually soften her stance toward him. Certainly, A.P. tried everything to win her back. He assured her, first of all, that he really and truly did not spend nights with his wife; the only reason he had gone to Ellis Street that night was because one of the children had been sick. This was almost certainly a lie, but Laura allowed herself to believe it. He also appears to have earned some pity because of his ongoing health problems. According to family letters, A.P. was in an accident of some kind late that winter, which left him rather seriously hurt. ("Your father's injuries might have been worse, but were quite bad enough," son-in-law Sidney Van Wyck wrote to his wife, Nannie, in February. "It is too bad that he should be so roughly treated at his age.") Crittenden also learned from his doctor that there was "something the matter with his heart."

In any case, the two lovers were eventually back together on their old terms, seeing each other every day—first, at a room at Mrs. Hammersmith's that A.P. rented just for this purpose, but finally, despite her earlier resolution, at Laura's rooms on Bush Street. "I gradually gave up trying to prevent him [from coming]," she would later explain, "and let it go on in that way, as he said it would be only a little while, and so we became just as friendly as we ever had been." But Laura did extract other concessions from him. One of the few surviving communications between them from this period is a genial but firm note from Laura asking A.P. to buy her a private box for a performance at the Pavilion, where famed violinist Camilla Urso was playing. Crittenden was not to attend the concert with her (she insisted she would have no escort), but she apparently expected him to pay for her to attend. "I ask this," she added at the end of the note, "supposing of course that the private boxes are the best and most fashionable—If they are not, you will know and will get what are the best."

Of course, she also expected him to keep his one big promise—

taking her east for the much-postponed divorce/marriage. Now Crittenden was claiming that this would happen in July of the current year (1870), when he would at last have arranged his affairs to allow him to end his current marriage. He even bought Laura $700 worth of new clothing for the trip, including a white wedding dress, which she accepted with alacrity. But her mother was disgusted by Laura's willingness to again make herself a married man's adulterous lover. According to Laura's later testimony, Mrs. Lane was constantly haranguing her with the fact that she was "utterly ruined" unless and until she parted from Crittenden for good.

Little wonder that Laura's health—never ideal even in the best of times—had only gotten worse after the high drama of her winter falling-out with Crittenden. Shortly after that incident, she had begun consulting a new physician—Dr. Benjamin Lyford, a rather pompous New Englander with shady academic credentials but a willingness to prescribe whatever his patients asked for. Over the course of the year, he diagnosed Laura with a raft of symptoms, including insomnia, anemia, dyspepsia, irregular menstruation, constipation, palpitations of the heart, and general nervous irritability, and put her on numerous drugs—including the hypnotic chloral hydrate, valerianate of ammonia, and strychnine—to address these problems. He also performed an unspecified surgery on her in early 1870, a surreptitious procedure after which Laura's housekeeper was asked to dispose of some material in a basin, suggesting that the operation may have been an abortion. This possibility was never explicitly discussed, either in letters or in later court testimony, but an unplanned pregnancy would certainly help to explain Laura's fierce determination to speak with A.P. on the night of the Ellis Street showdown.

Either way, Laura's mental and physical condition was fragile at best, and it did not improve when, as July approached, Crittenden again made noises about having to delay their journey east. Apparently he had made "a speculation in gasoline that failed." But he promised her that he was sending Clara and their daughter Carrie on an extended trip to Virginia to visit relatives, and that once they arrived there he would write to tell his wife that their separation was permanent.

But Laura had had enough of his broken promises. On Sunday, August 14, in a fit of exasperation and despair, she did something shocking: She married someone else whom she had met just ten days earlier.

. . .

The wedding had been her mother's idea. Jesse Snyder, newly arrived in California, was a fellow resident of the lodging house on Bush Street where Mary Lane lived with her daughter and granddaughter. Playing matchmaker, Mrs. Lane had introduced the two young people and encouraged a courtship between them. True, Snyder was rather hard-up and lacking either a fixed profession or great prospects, but he had the one quality that Mrs. Lane was seeking in a suitor for her daughter— he was unmarried. And Snyder seemed to have no objection to being fixed up with an attractive woman with a substantial bank account, even if she did come with a ten-year-old child and a rather question-able history attached. And so the two young people became friendly, with Mrs. Lane doing everything she could to put them together in hopes that some kind of chemistry might develop.

One evening, a few days after they had met, as Snyder was visiting Laura in their parlor at the Bush Street house, Mrs. Lane came in and said that Mr. Crittenden had come to see her. Laura excused herself and went out to the hallway to talk to him. "Who is in there?" Crit-tenden demanded. Laura told him that it was a Mr. Snyder, and that she wanted A.P. to come in and meet him. But Crittenden was in-stantly suspicious. "He shall not come to see you [anymore]," he stated flatly. A.P. said that he was going to go in and say as much to this Sny-der person. He would tell him that Laura was *his* wife and order him out of the house. This made Laura angry. She told A.P. that "after he had obtained his divorce he might order out whom he pleased, but that until that time he had no right." This in turn angered him, and when Mrs. Lane intervened and insisted that Crittenden leave and let Laura return to Snyder in the parlor, he exploded. Fine, he said, claiming that he didn't care anymore whom she saw. "But let me tell before you go," he snarled, just before storming out, "that I am going to send for my wife!"

That was it, then, Laura told herself—the end; Crittenden was going to reunite with his wife again. Over the next days, Laura confessed to Jesse Snyder that while she *had* been engaged to Mr. Crittenden, he had broken the engagement, and so she was entirely unencumbered by any other attachment. This seemed acceptable to him, and so he and Laura rushed into a marriage that—in Mrs. Lane's eyes, at least—would rescue her daughter and granddaughter from their current state of disrepute. Within a week, Laura Fair had become Laura Snyder, Lillian Fair had acquired a new father and protector, and the three had moved into a new suite of rooms in the same Bush Street house.

When he heard about the wedding, Crittenden nearly lost his mind. But since he could not go to see another man's wife at the other man's home, he had to wait until he could meet her in public. A few days afterward, he did see Laura walking on California Street, but given the changed circumstances, he felt he had to be circumspect. He told her simply that he had to talk to her privately: "I must see you—at whatever cost!" She replied that this was impossible, that she was Mrs. Snyder now and he must be content without her. The two parted, but that night Crittenden sent her a note: "No—I can *not*—*cannot* be content. You are to me sun—air—life—everything; and without you—as we are now—there can be no existence. I am wretched; insufferably, infinitely wretched . . . Day and night I wander about like a restless ghost. It is vain to tell me to be content."

In subsequent notes to her, he continued to insist that they meet: "See you I must . . . What you are doing is all wrong, and tends to raise a fearful barrier between us. To think you must stand in awe of some other man . . . My God! I never expected this to occur, and it cannot be right." But it was his last note that finally crushed Laura's resolve: "I can not wait. This night is perfectly decisive of our fate. It is now or never. If you won't see me to-night, we shall never meet on earth." Taking this as a suicide threat, she immediately went upstairs and told her mother that she was going to go see Mr. Crittenden. Mrs. Lane's reaction to this is unrecorded, but can easily be imagined.

Laura met her former lover at Mrs. Hammersmith's lodging house. He had again taken the same two rooms, and now she came to him there, after dark. Upon seeing her, he immediately took her hand. "Why have you done this thing?" he asked wildly. "Why have you put this barrier between us?" She told him it was his own fault, that she had decided to give him up when he'd said that he would call Clara back to San Francisco. No, no, he insisted, that was merely something he'd said in anger. He had tried to send Laura a message to that effect, after he'd had time to cool down, but by then it was too late—she had already married Snyder. According to Laura, hearing about this latest cross-communication "swept away all the foundation I had to sustain me." Her resolve to be finished with Crittenden instantly collapsed.

He sat her down and asked her directly whether she loved Jesse Snyder. She said that she did not. He asked her whether she still loved *him*. "I told him that I did love him, better than I did anything in the world." Convinced now that she had made a huge mistake, she asked what could be done about it. And, of course, Crittenden, the consummate lawyer, had an answer. He told her that if she agreed to come back to him, he could procure for her a divorce from Snyder inside of three months, "that it was a simple matter of two divorces now instead of one." He himself would handle the whole thing. All she had to do was go home and tell her new husband that she wished to end the marriage; she should move back into her mother's apartment and then never allow Mr. Snyder to be alone with her again. Meanwhile, Crittenden would see to everything else, ensuring at the same time that no one knew he was the impetus behind the whole plot.

It's uncertain exactly what manner of persuasion A.P. used on Jesse Snyder; one rumor held that it was a $10,000 bribe, though that seems unlikely, given Crittenden's financial condition. But the young man ultimately consented to sign a separation agreement with his wife of several weeks, each of them promising not to contest any legal action for divorce from the other. Then an arrangement was made with Snyder whereby two policemen "surprised" him in bed with another woman. Once this evidence was procured, it was easy enough to obtain a quick, uncontested divorce. On October 11, less than two months after the wedding, the marriage of Jesse and Laura Snyder (that name would never stick) was ended—in the courtroom of the Honorable Samuel H. Dwinelle, the judge who would later preside at her murder trial.

Unfortunately, the split from Snyder also led to a breach between Laura and her mother. Exasperated by her daughter's insistence on renewing her scandalous affair with a married man, the ever-thwarted Mrs. Lane decided to move away from San Francisco and take up residence in San Jose, a two-hour train ride south of the city. Unlike Laura, her mother did not have an endless capacity for forgiveness.

•   •   •

For some time after the divorce, things seemed relatively placid, even blissful, between the newly reunited lovers. Laura insisted that they not live under the same roof until they could be properly married, but with Clara and the children still in Virginia and the intractable Mrs. Lane out of the picture, Crittenden seemed to have no fears about being seen in public with his mistress. The two met regularly, and were often seen dining tête-à-tête in local restaurants or walking together arm in arm on the streets. Some weeks before her divorce from Snyder became official, Laura had moved to new rooms at the lodging house of an Englishwoman named Mrs. Letitia Marillier, at 229 Kearny Street, and here A.P. would visit her every day after leaving his office or the court. Often, according to Laura, he would come to see her twice or even three times in a day.

But then, one afternoon in late October, as Laura was arranging to have some furniture redone in her new rooms, the upholsterer, a man named Charles Volberg, let her know that he was also helping to refurnish a new house that A. P. Crittenden had rented as a surprise for Mrs. Crittenden, who would shortly be returning from the East. This news shocked Laura to the core. According to the upholsterer's later testimony, Mrs. Fair became very excited and began to complain loudly about how Crittenden was ruining her and her child. Volberg tried to calm her, insisting that Crittenden, whom he regarded as a friend, was a good man. But Laura was implacable. If you knew all, she informed him, you would think otherwise. Then, according to Volberg, she announced that if Clara Crittenden returned to the city, "one of us three should have to die."

When she confronted A.P. about it that same evening, he sheepishly confirmed that Clara was indeed coming back. But that fact didn't mean what Laura thought it did. In a moment of anger after Laura's marriage to Snyder, he said, he actually *had* written to his wife asking her to return. But then, after his reconciliation with Laura, he had repeatedly told Clara not to come. Unfortunately, however, she was coming anyway, and bringing little Carrie back with her.

While there was a shred of truth in what Crittenden told her that day, it was mostly a lie. The fact of the matter was that A.P. had never sent Clara away permanently; the plan had always been that she would go east for six months or so to visit family in Virginia and then return to San Francisco sometime in the fall. This was clear from a letter he'd written to Clara back in May, when she was still en route to Virginia. She'd had a bad experience on the Erie Railroad, so he advised her: "When you return, come back by the Pennsylvania Central and Pittsburgh, Fort Wayne, and Chicago roads. Bear this in mind and don't forget it when you come to plan your return." He'd even made his customary little jokes about their marriage: "I infer from your silence

on the subject that you got through Utah without being made a convert to the doctrine of polygamy, and through Chicago without being
divorced. Fortunate woman! . . . I must enquire a little into the law of
that state to see whether the stopping of a married woman in Chicago
for a whole day and night does not of itself, necessarily, dissolve all
bonds of matrimony." Given the state of their marriage for the last few
years, these jests about polygamy and divorce must have come like
cruel jabs to Clara's much-beleaguered heart.

Of course, Crittenden had also been lying to his wife during this
time: "I lead a rather humdrum life," he'd written to Clara in June. "It
is very quiet at my rooms—no, not *quiet,* for there is always more noise
on the street than I like, but it is very lonely. I stretch myself out in the
evening in the big chair and read the newspapers or a novel, and work
only when absolutely compelled to do so." One wonders how very
lonely he could have been while meeting so regularly with his mistress.

But Clara clearly knew that Laura Fair was still a danger to her marriage. In August, when A.P. had first learned about Laura's marriage to
Snyder, he'd written to his wife in a spirit of resignation, and in a way
that signals how much she knew: "I feel unusually light-hearted this
morning," he'd told her. "You too will feel so, for henceforth you can
have no fears or apprehension from the old source of trouble. Read the
enclosed slip from the *Alta,* and you will find the explanation." The
"slip" was the Fair-Snyder wedding announcement, which had appeared in the newspaper that very morning. "You have been a good,
brave, loving, and forgiving wife," he continued, "and I can never forget how much you have borne and forgiven." This was when he began
to urge her to come home. "Pray, how long do you expect to stay
away?" he asked two days later. "Have you forgotten me, and how
lonesome I am? I want you to come home . . ." He'd even told his
daughter Laura Sanchez, who knew all about the other Laura in her
father's life from their years in Nevada, that he'd urged Clara to come
home early. "I suppose you will be surprised to hear that Pa has written for Ma to come home—two months sooner than she expected,"

she wrote her sister Nannie. "He has become completely disgusted with the kind of life he is leading & says he wants a home again."

But Crittenden's disgust had proved fleeting, and once he'd hatched his plot to end his mistress's marriage and get her back, his tune changed immediately: "Don't come on the 15th of September [after all]!" he wrote Clara in late August. He claimed that he did not get the house he'd hoped to rent for her upon her return (he actually had—a house on the corner of Ellis and Hyde), and in any case, the weather in October would be much nicer for her return across the plains, which would still be very hot in early September. "All well and nothing going on," he assured her, with the epistolary equivalent of a straight face. Understandably bewildered by her husband's quick changes of mind, Clara had then gone back to her original plans, spending a little more time with her family in Virginia and with the in-laws in Kentucky before making any further arrangements for her return.

And now it was late October, and Laura had had to learn from an upholsterer—a tradesman!—that Clara would be back in San Francisco within days. Exactly when, she wondered, was A.P. planning to tell her this momentous piece of news? During their conversation about it that evening, Laura had become overwrought, notwithstanding her lover's assurances that his wife's return in no way represented any kind of reconciliation. Laura insisted that the stress and anxiety caused by Clara's mere presence in town would kill her, knowing that at any time he might decide to spend a night with her. Every moment that A.P. was not with Laura, she said, would be an unbearable agony.

Apparently impressed by the vehemence of this reaction, Crittenden, as usual, had a plan. He offered to take a room at Mrs. Marillier's house, where he could sleep every night, so that Laura need not worry that he was sleeping with Clara. It was still understood between them that Laura would deny him her own bed, at least until he was divorced. But since they would be sleeping under the same roof, if not in the same room, she would never have to worry about where he was spending his nights.

This plan seemed to mollify her, but even after Crittenden engaged the room the next day, paying in advance a month's rent of $40, Laura's mind was not easy. According to Mrs. Marillier, Laura slept very little in the days leading up to Clara's return and complained of acute headaches. Laura herself later claimed that she was taking valerian and chloral hydrate every night; she was also experiencing memory lapses. And on the day of Clara Crittenden's scheduled arrival—November 3—she was, according to Mrs. Marillier, "very excited and weepy."

A.P. had informed her that morning that he was going to meet Clara and Carrie when they got off the transcontinental train at the pier in Oakland across the bay. This was merely a courtesy, he assured her. Clara meant nothing to him; he had never really loved her; it was Laura who was "the only wife he had on earth." He couldn't stay with her until then, however, since he had to be in court that day. But he vowed to return to her late that afternoon, before heading over to the ferry terminal. Laura allowed him to go, but she was miserable all day, and filled with misgivings.

Shortly before 4 P.M., Crittenden left the Fifteenth District Court, where he had been arguing the real estate lawsuit of *McCauley v. Fulton*. After stopping briefly at his office, he went over to see Laura as promised at their lodging house on Kearny Street. He only had a few moments to sit with her before leaving to catch the five o'clock ferry to Oakland, and he was disappointed that Laura was still upset. "You have been crying again," he said, "[but] you have no reason to." He led her over to the sofa and sat down with her, but when he tried to kiss her, she wouldn't allow it. He asked why, and she said later, "I did not wish him to kiss me, and perhaps, a few moments afterwards, for all I might know, kiss her." That's when he said those words—"his words exactly," she claimed—that left such a deep impression on her: "Have I not assured you that you are my only wife, and I kiss no other?"

He had to leave then, but he promised that he would return and spend the evening with her—and sleep (if she insisted) in his rented room right there at Mrs. Marillier's. Before that, of course, he would have to escort Clara and Carrie from the train to the ferry to the Crittenden house on Ellis Street, and then dine with them and the other children—purely for the sake of appearances. Even so, it might be late before he got back to Kearny Street. But he assured her that he would come.

According to Mrs. Marillier, who saw them as they left, Laura and A.P. were affectionate together as they prepared to part ways until that night. A.P. asked for a night key, since he would be returning late, and the landlady gave him one. Then Laura announced that she was going to get an early dinner at the German restaurant across the street, and so she would go downstairs with him and see him off. The two were arm in arm as they descended to the street.

But then, just a few minutes later, Mrs. Marillier was surprised to hear Laura returning to the house. She seemed to be in a state of acute agitation and asked to borrow the landlady's cloak. Laura was going to follow Crittenden to the ferry, she said. She wanted to—she *had* to—see how he greeted his wife, to be sure that he would "meet her without kissing her."

· · ·

Clara Crittenden stood on the busy Oakland wharf, waiting with her family to board the *El Capitan* ferry. She and her little traveling party—consisting of her fifteen-year-old daughter, Carrie, and some new acquaintances named Captain and Mrs. Fithian—had gotten off the transcontinental train sometime earlier and had been met by two of Clara's sons, twenty-two-year-old Parker and thirteen-year-old Tommy. Parker and Tommy had come over from San Francisco on the four o'clock ferry in order to be there when the train arrived; A.P., claiming work burdens as always, had taken the next boat and joined them late. But now—at half past five, as the sun sank low over San Francisco Bay—they were all together, awaiting the signal to get back on the ferry for the return trip.

Had A.P. kissed his wife upon seeing her for the first time in six months? Because of the chaos following the ferry's docking, Laura had failed to witness the reunion, as she had hoped. A *San Francisco Chronicle* writer did later report that Crittenden "was affectionately embraced by his devoted wife, and fondly kissed by his loving and beautiful daughter" when they met. But this was probably a journalist's invention, since there would have been no reason for him to notice the Crittendens among the roughly four to five hundred passengers on the wharf at the time. Either way, husband and wife were now reunited, and Clara, at least, was happy about it.

It had been a long and tiring journey, made only a little more tolerable by having an adult female companion with her. She had met Mrs. Fithian when she was visiting the Crittenden in-laws in Frankfort, Kentucky, and had felt relieved to find a respectable woman headed to San Francisco with whom she could travel. Of course, Mrs. Fithian and her husband were northerners, but by now Clara had softened on that particular topic. ("[Mrs. Fithian] is a very pretty and graceful woman, and I liked her looks," Clara had written A.P. from Kentucky. "[I] could not help laughing at the idea of my traveling with a Yankee officer's wife, but we have to give up our prejudices.") Now Clara was more than ready to complete the final short leg of her protracted cross-country trek and get to the house on Ellis.

When the horn of *El Capitan* sounded a warning for departure, Clara took her husband's arm and together they followed the crowds onto the ferry and then up the steps to the open-air deck. Clara had a favorite place to sit—a bench near the starboard wheelhouse—and asked her husband if they could see if it was still free. It was, and so they all sat down together. Crittenden took a place between his wife and Mrs. Fithian, while Tommy and Carrie sat catty-corner on the connecting bench. Clara asked her son Parker to go below and make sure that everything was sorted with their luggage, and when the young man had gone she again took her husband's arm and began looking around the boat, content to have come back to a place she had long resisted but now thought of as home. She noticed a woman sitting not far away, dressed in what appeared to be a black waterproof cloak with her head wrapped in a black veil—which struck Clara as strange, since it had been a "bright, sunshiny afternoon." But she thought little more of it, and quickly turned back to join the conversation with her family and Mrs. Fithian.

She was not aware of the approaching figure until it was too late. In the deepening twilight, Clara saw only a pistol in a gloveless hand aimed toward her husband's chest. Before she realized what was happening, a blaze of light flashed in her face, and she heard the crack of the pistol, the shot so close that it singed her dress. Clutching his chest and moaning something incomprehensible, A.P. tried to rise from the bench, but instantly fell back against her. A heavy weight in her arms now, he slumped off the bench to the deck, dragging her down with him.

Only then did Clara look up to see who had fired the shot. It was the same black-clad figure she had noticed earlier. The woman was backing away now, dropping the pistol as she retreated. Her head was still mostly obscured by the veil, but Clara—helplessly sprawled on the cold deck beside her bleeding husband—didn't have to see the woman's face to know exactly who it was.

Part Four

A Woman in Name Only

(1870–1875)

This is not a subject to be turned off with a flippant sneer or an idle jest. It is the bounden duty of every honest man and woman in the land to keep high the standard of morality in the community, refusing to sanction either vice or violence, however disguised by fair repute or show of justice.

—*Daily Alta California*
"The Lessons of a Tragedy"
November 6, 1870

21

The Great Man Honored

ESTABLISHMENT SAN FRANCISCO was in shock. On the rainy Monday afternoon of November 7, 1870, the city's elite gathered at the flower-and-evergreen-bedecked Trinity Episcopal Church (the so-called Mother Church of the Pacific Coast) to bid farewell to one of its own. All of the law courts in the city had adjourned in the late attorney's honor, from the state and federal district courts right down to the county, municipal, and even the probate and police courts. Every presiding judge had eulogized the dead man in laudatory terms—words reprinted by nearly every newspaper in town: "The blow that struck him down extinguished one of the brightest intellects that ever cast its ethereal rays about us," intoned Judge Elisha McKinstry of the Twelfth District Court, in a particularly gushy encomium, "and forever stilled the very warmest heart that ever beat beneath so calm and cold an exterior."

Spectators thronged the sidewalks of Union Square, watching as the city's most distinguished personages entered the three-year-old Gothic Revival church, serving a parish first established back in 1849, the year Alexander Parker Crittenden came to California as a young legislator. The city's current mayor, Thomas Henry Selby, was among the mourners, as were the entire county board of supervisors, along with various business leaders, judges, and members of the San Francisco bar (including Judge S. H. Dwinelle and District Attorney H. H. Byrne, good friends of the deceased who would be representing the state in the upcoming trial of his murderer). When the ceremony began, two different Episcopal clergymen officiated, conducting the service as Clara Crittenden and her extended family wept in the front pew. Afterward, the pallbearers carrying the elegant casket to the hearse included two state supreme court justices, the head of the San Francisco Stock and Bond Exchange, the general superintendent of the Central Pacific Railroad, and, of course, the great city-builder himself—William Ralston—who took a place of honor at the head of his old friend and client's bier.

It had been four days now since the horrendous shooting on the *El Capitan* ferry, and the city had been abuzz with the news ever since. People had talked about it incessantly from the moment the ferry reached the San Francisco wharf on Thursday evening. There had, after all, been a dozen witnesses to the act itself, and hundreds more to the events that immediately followed it. Drawn to the starboard wheelhouse by the sound of the single shot, numerous passengers had looked on in morbid curiosity as the distraught middle-aged woman sat on the deck with a man's head in her lap, crying out that her husband had been shot. Capt. William Kentzel, the head of the harbor police, had quickly taken control of the scene. Others in authority kept the crowds at bay—among them the steamer's captain, William Bushnell, and former California governor Leland Stanford, who just happened to be a passenger that night on the ferry owned by his Central Pacific Railroad. A doctor on board named Nelson J. Bird appeared and offered to examine the victim. He unbuttoned Crittenden's vest and shirt and saw the gunshot wound in the right breast just above the nipple. The trajectory of the bullet appeared to angle down toward the man's heart, and when the doctor found no perceptible pulse at the wrist, he knew the situation was dire. "This man is dying," he said aloud, and then called for some kind of stimulant to administer to the rapidly failing victim.

Meanwhile, Parker Crittenden, having returned from his errand with the luggage to find his parents at the center of this terrible commotion, ran up to try to help his father. Parker inferred instantly who was responsible for the assault, even before his mother spoke the name. Turning and approaching Captain Kentzel, who was now interviewing witnesses, he said he knew the woman who had fired the shot. This was all Kentzel needed to hear. Enlisting Parker's aid, he and the young man went off together to find her, Kentzel now holding the assailant's small pistol, which a teenage boy had picked up off the deck and passed on to him.

It took just a few minutes to find her. Laura Fair was sitting quietly on a bench in the cabin near the forward saloon, her veil pulled back from her face now, looking dazed and upset. "This is the woman," Parker announced, pointing toward her. "I accuse her of the murder of my father. Arrest her."

Laura looked up at them. "Yes, I did it and I don't deny it," she said, in a tone of barely suppressed agitation. "He ruined both myself *and* my daughter."

With that, Captain Kentzel "took hold of her," as he later testified, and escorted her out of the cabin. Pushing onlookers aside, he brought her to the aft portion of the ferry and sat with her there, while another police officer on board, William Kelly, kept curious onlookers at a distance. The prisoner started talking nonstop then, asking to go see Crittenden, accusing him again of ruining her, and of ruining her daughter's future. Then she began frantically urging someone to relay her apologies to him. At one point, she warned Kentzel that she was going to have a "spell" and needed drops from a pharmacist on Pine and Kearny Streets. The police captain tried to keep her calm, but she continued carrying on in this frenzied manner for the remainder of the trip across the bay. When they finally docked at the San Francisco wharf, Kentzel immediately whisked her off the ferry. Officer Kelly managed to commandeer a carriage and the two of them accompanied the prisoner to the station house and then on to City Prison.

The wounded Crittenden required more time to evacuate. Shortly after the shooting, a deckhand had found a mattress belowdecks and the victim had been carefully lifted onto it, though he was unconscious by now and likely didn't know the difference. Once the steamer had docked, a half dozen volunteers hoisted this makeshift stretcher and carried it down the gangway and along the wharf to shore, as Clara and the children followed. A wagon was procured to transport both man and mattress, along with Clara, Parker, Dr. Bird, and another physician. In this age before hospital emergency rooms, trauma cases were often sent to the prison infirmary, where there was always a doctor on duty. Well-off individuals, however, were typically treated at home, so the wagon headed immediately to the Crittenden residence on Ellis Street. Here more doctors were summoned to attend to him, but since they could not locate the bullet in the victim's chest, there was little that they could do besides administer chloroform and injections of morphine and hope for the best. Crittenden did regain consciousness shortly after arriving at the Ellis Street house, but although he appeared to recognize members of his family, he could not speak. And his suffering appeared to be acute. At 6 P.M. on Saturday, November 5—despite round-the-clock efforts by his doctors—A. P. Crittenden died, after nearly two full days of agony.

By that time the city's clergy and newspapers had worked themselves up to a fever pitch of outrage. Murder was common enough in San Francisco at this time, with one or two occurring every month, but murders with a female perpetrator were much rarer—perhaps one or two per year. And seldom if ever was the victim as high-profile a character as A. P. Crittenden. As a result, emotions were running high. The narrative being spun from the city's pulpits and editorial columns portrayed Crittenden as a flawed but brilliant jurist and upstanding family man brought down by a brazen Jezebel. Journalists who had once derided Crittenden for his imperfectly concealed Confederate sympathies now depicted him as a founding father of California jurisprudence, his only blemish an unfortunate susceptibility to feminine wiles. And this interpretation of events was uncritically accepted by newspapers nationwide, as articles from the local press were reprinted in papers ranging from the *New York Times* and *Chicago Tribune* to the *Memphis Public Ledger.*

Granted, a few accounts, like one that appeared in the *San Francisco Chronicle* two days after the shooting, did acknowledge the double standard in how society treated adulterous males and adulterous females. "It is reckoned a very slight offense, if an offense at all," the newspaper noted, "for a man to be unfaithful, to devote to another woman the love and attention that he has pledged before the altar of God to his wife. But the partner in his offense, who may be, and in most cases is, more sinned against than sinning, is outlawed from all society and regarded as a moral leper." But while the *Chronicle* lamented the unfairness of this situation, that sentiment didn't prevent the paper from doing precisely the same thing, praising Crittenden as "a gentleman of education and refinement, of high standing in an honorable profession, moving in the very best society," while his mistress was "notoriously of bad antecedents and violent disposition"—in short, a "Bold, Bad Woman," as she was called in one article's sub-headline.

Laura Fair was further depicted as a living symbol of lawlessness, greed, and base immorality, as accounts of her past became increasingly hyperbolized. According to one paper, her run-in with toy-store owner Dale in Virginia City had been fatal—Fair had shot him down in cold blood, the paper reported, after he had the audacity to raise the American flag at his store. Another reporter identified Lillian as Crittenden's love child, failing to calculate that the child had been born three years before her two alleged parents even met. But the most preposterous story came from the *Chronicle,* which reported that Laura Fair had once paraded half-naked through the streets of Virginia City, brandishing a Confederate flag in one hand and a pistol in the other, daring anyone to stop her.

The woman who inspired these prodigious flights of imagination was now incarcerated at City Prison, confined in a cell made of sheet-iron incongruously painted pink. Under the constant care of a nurse, she seemed to be suffering a protracted version of one of her "spells," drifting in and out of consciousness, moaning, tearing at her hair, and talking incoherently about her child and the man she loved, both of whom needed her, she claimed. The papers were convinced that the onetime actress was shamming insanity, but if so, it was a bravura performance. At times, it took the efforts of several strong policemen to hold her down; once, when her doctor tried to administer an oral sedative, she bit a chunk out of the thick glass tumbler he held to her mouth. This extreme behavior (described disapprovingly by the *Alta* as "unladylike") continued for several days, at which time she was diagnosed with "brain fever" by the ever-obliging Dr. Lyford and prescribed even larger doses of chloral hydrate.

The slow-moving gears of the justice system were meanwhile grinding along. The coroner's inquest took place a week after the shooting—convening first in the elegant dining room of the newly completed Crittenden home on Ellis Street, where members of the family could be examined privately and respectfully. Next day, the proceedings moved over to the coroner's office. Here evidence was heard from Captain Kentzel, Dr. Bird, and other witnesses from the ferry. Finally, after a few more days of testimony, the coroner's jury reached its verdict: Alexander Parker Crittenden, a native of Kentucky aged fifty-four years, "came to his death from a gunshot wound, which shot was fired from a pistol in the hands of Laura D. Fair." At this point (according to the procedures of California law as written two decades ago by the victim in this case), the accused would await a grand jury inquiry to see whether the case would go to trial—an outcome that was considered a virtual certainty.

As for the accused, she was doing what she could to assemble a defense—or, rather, her mother was, since Laura Fair herself, now in possession of at least some of her wits, professed to be too distraught to even care. In an interview conducted in City Prison, the now-thirty-three-year-old prisoner insisted, between fits of convulsive weeping, that she just wanted to be left alone. When asked if she wished to make a statement, she grew angry: "No! I have nothing to say . . . They have said so many things about me already, and now not even a single lawyer will do anything for me. All I want to do is to arrange my money affairs to secure my little girl, and then I want the doctor to give me drugs until I die."

Laura was exaggerating only slightly about being unable to find a lawyer to represent her. Mrs. Lane, who had come up from San Jose to take care of her grandchild and help with her daughter's defense, had approached a number of attorneys about taking the case, with little success. The entire San Francisco legal community seemed to have closed ranks, refusing to defend the killer of a member of their close-knit fraternity. According to rumor, even an offer of $10,000 was not enough to tempt any of the victim's former colleagues. But eventually, for the fabulous sum of $15,000 (the equivalent of over $350,000 today), Mrs. Lane was able to secure the services of not one but two creditable jurists. Prominent criminal attorney Elisha Cook, forty-seven years old and the scion of a notable New York family of lawyers, would serve as principal, and the New England–born Leander Quint, a former judge who had served in the mining districts during the heyday of the Gold Rush, would provide backup whenever the former's rheumatoid arthritis kept him home in bed.

The Crittenden family, meanwhile, was still reeling from the death of the family patriarch. For Clara in particular, the loss had been devastating, coming just when she and her husband were reunited after a six-month separation. In fact, she had been so beside herself in the days after the death that she'd fallen down the stairs one night (in the brand-new house that her husband had been furnishing for her) and had nearly broken her arm. Naturally, the family was determined not to let the author of their grief go unpunished, and so, advised by A.P.'s many friends and business associates, they were lining up some additional legal talent of their own. Although the people of the state of California would be officially represented by District Attorney Harry H. Byrne, the family would be hiring its own attorney to "assist" him—Alexander Campbell Jr., a good friend of the deceased and an extremely sharp criminal lawyer who had represented enough defendants to know every trick or stratagem the defense might devise. Because Byrne, like his opponent Cook, was in ill health, it would be Campbell who'd do most of the nuts-and-bolts prosecuting in the trial to come, with Byrne reserved mainly for moments when his talent for high-flown rhetoric would be needed to impress the jury.

In early February 1871, a San Francisco County grand jury issued its murder indictment against Laura Fair. There had been some controversy early on over whether she should be tried in Alameda County instead of San Francisco, given that the shooting had occurred just minutes after *El Capitan* had pulled away from the Oakland wharf. But it was ultimately determined that the ferry had already left Alameda County by the time of the shooting. This was therefore San Francisco's case to try.

The prisoner was transported to the Fifteenth District Courthouse to be arraigned before Judge Samuel H. Dwinelle, in whose courtroom A. P. Crittenden had argued countless cases. Hoping to avoid a mob scene outside the building, the judge had quietly moved the hearing from its scheduled 3 p.m. slot to 9:30 a.m., but still there were a few reporters who witnessed the arrival of the now haggard-looking defendant and her lawyers. According to the *Chronicle*'s writer, "She looked very pale and worn, and her face bore an expression of great sadness, which was doubtless genuine enough." When Dwinelle asked for her plea, the accused could not even muster the energy to rise from her chair and speak. So Cook answered for her: "Not guilty." The plea was recorded and the date set for the start of the trial—March 28, approximately one month hence.

That gave the lawyers on both sides a full four weeks to develop their strategies. For Cook and Quint, the general line of defense was clear. Their client had obviously fired the shot that killed the victim, so they would have to focus on extenuating circumstances—that is,

Crittenden's tormenting treatment of the defendant over the course of seven years and the mental and physical ruin it ultimately caused. Specifically, they'd have to make a persuasive case that the defendant was in such a compromised mental state at the time of the shooting that she could not, and should not, be held responsible for her actions.

The prosecution, on the other hand, had much higher ambitions. Byrne and Campbell understood that this trial had to be more than just a matter of punishing a disreputable woman for a crime she had indisputably committed. There was an important point to be made here, a signal to the rest of the world about what San Francisco was and what it would become. By the early 1870s, after all—even with its well-publicized transformation from frontier settlement to major urban center—the city still had some image problems in the rest of the country. For every visiting journalist writing paeans to the advanced economic and social environment of the great western metropolis, there were others who emphasized the lingering social disorder and lawlessness. One influential writer, for instance—Samuel Williams, writing for the New York–based *Scribner's Monthly*—charged that San Francisco society, though changing for the better, was still far too "mixed": "The lines of class and caste are often vague and shadowy," he insisted. "Your coachman of yesterday may be your landlord today . . . Bridget, who was your maid of all work when you first came, [now] lives in a grand house [and] rejoices in a coachman in livery." Williams also noted the prevalence of "bummers" (in other words, the unemployed and unhoused) on the city's streets, along with all kinds of idle eccentrics and ne'er-do-wells. Worst of all was his focus on so-called hoodlums, "a distinctive San Francisco product," whose rise in this particular city was indicative of "a screw loose somewhere in our social mechanism . . . Hoodlumism is a disease so virulent, so rapid in its spread, that moral physicians are at their wit's end how to treat it."

For the prosecution, then, it was critical to show the world that San Francisco was no longer the kind of place that would tolerate a deviation from social norms like Laura Fair's. The time had come to relegate that image of the city to the past, to show that this was no longer a community where, as a young Mark Twain had complained back in 1865, "punishment of lawbreakers is, in some favored cases, almost obsolete." San Francisco was now a stable and dependable American city where law and order reigned, where respectability was valued, and where justice was served. To drive this point home, the prosecution would have to convince a jury of twelve men to find Laura Fair guilty of murder in the first degree. And they would have to ensure that the judge made an example of her—by sentencing her to become the first woman in California history to be executed by the state. Laura Fair, in other words, would have to be hanged.

22

Dueling Clichés

Yesterday, in the Fifteenth District Court, Mrs. Laura D. Fair was put upon her trial for the alleged killing of Arthur [*sic*] P. Crittenden, upon the Oakland ferry boat, on the evening of the 3d November last. Although this event happened several months ago, and we are not in the habit, in California, of burdening our memories for a very long time with even the most sensational events, the affair in question must yet be fresh in the minds of our readers . . .

—*The San Francisco Chronicle*

T HE SUFFRAGISTS WERE THERE FOR LAURA, both literally and figuratively, from the start. At a time when few respectable women dared to attend courtroom trials as spectators—the matters discussed being regarded as too unseemly for female consumption—members of the California Women's Suffrage Convention had resolved to attend every session of the Fair-Crittenden trial. Led by the organization's president, the formidable twenty-nine-year-old Emily Pitts Stevens, they hoped to show their unwavering support of the defendant, whom they felt had been unjustly persecuted by the male-dominated press ever since her arrest. How these women bypassed Judge Dwinelle's strictures on admission to the spectators' enclosure is a mystery; perhaps, as editor and publisher of *The Pioneer* ("a woman's paper produced entirely by women"), Pitts Stevens was permitted to enter as a representative of the press, bringing her entourage in tow. In any case, the convention members were likely among the few ardent supporters of the defendant in the building. As such, their presence was treated with much amused condescension in the local mainstream press. "Strange as it may seem," the *Daily Alta*'s reporter said of these determined women, "several of them were very good-looking."

Of course, women's rights had been an object of male derision ever since the 1848 Seneca Falls Convention, whose widely distributed "Declaration of Sentiments," a manifesto demanding equality for women, essentially launched the American female suffrage movement. But the experience of the Civil War—when women were forced to assume many traditionally male roles while their husbands, sons, and fathers took up arms—had advanced the cause significantly. Just four years after the end of the conflict, Pitts Stevens had founded *The Pioneer* with a very straightforward purpose: "We defend the rights of women fearlessly and to the best of our ability," she wrote in her "Salutatory" editor's note in 1869. "We shall insist upon women's independence— her elevation, socially and politically, to the platform now solely occupied by man. We shall claim for her each privilege now given to every male citizen of the United States."

Being tried by a jury of one's peers was one such privilege. But since Laura Fair was being tried by a jury of men, before a male judge and under the questioning of male prosecutors and defense attorneys, it was up to Pitts Stevens and her associates to see that the defendant was fairly treated. *The Pioneer* had thus been overwhelmingly sympathetic to her, questioning the wild tales about her previous behavior and challenging the image of her as a "Bold, Bad Woman" propagated by the mainstream press, local clergymen, and other opinion-makers. Even so, it's doubtful that Pitts Stevens had changed many minds about the Fair case. The vast majority of San Franciscans—not least the twelve sturdy businessmen who had been chosen as the jury—were unlikely to have drawn their impressions of the defendant from a regional suffragist newspaper.

The first few days of the trial had run with surprising efficiency. Jury selection had required only a day and a half, and District Attorney

Harry Byrne's opening statement had been brief and to the point—unusual in a prosecutor notorious for indulging in flights of oratory that could go on for hours at a time. And when he turned the case over to his fellow prosecutor, Alexander Campbell, matters moved along in an even brisker and more businesslike manner. Just about the only excitement erupted when, at the end of the second day of the proceedings, Judge Dwinelle announced that he had decided to sequester the jury for the duration of the trial, in order to preserve "the reputation of the Court" and to "prevent scandal"—a clear indication that he feared that the jury might be bribed. Sequestration was a practice unprecedented in California legal history to that date, and it was met with considerable displeasure by the jurors themselves, almost all of whom had businesses to run.

As Byrne had indicated in his opening statement, the first several days of the prosecution proceeded with inexorable logic. Campbell, who did most of the questioning, built a case as if assembling a mosaic, piece by piece, so that the desired picture would emerge gradually. First, the witnesses from the ferry were called to the stand—William Kentzel, the arresting officer; William Bushnell, the captain of the ferry; Tommy and Carrie Crittenden, who had been with their father when he was shot; and other passengers who had seen the defendant's arrest and verbal confession. Campbell called these witnesses mainly to establish beyond any doubt that it was indeed Laura Fair who had pulled the trigger on the evening of November 3. Also called were witnesses to prove that the act was premeditated—the gunsmith who had sold her the murder weapon several days before the shooting, along with the cabdriver whom she had engaged the day before to take her to and from the ferry.

To show malicious intent, Campbell also called those witnesses who had heard the defendant make threats of violence at various times in the past, so that the defendant's own words could be used against her. Most damaging was upholsterer Charles Volberg, who, just days before the crime, had goaded Fair about Clara Crittenden's rumored return. Laura's response at that time—that "one of us three should have to die"—provided a clear motive for the defendant's actions: Her lover was apparently reconciling with his wife, and Fair would rather kill him than give him up to her hated rival. Campbell also spent a good deal of time questioning two of the victim's adult children, Parker Crittenden and Laura Sanchez, who were witnesses to the ugly late-night confrontation at the Crittenden home in November 1869. Here again, the defendant's threat—that if police were called to eject her from the house, "there will be bloodshed here"—would surely weaken any claim that the shooting a year later was purely impulsive and un-premeditated. And, of course, the defendant's statement at the time of her arrest—"Yes, I did it and I don't deny it. He ruined both myself *and* my daughter"—was something that Campbell wanted the jury to hear as many times as possible. He suspected that Fair's lawyers were planning some kind of insanity defense, and so he elicited accounts of this incriminating admission from every witness possible, since it was a sign that Fair was fully aware of her actions just moments after the crime.

Laura's defense attorneys did what they could on cross-examination to defuse some of this damning testimony. Elisha Cook managed to get Volberg to admit that he had recently filed a lawsuit against Mrs. Fair for nonpayment of a bill, making the upholsterer anything but an un-biased witness. And the lawyer also induced several witnesses, including little Tommy Crittenden and his sister Carrie, to admit that their testimony on the stand was slightly inconsistent with their testimony at the coroner's inquest several months earlier. But these were clearly desperation tactics and did little to undermine the methodical case for premeditated murder that the prosecution had assembled.

It was only when Clara Crittenden was called to the stand on the third day of the trial that the prosecution's deeper, more psychological strategy began to unfold. Prosecutor Campbell plainly intended to draw a stark contrast between the *real* Mrs. Crittenden and the pre-tender to the title. And Clara played her role perfectly. Clearly coached beforehand by the prosecution, she emphasized her loyalty and devotion to duty at every opportunity. When asked by Campbell to describe the moments just before the shooting, the widow made sure to include a few reverential comments about her much-criticized husband's character:

> CLARA CRITTENDEN: I turned from her [that is, the veiled woman she had noticed sitting nearby] as I would from any indifferent person . . . and carried on some conversation between my husband and myself and Mrs. Fithian; and the last act of his life was one of the usual acts of gentlemanly courtesy which he paid to everyone; he turned to Mrs. Fithian and said, "Madam, allow me to take your traveling bag" . . . which was his usual way of being courteous to every person that bore the name of woman . . .

Only once did she slip up, when she described going to see Mrs. Fair in June 1865—during Clara's final sojourn in Virginia City, when she tried to convince her husband's "landlady" to give him up. Cook was cross-examining her about the visit:

> ELISHA COOK: Did you go to her house then?
>
> CLARA CRITTENDEN: I did, against my husband's express orders . . . or request, rather.
>
> COOK: How?
>
> CRITTENDEN: His request, not his orders. I always obey them [that is, his orders].

How different was this steadfast Victorian wife from Laura Fair! Here was the ill-treated Mrs. Crittenden, defending her family and yet still respectful of and obedient to her husband, no matter what his weaknesses or how much his peccadilloes had hurt her. Meanwhile, Laura Fair seemed to think that marriage was defined simply by the intensity of ardor she inspired in a man, rather than by the laws of the land and the duties they embodied. Even more outrageous, when the defendant's lucrative little "marriage by God" was threatened by signs that the man might return to duty and reembrace his lawful wife, she felt justified in gunning him down in public. What could be more calculating, more vengeful, or (to cite adjectives that Campbell used frequently in his various speeches to the jury) more "bold," "bad," "manly," and "unfeminine"?

It was an effective strategy. Having thus established a neat contrast between two familiar Victorian clichés of womanhood—the noble, long-suffering, but ever-loyal wife versus the worldly, brazen, and manipulative seductress of dubious reputation—the state completed the initial presentation of its case. On the afternoon of the trial's fourth day, after calling a few medical witnesses to verify that it was indeed the gunshot that had caused Crittenden's death, the prosecution rested and turned the floor over to the defense.

• • •

In laying out their defense over the next ten days of the trial, attorneys Cook and Quint tried to create for the jury a very different narrative connecting the events in evidence. It was a variation on a defense narrative that had proved successful in several high-profile murder trials over the past ten years, securing acquittals for male defendants based on the Victorian concept known as "the unwritten law"—the notion, as one historian has defined it, "that an outraged husband, father, or brother could justifiably kill the alleged libertine who had been sexually intimate with the defendant's wife, daughter, or sister." In the celebrated court cases of New York congressman Daniel Sickles in 1859, former Civil War general George W. Cole in 1868, and New York lawyer Daniel McFarland in 1870, the accused was in each instance acquitted of murdering his wife's lover. The justification was the same each time—namely, that the insult to the sanctity of the defendant's home and family caused a state of temporary insanity in the incensed husband, rendering him incapable of being responsible for his actions. In each of these three cases, the acquittals were met with almost universal approval in the press and among the public, the true guilty party being seen as the adulterer who won the woman's affections and destroyed her reputation and that of her family.

Of course, the Laura Fair case was different from these other cases, not least because the killer was a woman. But the idea that someone could succumb to an exculpatory bout of insanity in the presence of a dire threat to reputation and the sanctity of family ("He ruined me *and* my daughter," as Laura said after the shooting) was one the defense lawyers were counting on. And so, in framing their alternative explanation for the shooting, they indulged in a few Victorian clichés of their own. Cook, in his opening statement, made certain to give the jury a very different picture of the defendant from that drawn by the prosecution. Far from being the seducer in this relationship, Laura Fair had been the seduced—the classic helpless female of nineteenth-century melodrama, without a male protector to shield her from the guiles of an older, more powerful, and unscrupulous man. Yes, A. P. Crittenden was indeed a consummate lawyer and a great mind, just as his defenders claimed, but in this case he employed his vaunted powers of persuasion to lead an unfortunate young woman astray. "Gentlemen of the jury," Cook reminded the panel, "for ten months after her introduction to and acquaintance with Mr. Crittenden, Laura Fair was unaware of the fact that he was a married man. It was a matter that he concealed from her, and in those moments he gained her affections."

Once he had secured those affections, however, something happened. The seducer himself fell in love, and the woman he had cynically deceived into becoming his mistress turned into his soul mate. "No two living beings on the face of God's footstool," Cook insisted, "ever cherished for each other greater, more sincere, or deeper love than these two did." And so Crittenden felt he had to hold on to her, whatever the cost. He became jealous and controlling, preventing her from receiving the attentions of any other admirer, forcing her to break off an engagement with one man in Havana (Mr. Sauers) and convincing her to divorce an actual husband (Jesse Snyder) in San Francisco just a year before the shooting. Meanwhile, he kept her bound to him by repeated promises that he would divorce his unloved wife and marry Laura. In this way, he put the defendant into a morally degraded position from which she ultimately had no escape.

As for the prosecution's depiction of Mrs. Fair as a greedy, kept woman using her sexual powers to bleed her paramour's finances, the facts painted a different picture. As attested to by the lovers' letters to each other (letters that the prosecution was struggling to keep out of evidence), Laura Fair had earned her substantial wealth herself, as a businesswoman and a savvy investor in mining stocks. In fact, this alleged gold-digger sometimes found herself in the position of lending money to her supposed victim. Surely this could not be the heartless adventuress described by the prosecution.

But then Cook came to the crux of his argument for acquittal: "Gentlemen of the jury, I say we shall show that Mrs. Fair was insane . . . We shall establish before you that Mrs. Fair—not only at the time of the shooting, but for twelve months before, at stated periods—was not a responsible being. She had what is called partial intellectual insanity, and partial moral insanity." Here Cook unleashed another Victorian stereotype—of Laura Fair as a hysterical woman unhinged by her own body chemistry. Specifically, she suffered from retarded menstruation, a condition that at its worst could send her into fits of violent madness: "For twelve months prior to the commission of this act," Cook continued, ". . . from that time down to the present day, she has not had a menstrual term without becoming a perfect maniac—furious! . . . We will show it by her physicians, by her mother, by those who know all about it." By the day of the shooting, this condition, exacerbated by two or three weeks of near total insomnia and anxiety over her repeated disappointments, rendered her unconscious of her actions and subject to irresistible impulses. "If she had possession of her faculties," he concluded, "[Clara Crittenden] was the person she would have shot. She was the only intervention between the marriage of herself and Mr. Crittenden. But, gentlemen of the jury, the fact that she shot past Mrs. Crittenden—so close even as to burn her dress—and killed the idol of her own heart—is not that the strongest evidence, the strongest fact that could be introduced in this case, to establish the fact that reason had been dethroned?"

Having laid this groundwork in his opening statement—and after engaging in the first of several tussles with the prosecution and Judge Dwinelle over the admissibility of the lovers' correspondence—Cook began calling the defense witnesses. To support the claim of temporary insanity, he first questioned a number of people who had observed Laura's wild and irrational behavior just after her arrest—the policemen who dealt with her at City Prison, two reporters who tried to interview her in the first days of her incarceration, and the nurse who cared for her in her cell. The woman these witnesses described certainly *sounded* insane, gibbering incomprehensibly at times, tearing at her hair, holding conversations with imaginary persons, and raving so fiercely that even several large men working together could not restrain her. A number of people described the episode in which she bit a chunk out of a tumbler held to her mouth, requiring attendants to wrestle the shard of glass from her mouth. The nurse, a Mrs. Jane Morris, claimed that the defendant became so agitated at times that she (Morris) feared for her own safety and banged on the cell door to be let out. "I was so much afraid that she would injure me or herself," the nurse testified, "[that] I had a knife then which I held in my hand to defend myself from her, because I was actually scared."

Laura Fair's most recent landlady, Letitia Marillier, was called then to confirm the defendant's mental and physical condition just *before* the shooting. "She was not well for five weeks previous," the young but supremely self-possessed Englishwoman revealed. "She complained of want of rest and very much of her head—distress in her head; that was the great complaint, and that she could not sleep . . . She seemed very much distressed." On the actual day of the shooting, "she was very much excited and she cried frequently." This was not particularly strong testimony with regard to the temporary insanity issue, but Mrs. Marillier's real value as a witness was that she could confirm that Crittenden and Fair, contrary to the prosecution's claims, were still very much on terms of affectionate intimacy to the very end. Indeed, the lovers had spent the two nights before the shooting together, in a room he had recently rented in Mrs. Marillier's house for this express purpose. What's more, Crittenden had explicitly told the landlady— just before heading to the Oakland ferry on November 3—that he intended to divorce his wife and marry Mrs. Fair. Since this intention was only alluded to indirectly in his letters to Laura, having a disinterested witness corroborate Crittenden's promise was critical to the defense.

At this point, Cook and Quint brought in two of Laura's doctors and several expert witnesses, ostensibly to talk about the "science" behind the defendant's temporary insanity. But this part of the defense quickly turned into something of a fiasco. The first witness was Benjamin Lyford, Laura's personal physician in the months before the crime, and from the start he proved to be a terrible witness. By turns evasive, arrogant, and self-important, he was so soft-spoken that he had to be asked several times to speak loud enough for the jury to hear. It didn't help that one of the first simple questions Cook asked him— What is your age?—seemed to flummox him. "It is thirty-five, sir," he answered, then corrected himself: "Thirty-two." Then, when asked to describe Mrs. Fair's general physical condition, he unleashed a torrent of medical jargon—beginning with "retrocedent gout" and ending with "antiversion and neuralgic type of dysmenorrhea"—that must have left the jurors reeling. Realizing this, he addressed himself directly to the jury box: "It is to be expected that many of these medical terms you do not understand," he said, rather condescendingly. "Still, it is necessary to give them in this way and manner, upon which medical experts can predicate an opinion."

The upshot of his abstruse testimony, rendered into plainer language, was that Mrs. Fair's many disorders, in particular her chronic experience of suppressed or retarded menstruation, often pushed her into a state of the "most positive, absolute mania," which in turn could "induce her to commit almost any insane act." On the day of the shooting, Lyford reported, the patient's menstrual period was already twelve days late (it would in fact not occur until four days after the shooting). Given this condition, complicated by her extreme insomnia and anemia, an outbreak of un- or semiconsciousness would not be surprising. "The suddenness of an outbreak of that kind, sir, with a person of the strongest emotional sensations, which this unfortunate female possesses—there is no estimating as to what might be done. I consider that anything striking the system [unfavorably] would constitute a complete and positive interruption to those nervous forces to such an extent to make her perfectly unconscious of her immediate surroundings."

On cross-examination, Prosecutor Campbell, who would later refer to Lyford as a "professional mountebank," proceeded to dismantle the good doctor's testimony, first by questioning his credentials. According to his testimony, Lyford had begun practicing medicine at the advanced age of twenty-three, so Campbell pounced on the issue of the young man's medical training:

CAMPBELL: Where did you study your profession?

LYFORD: Various places, sir.

Q: What places?

A: In Canada, and the United States.

Q: When did you commence the study of medicine in Canada?

A: About the year—I do not recollect the year, sir. Perhaps 1856 or 1857.

Q: At what place and what institution?

A: That was not at an institution.

Q: Well, under whose supervision, or what supervision, if any?

A: Of a physician.

Q: What physician?

A: The first one was Dr. Rutherford by name, sir.

Q: Were you a student in his office?

A: Yes, sir.

Q: How long did you study your profession under him?

A: I can not tell you, sir.

Q: *About* how long?

A: Off and on for perhaps a year; perhaps less than that, a little.

Q: How do you mean by "off and on"?

A: I mean this, sir—that I had other business, and devoted my leisure moments, every leisure moment I had, to the study of my profession.

Q: What was your "other business"?

A: I was a chemist, sir.

Q: Was that your profession?

A: There was . . . I did a good deal of that kind of business.

Q: When did you commence the study of chemistry?

A: I cannot tell you that, sir.

Q: Did you have any establishment of your own?

A: No, sir. I was not a professional chemist; I do not call myself a professional chemist . . . I am a self-made individual, sir, what you see of me here.

It went on in this excruciating manner for a long while, as Campbell painfully extracted the admission from Dr. Lyford that the only formal medical training he'd ever had was several months at an institution called "the Philadelphia University," from which he'd received a diploma, although he couldn't remember what year he had received it. Granted, this was an age when the prerequisites for practicing medicine were few and ill-defined, but even by nineteenth-century standards, "Dr." Lyford's credentials seemed dubious at best.

Having effectively demolished the man's credibility as a physician, Campbell proceeded to poke holes in his diagnosis and treatment of this particular patient. The prosecutor insisted that the witness explain the function of the various medicines he had prescribed for her. Needless to say, he could not, at least not to Campbell's satisfaction. And when Lyford claimed that, in the three weeks leading up to the shooting, Mrs. Fair was suffering a condition of "nervous irritability," which led her to "capricious" behavior, Campbell asked him—not once, not twice, but over a dozen times—to be more specific, but to no avail:

CAMPBELL: Now, I ask my question once more. I ask you what she ever said or did during any of those periods that led you to believe that she was in a capricious, nervous, or irritable state? State one thing she said, or did.

LYFORD: That would be a matter of impossibility, sir. I could not begin to do that.

Q: Can you state any of it? You said that nothing seemed to go right with her—now, what seemed to go wrong?

A: Everything.

Q: If everything went wrong, can you not tell us of something that went wrong?

A: Well, sir, it would be very hard to tell you of anything that went right.

Q: Then I suppose it is very easy for you to tell us one thing that went wrong?

A: No, I could not, really.

Dr. Lyford's testimony was, in short, a debacle—and one that must have humiliated him sorely, since, when needed for further testimony later in the trial, he repeatedly claimed to be too ill. In fact, this key witness—the defendant's primary physician in an insanity trial—could never be coaxed into the courtroom again for the duration of the trial.

The defense had somewhat better luck with the other expert witnesses. Dr. John Trask, an older and seemingly more trustworthy physician, had been called in to examine the defendant at City Prison shortly after her arrest. At first, being predisposed to think ill of the defendant, he had believed that she was feigning insanity. But after seeing her more frequently—particularly after becoming her attending physician in late December, when Dr. Lyford had to go out of town for several weeks—he became convinced that her behavior was entirely genuine. He diagnosed her with "hysterical mania," a condition which, he claimed, could cause the most extreme irrational behavior. "I have seen [a hysterical woman] divest herself of every particle of clothing, and spring out of bed, out upon the floor, in a perfectly naked state, and totally uncontrollable . . . [Even] cases of murder are not infrequent during these attacks of hysteria from menstruation."

In his cross-examination, Campbell tried to make something of Trask's initial judgment that Fair was shamming insanity, but the doctor would not budge on this. His first impressions, he insisted, had been distorted by prejudice against the defendant; subsequent observations and examinations had convinced him that there was no playacting here. Therefore, his ultimate conclusion—supported by the testimony of two other expert witnesses, one of whom opined that "the majority of the insanity of females results from uterine disease"—was that the defendant's violent act on November 3 was unconscious and involuntary. She committed it while in a fit of temporary insanity over which she had no control and for which she could not be held responsible.

Did the defense make a convincing case that Laura Fair was insane at the time of the shooting? Given the confidence with which these medical men made their pseudoscientific and baldly misogynistic pronouncements, at least some of the jurors may have been convinced. But in any case, the twelve would soon be able to judge the woman for themselves. For contrary to California law until just recently, Cook and Quint decided to have the defendant testify on her own behalf. Late on the morning of Tuesday, April 4—the eighth day of the trial—the accused murderess Laura D. Fair was summoned to the stand.

23

A Female Hercules

IN PRESENTING THEIR MULTIPLE VERSIONS of Laura D. Fair to the jury—Fair as unprotected female seduced by a powerful man, Fair as successful entrepreneur with no need of a paramour's money, Fair as physically and mentally beleaguered hysteric often susceptible to irrational impulse—the defense may have just confused their case more than bolstered it. After all, could one person really be defenseless, supremely capable, *and* insane? Certainly, the defendant herself had been providing illustrations of all three images during the first week of the trial. Much of the time, Mrs. Fair had merely looked on from the sidelines with sorrowful equanimity. But at various moments throughout the proceedings, something said by Alexander Campbell or one of the prosecution witnesses would send her off into outbursts of "sighs and tears and groans." These eruptions would often be addressed by Dr. Trask with the administering of a shot of whiskey or even a warm footbath under the defense table. The ornate lounge chair that had been brought into the courtroom, so that Mrs. Fair could recline whenever she began suffering one of her "spells," had received little use; Judge Dwinelle eventually refused to proceed with the trial unless the defendant remained vertical. But that just meant that court had to be adjourned, sometimes for hours at a time, whenever the defendant felt overwhelmed by emotion or too weak to proceed.

All of this emotional instability was being regarded with considerable skepticism, not to mention a little sardonic amusement, by the press—both local and national. The *San Francisco Chronicle*—which provided the most complete coverage of the trial, reproducing the proceedings of each morning and afternoon session almost verbatim—professed to be withholding judgment until the verdict. Noting that the trial was "the chief topic of conversation" all over town, the paper claimed that, "for obvious reasons, we do not reproduce the opinions expressed . . . nor introduce any comments of our own." But the paper had subtler ways of making its opinions known, dropping ironic references to the defendant's courtroom dramatics and her brief career as an actress. And the more distant newspapers felt little compunction about weighing in pre-verdict on the credibility of the defendant. The *New York World,* for instance, made light of Mrs. Fair's personal tribulations, noting that she should have just continued ending her marriages by driving her husbands to divorce or suicide, "but unfortunately she ventured to vary the monotony of perpetual marriage by a little adultery and subsequent homicide." Even the more staid *New York Times,* which had been perfectly willing to accept the jury verdicts in the Sickles and McFarland cases, disparaged the attempts by Mrs. Fair and her lawyers to build a case for temporary insanity: "We would call attention to [the strategy's] flimsy character, and to the growing danger that the acceptance of such a line of defense will defeat the ends of justice."

Only the women's press seemed to regard the defendant as something other than a kind of seductive con artist. Throughout the trial, the local suffragists' newspaper, *The Pioneer,* had been propagating its own version of Laura Fair, very different from the versions being presented by prosecutors, defense attorneys, or the mainstream press. For Emily Pitts Stevens, the defendant was something of a hero, a courageous woman driven to a desperate but justifiable act of defense against an oppressive, male-dominated world. "May not a woman," Pitts Stevens wrote, "be allowed the same right [as a man] to judge of her own wrongs, and to avenge them according to her ideas of justice?" The national suffragist press, meanwhile—at least as represented by *The Revolution,* Susan B. Anthony's short-lived weekly newspaper—was a little more doubtful of Mrs. Fair's heroism, but nonetheless echoed *The Pioneer*'s call for equal treatment of the sexes. "There are grievous sins on Mrs. Fair's head," the paper pointed out as the trial wore on, "and so there were on the head of Daniel McFarland, but he received the tenderest sympathy from members of the bar, not to speak of the consecrated occupants of pulpits . . . In our estimation, McFarland and Mrs. Fair stand on much the same level. If the law could excuse the one from punishment, it would be monstrous to condemn the other."

But the woman who stepped up to the witness box on the eighth day of the trial—setting off a rustling of anticipation among Emily Pitts Stevens and that group of "strong-minded" female spectators in particular—seemed to defy all of the stereotypes currently circulating and present herself as merely a model of dignified and unruffled composure. Under Cook's kind and somewhat avuncular guidance, Mrs. Fair answered an initial series of straightforward questions, speaking in a "loud and determined tone of voice" as she established facts like her age, her various residences, and the circumstances under which she had come to know the deceased. When Cook moved on to the subject of her health, specifically regarding the "difficulty with [her] menses," she maintained her cool demeanor. This topic, of course, was an extremely delicate matter to be discussing in public, especially in a Victorian-era courtroom, but Fair handled it with grave matter-of-factness. Her account of how events had played out on the evening of the shooting, moreover, was a marvel of vivid but dispassionate narration, her descriptions of her distraught mental state becoming vaguer and dreamier as the moment of the crime came closer. ("I know I reached my hand out and touched something cold; that made me remember, and I thought to myself, 'I never put my gloves on yet, for now my hand is wet.' The glass seemed to be wet, and I can remember nothing after that . . .")

She did at times get emotional, when the questioning turned to certain aspects of her affair with Crittenden. There were wistful tears in her eyes when she explained how the deceased had told her that she was the only real wife he had on earth, and that if he had ever committed adultery, it was with Clara, not with Laura. But this tenderness of feeling on Crittenden's part apparently came with a darker side of jealousy too. When, after her return from Havana in early 1868, she mentioned her provisional engagement to the commission agent Mr. Sauers, Crittenden had put the fear of God into her: "He said he would kill any man who married me, and kill me," she admitted. "He had written letters that he would kill any one who came between us."

There was even one moment when Mrs. Fair displayed some of the quick-tempered boldness for which she was notorious. Referring to a snide comment made by prosecutor Campbell a few days earlier about her reputation, she blurted that if Crittenden had been alive to hear the prosecutor insult her in court, "he would have made Mr. Campbell— on his bended knees—apologize for it!"

At this, Emily Pitts Stevens and her entourage burst into applause and foot-stomping. It was likely the tone of Fair's comment, more than its content, that prompted their noisy approval; Fair's alleged impudence was a welcome show of female defiance in this courtroom full of men. But their demonstration of solidarity was too much for Judge Dwinelle to tolerate. "Silence!" the judge shouted to the spectators' enclosure. He demanded that those responsible for the disturbance come forward. Eventually, and reluctantly, Pitts Stevens and another woman made themselves known to the court. The judge promptly fined each of them $25—at which point Fair announced that she would pay both fines. "You will have to draw heavily on your bank account if you pay the fines of all of them," Judge Dwinelle tartly observed, before ordering that she resume her testimony.

When the prosecution took its turn for cross-examination, Alexander Campbell knew exactly what aspect of the defendant's narrative he wanted to emphasize—namely, her subversive and outrageous views on the institution of marriage. The prosecutor did spend some time underlining the defendant's apparent tendencies toward physical violence, reprising the slashing incidents in Virginia City and the night she fired a gun at Crittenden. But it was the social danger she posed to the community that he wanted to really bring out. So when, in the course of answering a question, she again asserted that she was Mr. Crittenden's wife, the prosecutor pounced:

CAMPBELL: I beg your pardon—what did you say?

FAIR: I was Mr. Crittenden's wife.

CAMPBELL: You were?

FAIR: Yes, sir.

CAMPBELL: When were you married to him?

FAIR: Well, God married me to him when we both were born. God made me for him, sir; and he for me.

After asking her for more clarification of that statement, he went on:

CAMPBELL: In other words, you repudiate the ordinary institution of marriage?

FAIR: I do not repudiate it, but I simply say, in the sight of God, standing up before a minister does not always make us married. If we go there with no love, it is not a marriage—in the sight of God, it cannot be.

CAMPBELL: Then as I understand it, you were Mr. Crittenden's wife because you loved him—is that it?

FAIR: Because my very life was bound in his, and his in me. He often said that I was his only wife—the only woman he had ever loved, he said.

This statement, which must have been exceedingly painful for Clara Crittenden to hear, was, of course, shocking to most people present in the courtroom, so Campbell pressed her further.

CAMPBELL: Then your idea is, that if a man is married to a woman he does not like very well, and finds one that he does fall in love with, and who falls in love with him, his marriage is not any marriage—is that it?

Perhaps feeling cornered, the defendant turned somewhat prickly, and tried to emphasize that this was not *her* idea alone:

FAIR: He told me that, the last time I saw him—that I was the only wife he had, and he kissed no other. If you remember, I told you that.

CAMPBELL: I do not wish, of course, to say anything which can be construed as annoying you in any way.

FAIR: [with, one assumes, heavy sarcasm] I know you have been very kind, Mr. Campbell.

Campbell's "kindness" continued for another day and a half of cross-examination, as he tried to paint a picture for the jury of a woman whose actions were consistently manipulative, mercenary, and subversive of societal norms. Fair tried to counteract his efforts, insisting that the letters between herself and Crittenden, if only they could be put in evidence, would corroborate her claim that her love for him was genuine, and that he felt the same way she did. What followed was an extended bout of legal wrangling over whether or not the letters could be or should be admitted. Over two full days of haggling, during which time the opposing attorneys grew downright testy with each other, the defense insisted that the letters were crucial to rebutting the prosecution's contention that Crittenden had been the hapless victim of a shameless seductress. The letters, they insisted, would demonstrate that it was he, not she, who did most of the manipulating, even to the point of thwarting her two desperate attempts to achieve respectability by becoming engaged to—and once even marrying—a more appropriate suitor. The prosecution countered that, as the product of an adulterous affair, the letters were "irrelevant and immaterial." They argued (somewhat illogically) that making the letters public would in essence constitute a second assassination—of Crittenden's character this time rather than of his body—and would give rise to accusations the dead man could not respond to.

Finally, however—perhaps anticipating that the letters might actually help their case more than hurt it, by demonstrating the shamelessness of the victim's mistress—Campbell and Byrne relented, removing their objections and allowing seventy-seven letters and a telegram into evidence. This, of course, meant that the correspondence would be made public and thus available to the press. Appalled by the letters' sensational and sometimes salacious contents, two newspapers—the *Chronicle* and the *Bulletin*—decided to show their outrage by reprinting an extensive selection of the juicier missives ("a rich feast of gushing sentimentality," as the *Chronicle* described it). Meanwhile, the newspapers' readers, equally outraged, proceeded to register their own disapproval by reading every single one of them, to the Crittenden family's acute mortification.

On Tuesday, April 11, after nine full days of defense testimony, Cook and Quint rested their case and the rebuttal witnesses for the prosecution could be heard. Clara Crittenden was recalled to the stand in order to contest the defendant's version of their various encounters over the years. This was when Clara gave her account of their first meeting at the Occidental Hotel in 1864, during which (according to

Clara) the younger woman kissed her hand in gratitude for agreeing to meet with her. "Mrs. Fair's eyes blazed in fury" at this, the *San Francisco Chronicle* reported, and her outburst of "That's a lie!" created such a sensation in the courtroom that the proceedings had to be paused for several minutes before order was restored. And although Emily Pitts Stevens and the other suffragists apparently escaped punishment this time around, Laura herself was ultimately fined $250 for what Judge Dwinelle described as a "gross insult" and a "contempt of Court."

At this point, prosecutors Campbell and Byrne made what would prove to be a big mistake in their case, calling a series of witnesses to testify to Laura Fair's general reputation in the community. Cook immediately objected to this tactic, citing several precedents that such testimony cannot be used as rebuttal when the defense has presented no witnesses to the defendant's *good* character. However, Dwinelle overruled the objection and allowed Campbell to go ahead. What followed was a parade of well over a dozen prosecution witnesses, all of whom claimed, ad nauseam, that Laura Fair was widely spoken of as having a bad reputation of one kind or another. It was overall a humiliating experience for the defendant, and of dubious relevance to the question of her sanity at the time of the shooting. Even so, the effect of this copious testimony, much of it from respectable business associates of the deceased and other community elites, could not have been anything but detrimental to the defendant's case.

On Saturday, April 15—the eighteenth day of the trial—the last rebuttal witnesses were heard and closing arguments could begin. In a decision that he would later regret, Judge Dwinelle ruled that the prosecution would give the first and last statements to the jury, sandwiching the two defense statements in between. Cook objected strenuously to this decision, but the judge refused to reconsider. In any case, whatever the order of presentation, each lawyer would be given as much time as he needed to make his final appeal to the jury. Together, in fact, the four closing arguments would end up filling nine entire days of court time (prolixity being considered no vice in a Victorian courtroom).

Campbell, who delivered the first closing, began by making explicit the prosecution's main theme—that this was no ordinary murder trial but rather a kind of referendum on the community. Since the defense of the accused was built on "doctrines and principles which we regard as utterly subversive of all social peace, harmony, order, and decency," it was up to the jury, as representatives of that community, to show the world that such outrages would not be tolerated here. By turns scornful and sarcastic, Campbell ridiculed the notion that Laura Fair had been insane when she pulled the trigger, pointing to her self-assured, unfeminine, and utterly rational demeanor on the stand. This was no insane person, he insisted, and hers was no act of involuntary impulse. Rather it was a brazen assertion by a depraved "outcast from society" of "a new system of morality of her own," one whereby a "woman who takes a fancy to another woman's husband may drag him forth from his home, or murder him if he refuses to go." No, Campbell insisted, the threat to the mores and institutions of civilized society posed by this kind of "free love" doctrine had no place in a courtroom, and certainly should not be used as the excuse for some sham pretense of temporary derangement. Thus, the jury's duty was clear: "That your verdict will be such as to sustain the purity, virtue, and honor of this community, is to me a question of no doubt," Campbell concluded. "I submit this case with confidence [as] to your decision."

The closings of defense attorneys Quint and Cook unfolded over the course of the next six days. Quint, who spoke first, spent a number of hours reading aloud many of the love letters exchanged between the victim and the defendant, all of which, he maintained, provided ample evidence that the two did love each other deeply, and that Crittenden emphatically did not love his wife. This notion that Laura was his "true wife," the lawyer pointed out, was not just some eccentric notion of the defendant's, but one that Crittenden explicitly asserted himself. Thus it was no surprise that Laura had acted as a spouse would, responding with involuntary fierceness to a perceived threat to her marriage. Here Quint cited as precedents those recent court cases—the

Sickles, Cole, and McFarland trials—in which a husband had killed his wife's adulterous lover in a fit of blind outrage, but was eventually acquitted on a plea of temporary insanity. Could not the so-called "unwritten law" excuse a *woman* who likewise lost her reason at such a threat to her home and happiness? And besides, if this idea of temporary insanity was such an outrageous concept, why had the prosecution not produced their own expert witnesses to contradict the defense's experts?

In his own closing statement, which followed directly after Quint's, Elisha Cook pointed to the logical inconsistencies in the narrative that the prosecution had been trying to construct. Why, he asked—if Mrs. Fair did indeed have such a bad reputation—did a man like A. P. Crittenden allow his ultra-respectable wife to dine with her in front of hundreds of witnesses in the Occidental Hotel dining room? Why, if the shooting was premeditated, had Mrs. Fair chosen to murder her lover so publicly, in a place from which it would be impossible to effect an escape, when she'd had every opportunity to do it far from the eyes of any witnesses? And why, if Crittenden had truly decided to abandon Laura and return to his wife, had he rented a room for himself in the very same lodging house as the woman he was supposed to be leaving behind? No, it made no sense. Laura Fair clearly perceived A. P. Crittenden "as her protector, as the only person on earth that she did love." How, except in a fit of madness, could she have killed her only hope of happiness?

Finally, it was Harry Byrne who had the last word, rising again—gingerly, since he had clearly been in pain for much of the trial—to give the prosecution's final statement. Always more an orator than an interrogator, the DA proceeded to fill the next two days with a grandiloquent recitation of the grave stakes hanging on the jury's upcoming decision, supporting his argument with high-flown quotations from Immanuel Kant, Lord Byron, Julius Caesar, Abraham Lincoln, John Locke, and any number of other legal and extralegal authorities. Citing the current case as "the most important trial in the annals of criminal jurisprudence in the United States," Byrne again tied its out-come directly to the welfare of the community, arguing that the de-fense offered by the accused's lawyers "strikes at the very foundation of morality, religion, and of the safety of the land."

The evidence in the case, which he reiterated in great detail, proved that the defendant was hardly an innocent girl succumbing to a se-ducer, but rather an experienced manipulator of men. Employing a tactic common in efforts to marginalize threatening women—one that had been used, consciously or unconsciously, against figures like Mary Ellen Pleasant and the madam Ah Toy—the DA harped on the manly assertiveness evidenced by Mrs. Fair's every action and utterance, not least being the cold-blooded assassination of her lover when duty called him back to his wife and family. This kind of confident authority proved that Laura Fair was no true woman; she was, on the contrary, "the greatest man that ever entered this courtroom." Moving danger-ously close to the edge of absurdity, Byrne went on to pronounce her "a female Hercules," capable of seducing "a regiment of Crittendens," none of whom could resist her carnal attractions. How could this overt menace to civilized society be allowed to go free?

"Why, gentlemen, this community would be struck with a moral earthquake, your whole system of morality would be undermined" if she were declared innocent, he insisted. A guilty verdict was therefore an absolutely necessity: "The demands and exactions of society require it; the tranquility of the community demands it; the reputation which our city bears in the estimation of the civilized world authorizes it."

With that grandiose coda, District Attorney Byrne brought to a close the state's case against Laura D. Fair. For the members of the jury, it marked the culmination of four exhausting weeks of evidence and argument, relieved only by weekly trips to church on Sundays and once, as a special treat, an excursion to Maguire's Opera House to see a performance of *Othello* (a play, as the *Chronicle* slyly noted, in which the title character kills his lover "in a fit of temporary insanity"). But now they would finally have to weigh it all and decide on the defen-

dant's fate. At 3:25 P.M. on Wednesday, April 26—after final instructions from Judge Dwinelle—the twelve men retired to the jury room.
And although it was expected that they would be out for at least a
couple of hours, and many people left the courtroom in anticipation
of a long wait, it didn't take the jury very long at all to reach a verdict.
To everyone's surprise, they were back after only forty minutes of deliberation. Despite hearing weeks of sharply conflicting narratives
about what had happened between A. P. Crittenden and Laura Fair,
the jury apparently had few doubts. Their verdict had been unanimous
on the first ballot: The defendant, foreman B. F. Sterett announced,
had been found guilty of murder in the first degree.

A wave of excitement swept through the packed courtroom as this
verdict was announced. At the defense table, Mrs. Lane and ten-year-
old Lillian burst into tears; even some of the jurors, according to the
Chronicle's reporter, were seen to wipe their eyes, since a sentence of
death in the case was now all but assured. Only the defendant herself
remained impassive, staring dry-eyed and grim-faced—until the jury
was discharged and a sentencing date was set, at which point Mrs. Fair,
the alleged female Hercules, collapsed in a fit of weeping.

24

Neither Saint nor Demon

F OR THOSE INVESTED IN BOLSTERING San Francisco's
reputation as an upright and well-ordered place, the outcome
of the Fair trial was extremely gratifying. The jury's swift verdict
seemed tailor-made to send the desired message, and the country at
large seemed to be receiving it with approval. Within hours of the
trial's conclusion, the reviews (as it were) came pouring in from all
over the nation, and they were predominantly raves. In New York,
that all-important wellspring of capital and commerce, the major
newspapers were virtually unanimous in their support of the jury's
decision. The *New York Times* offered high praise—and on page 1,
no less. "It may not be improper to say that this verdict . . . was not
generally believed possible, nearly everybody expecting the trial to
prove a farce," the paper marveled, adding that "nine-tenths of the
community [here] regard the verdict as just and a proper vindication
of the law."

The local response in San Francisco was equally enthusiastic, at least
to hear the major daily newspapers tell it: According to the *Daily Alta
California,* "The verdict of the jury . . . was a triumph for justice, law,
and morals, and [was] hailed as such by the people." The *Chronicle*
agreed: "Upon the streets, in saloons, in the restaurants, at home in the

parlor and at the dinner table, old and young discuss the verdict and we have yet to hear a single opinion against its justice."

Perhaps the papers' reporters should have been listening more carefully. For while the members of the establishment press may have perceived unanimous civic approval of the verdict, there were many in the city (beyond Emily Pitts Stevens and other suffragists) who felt that Fair had been tried unjustly, and that, given how Crittenden had led her on for so many years, she didn't deserve death for her crime. Several days after the trial, one of the jurors, a wood and coal dealer named Thomas Horabin, told the *Chronicle* that several of his best customers had told him that they were taking their business elsewhere because of the verdict. "I will never buy another lump of coal or stick of wood from you to save your life," one woman said. "You are a heartless, cruel man." And these dissenters would become more numerous as the months passed. "My sympathies are all with the defendant," a Bay Area lawyer and notary named F.L.B. Goodwin claimed in a letter to his sister several months after the trial. "I have been writing some articles to try and shape public opinion, which is beginning to turn in her favor."

As for the Crittenden family, they naturally felt considerable satisfaction with the outcome of the trial, though the shock of the death and the subsequent ordeal of the court case had been grueling for all of them, Clara in particular. "These six months of sorrows, afflictions, and troubles have certainly left their mark upon her," Laura Sanchez said of her mother in a letter to sister Nannie. And while Clara had held up remarkably well in public during the trial, in the privacy of lawyer Campbell's office after hours, she'd often been "totally prostrated," particularly on days when she'd been called on to testify.

Adding to Clara's woes was the fact that their shared tragedy, rather than bringing the family together, seemed instead to be fracturing it along gender lines. The three Crittenden daughters—Laura, Nannie, and Carrie—were standing by their mother and honoring their father's memory. Laura, now thirty-two, was particularly loyal, viewing the family patriarch's seven-year dalliance with "that woman" as merely "one error during a lifetime of all that was good, generous, and noble." Apparently forgetting some of the harsh words she'd previously directed at her "Pa," Laura was now playing the dutiful Victorian daughter. "His name shall always be sacred and revered by me," she told Nannie, "let this world say and think what it may."

The two oldest males of the family, however, were engaging in all sorts of bad behavior in the wake of their father's death. When A.P.'s will was probated shortly after the shooting, it was found that the deceased had left his entire estate to Clara, with no provision for any of the children. The estate, after all, was mired in debt, and as Crittenden frankly admitted in the will, he simply could not provide anything for his seven surviving children. Even so, that didn't prevent James, now thirty years old and a practicing attorney, from commandeering his father's large and expensive law library for his own use. Eventually, Clara was forced to get A.P.'s old associate Solomon Heydenfeldt to send her son a formal letter demanding the library's return. James was instructed to deliver the books directly to the bookstore of Bancroft & Co., where presumably they'd be sold to pay off some of the estate's debts.

And Howard, too, was adding to the family's heartache. Now twenty-six, married, and living in Texas, he had not even come back to California for his father's funeral or the murder trial. Depressed and still debilitated from the gunshot wound he'd suffered at a friend's New Year's Day hunting party in 1859, he'd cut all ties with the family after Clara accused him of dishonoring his late father. "You all need not expect to hear from me for many months and even years," he wrote Clara in a melodramatic farewell letter in 1871. "I trust, dear Mother, that some years hence, when you think that my honor has been restored, that we may meet; until then I fear we will not see each other. From today, the past is buried."

But while the various Crittendens may have been eager to put the whole Laura Fair matter behind them, San Francisco—not to mention the nation at large—was not quite done with it yet. For one thing, Fair's lawyers were still doing everything they could to make sure that their client didn't hang. In May, Cook and Quint filed a motion before Judge Dwinelle for a new trial, citing numerous errors in the court's conduct of the case. The defense lawyers also warned that they intended to file an appeal to the state supreme court. Naturally, if this appeal were accepted, the justices would take months to issue a ruling, but Judge Dwinelle decided that he had no choice but to move on with his job until told to do otherwise. On June 3, Dwinelle denied the defense motion for a new trial, claiming that "the case has been very carefully tried" and that "the prisoner has had every advantage that could be given her." He then proceeded to set July 28 as the date on which Mrs. Fair would be "hung by the neck until you shall be dead—and God have mercy upon your soul." According to the *Alta,* there were tears in his eyes as he said this.

"You have got what you want now, haven't you?" a bitter Mrs. Lane told several reporters as she accompanied her grief-stricken daughter from the courtroom. "You have got her hung. It gives you great joy, I hope."

As these legal machinations went on, the public's fascination with the case showed no signs of tapering off. Entrepreneurs tried to capitalize on the interest, selling transcripts of the trial testimony at bookstores and charging admission to see "the only correct likeness of Mrs. Laura D. Fair" on exhibit at Shaw's New Photographic Studio on Kearny Street. Even Benjamin Lyford was taking advantage of his new notoriety as Laura Fair's "doctor"; the enterprising expert witness ran several newspaper ads in the month after the trial, touting his new patented embalming process, which would render cadavers "FIRM AS STONE, WITH COLOR AND EXPRESSION OF LIFE." And the residual obsession with the case was not just local: In June, a man rushed into the New York City coroner's office claiming that he was sent by Jesus Christ to save Laura Fair, whom he insisted was his wife in God's eyes. Whether this was lunacy or satire is unclear.

The object of this universal fascination, far from retiring quietly from the public eye, was actively adding to her notoriety even as she sat on the Gilded Age equivalent of Death Row. In the first of many civil cases generated by the murder trial, Mrs. Fair's second doctor, John Trask, sued her for nonpayment of $2,100 in medical services. When court officers went to the Bank of California to attach the defendant's assets, however, it was discovered that she had no money at all in the bank. Laura, it turned out, had astutely consigned her fortune over to her mother, ostensibly in trust for young Lillian; the hapless Dr. Trask ended up winning a judgment of just $312.50—at which point Fair turned around and sued her mother to get the consigned money back, since Mrs. Lane seemed doggedly reluctant to return it.

Several weeks before the scheduled hanging, Fair's lawyers presented Judge Dwinelle with "new evidence" about alleged misrepresentations by several jurors during voir dire—an issue that, in their opinion, made a new trial necessary. Dwinelle again rejected their petition, but since they had now filed an appeal to the California Supreme Court, the matter was out of his hands. On July 10, Chief Justice A. L. Rhodes of the supreme court issued an indefinite stay of execution, an expected development that would postpone any action until the higher court had made its decision.

Given this reprieve, Laura apparently began making herself at home in her cell—one report even had her busily writing a four-act dramatization of Owen Meredith's verse novel *Lucille*. She was also taking satisfaction in her new fame as an icon of defiant femininity. In fact, renowned anti-suffragist Horace Greeley, the influential editor of the *New York Tribune* (noted for his famous bit of advice to "Go west, young man"), seemed to have adopted Fair as his own personal bête noire. Greeley, an early ally of women's rights advocates, had in recent years turned sour on issues like female suffrage, and he was appalled by "the advanced views of womanhood" espoused by Fair and her supporters. "Those fantastic theories which strip woman of the proverbial attributes of the sex," he wrote in an editorial just after the trial, "can have no other logical result in practice than to reduce woman to the condition of a monster."

Months later, Greeley was still talking about the monster of San Francisco. "The Advanced Female of the Laura Fair type," he wrote in a letter reprinted in the *Golden Age* and in many other newspapers nationwide, "who kills the paramour . . . and gives the lie in open Court to the wife she has doubly widowed, is my pet aversion." By now, Greeley was holding Fair up as a symbol of all "strong-minded women" who aimed to destroy the institution of marriage by asserting their alleged rights. To this, the famed suffragist Elizabeth Cady Stanton had a swift response: "What has that to do with our movement?" she wrote in a follow-up letter to the papers. "There are no Laura Fairs on our platform; the right of suffrage and [that of] shooting are entirely distinct." On the contrary, Stanton insisted, to find the root cause of misdeeds like the Crittenden killing, Greeley need only look in a mirror. "The Mrs. Fairs [of the world] are the product of man's moral code and not of the suffrage movement."

The name of Laura Fair had become so prominent in the ongoing national debate over women's rights that when Stanton came to California on a lecture tour with Susan B. Anthony in July, the two insisted on being taken to visit the now-famous figure in jail. Emily Pitts Stevens was happy to accompany them, and after sitting with the prisoner for over half an hour and hearing her story from her own lips, all three activists were livid. "Mrs. Fair may not have been a saint but she cannot have been a demon," Stanton told a reporter. "The treatment of this woman is an outrage and a disgrace to the city of San Francisco." Pitts Stevens was even more emphatic in her subsequent editorials in the *Pioneer:* "It was A. P. Crittenden, that notorious roué and adulterer, who advanced the unholy doctrine of free love," she pointed out, "as a married man living in open adultery with Mrs. Fair." And yet, "the best of San Francisco society had its arms open for the warm reception of this free-lover," while showing no mercy to his ailing and friendless partner. "Hang this woman," Pitts Stevens concluded, "and the very name of San Francisco will be odious for ages to come!"

The night after this visit to jail—when Susan B. Anthony referred to the Fair case in her lecture, showing sympathy for the condemned woman—the audience at Platt's Hall erupted in hisses and catcalls. Uncowed by this response (and perhaps aware that Laura Fair's mother and ten-year-old daughter were in the audience), Anthony was defiant: "Woman must not depend on the protection of man," she insisted. "[She] must be taught to protect herself, and here I take my stand." But although she didn't show it on stage, the intrepid social reformer was clearly shaken. "Never in all my hard experience have I been under such fire," she wrote in her diary that night. "I never before was so cut down."

Fair's lawyers were also doing their best to defend the beleaguered prisoner. In November they finally got to make their appeal to the state supreme court, which by California law received direct appeals for all criminal cases involving the death penalty. Elisha Cook laid out his strongest arguments for nullifying the verdict, at great length and at great cost to his health, which was noticeably failing. After the briefs were filed, the justices retired to review the case. And then all of those involved—the lawyers, the Crittenden family, and the woman sitting in jail—could only sit back and wait for a decision.

It came the following February, and the ruling was, for many, a shock. The supreme court overturned the results of the first trial, citing two errors by Judge S. H. Dwinelle: First, the judge should not have allowed the prosecution to present the final closing argument before the jury, which was the defense's prerogative; and second, he should not have permitted testimony about the defendant's reputation for chastity, which was both prejudicial and irrelevant to the charge under consideration. The decision in sum: "Judgment reversed and cause remanded for a new trial."

In other words, Laura Fair would get a second chance.

. . .

The second trial of Laura Fair for the murder of A. P. Crittenden began, after numerous postponements, on September 9, 1872. By that time, a number of circumstances surrounding the case had changed. For one, the woman who was to have been executed in July 1871 had ended up outliving half of the lawyers involved in her original trial. Lead defense attorney Elisha Cook had died on December 31 (of "rheumatic gout"), followed two months later by DA Harry Byrne (of Bright's disease). This latter death provided plenty of fodder for anyone cynical about the prosecution's outbursts of moral outrage during the first trial. For when Byrne's estate was probated, it turned out that the man who'd excoriated Laura Fair for her marital misdeeds had committed a few of his own. Byrne had left the impressive sum of $5,000 to a certain Miss Mary Cross from Philadelphia, who appeared to be the late prosecutor's mistress. Then an actress named Matilda Heron arrived from New York to contest this will, claiming to be Byrne's wife whom he'd walked out on eighteen years earlier without ever fully completing divorce proceedings. To add icing to this sumptuous cake of hypocrisy, moreover, the lawyer representing Byrne's estate was none other than Alexander Campbell, the man who had insisted that Laura Fair was a bigamist because of a technical flaw in her divorce from Thomas Grayson. This staunch defender of strict adherence to marriage law now argued that Harry Byrne's failure to finalize a divorce from Heron meant nothing—certainly not that the deceased's unwanted wife was entitled to a claim on the estate as Byrne's widow.

As for the defendant herself, contrary to sensational reports of her alleged death in early April, Laura Fair had recovered enough of her health to appear in court punctually on the first day of the trial, though, according to the *Alta,* she still appeared "pale and emaciated." At her side was her old stalwart, Leander Quint, again assisting in her defense, along with her new lead defense lawyer, N. Greene Curtis. A native

North Carolinian who had come west in the Gold Rush years, Curtis was a respected jurist and former state legislator, causing some observers to express puzzlement that he would take on such a seemingly hopeless case. Doubtless he had been promised a handsome fee by the still-wealthy defendant—though, in light of her history of not paying bills, it was an open question whether he would ever collect. On the other side of the aisle, the redoubtable Alexander Campbell would reprise his role as co-prosecutor, this time assisting Byrne's successor as district attorney, Daniel J. Murphy. These four would again be arguing in the Fifteenth District Court, but before the judge of the Fourteenth District, T. B. Reardon, a veteran California jurist originally from Maryland, since Judge Dwinelle could naturally not return after the flawed first trial.

As expected, the courtroom on the first day of the trial was extremely crowded, though this time the throng consisted largely of potential jurors. Given the extremely high profile of the Fair-Crittenden saga over the past two years, court officers had reckoned that it wouldn't be easy finding jurors who did not have a fixed opinion as to the defendant's guilt or innocence. They had therefore summoned no fewer than four hundred candidates for the voir-dire examinations. And yet even then the task of finding twelve acceptable jurors proved difficult. It would require a full eight days of court time before a complete panel could be seated; some days, not a single juror was selected, despite scores of examinations. Judge Reardon had to resort to some desperate measures: when the initial group of four hundred was exhausted, further calls went out for potential jurors, and anyone failing to answer the summons without an acceptable excuse was fined the stunning sum of $200 (or about $5,000 today).

Finally, on September 17, a twelfth person managed to survive both defense and prosecution challenges and was selected. The jury was now complete, but the consensus—in the newspapers, at least—was that those ultimately chosen were hardly the cream of the crop. As the writer for the *Chronicle* put it, the task of jury selection had been about finding twelve men "willing to confess that they are idiots." What else would you call men with no fixed opinion on a subject that had been discussed obsessively in the press and in offices and homes for months? ("I take the paper but don't read it," one typical juror claimed during voir dire. "I read the headings, that's all," the man admitted. "I'm not much of a reader.") Little wonder that Mark Twain—who was apparently watching this trial closely, though regrettably not writing about it—would soon quip to a friend: "The humorist who invented trial by jury played a colossal joke upon the world . . . A criminal juror must be an intellectual vacuum attached to a melting heart."

By the time the last juror was impaneled, Laura Fair, who had been watching from the defense table, was barely upright in her chair and weeping bitterly—for what precise reason no one knew. Deeming the defendant "ill," DA Murphy (who was probably tempted to do some weeping himself by this point—from frustration) moved for an adjournment. Judge Reardon complied, declaring that the case would resume at ten o'clock the next day, when the prosecution's opening statement would be heard.

The trial that followed played out much the way the first trial had, with many of the same witnesses testifying to many of the same facts. There were, however, a few key differences. For one thing, both prosecution and defense moved things along at a much more rapid pace this time. "There was a general feeling manifested to present the case without unnecessary delay," the *Alta* reported, "and [without] the long, tedious examination and cross-examination on points not material to the main issue." In fact, DA Murphy presented the prosecution's case in a single day. He gave his opening statement and ran through his list of witnesses, all of whom had appeared in the initial trial and given similar testimony, with only the briefest interruptions for cross-examination from lawyers Curtis and Quint. The defense case was not quite as brisk, occupying three and a half days of court time before the judge moved on to rebuttals. But even the notoriously long-winded Dr. Lyford, when called to the stand to describe his patient's physical and mental state before the shooting, was remarkably clear and succinct. And this time, he even remembered what year he had studied medicine at the supposed "Philadelphia University."

And there were other differences besides the speed of the proceedings. With the supreme court's objections in mind, prosecutor Murphy was careful not to repeat Campbell's mistake of bringing the defendant's alleged bad reputation into evidence. And he made sure to put up a series of his own expert medical witnesses (to whom the state of California paid $250 each) to rebut Lyford, Trask, and the defendant's other experts on the temporary-insanity issue. As for the new defense case, Curtis put Laura Fair's mother on the stand (the fact that she had not been called in the first trial had been considered a mistake). True, mother and daughter were not on the best of terms, given their ongoing lawsuit, but Mrs. Lane did give important and highly affecting testimony on the stand. "[Laura] would act very violently," a teary-eyed Mrs. Lane explained, describing her daughter's behavior at times of great stress. "[She would] tear her hair and act as if in frenzy." Mother and doctors had tried to keep Laura's outbursts secret from the neighbors, but there was only so much they could do. "[Laura] would be raving, rambling, tear at her own and my clothes—at one time she tore the window curtains." And although Mrs. Lane had trouble delivering some of her testimony—"At times she could not find her voice, being choked with emotion," the *Chronicle* reported—she was nonetheless able to provide critical evidence about a history of insanity in the Hunt family, as well as Laura's past suicide attempts, threats of violence against her loved ones, and irrational behavior during her "spells."

Perhaps the most significant difference in the defense's strategy this time, however, was Curtis's presentation of a more focused and less alienating image of the defendant. Right from his poignant opening statement begging the jury to be merciful (which apparently moved several of the jurors and spectators to tears), Curtis played up his client's victimhood as an emotionally unstable "dependent child" without any man to protect her. Gone was any sign of the "unwomanly" competence that had enabled her to make her own fortune as an entrepreneur and investor. Instead of that "female Hercules," the person standing before the jury now was an ill and ill-used young woman. She was a victim, an example of "poor, frail, unfortunate humanity"—subject to mental illness even in the best of times, but driven by her circumstances to an explosive and involuntary act of violence. Contrary to Laura's own wishes, Curtis insisted that she not testify this time, lest she contradict this image of passive female helplessness and battered victimhood with any signs of "manly" capability on the stand. And in his closing, Curtis pleaded with the jury to remember the words of "the God-Man of Nazareth" and show forgiveness: "Hasn't she been punished enough [with nearly two years of incarceration]," he asked. "San Francisco, with its great throbbing heart and its great interests . . . does not demand her blood."

Was this true? Had San Francisco grown beyond its need to make an example of an obviously disturbed and beleaguered woman? Were Elizabeth Cady Stanton and Emily Pitts Stevens perhaps right when they warned that hanging Laura Fair would disgrace the city, hurting rather than helping its reputation in the wider world? Somehow, the whole matter looked a little different with the hindsight of an extra year and a half. As Curtis pointed out in his opening and closing statements: The prosecution's point had been made; the outrage of the community—which had been "understandable and natural" in the heat of the moment—had found adequate expression in the earlier verdict. But the city had since moved on. "There are other and more vital interests occupying the attention of the citizens of this great city today," he insisted. The defendant's mind in this case had clearly been "crazed by the man who had her in his grasp." So wasn't the important thing now for the community to put aside its outrage and make sure "that disease shall not be mistaken for and punished as crime"?

This was the question that the jurors now had to decide—and they apparently found it a more difficult one than their predecessors had. On Friday, September 27, Judge Reardon gave them their final instructions and the panel retired to deliberate. But unlike the first jury, they did not return within an hour. Nor did they return later that day, or the next. At one point, the full twelve filed back into the courtroom, but only to ask for further instructions from the judge about the burden of proof for insanity. Reardon answered their question and immediately sent them back to deliberations. But even then there was no ready decision. Rumors began flying—that the jury was hopelessly deadlocked; that two disagreeing jurors had almost come to blows in the locked deliberation room. There was even one report that a two-gallon jug of whiskey provided for the jury's comfort had been stolen. According to the *Alta,* "Threats were made against the thief, if he ever should be caught."

Finally, more than sixty-four hours after deliberations had begun, the panel of twelve reappeared—at 9 A.M. on the following Monday— at which point almost everyone believed that they would report themselves at a hopeless impasse. But the foreman, H. W. Byington, claimed that the jury had indeed reached a verdict. He handed a slip of paper to the clerk of the court, who took it to Judge Reardon. The judge read the paper, then handed it back to the clerk and instructed the defendant to rise.

When the clerk read the words on that paper aloud, Laura Fair— amid a general commotion in the courtroom—moaned aloud and collapsed into the arms of her lawyer.

25

The Lady Triumphs

MURDER LICENSED

The Crittenden Tragedy Ends in Jury Farce

The most remarkable, surprising, and outrageous verdict ever pronounced in a criminal case was that rendered yesterday in the case of Laura D. Fair for the murder of Alexander P. Crittenden . . .

—*The Daily Alta California*

THE *ALTA*'S INCREDULOUS REACTION was typical of the overall press response to the Crittenden jury's verdict of not guilty. Although the *San Francisco Examiner* and one or two other papers praised the jurors' reluctance to condemn a woman to hang, the *Chronicle,* the *Bulletin,* and most other major California dailies were appalled that Laura Fair would now be free to walk the streets without any consequences at all for her actions. Like many ordinary San Franciscans whose anger toward the defendant had cooled in the months between the two trials, the editorial writers insisted that they would have been content to see the convicted woman spared the noose, as long as she was given some lesser punishment—life in prison, say, or else confinement in a mental institution. Even a mistrial resulting from a deadlocked jury would have been an acceptable, if less than satisfying, outcome. But total exoneration was a travesty, and precisely the wrong message the city wanted to send to the world.

"By the first trial and its result," the *Alta* maintained, "the State of

California and the city of San Francisco rose abroad in public estimation a hundred percent . . . Thousands began to think that the old stories of lawlessness and crime were figments of the imagination, or
things of the dead past. But now! Who after this can look the world in
the face and say one word in favor of our criminal laws, courts, trials,
or of the public morals, which in and out of courts permits a whole
people to be disgraced?"

And sure enough, the city's reputation was already paying the price.
Newspapers nationwide expressed their disgust with the jury's verdict.
"The result is nothing less than a most ridiculous and shameful miscar-
riage of justice," sputtered the *New York Times,* noting that the acquittal
"turns loose upon society a woman who has outraged nearly all the
fundamental principles on which society rests." The *Dallas Weekly Herald* put it more bluntly: "The jury in her case were not even hung,
although they ought to be. There is now encouragement held out to
every dissolute woman to kill her paramour when he deserts her."

The general impression was that the "marvelously ignorant San
Francisco jury," as the *Times* called it, had been duped. Made up entirely
of men ignorant enough to survive defense challenges during voir dire,
the jury had been easy prey for the defendant's lawyers, falling for their
flat-out false depiction of Fair as helpless, dependent, and temporarily
insane. And it *was* true that Curtis and Quint had cleverly given the
jurors an easy narrative to swallow—of a weak and sickly woman ma-
nipulated by a powerful man who eventually received his just deserts.
Thus convinced that "it served him right," the jurors could then justify
acquitting his murderer as an appropriate response, as "a revolt against
the looseness of living which had long been condoned by a too tolerant community." The defense narrative, in other words, allowed the
jurors to feel that they were expressing the community's moral outrage
by freeing, rather than hanging, the defendant—excusing a woman
who, in a moment of uncontrollable impulse, punished a libertine for
his inexcusable behavior.

But most observers outside the courtroom did not buy this image of Laura as victim. And indeed, "the Fair Lunatic," as the *Chronicle*'s headline-writer began calling her, was soon showing little resemblance to the figure of feminine frailty and vulnerability conjured by her lawyers. Granted, her "spells" and bouts of so-called hysteria did not disappear immediately. At the county jail, where she was taken immediately after the verdict (and where her appearance set off an exuberant celebration among the prisoners, who created "the most infernal din ever heard in a prison or outside of it"), Mrs. Fair reportedly succumbed to another swoon that left her debilitated for several hours. But her health—both mental and physical—seemed to improve steadily after her release. Soon she was being seen out and about in downtown San Francisco, taking care of various bits of unfinished business. Even rumors that the always volatile James Crittenden, eager to avenge his late father's death, was threatening to gun her down in the streets did not deter her from venturing back into the world.

Contrary to her lawyers' promises that the defendant, if acquitted, would quietly leave the city and "return to her native land" (New Orleans), the freed prisoner seemed to have no plans to slink away in shame. Reverting to her old brazen, "unwomanly" ways, she sued a cartoonist who had created a satirical poster about the trial, and even demanded that authorities return the pistol she'd used to shoot her lover. Apparently she succeeded in the latter effort, for there were soon reports of her traveling on the San Francisco streetcars, "looking defiance" at anyone who glanced her way, while the handle of that very same pistol peeped conspicuously out of her pocket. In one incident described in the *Chronicle* just weeks after her acquittal, Mrs. Fair was observed on one of the cars of the North Beach and Mission Railroad, angrily scolding the conductor for not stopping at the corner where she wanted to get off. "I suppose nowadays to stop the car," Mrs. Fair sneered, her eyes flashing fire, "a lady must carry and blow a policeman's whistle!" To which the blandly smiling conductor replied, "No necessity for a whistle, madam; just fire off that little memento you are in the habit of carrying and I'll hear you."

Perhaps her most unwomanly affront to Victorian sensibilities, however, was her bold return to the stage—not as an actor this time but as a lecturer. Hoping to clear her name among the lingering doubters (or else to reap the lucrative returns that many lecturers enjoyed at this time), Fair wrote "Wolves in the Fold"—an account of the ways in which she had been persecuted by judges, prosecutors, newspaper publishers, clergymen, and any number of other, mostly male, enemies. This she hoped to present as a public lecture—for a reasonable admission fee—to the people of San Francisco. Consisting of a "calm statement of plain facts," the lecture was intended to "give proof that the base slanders heaped upon me by my revilers and enemies are deliberate, premeditated, and false, from alpha to omega." To supplement her own accounts of episodes like the Virginia City flag incidents and the death of William Fair, she produced affidavits from others— Colonel Fair's stepmother, the clergyman who married them, a Yreka colleague of her late husband's, and so on—all of whom vouched for her respectability, her blamelessness, and her reputation as a "true and pure woman." And she did not stint on striking back, often with dripping sarcasm, at her many hateful ill-wishers, particularly the journalists who had dragged her name through the mire from the very beginning: "These chivalric gentlemen of the press, these courteous, polished, and gallant knights of the quill, have made a most ignoble record for themselves," she wrote. "They lavishly fed public opinion out of the abundance of that mental dross with which they are so prolific . . . They attempted to poison my life with their vindictive wrath; and, true to their generous, noble, and manly instincts, cried out, 'crucify her! crucify her!'"

"Wolves in the Fold," in short, was to be the thorough and impassioned self-defense that N. Greene Curtis would not allow her to make on the stand in the second trial, and so she engaged Platt's Hall for the night of November 21 to make it there. Unfortunately, however, an unruly crowd of some 1,500 people gathered around the hall in the hours before the lecture. According to the *Alta,* they were "not of the

class which usually attends lectures, but rather of the one which pa-
tronizes prize-fights, horse-races, and amusements of that character."
Eventually the crowd grew so menacing that the Platt's owners, who
had already received hate mail and bomb threats, were forced to lock
the doors for fear of a riot. Determined to go on no matter what, Fair
sent to the chief of police for a bodyguard, but her request was refused.
And when the police already on the scene told her that they could not
guarantee her safety if she proceeded to the hall, she wisely canceled
her plans (though she would later sue the music hall—and win).

Undeterred, Fair then tried to reschedule the event for a venue in
Sacramento, where the feeling against her was somewhat less extreme.
But when no local hall would consent to host it, she ended up presenting the lecture in a noisy beer saloon for no charge. Despite the
alcohol-soaked environment, no violence erupted, so she was eventually able to engage Hamilton Hall in Sacramento and Hansel Hall in
Stockton, where she succeeded in speaking her piece to a small but
paying audience. Ultimately, she published the lecture as a two-part
pamphlet, with an added section about the aborted lecture at Platt's
Hall, blaming the editors and owners of the San Francisco press for
inciting the mob against her. But the pamphlet drew little notice from
the public, who seemed to be more interested in the woman herself
than in her claims of innocence, and she ended up losing money on
the publication.

Even after this setback, however, Laura Fair refused to sink into
obscurity. She still had money, for one thing. According to one January
1874 report in the *New York Times* (written by the same "Podgers"
who had taken the early transcontinental train journey with A.P. and
his companions back in 1869), Fair had just realized a $75,000 gain
from the sale of her stock in the Ophir mine. Whether or not this
particular report was true, she apparently was still quite wealthy, and
this was enough to convince at least some people in San Francisco
society that she was worth knowing. "[Mrs. Fair] lives in style, gives
balls, and speculates in stock," one visiting British journalist reported in

1875. "Few ladies are so often named at dinner tables, and the public journals note her doings as the movements of a duchess might be noted in Mayfair."

. . .

One of the people doing the most to keep the ersatz duchess in the public eye was her old neighbor from Virginia City, Mark Twain. Now married and living in Hartford, Connecticut, Twain was prospering, his fame and fortune still on the rise, though not yet near its peak. Although there's no evidence that he ever wrote anything about the Fair trial while it was happening, he had been acutely aware of it. In January 1873 he even decided to adapt Fair's story for *The Gilded Age*, a novel he was writing with his neighbor Charles Dudley Warner. Disgusted by the moral state of the nation in the post-bellum era, Twain and Warner, editor and co-owner of the *Hartford Courant*, intended their book to be "a thoroughgoing exposé of its times." With each writer contributing his share of the ideas, plotlines, and actual writing, the novel aimed to lay bare the widespread corruption and hypocrisy evidenced by recent high-profile scandals like the Credit Mobilier affair and the shocking accusations of adultery leveled against the famous clergyman and social reformer Henry Ward Beecher.

To Twain's mind, the outrage of the Laura Fair verdict was just another manifestation of this overall societal decay. For some years, he had been railing against American juries in general and the insanity plea in particular—most notably in *Roughing It,* his second travel book, which had been published to much acclaim the year before. "The jury system," he'd asserted in that book, "puts a ban upon intelligence and honesty, and a premium upon ignorance, stupidity, and perjury." Now he wanted to illustrate the point by basing one of the novel's two major plot threads on the real-life story of the Crittenden shooting, with a beautiful young woman named Laura Hawkins gunning down her married lover and ultimately being acquitted for the crime on an insanity plea. The book was written and published very quickly, appearing in May 1873, just four months after it was begun. The haste shows in the writing—reviews were mixed to scathing—but the novel ended up selling fairly well. And it was topical enough for one would-be plagiarist (the drama critic for the *Golden Age* newspaper, as it happened) to put on an unauthorized stage adaptation in a San Francisco theater. Twain's lawyers successfully stopped the production, but Twain apparently liked the idea of a theatrical version and soon produced his own adaptation under the title *Colonel Sellers.* The play, which features the fictional Laura shooting her old lover right onstage—and then vacantly uttering, "I have killed the only man I ever loved"—was an immediate hit when it opened on Broadway and went on to spawn many more productions all over the country.

Whether or not the real-life Laura ever saw *Colonel Sellers* is a matter unknown to history; one imagines her and young Lillian boldly striding to their front-row seats at the San Francisco premiere. But the notorious Mrs. Fair's season of triumphant defiance would prove to be fleeting, and her ultimate downfall was tied to that of her fellow San Francisco icon William Ralston. By the mid-1870s, the illustrious city-builder was slipping in the public's esteem, mainly because of some shady dealings involving a water company he'd tried to sell the city at an inflated price. A surprise 1873 audit of the Bank of California's books, meanwhile, revealed that Ralston had secretly lent large sums of the bank's money to three of his own private ventures, with no security provided to back the loans. But it took a local stock market collapse in late August 1875 to finally bring the hopelessly overextended Ralston down. To his horror, he took the Bank of California with him. The bank's failure was a scandal that shocked the entire city, but residents didn't have much time to revile the man responsible for it. After a touching and penitent farewell address to his suddenly jobless employees on August 27, Ralston went out for his daily swim from the Neptune Bath House in North Beach. A few hours later, his body was found floating in the bay. Naturally, many people suspected suicide, though an inquest and autopsy revealed evidence of an apoplectic stroke. Whatever the case, it was a suitably ambiguous end for an often morally ambiguous figure. But as his old friend William Tecumseh Sherman would later say of him: "No matter what he has done, I hope he has gone to Heaven. He did so much for your city."

(A final irony: Sherman made this statement on a return visit to the city in 1876, addressing a crowd from his balcony at the Palace Hotel, the vastly expensive project that had played a large role in Ralston's financial ruin. The hotel had opened with great fanfare just two months after its builder's death—and quickly became the latest symbol of San Francisco's arrival as a world city.)

With the failure of the Bank of California came the demise of Laura Fair's fortune, which had always been inextricably tied up with Ralston's affairs. And so the once-destitute woman became destitute again. Even in her newly reduced circumstances, however, she still found it difficult to stop dabbling in stocks, since she was soon being sued by a certain Lizzie C. Adams for $1,200—money advanced to Fair as an agent to buy Imperial mining stock. By mid-April 1877, beholden to over two dozen creditors, including the defense lawyer who had arguably kept her from the gallows, she was forced to declare bankruptcy. By then her stated assets were worth far less than the $21,334.66 she owed, and her days of throwing stylish balls were over.

But while Laura Fair essentially left the public eye at this point, the significance of her ill-fated life remained a source of contention for years afterward. Was this woman, as many believed, a reckless and amoral threat to society—a remnant of the old Wild West days that San Francisco hoped were well behind it? Or was she a victim of misfortune, prejudice, and exploitation, pushed by her thwarted ambitions and her own personal demons to commit an unspeakable act of violence? The answer depended largely on the perspective of the person asked. Perhaps all that can be said for certain is that Laura Fair did what she deemed necessary, however misguided, to further her goal of a secure and respectable existence for herself and her orphaned child, despite adversity and betrayal by the man she loved. Her own final words in "Wolves in the Fold" would prove apt: "We have, all of us, immense desires . . . But Ah! what limitations to our desires. We are creatures of circumstance. We must, then, endure our destiny as allotted to us; and whatever that is (darkness or sunshine, calms or tempests), accept it without murmur or complaint, as the inevitable."

Epilogue

The New York of the West

Marvelous has been the growth of San Francisco. Its story reads like a chapter from the "Arabian Nights." Yesterday a dreary waste of sand—today a city of a quarter of a million souls, with an aggregate wealth of five hundred millions. The men who laid its foundations—who were present at its birth and christening—are hardly past the prime of life.

—Samuel Williams

On July 4, 1876, 200,000 people from all over Northern California thronged the streets of San Francisco for what the *Daily Alta California* called "the most imposing pageant yet witnessed in our city"—the Centennial Fourth of July celebration. "The city seemed almost smothered with flags, bunting, and other gay decorations," the paper gushed. "Never, since the triumphal entrance of the Caesars into Rome, has there been such a magnificent display of decorations—and probably not then."

The *Alta*'s reporter may have been guilty of a bit of hyperbole, but there was indeed a special feeling to the day's celebration in San Francisco. For while every other city in the country was commemorating just the hundredth anniversary of the Declaration of Independence, San Francisco was also marking the centennial of its own founding. It was on June 29 of 1776 that Father Francisco Palou conducted the Mass that established the Mission of San Francisco of Assisi, aka Mission Dolores, the first colonial settlement on the site of the future metropolis.

To say that the city had come a long way in that century would be a ridiculous understatement. From virtually nothing, it had grown to a community of over 200,000 people—the tenth largest in the nation and "the commercial metropolis of the Pacific coast," producing 60 percent of the entire region's manufactured goods. And most of that growth had occurred over the span of just three decades. As *Scribner's* magazine declared in 1875, "The stranger . . . will find it difficult to realize that he is in a city only a quarter of a century old." True, the dives and brothels of the Barbary Coast neighborhood were still a blot on the city's escutcheon, and one still heard complaints from visitors about the relative lack of parks, gardens, and other public open spaces within the very businesslike city. One particular foreign visitor— Anthony Trollope, who traveled through in September 1875—had in fact been profoundly unimpressed with the whole town: "I don't know that in all my travels I ever visited a city less interesting to the normal tourist," the novelist wrote. "There is almost nothing to see in San Francisco that is worth seeing."

And yet the city was ahead of its time in other ways. The first of San Francisco's distinctive cable-car lines, for instance, was already running up and down the virtual ski slope that was Clay Street. The brainchild of an engineer named Andrew Hallidie, the car line employed a woven-wire rope technology that Hallidie had initially invented to convey heavy ore skips around the mountainous mining districts; now he used the same idea to address San Francisco's need for steep-uphill public transportation. The Clay Street cable cars quickly opened up Nob Hill, a previously impractical section of the city, to upscale development. It proved to be a perfect neighborhood for the city's new class of railroad and mining multimillionaires, who soon built megamansions atop the hill from which they could look down upon the more modest dwellings of the hoi polloi below.

Many of the well-known neighborhoods of today—Haight-Ashbury, Eureka Valley—were still largely agricultural, but more central areas like the Western Addition and the Mission District were growing increasingly dense to accommodate the incoming population. And the downtown areas closest to the bay shore—a sea of shacks, shanties, and tents just thirty years earlier—now had the look of a centuries-old metropolis. "It is New York," writer Helen Hunt Jackson remarked upon first seeing downtown San Francisco in the 1870s, "a little lower of story, narrower of street, and stiller, perhaps. Have I crossed the continent only to land in Lower Broadway on a dull day?"

And yet this awkward adolescent city was already outstripping even New York in certain civic improvements, like the electrification of its streets. That very Independence Day, a one-block stretch of Market Street was illuminated by electric lights for the very first time—the pet project of Jesuit science professor Joseph Neri of the Saint Ignatius Church. Father Neri's groundbreaking demonstration of arc-light technology would soon prompt San Francisco to build the country's first central electricity-generating station, distributing power to businesses, theaters, and hotels in the main downtown area, years before Thomas Edison would do the same for New York City.

Under Father Neri's three buzzing arc lights on Market Street—shedding a "startling white radiance" even in the daytime—there now passed some ten thousand Independence Day marchers. The parade began with an advance group of dignitaries, including the first and the present governors of California, various high-ranking military officers, consuls from a score of foreign nations, and a number of local luminaries, including Andrew Hallidie himself. Then came several regiments of National Guardsmen, followed by a full sixteen divisions of assorted societies, organizations, and clubs representing a range of the nationalities and ethnicities that had helped to build the city over the past century. These included such groups as the Sons of the Emerald Isle, the Lodge of Orangemen, the Ancient Order of Hibernians, German Dragoons, the Garibaldi Guard, Swiss Sharpshooters, the Scandinavian Society, and the Portuguese Benevolent Association. Noticeably underrepresented were non-white populations, which had played a large role in the city's history but, for some, did not fit comfortably into its new conception of itself. Black Americans were represented by a single group—the Young Men's Union Benevolent Society—escorted by an eight-person Centennial Guard. Marching groups of Chinese or Latin American societies were nowhere in evidence. And as for Native Americans, they were "honored" by a large contingent from the Improved Order of Redmen, the oldest fraternal organization in the country, consisting entirely of white men.

The irony of this last group's name should have been painfully evident, given that the state and federal governments had been systematically trying to eliminate California's Indigenous populations for decades, most recently in the so-called Modoc War of 1872–1873. The dearth of Latin American marchers was similarly emblematic of attempts by this new, forward-looking metropolis to erase inconvenient aspects of its past. Meanwhile, Black participation in the city's Independence Day celebrations, as Bret Harte had pointed out some years earlier, typically faced fierce opposition from segments of the city's Irish and southern populations, perhaps explaining the merely token representation of African Americans in that day's parade. But the total absence of Chinese marchers was no surprise. Conflict between white and Chinese laborers had only intensified in recent years, as the state suffered under a 25 percent labor unemployment rate and anti-Chinese rallies erupted all over the region. Any official Chinese presence in the parade would likely have resulted in violence.

It was Harte—the "Pacific Coast's conscience"—who had most tellingly exposed this rising tide of anti-Asian sentiment in California. Sometime in late 1870 (shortly before Laura Fair shot her lover), Harte had written a brief satiric poem called "Plain Language from Truthful James." Better known as "The Heathen Chinee," the poem tells the story of a Chinese immigrant named Ah Sin who successfully outswindles a pair of would-be cardsharps in a game of euchre. A negligible bit of doggerel that Harte published in the *Overland Monthly* mainly to fill some column inches, the little lyric proceeded to do the nineteenth-century equivalent of going viral. Picked up and reprinted by newspapers nationwide, "The Heathen Chinee" became a phenomenon, quoted on the floor of Congress and parodied countless times (including once as "The Heathen Greelee," mocking Horace Greeley's 1872 presidential ambitions). But although the poem was intended by Harte as a satire of the anti-Chinese prejudices of Irish laborers, many people read the poem as satirizing the Chinese themselves—a misreading that just emphasized the widespread prejudice that Harte was lampooning.

Misinterpreted or not, "The Heathen Chinee" is what ultimately led to Harte's abandonment of the city whose literary culture he more or less put on the map. Flooded with offers of employment from eastern publications in the wake of the poem's extraordinary popularity, Harte soon decided it was time to follow the example of his friend Twain and head east. In February 1871, he left San Francisco for good. And although his career never reached its potential in the East ("Like a transplanted piñon tree," as one of his biographers put it, "he failed to take root and flourish in unfamiliar soil"), it was probably time for him to move on in any case. The new incarnation of San Francisco was of little interest to the writer. Shortly before his departure, in turning down an offer from the *New York Tribune* to be its California correspondent, Harte had complained about the city of the 1870s: "Society [here], as it has gained in respectability, . . . has lost in picturesqueness, and differs now but little from that of most American second-rate towns."

And Harte may have been right, at least judging by the homogenous, socially regimented parade on that Fourth of July in 1876. San Francisco's elites had in many ways created the city they wanted—an orderly place where men were men, women were submissive, and those holding the reins of wealth and power were almost exclusively white males. In other words, a respectable Victorian metropolis.

• • •

Even so, this unique city still was—and always would be—a magnet for border-crossers, mavericks, eccentrics, and nonconformists of all types, despite efforts to enforce strict social norms. And while some of its resident "social outlaws," like cross-dresser Jeanne Bonnet, came to bad ends, others had happier outcomes. Ah Toy, for instance—the Chinese madam who had gone from being a frequent plaintiff in the city's courtrooms in the 1850s to being a frequent defendant in the 1860s—apparently retired from the profession around 1871. Though she largely disappears from the historical record after this, it's known that she moved to San Jose and married a wealthy Chinese man named One Ho around this time. She thus avoided being directly affected by the passage of several federal laws in the 1870s, like the Page Act of 1875, specifically targeting Chinese prostitution and immigration. After the death of her husband around the turn of the century, Ah Toy moved to a small cottage in Alviso, a waterfront district in San Jose. Here, according to the *Oakland Tribune,* she kept house for her late husband's brother and sold clams to tourists and yachting parties, to whom she was condescendingly known as "China Mary." She died on February 1, 1928—three months before her one hundredth birthday.

Moy Jin Mun, the former gardener for Leland Stanford who later became a miner, was less insulated from the rising tide of anti-Chinese sentiment. During one of many anti-Chinese riots that erupted in the mid- to late 1870s, Moy was nearly caught and killed by a roving band of Irish union members in Truckee, Nevada, saved only by a friendly Irish policeman who sheltered him in his own home until the violence abated. Sometime later, after trying his hand at farming for a few years, Moy returned to San Francisco and opened an import-export emporium on Dupont Street (now Grant Avenue) with his wife, whom he finally retrieved from China in 1881, just before the first federal Chinese Exclusion Act of 1882 virtually ended Chinese immigration. Moy's Dupont Street business prospered, and, along with his work as a government translator and interpreter, ultimately made him wealthier than gold mining ever had. Eventually, he became a leader of the Chinese Six Companies and the Chinese Peace Association, acting as a mediator with the warring triads of Chinatown whenever conflict broke out among them. At one point, he even became co-owner of Shanghai Low, the San Francisco nightclub where Orson Welles would later film much of *The Lady from Shanghai*. And although he was all but ruined in the 1929 stock market crash, Moy remained such a prominent fixture in the city's Chinese community that when he died in 1936 at the age of eighty-six, he was eulogized as "unofficially the 'mayor' of Chinatown."

•   •   •

For the rest of Mary Ellen Pleasant's lifetime, her standing as an influential and financially thriving African American woman continued to be difficult for most white San Franciscans to accept. Though her political activism seems to have waned after the streetcar campaigns of the 1860s, she continued to promote the local Black community by acting as a kind of employment agent for new arrivals in town and contributing money to nascent Black-owned businesses and institutions. Thanks in part to her unusual partnership with the banker Thomas Bell, she was apparently making plenty of money on her investments, which she used to buy and build on property both in and out of town. Most lavish of all was the opulent ten-room Victorian mansion on the corner of Octavia and Bush Streets, which she co-occupied with Bell once it was completed in 1879. This living arrangement, as we've seen, excited much indignation and comment, and eventually there were all kinds of fantastic rumors circulating about goings-on in the so-called House of Mystery. Plausibility was no requirement for these stories: "As Voodoo Queen," one supposed witness told a latter-day researcher, "Mammy held horrible orgies in the basement at Octavia Street. They [that is, the participants] sang Voodoo songs while Mammy stood on a box with a snake in it and made the calls."

Such nonsense aside, Pleasant admittedly did much to contribute to her own notoriety among San Franciscans, often playing into stereotypes as either an unthreatening mammy or a dangerous sorceress whenever it served her interests. ("I am a whole theater in myself," she once admitted.) At one point in the 1890s she was prominently involved in four simultaneous court cases, including one in which a protégée of hers sued the former banker William Sharon, now a U.S. senator, for adultery, claiming to be his secret wife.

Then, one night in October 1892, Thomas Bell tumbled to his death down the stairs at the Octavia Street mansion. The rumor mills instantly went into overdrive. Pleasant was, of course, accused of having thrown Bell down the steps herself, and there were any number of alleged witnesses willing to relate their version of the tale to eager listeners.

The accusations were never proved or even taken seriously by police. But since her business affairs were so entangled with those of her late partner, Pleasant did lose much of her fortune in the financial wrangling that followed Bell's death and the challenging of his will. Eventually, she was evicted from the Octavia Street mansion she herself had built. In fact, the Bell estate was still not settled by the time Pleasant died in 1904 at the age of eighty-nine—still hating the name "Mammy" that clung to her legend. ("Listen," she told an interviewer late in life, "I don't like to be called Mammy by everybody. Put that down. I'm not mammy to everybody in California.") Today San Francisco remembers her more respectfully as a civil rights pioneer, with a memorial park named in her honor on the site of her old Octavia Street mansion, featuring a line of tall eucalyptus trees and a plaque honoring the "Mother of Civil Rights in California." Since 1964, moreover, her gravestone—as she requested on her deathbed—identifies her as "A Friend of John Brown."

· · ·

As for Laura D. Fair, she never returned to her native South as promised during her trials, but instead remained a resident of the city she had outraged for the rest of her days. For several years, up until Clara

Crittenden's death from apoplexy in 1881, she even had the temerity to live just a few blocks away from the woman she had made into a widow. She suffered no lasting consequences regarding her alleged bout of temporary insanity in 1870, and was permitted to reside in the community free of probation or any other kind of official supervision—something that infuriated many people, both in California and across the country. In the years following Fair's acquittal, in fact, many state supreme courts ruled to disallow or at least restrict the use of the insanity defense that had secured her acquittal; in latter days, it has become a rare, and even more rarely successful, defense tactic in American courtrooms.

After her bankruptcy in 1877, however, Fair was never able to recover her former financial position, although not for lack of trying. She even made another attempt at a lecture tour in 1879. Traveling to New York and several other eastern cities, she was able to successfully deliver her new lecture, "Chips from California" (a "sharp, sarcastic, and bitter" performance, according to the *Alta*), to sizable audiences and generally good, if somewhat condescending, reviews. The most quoted line from the lecture was characteristically provocative: "The woman in San Francisco who has not some scandal sticking to her skirts," Fair proclaimed, "is as hard to find as a white blackbird or an honest New York politician."

Information as to her doings after this lecture tour is spotty, but she appears to have lived on in reduced circumstances, making the papers every so often on a slow news day. It's hard to know how much in these articles is fact and how much is purely fanciful. One piece in the *Reno Weekly Gazette* in 1879, later picked up by the *Alta,* reported that Fair had invented some kind of improved baby carriage, the patent for which she'd sold to an eastern firm for $14,000 (almost certainly false); another article, in the *Santa Cruz Weekly Sentinel* in 1882, claimed that she had been thrown down the stairs of her daughter Lillian's home by the latter's drunken husband, A. W. Hines (perhaps more plausible, alas). After that, the notices were mainly reports of Laura Fair sightings on the street—usually remarking on how much she had aged—or else anniversary rehashes of the 1870 shooting, typically with a few major details wrong. One error-filled article even had Fair shooting *James* Crittenden instead of his father.

Despite her much-discussed chronic ill health, Fair survived for many more years, long enough to see San Francisco lose much of its old "ingenuous charm," as one longtime resident put it in the 1890s, in favor of a "new cosmopolitanism" patterned on that of New York. Fair lived on to witness many of the more notable developments in the city's latter-day history, including an epidemic of bubonic plague in Chinatown, the inauguration of the Pacific cable between San Francisco and Honolulu, and the invention by assorted San Franciscans of everything from chop suey to the Murphy bed to the poem "Casey at the Bat." She hung on long enough to see the now-great city destroyed by the earthquake and fire of 1906, and to witness its second bout of explosive (re)growth. And this onetime icon of women's rights even lived to see the culmination of the suffragists' work—the passage of the Nineteenth Amendment, granting women the right to vote. In fact, this "most notorious woman in California history" ended up outlasting her mother, her daughter, and virtually all of her countless enemies, dying of heart failure at the age of eighty-two in October 1919 at her home on Market Street. At her death, her entire estate consisted of just $1,100 in a savings account—at San Francisco's Bank of Italy (precursor of the Bank of America), an institution she apparently trusted more than the revived Bank of California, which had ruined her.

Notes

xvii   **"I kiss no other . . ."** All quotations and subjective thoughts or feelings in this prologue as reported in Laura Fair's own testimony at her first trial. Marsh and Osbourne, *Official Report,* 105–107. Other details from the testimony of Fair's landlady, Mrs. Marillier, in *Official Report,* 64–65.

1   **"At ten minutes to ten . . ."** As quoted in Marsh and Osbourne, *Official Report,* 2.

1   **a brisk, cloudless spring morning . . .** San Francisco weather as per the *Daily Alta California* (hereafter DAC) of March 28, 1871. The main sources for the trial details are the local newspapers and the trial transcript as published in the *Official Report* by court stenographers Marsh and Osbourne.

2   **The man principally responsible . . .** Shuck, *History of the Bench and Bar,* 442–445.

3   **"I think any man who acts that way . . ."** Marsh and Osbourne, *Official Report,* 4.

4   **"Her expression . . ."** Marsh and Osbourne, *Official Report,* 2.

4   **"That, gentlemen . . . is substantially the case . . ."** Marsh and Osbourne, *Official Report,* 6–7; see also *Sacramento Daily Union* (hereafter SDU), March 29, 1871.

4   **gender was still enough of a novelty . . .** For the small percentage of female defendants in California courts at this time, see Haber, *Trials of Laura Fair,* 277 (*n*16); for women and the public sphere, *Trials of Laura Fair,* 3.

6   **"the most important case . . ."** Marsh and Osbourne, *Official Report,* 295.

9   **one of the most distinguished and reputable families:** Genealogy of the Crittendens and career of John J. as per Eubank, *Shadow of the Patriarch,* ix, 1–2; see also https://www.familysearch.org/tree/person/details/G9TR-2Z8/.

10   **Thomas T. Crittenden . . .** CFP, Box 1, Folder 2; Find a Grave, database and images (https://www.findagrave.com/memorial/188613427/thomas-turpin -crittenden: accessed 14 April 2022)/.

10   **precarious amounts of debt . . .** CFP, Box 1, Folder 45.

10   **cobbling together an education** . . . Crittenden's education as per his hand-written entry in "Biography of the First California Legislature" (http://www
.archive.org/details/biographyoffirst00sacr), original in California State Library;
see also DAC obituary for Crittenden, November 6, 1870.

10   **"You are the kind of material . . ."** Shuck, *History of the Bench and Bar,* 403.

10   **army life proved to be incompatible** . . . Copy of his military record in Crit-tenden Family Miscellany, 1862–1874 (CFM), Society of California Pioneers Ar-chives.

11   **Clara Jones** . . . For details about Clara's family, see https://www.familysearch
.org/tree/pedigree/landscape/LYHK-RRK (NB: Clara would ultimately have
twelve siblings); handsome, intelligent, talkative . . . CFP, Box 1, Folder 38;
"Imagine all the affection . . ." Crittenden's love letters to Clara, CFP, Box 1,
Folders 16 and 17.

11   **Clara was hesitant** . . . CFP, Box 1, Folders 27, 43; "Knowing you are fond . . ."
CFP, Box 1, Folder 27; "poor lovesick swain" . . . Box 1, Folder 45; "he never has
and never . . ." CFP, Box 1, Folder 21. For their exact wedding date, see Box 7,
Folder 70.

12   **Texas seemed to offer an ideal opportunity** . . . "I want to become a great
statesman . . ." letter reprinted in Willett, *Texas That Might Have Been,*132;
"Where there is neither law nor gospel" . . . CFP, Box 1, Folder 51; fourteen
children . . . Finding Aid for Crittenden Family Papers, 2.

12   **getting help from some old family friends** . . . Hay, *Papers of Henry Clay,* 481.
(Thanks to the National Archives for supplying a scan of the complete handwrit-ten letter.) "Money, you may recollect . . ." as quoted in Willett, *Texas That Might
Have Been,* 102.

14   **"Keep up your spirits, old lady . . ."** CFP, Box 1, Folder 60.

14   **Official mail service was nonexistent** . . . For mail delivery generally, and the
specific route of this one letter, see Marvin, "Special Delivery," 36–37.

14   **Crittenden's own journey** . . . "The heat has been trying" and other details of
Crittenden's trip across Texas from CFP, Box 1, Folder 63.

15   **"It would remind you . . ."** . . . distinctly more exotic CFP, Box 1, Folder 61;
"We are now in the region . . ." CFP, Box 2, Folder 3.

15   **droll observations and anecdotes** . . . "We traveled for a day or two . . ." and
"The Comanches are the beauties . . ." CFP, Box 1, Folders 61 and 62.

16   **"The greatest source of misery . . ."** CFP, Box 1, Folder 62.

16   **"There was no alternative . . ."** CFP, Box 2, Folder 1.

16   **"desperate fight"** . . . CFP, Box 2, Folder 3.

17   **"I am in most excellent health . . ."** CFP, Box 2, Folder 5.

17   **an old West Point friend** . . . The story of meeting Coutts and APC's early
political career, see Shuck, *History of the Bench and Bar,* 402–404. "Where every-thing was in a ferment . . ." CFP, Box 2, Folder 20.

18   **a mere 258 votes** . . . See Tennis, "California's First State Election," 357–398.
For other election info, see www.joincalifornia.com.

18   **a seventy-five-passenger schooner** . . . CFP, Box 2, Folder 6.

19   **"an odd place . . ."** Lotchin, *From Hamlet to City,* 291.

19   **assorted communities of Ohlone** . . . Solnit, *Infinite City,* 13; Pfaelzer, *Slave
State,* 31–38. "Instead of finding a country . . ." Browning, *San Francisco Yerba*

Buena, 50. Borrowed boat and gunpowder . . . Browning, *San Francisco Yerba Buena,* 55–56, 80.

20   **confiscated from the Franciscans** . . . Godfrey, *Neighborhoods in Transition,* 56; "What a country this would be . . ." Dana, *Two Years Before the Mast,* 237.

21   **a British seaman named William Richardson** . . . See Browning, *San Francisco Yerba Buena,* 102–106, and Byington, *History of San Francisco,* 80–83; Mission Dolores closed as church, Presidio abandoned . . . Richards, *Historic,* 37.

21   **"The country will fall into other hands . . ."** Browning, *San Francisco Yerba Buena,* 93.

22   **the natural entrepôt of the region** . . . The literature on the Gold Rush is vast, and the subject is too well covered to be discussed at length here. The best first-person accounts I found are the famous Bayard Taylor book (*El Dorado: or, Adventures in the Path of Empire*) and the lesser-known but equally vivid *Three Years in California* by Englishman John David Borthwick.

22   **"grown out of the Mexican pueblo . . ."** As quoted in Barker, *Eyewitness,* 1; "I can hardly give you any description . . ." CFP, Box 2, Folder 6.

22   **the vast majority of buildings** . . . Customhouse, shacks, sleepers in blankets, etc., in O'Meara, "Early Days," 130–136; Richards, *Mud,* 2, 26–27.

22   **the whole frenzied town was littered** . . . Rats and beach strewn with garbage in Borthwick, *Three Years,* 54; Richards, *Mud,* 27.

23   **most thoroughfares remained pure dirt** . . . Muddy streets, etc., in O'Meara, "Early Days," 135–136; drowning horses in Asbury, *Barbary Coast,* 12.

23   **"Yankees of every possible variety . . ."** Taylor, *El Dorado,* 43; "It is the wonder of the age . . ." CFP, Box 2, Folder 6.

24   **the tale of Talbot Green** . . . See Hussey, "New Light," 35–39; Stewart, *California Trail,* 28. (NB: Some sources say it was Gettysburg, not Philadelphia.)

24   **Another emblematic character** . . . Details about Leidesdorff come mainly from Adkins, *African Americans,* 10–11 and de Graaf, Mulroy, and Taylor, *Seeking,* 7–8; see also a self-published book-length treatment of his life by Gary Mitchell Palgon, which reproduces many primary documents from Leidesdorff's life.

25   **"swarthy"** . . . see, for instance, Swasey, *Early Days and Men,* 155–156, who seems unaware of Leidesdorff's African heritage.

25   **Mifflin Wistar Gibbs** . . . Gibbs, *Shadow and Light,* 36–45.

26   **George Washington Dennis** . . . See Adkins, *African Americans,* 17–18, and de Graaf, Mulroy, and Taylor, *Seeking,* 17.

26   **Alvin Coffey** . . . See Lapp, *Blacks,* 42, 70ff.

26   **abolished Black slavery** . . . Lapp, *Blacks,* 3; granted full rights . . . de Graaf, Mulroy, and Taylor, *Seeking,* 74; Pio Pico . . . de Graaf, Mulroy, and Taylor, *Seeking,* 84; "With thrift and a wise circumspection . . ." Gibbs, *Shadow and Light,* 45–46.

27   **eight of the forty-eight delegates** . . . Delmatier, *Rumble,* 4; slavery unchallenged in de Graaf, Mulroy, and Taylor, *Seeking,* 9, 102; other discriminatory laws in de Graaf, Mulroy, and Taylor, *Seeking,* 88, and Delmatier, *Rumble,* 7; extended to the Chinese in Heizer and Almquist, *Other Californians,* 129; the assault on Lester described in Gibbs, *Shadow and Light,* 46.

27   **"This will inform you . . ."** *Liberator,* February 15, 1850; 1852 population figures from Lapp, *Blacks,* 22 (statewide population) and de Graaf, Mulroy, and Taylor, *Seeking,* 11 (San Francisco only).

28   **general air of economic optimism . . .** CFP, Box 2, Folders 6, 7, 8.

29   **an act of characteristic bravado . . .** CFP, Box 2, Folder 9.

30   **opportunities were already changing . . .** Shovel prices in Byington, *History of San Francisco,* 142; $96 bedpan in Richards, *Mud,* 54; journalists' newspapers in Taylor, *El Dorado,* 44; "When the sufferings of the emigrants . . ." Starr, *California Dream,* 57–58.

31   **"In the course of a month . . ."** In Borthwick, *Three Years,* 40, 49

31   **"The town seemed running wild . . ."** Browning, *San Francisco Yerba Buena,* 188. "It is a noisy, drinking, gambling place . . ." CFP, Box 2, Folder 20.

31   **being built at breakneck speed . . .** Bayard Taylor estimated that some fifteen to thirty new houses were going up daily. See Taylor, *El Dorado,* 45; underground pipes laid in 1858 and water sold door-to-door, see Richards, *Mud,* 43–45, and Barry and Patten, *Men and Memories,* 43; sewage and garbage disposal in Richards, *Mud,* 27–28.

32   **"We are not burdened . . ."** Richards, *Mud,* 144–146.

32   **"the promised land of gamblers . . ."** Browning, *San Francisco Yerba Buena,* 170.

33   **"In no respect . . ."** CFP, Box 2, Folders 20, 26.

33   **establishing its new legal code . . .** Grenier, " 'Officialdom,' " 143. See also Ellison, *Self-Governing Dominion,* 72; JoinCalifornia.com, Election History for the State of California; California State Assembly 1849–50 Journal.

34   **"reckless and daring spirit . . ."** Taylor, *El Dorado,* 233.

34   **"Every sort of accident . . ."** CFP, Box 2, Folder 17.

34   **"a whole series of blunders . . ."** CFP, Box 2, Folder 19.

34   **two unfortunate career mistakes . . .** For the vote count in his run for attorney general, see Davis, *History of Political Conventions,* 10–11; other details are from CFP, Box 2, Folder 19.

35   **"It did not last more than three or four hours . . ."** CFP, Box 2, Folder 10.

35   **"Well, I have been burnt out again . . ."** CFP, Box 2, Folder 11.

36   **"It was a desolate-looking site . . ."** CFP, Box 2, Folder 27.

36   **very worst of the series of fires . . .** Estimate of the amount of destruction is from Lotchin, *From Hamlet to City,* 175–176; "Even while his house is burning . . ." quoted in Barker, *Eyewitness,* 286; city's ban of tents and wooden buildings in Lotchin, *From Hamlet to City,* 12; "Like so many other emigrants . . ." quoted in Lewis, *This Was San Francisco,* 123.

37   **"I shall do nothing . . ."** and "country of sudden changes" in CFP, Box 2, File 20; "I am content to live anywhere . . ." CFP, Box 2, File 26.

38   **typically exaggerated . . .** Mullen, *Justice,* xiv–xix, 17, 27; see also Mullen, *Dangerous Strangers,* 15–19, and Lotchin, *From Hamlet to City,* 205–206; "Death of the Oldest Inhabitant . . ." as cited in Richards, *Mud,* 22.

38   **"perhaps the worst governed . . ."** as quoted in Sears, *Arresting Dress,* 52; "without a single requisite . . ." John Geary, as quoted in Byington, *History of San Francisco,* 185.

38   **situation had improved dramatically . . .** Prison built in 1851, in Byington, *History of San Francisco,* 207; Brig *Euphemia,* in Soulé, *Annals,* 233; thirty-man police force in Mullen, *Justice,* p. 77; Mullen is probably the best source for the Vigilance Committees. See *Justice,* 139–223; also see Byington, *History of San Francisco,* 217–226.

39   **starting to offer the kind of amenities . . .** Omnibus line, steamship to Oakland, steam shovels in Lotchin, *From Hamlet to City,* 25.

40   **Crittenden took the so-called Panama route . . .** CFP, Box 2, Folders 30 and 31.

40   **finally steamed into San Francisco Bay . . .** The Crittendens' arrival on the *Golden Gate* was reported in the DAC of January 10, 1852.

41   **Crittenden was still reassuring . . .** "The great difficulty is over . . ." CFP, Box 2, Folder 33; "You have endured . . ." CFP, Box 2, Folder 26.

41   **a small house in San Jose . . .** Trying to find a place in Sacramento in CFP, Box 3, Folder 3; for the moving of the state capital, see *California State Assembly Journal* for 1852.

42   **"I have just received your letter . . ."** CFP, Box 2, Folder 34.

42   **their ninth child . . .** Two of the Crittendens' earlier children had died in infancy per https://www.familysearch.org/tree/pedigree/landscape/LYHK-RRK; "entertaining gloomy feelings" in CFP, Box 2, Folder 42; "I am fixed . . ." CFP, Box 2, Folder 53.

43   **"Society I care nothing for . . ."** CFP, Box 2, Folder 35.

43   **"Now there is rising a distinction . . ."** CFP, Box 2, Folder 26.

43   **William Tecumseh Sherman . . .** For details about Sherman's first time in California, see McDonough, *In the Service of My Country,* 133, 137–138; and Sherman, *Personal Memoirs,* Vol. 1, 68. "A poor contemptible village" as quoted in McDonough, *In the Service of My Country,* 171; "having passed through a war . . ." in McDonough, *In the Service of My Country,* 125; "I have seen mules stumble . . ." in McDonough, *In the Service of My Country,* 144.

44   **"San Francisco was on the top wave . . ."** and other quotes in this paragraph are from McDonough, *In the Service of My Country,* 171, 181.

45   **a young Chinese immigrant known as Ah Toy . . .** Details about Ah Toy come from a number of sources, most notably Tong, *Unsubmissive Women,* 6–12; Cilker, "A Little China Leader," 37–61; Jeong, "Ah Toy, Pioneering Prostitute," 90–91; and Hurtado, *Intimate Frontiers.*

46   **"Search the city through . . ."** As quoted in Richards, *Mud,* 158. "They are among the most industrious . . ." is from the DAC of May 12, 1851. The ceremony honoring the Chinese is in Soulé, *Annals,* 158; other ceremonies in O'Meara, "Chinese," 478–479.

46   **"Atoy came into court . . ."** DAC of December 14, 1851; for Ah Toy's court appearances, see, for instance, Tong, *Unsubmissive Women,* 6–12.

47   **conflict with the nascent Chinese tongs . . .** For *Ah Toy v. Norman Ah-Sing,* see Cilker, "A Little China Leader," 58–59; also see the DAC of March 6 and 8, 1851.

47   **"one of the most worthy classes . . ."** as quoted in McClain, *In Search of Equality,* 10; Rouse says the Chinese in California numbered about 25,000, though this number (with no source cited) seems too high; Governor Bigler's address was reprinted in its entirety in the DAC of April 25, 1852. Norman Ah-Sing's open letter was published in the DAC of May 5, 1852.

48   **the mistress of a white man . . .** For the affair with Clark, see Jeong, "Ah Toy, Pioneering Prostitute."

49   **ever-increasing hostility from the tongs . . .** Tong, *Unsubmissive Women,* 9; suicide, in Cilker, "A Little China Leader," 61.

49   **"My dear Clara . . ."** Quotes from this November 7 letter are in CFP, Box 3, Folder 1.

50   **alone with the children . . .** For the Crittenden children and their birth years, see the Finding Aid for the CFP; San Francisco's "brutalizing vulgarity" in Brechin, *Imperial San Francisco,* 280. (NB: The college was first located in Oakland before finally moving to Berkeley.)

50   **a series of losses . . .** CFP, Box 3, Folders 4, 5, 6 (unfortunately, none of Clara's letters from this time survive); see also familysearch.org for the children lost in infancy.

50   **"If I find a wrinkle . . ."** CFP, Box 2, Folder 26.

52   **southerners had been able to keep enslaved people . . .** For Robinson's servant, see CFP, Box 2, Folder 18 (for more on Robinson, see: https://www .familysearch.org/tree/person/details/2MGY-7DR); newspaper ads—Lapp, *Blacks,* 132–134; Beasley points out that the original state constitution contains a section claiming that "neither slavery nor involuntary servitude, unless for the punishment of crime, shall ever be tolerated in this state" (Beasley, "Slavery in California," 38); also see Stacey Smith's "Remaking Slavery in a Free State" on how the ambiguous status of slavery in California enabled many enslaved people to renegotiate the terms of their enslavement.

53   **a young enslaved man named Frank . . .** The Frank case as per the DAC of March 31, April 1 and 2, 1851; see also Lapp, *Blacks,* 138–139, which cites the quotation from the *Herald.*

53   **"The wealthy California negroes . . ."** As quoted in Lapp, *Blacks,* 137; I have altered the original translation, which (to my mind) inappropriately translates the German "Entführung" as "stealing" rather than "abduction."

54   **a Caribbean "voodoo priestess" . . .** One of the principal perpetrators of this folklore was Helen Holdredge, the author of a mean-spirited and exploitative "biography" of Pleasant published in 1953. Holdredge appears to have done extensive research on Pleasant's life, but her unfootnoted book, *Mammy Pleasant* (which sold well enough to inspire a *Mammy Pleasant Cookbook*), strikes me as extremely unreliable, peddling racist stereotypes, barefaced innuendo, and a kind of tabloid sensationalism that make it all but unreadable to modern audiences (for this reason, I do not include it in the bibliography). Pleasant is far better served by her more recent biographers, especially Lynn M. Hudson, whose *The Making of "Mammy Pleasant": A Black Entrepreneur in Nineteenth-Century San Francisco* is the source for many of the details in my account. Susheel Bibbs's *Heritage of Power: Marie LaVeaux to Mary Ellen Pleasant* is also useful. "A native Kanaka," "a full-blooded Louisiana negress," and other details from Pleasant's memoir as published in Davis, ed., *Pandex of the Press,* 5–6. "Colored school" is in Wills, *Black Fortunes,* 13–26. "I have run across a good many highly educated people . . ." from *Pandex,* 6.

55   **"to better my condition . . ."** All quotes in this paragraph from Wills, *Black Fortunes,* 20–21.

55   **"my husband frequently . . ."** Quoted in Wills, *Black Fortunes,* 22–23. The very circumspect Hudson points out that no census information or evidence of a will can be found for Smith.

56   **$15,000 in gold coins . . .** and the quote ("They put out the money . . .") are

from an interview Pleasant gave in the *San Francisco Examiner* of October 13, 1895.

56   **often apart for extended periods** . . . Most information about John James Pleasants is from Hudson, *Making,* 27–30, and Wills, *Black Fortunes,* 113–114.

56   **a role less threatening** . . . Hudson, *Making,* 32–34.

57   **ready to put her wealth to work** . . . For Pleasant's activist work with the local Black community, see Hudson, *Making,* 34–38.

57   **a relatively low profile** . . . Hudson, *Making,* 46; "Black City Hall" in Wills, *Black Fortunes,* 113.

58   **the notorious William Walker** . . . There are a number of book-length treatments of Walker's escapades; I relied most heavily on Albert Carr's *The World and William Walker,* Scott Martelle's *William Walker's Wars,* and on Walker's own memoir, *The War in Nicaragua.* For Crittenden's participation, see the Crittenden and Jones depositions from *McDonald v. Garrison and Morgan* in the New York Public Library's Isaiah Thornton Williams Papers.

58   **1856 faced a kind of insurrection** . . . The literature on the San Francisco Vigilance Committee episode of 1856 is extensive. Particularly useful (since it offers three different perspectives on the events) is Nunis Jr., ed., *San Francisco Vigilance Committee of 1856: Three Views.*

59   **caught up in the episode** . . . Crittenden's role and "I am utterly heartsick . . ." in CFP, Box 3, Folder 9 (NB: Crittenden's professed belief in the authority of legitimate governments apparently did not extend to the governments of Central America); see also Frajola, *Crittenden Correspondence,* 19.

61   **"As it was announced . . ."** DAC of April 1, 1871.

61   **the spectators came** . . . The scene in the courtroom, including all quotes and testimony, are from the trial transcript (Marsh and Osbourne, *Official Report,* 99–100, with some editing for clarity and concision) and supplementary material from the DAC of April 5, 1871.

65   **Holly Springs, Mississippi** . . . Callejo-Pérez, "Chapter Three," 21–22; details about Laura's early life come primarily from her own court testimony (Marsh and Osbourne, *Official Report,* 124–125); see also Haber, *Trials of Laura Fair,* 12–15, and the *New York Times* (hereafter NYT) of July 18, 1871. (NB: Haber says the Hunts were a family of four, but the NYT article mentions the sister, Mary Jane [Hunt] Payne, while O.D. is frequently referred to in letters and testimony.)

66   **a disastrous husband** . . . Details about the separation and divorce from Stone come mainly from the NYT story of July 18, 1871. "a dissipated man . . ." is in Marsh and Osbourne, *Official Report,* 124.

66   **Still a teenager** . . . The details of Laura's marriage to Grayson "to support myself and my mother . . ." and "to show what a good marksman . . ." and "fifty at a time . . ." are in Marsh and Osbourne, *Official Report,* 124–125. The agreement between Laura and Grayson re: the divorce as per Laura's testimony, Marsh and Osbourne, *Official Report,* 133–134.

67   **"To suffer and to be silent under suffering . . ."** As quoted in Haber, *Trials of Laura Fair,* 14.

67   **decided to leave New Orleans** . . . Haber, *Trials of Laura Fair,* 15.

67   **a very different city** . . . fifty thousand population; New York 190 years, etc., in Lotchin, *From Hamlet to City,* 30, 102; urban sorting of population in Berglund,

Making San Francisco American, 12, see also Lotchin, *From Hamlet to City,* 17; "morally inviting" as quoted in Lotchin, *From Hamlet to City,* 79.

68 **Laura Grayson and her mother** . . . Staying at Rassette House per Marsh and Osbourne, *Official Report,* 112; unattached women keeping house is in Haber, *Trials of Laura Fair,* 16; called "Little China" at the time per Seligman, *Three Tough Chinamen,* 22; family friend and two music students living with them is per Marsh and Osbourne, *Official Report,* 112.

69 **a bust cycle** . . . empty buildings and real estate plummeting in Byington, *History of San Francisco,* 250; Lavender, *Nothing Seemed Impossible,* 79; WTS closing bank and leaving is in McDonough, *In the Service of My Country,* 207–208, 213; "The whole town is for sale . . ." in Lavender, *Nothing Seemed Impossible,* 115.

70 **managed to buy a nicer house** . . . The Crittendens may have lived on the corner of Dupont (now Grant) and Post between the Pacific and Taylor houses— see advertisement in the DAC of January 30, 1857; almost climbed out of debt in CFP, Box 4, Folder 21; new house per CFP, Box 3, Folder 21.

70 **his political career** . . . For Crittenden's attempt to become a senator, see Hittell, *History,* vol. 4, 203, and O'Meara, *Broderick and Gwin,* 160–161; "I think the prospect of my success . . ." per CFP, Box 3, Folder 12.

71 **concerned with her own economic survival** . . . Laura's move to Shasta per Haber, *Trials of Laura Fair,* 17; for William D. Fair's service in the first state legislature, see the California State Assembly Journal for 1849–50; William Fair's checking the divorce is in Laura Fair's "Wolves in the Fold," 22–23; "by nearly all the first ladies" is in Fair, "Wolves," 28.

71 **invented many key aspects** . . . Fair's background and lies are per Haber, *Trials of Laura Fair,* 17; is in Fair, "Wolves," 23.

73 **a sweat-soaked rider** . . . For the Pony Express rider and the telegraph line over the Sierra, see Lavender, *Nothing Seemed Impossible,* 150.

73 **fourteenth-largest city** . . . Starr, *California Dream,* 239; for the power of Southern Democrats, see Lavender, *Nothing Seemed Impossible,* 150; bill passed to split California in Richards, *California Gold Rush,* 225.

74 **the last notable duel** . . . The main source for the Broderick-Terry duel is Richards, *California Gold Rush,* 4–7, 215–225. See also Matthews, *Golden State,* 40ff, and Delmatier, *Rumble,* 21.

75 **"There was nothing political . . ."** CFP, Box 4, Folder 62.

75 **a divided Democratic vote** . . . For the election results, see Monzingo, *Thomas Starr King,* 61, 71.

75 **not always predictably aligned** . . . Crittenden's views on Lincoln and "as I would study any question of law . . ." CFP, Box 5, Folder 77; "that old abolitionist fool and humbug," CFP, Box 6, Folder 33; "I hope there will be no secession . . ." CFP, Box 5, Folder 77.

76 **family who found themselves on opposite sides** . . . For Crittenden family loyalties, see, for instance, Eubank, *Shadow of the Patriarch,* 46–47; Jones family loyalties in CFP, Box 6, Folders 27, 32, 40; Box 7, Folders 3 and 12.

76 **disturbing signs of disagreement** . . . Churchill and James at school in the East in CFP, Box 3, Folders 34, 38, 51, 62; "Don't worry, I won't change loyalties . . ." CFP, Box 3, Folder 73; "James will always be a Southerner . . ." CFP, Box 4, Folder 35; "You speak of slavery as a curse . . ." CFP, Box 4, Folder 50.

77   **a constant source of anxiety . . .** For the various mishaps suffered by the Crittenden children, see CFP, Box 3, Folder 87, and Box 4, Folders 1, 2, 9, 10, 13, and 20; for Crittenden's own health complaints, see CFP, Box 5, Folder 3.

78   **bonanzas at the Comstock Lode . . .** See Lavender, *Nothing Seemed Impossible,* 136, 147; Crittenden's personal fee of $18,000 is per CFP, Box 4, Folder 49.

78   **"The whole city has improved immensely . . ."** CFP, Box 4, Folder 75.

78   **just under fifty-seven thousand . . .** San Francisco population in 1860 as per U.S. Census figures (https://www2.census.gov/library/publications/decennial /1860/population/1860a-06.pdf);" well built, magnificently laid out . . ." as quoted in Barker, *More,* 109; "Imagine my astonishment . . ." Barker, *More,* 111–112.

79   **trappings of sophisticated urban living . . .** For Platt's, see the DAC of July 28, 1860; for other theaters, see also http://sanfranciscotheatres.blogspot.com/; for the Western Addition, see Byington, *History of San Francisco,* 274.

79   **Bret Harte . . .** For Harte's early life, see Tarnoff, *Bohemians,* 22–24; "It was a terrible experience . . ." Tarnoff, *Bohemians,* 22. See also Merwin, *Life of Bret Harte,* 16–17.

80   **a fine job of educating himself . . .** Shakespeare by age 6, etc., per Scharnhorst, *Bret Harte,* 5; "I was fit for nothing else" in Tarnoff, *Bohemians,* 24.

80   **job as a printer's apprentice . . .** Merwin, *Life of Bret Harte,* 30. (NB: Arcata was known as Union or Uniontown before 1860.) See also Duckett, *Mark Twain and Bret Harte,* 11–12; "Turn that pensive glance . . ." as quoted in Scharnhorst, *Bret Harte,* 11.

81   **a brutal massacre . . .** The figures of between 9,000 and 16,000 killed are given in Heizer and Almquist, *Other Californians,* and Madley, *American Genocide,* 47.

81   **Humboldt Bay Massacres . . .** "a scene of atrocity . . ." Quoted in Heizer and Almquist, *Other Californians,* 30; see also Pfaelzer, *Slave State,* 181–202. "Neither age or sex . . ." as quoted in Madley, *American Genocide,* 560 Harte's flight is per Tarnoff, *Bohemians,* 26.

82   **the young author was forced to flee . . .** "The event ended his life as a wanderer" in Merwin, *Life of Bret Harte,* 31; composing at the type case per Scharnhorst, *Bret Harte,* 16; other details, including the Twain quote, are from Tarnoff, *Bohemians,* 26–28.

83   **"The literary West . . ."** Henry Seidel Canby, as quoted in Scharnhorst, *Bret Harte,* xiii.

83   **an eruption over Lincoln's election . . .** Kibby, "California, the Civil War, and the Indian Problem," 191.

83   **at least thirty thousand men . . .** Kibby, "California, the Civil War, and the Indian Problem," 189 (citing an earlier author), attributes the statement to A. P. Crittenden himself, but since Crittenden was neither a resident of El Dorado County nor a member of the legislature at this time, this is almost certainly wrong.

84   **the so-called Crittenden Compromise . . .** See, for instance, Davis, *History of Political Conventions,* 159.

84   **a report reached San Francisco . . .** For the twelve-days-late arrival of news about Fort Sumter, and the quotes ("fever of excitement," "Madness rules the hour . . .") see Monzingo, *Thomas Starr King,* 82–83.

85   **"We have so many inhabitants . . ."** James V. Mansfield Papers, Notebook 17.

87   **a small group of determined southerners . . .** For the rumored coup, see
      Harpending, *Diamond Hoax,* 28–38; also Monzingo, *Thomas Starr King,* 86, and
      Byington, *History of San Francisco,* 306.

87   **different choices . . .** Kibby, "California, the Civil War, and the Indian Prob-
      lem," 197–198; according to Harpending, *Diamond Hoax,* 35, it was Johnston
      who discouraged the committee from going forward with the coup, claiming that
      he would defend the property of the United States as long as it was his duty to
      do so.

88   **becoming a member . . .** Breckenridge Democratic State Committee per
      Davis, *History of Political Conventions,* 165, 188; "I am amazed . . ." CFP, Box 6,
      Folder 6.

88   **James was less compliant . . .** James's arrest is per CFP, Box 6, Folder 27; "to
      save our noble country . . ." in John J. Crittenden Papers, Library of Congress
      (Letter of May 14, 1861, from James Crittenden to John J. Crittenden).

89   **the man who kept California in the Union . . .** see Monzingo, *Thomas Starr
      King,* ix; references to Lincoln's regarding him as such are ubiquitous in the lit-
      erature, if not authoritatively proved.

89   **diminutive and sickly clergyman . . .** King's height and weight per Monzingo,
      Thomas Starr King, 9; five pastors, lack of Harvard credentials per Starr, *California
      Dream,* 97–98; debut sermon; flooded with requests per Monzingo, *Thomas Starr
      King,* 13, 20.

90   **"The old Declaration of Independence will live . . ."** quoted in Monzingo,
      Thomas Starr King, 103; death threats per Monzingo, *Thomas Starr King,* 93; "He
      is a torrent of eloquence . . ." Monzingo, *Thomas Starr King,* 121; "I am so fond
      of King . . ." in James V. Mansfield Papers, Notebook 7.

90   **Republicans triumphed in the state elections . . .** See de Graaf, Mulroy, and
      Taylor, *Seeking El Dorado,* 12, and Heizer and Almquist, *Other Californians,*
      124–126; for the September 1861 state election results, see http://www.join
      california.com/election/1861-09-04.

90   **began lifting some of the restrictions . . .** For the repeal of the testimony ban,
      see Fisher, "The Struggle for Negro Testimony," 322; the turn to other issues in
      Hudson, *Making,* 45.

91   **at least one witness . . .** Hudson, *Making,* 37–39.

91   **journey to Canada . . .** Re: buying property in Chatham, see Hudson, *Making,*
      39. All quotes in this paragraph are from Davis, *Pandex of the Press.*

92   **probably apocryphal . . .** Details and all quotes are from Davis, *Pandex of the
      Press,* no page numbers.

93   **"Black or white . . ."** as quoted in Bennett, "Mystery," Part 1, 90.

93   **back to local issues . . .** For Pleasant's return to San Francisco and the makeup
      of the Black community in the early 1860s, see Hudson, *Making,* 44–46. (NB:
      The *Pacific Appeal* was a continuation, under a different name and ownership, of
      the earlier *Mirror of the Times.*)

94   **considered a victory . . .** See *Brown v Omnibus Rail Road Company,* California
      Historical Society.

94   **one Black reader insisted . . .** Hudson, *Making,* 50; see also the Charlotte
      Brown biographical file, California Historical Society.

95   **he and Laura decided . . .** For details of the Fairs' move back to San Francisco, see the trial transcript (Marsh and Osbourne, *Official Report*, 32); Haber, *Trials of Laura Fair*, 17; Lamott, *Who Killed*, 10–12; and Fair's own account, "Wolves," 23–26.

95   **One night toward Christmas . . .** The Fairs' meeting at Dr. Murphy's office is in Lamott, *Who Killed*, 12; Hitchcock finding the body in Fair, "Wolves," 26.

95   **Laura rushed over . . .** "Crazed and frantic" and "I was immediately surrounded . . ." Fair, "Wolves," 27; "domestic troubles" as quoted in Haber, *Trials of Laura Fair*, 18.

96   **desperate straits . . .** The boardinghouse on Mission, etc., per Lamott, *Who Killed*, 13-14; "I am surprised, Madam . . ." and "My indignation rendered me speechless . . ." is in Fair, "Wolves," 38.

96   **unpaid bills kept accumulating . . .** The wood and coal man incident is in Marsh and Osbourne, *Official Report*, 122. "God and my own soul alone . . ." per Fair, "Wolves," 38.

97   **two pieces of good news . . .** For the simultaneity of the aqueduct opening and Lincoln's signing of the railway act, see Brechin, *Imperial San Francisco*, 78.

98   **"Debut of Mrs. W.D. Fair . . ."** DAC of March 13, 1863.

99   **an actor named McKean Buchanan . . .** Lamott, *Who Killed*, 15, claims that Buchanan was a friend of a lodger, rather than a lodger himself, though most other sources say the latter; "world-renowned tragedian" in Haber, *Trials of Laura Fair*, 235*n*.

99   **proved to be a natural actress . . .** "excellent conception and . . ." DAC of March 14, 1863; playing in *The Marble Heart* in *Marysville Daily Appeal* of March 19, 1863.

100   **a disreputable profession . . .** For the status of stage actors, see Haber, *Trials of Laura Fair*, 20.

101   **brand-new boomtown . . .** For the discovery of silver in the Washoe, see Lavender, *Nothing Seemed Impossible*, 131–134 and James, *Roar*, 1–9; "annoying blue stuff" per James, *Roar*, 9.

101   **silver strikes were not conducive . . .** For the more capital-intensive type of mining required in the Washoe, see James, *Roar*, 8–9; Lyman, *Ralston's Ring*, 2–4; Lavender, *Nothing Seemed Impossible*, 135.

102   **the most influential capitalist . . .** Most of the details of Ralston's life come from the excellent biography by David Lavender; $50,000 capital is in Lavender, *Nothing Seemed Impossible*, 110.

102   **the Ophir Mining Company . . .** Details per Lavender, *Nothing Seemed Impossible*, 136.

103   **one Samuel Clemens . . .** Most of the details of Clemens's early months in Nevada are from Powers, *Mark Twain*, 101–117.

103   **"My back is sore . . ."** Powers, *Mark Twain*, 108; "had been living on alkali water and wang leather" . . . Nevada politician Rollin M. Daggett, as quoted in Williams, *Life in Virginia City*, 9.

104   **"Rather than focus on the facts . . ."** Powers, *Mark Twain*, 112.

104   **"The Unreliable" . . .** For the Clemens-Rice "feud," see Powers, *Mark Twain*, 115–117.

105   **the political situation in California . . .** California 1862 elections in http://www.joincalifornia.com/election/1862-09-03; also Davis, *History of Political*

Conventions, 188; "hateful Yankee community" as quoted in Matthews, *Golden State,* 197; California contribution to Sanitary Commission per Monzingo, *Thomas Starr King,* 213–214.

106 **"It perhaps hardly lies . . ."** CFP, Box 4, Folder 95.

106 **"You have been to me a true and loving wife . . ."** CFP, Box 5, Folder 31.

106 **being claimed by both . . .** For the bizarre disagreement about whether Aurora was in California or Nevada, see Stewart, *Aurora,* 11–25, and CFP, Box 8, Folder 60; "rough, struggling place" is from Frajola, *Crittenden Correspondence,* 1.

107 **"Dearest mother . . ."** CFP, Box 6, Folder 55.

107 **"save [our] native land . . ."** CFP, Box 6, Folder 57; other details from Box 6, Folders 62, 67, and 76; "Have I not been fortunate . . ." Box 6, Folder 67; "we must do our duty . . ." Box 6, Folder 57.

108 **silver wedding anniversary . . .** The anniversary party is described in a letter from Nannie to her husband, Sidney Van Wyck, CFP, Box 7, Folder 70; "It is nothing strange for Pa . . ." CFP, Box 7, Folder 74.

108 **"If I am fortunate in my speculations . . ."** CFP, Box 7, Folder 36; "Pa thought you would be uncomfortable . . ." CFP Box 8, Folder 2.

109 **passed a series of new laws . . .** Matthews, *Golden State,* 185; for the loyalty oaths, see especially Chandler, "California's 1863 Loyalty Oaths"; "Pa says he had had some very handsome offers. . . ." CFP, Box 7, Folder 88.

109 **Crittenden pulled up stakes . . .** According to Franklin, "Crittenden Correspondence Revisited," 14, a warrant for Crittenden's arrest had been issued, unbeknownst to him, for his treasonous fundraising activities; see also CFP, Box 8, Folder 62; "I can no longer practice law in California . . ." CFP, Box 8, Folder 40; "It will be almost impossible to get a house . . ." CFP, Box 8, Folder 65.

109 **Virginia City in the summer of 1863 . . .** Population growth is in Lavender, *Nothing Seemed Impossible,* 168; Clemens sleeping at newspaper offices per Powers, *Mark Twain,* 114; 10th Baron Fairfax per Lamott, *Who Killed,* 19–20.

110 **two rooms on the second floor . . .** Details about Crittenden's suite in Fair, "Wolves," 30. According to Laura Fair's court testimony in Marsh and Osbourne, *Official Report,* 99, 114, Crittenden insisted he was a widower when they were first introduced.

110 **"I have made up my mind to settle here . . ."** Franklin, "Crittenden Correspondence Revisited," 17; see also CFP Box 8, Folder 65; thirty-hour coach ride away is per Goldman, *Gold Diggers,* 12.

111 **Tahoe House proved ideal . . .** Details about Tahoe House and her monthly profit from Fair's court testimony in Marsh and Osbourne, *Official Report,* 100–101, 113–114; see also Haber, *Trials of Laura Fair,* 26, and Lamott, *Who Killed,* 29. (NB: Tahoe House still operates as a hotel in Virginia City; this book's author stayed there for a few nights in the summer of 2021.)

112 **One tenant in particular caught her eye . . .** For the start of the affair, see Fair's testimony in Marsh and Osbourne, *Official Report,* 114.

112 **In late October . . .** Selling the Taylor Street house and moving Clara and children to Aurora is in CFP, Box 8, Folders 53, 55, and 64. "It will be almost impossible . . ." CFP, Box 8, Folder 58.

112 **"I have rooms . . ."** CFP, Box 8, Folder 79.

113 **"He courted me as a single man . . ."** Marsh and Osbourne, *Official Report*, 114; Howard's visit is in CFP, Box 8, Folders 96, 97, and 98; "I supposed he [A.P.] was a widower . . ." Marsh and Osbourne, *Official Report*, 114.

113 **a man named Dale . . .** For the December incident with Dale, including the quote ("I paid five hundred dollars a month . . ."), see Marsh and Osbourne, *Official Report*, 122.

114 **On February 4 . . .** Clara's arrival is from her court testimony in Marsh and Osbourne, *Official Report*, 162; details about the new house from CFP, Box 8, Folders 87, 90, 103; for Crittenden's business trip to San Francisco, see Frajola, *Crittenden Correspondence*, 5.

115 **Sometime after A.P.'s San Francisco trip . . .** All details and quotes in the paragraph ("I asked him if he was divorced . . .") are from Fair's court testimony, Marsh and Osbourne, *Official Report*, 100.

115 **"very miserable . . ."** and "He said it would be an evidence of my love . . ." are from Marsh and Osbourne, *Official Report*, 100.

115 **she always swore . . .** Clara's return to San Francisco and the interruption are in Marsh and Osbourne, *Official Report*, 162.

116 **another high-profile brouhaha . . .** For the article clipping and the quote, see CFP, Box 9, Folders 23 and 25.

116 **rapidly maturing San Francisco . . .** For the changing ratio of women to men, see Hurtado, *Intimate Frontiers*, 76; for the "good morals and decency" program, see Graves and Watson, *Citywide Historic Context Statement*, 16; for the new city ordinances and efforts to confine vice and separate races, see Sears, *Arresting Dress*, 2, 44, 70; Barnhart, *Fair but Frail*, 32; Asbury, *Barbary Coast*, 90.

117 **being doubly condemned . . .** See Jeong, "Ah Toy, Pioneering Prostitute"; "This city boasts of its loyalty . . ." per Mansfield Papers, Notebook 17.

117 **to police sexuality and gender expression . . .** For fourteen years for sodomy, see *Laws of the State of California 1855*, 105, ch. LXXXII, enacted Apr. 10, 1855; "in a dress not belonging . . ." and the penalty for cross-dressing per Graves and Watson, *Citywide Historic Context Statement*, 16; "European cult . . ." is in Wright, "San Francisco."

118 **Anxiety over gender uncertainty . . .** For two-spirits, see especially Stryker and Van Buskirk, *Gay by the Bay*, 11–12; Graves and Watson, *Citywide Historic Context Statement*, 5–7. For the Mission San Antonio story, see Hurtado, *Intimate Frontiers*, 7–8.

118 **atypically tolerant . . .** For cross-dressing and homosexuality in Gold Rush San Francisco, and the quote, see Wright, "San Francisco," 165–166; also see Sears, *Arresting Dress*, 29.

119 **"A tremendous sensation . . ."** and "As the police arrest . . ." DAC of May 9, 1866; other DeWolf details per Castañeda and Campbell, *News and Sexuality*, 4–5; over a hundred arrests, more than for sodomy, is in Sears, *Arresting Dress*, 62.

119 **Jeanne Bonnet . . .** Though much of what we know about Bonnet comes from sometimes unreliable newspaper accounts, there are several good secondary sources to be consulted, including Sears, Mullen, the San Francisco Lesbian and Gay History Project, and Donoghue (whose excellent novel *Frog Music* has an online bibliography that was particularly useful); I also drew on the notes and

clippings in the Allan Bérubé and Eric Garber Collections; Bonnet's twenty arrests in Duberman, *Hidden from History,* 188; "Her career and fate furnish an illustration . . ." SFC of September 16, 1876.

120   **Adah Isaacs Menken . . .** See Graves and Watson, *Citywide Historic Context Statement,* 24 ("idealized duality of sex"). Description of Mazeppa's climax, Stoddard's admiration of her "half-feminine masculinity," and his journal entry are in Tarnoff, *Bohemians,* 52–53.

121   **"Here every tongue sings . . ."** in Branch, *Clemens,* 94; "pack-mule after his burden is removed" as quoted in Tarnoff, *Bohemians,* 53.

121   **"How I hate everything . . ."** As quoted in Branch, *Clemens,* 7. "After the sagebrush and alkali deserts of Washoe . . ." Tarnoff, *Bohemians,* 10; "If there were no fires to report . . ." Branch, *Clemens,* 17.

123   **"On this coast . . ."** as quoted in Tarnoff, *Bohemians,* 59; October 1863 issue, next to Thoreau per Scharnhorst, *Bret Harte,* 19.

123   **"to wage an all-out war . . ."** Tarnoff, *Bohemians,* 65; Golden State Trinity is per Scharnhorst, *Bret Harte,* 31; "Bohemian's Protective Union" and "Any author expecting pay . . ." in Tarnoff, *Bohemians,* 65–66.

123   **"His head was striking . . ."** Harte and Twain, *Sketches,* viii.

124   **"He was distinctly pretty" . . .** Powers, *Mark Twain,* 147; "trimmed & trained & schooled me . . ." Scharnhorst, *Bret Harte,* 30.

124   **an especially trying time . . .** Branch, *Clemens,* 23, 285.

125   **at a hotel bar . . .** For the story behind the jumping-frog story, see especially Powers, *Mark Twain,* 149–156; Tarnoff, *Bohemians,* 110–113. (NB: The story was originally published in the *New York Saturday Press* under the title "Jim Smiley and His Jumping Frog.")

125   **"Harte strove . . ."** Tarnoff, *Bohemians,* 60.

126   **"This morning the only man I ever worshiped . . ."** Mansfield Papers, Notebook 26.

126   **"Yankee Poodle" . . .** Monzingo, *Thomas Starr King,* 114. Other details and quotes in this paragraph are also from Monzingo, *Thomas Starr King*: 118 (collapse), 140 ("I am worn out . . ."), 210 ("As soon as [the new church] is paid for . . .").

126   **For a full three days . . .** Details about King's funeral are mainly from Tarnoff, *Bohemians,* 66–68, and Monzingo, *Thomas Starr King,* 219, 222–226, 231; "Let the church, free of debt . . ." is in Monzingo, *Thomas Starr King,* 219.

127   **"I have had three horses killed . . ."** Crittenden Family Letters (University of Washington Digital Collections, Civil War Letters, Accession No. 256-1); letter from Churchill to Clara, January 14, 1864.

128   **picking up large contracts . . .** $30,000 from the U.S. government, $10,000 from Savage, CFP, Box 8, Folder 78; "Have been dipping deep into Baltic stock . . ." CFP, Box 8, Folder 79; "Yesterday or two days ago . . ." CFP, Box 8, Folder 81.

128   **playing the market . . .** Laura's investing in Marsh and Osbourne, *Official Report,* 139–40; California's constitution allowing women to own property, see Schuele, "'None Could Deny,'" 169–176. (NB: Throughout the mid-1800s, other states began allowing women property rights through legislation and statutes.) "mud hens" per Neville, *Fantastic City,* 158; "In all I have borrowed . . ." CFP, Box 8, Folder 81.

129 **scattered widely over the globe** . . . Howard in Saxony per CFP, Box 9, Folder 11. Churchill and James in Crittenden Family Letters (University of Washington); "True, it is a wretched life . . ." CFP, Box 9, Folder 27.

130 **no longer attempting much discretion** . . . Marsh and Osbourne, *Official Report,* 115.

130 **some fancy explaining** . . . Marsh and Osbourne, *Official Report,* 163.

131 **"he wished to ask a sacrifice"** . . . Marsh and Osbourne, *Official Report,* 115.

131 **"as an evidence"** . . . Marsh and Osbourne, *Official Report,* 115.

133 **"The Assassin of the late Hon. A. P. Crittenden . . ."** DAC of April 11, 1871.

134 **On the morning of the fourteenth day** . . . All quoted testimony in this section is from the transcript (Marsh and Osbourne, *Official Report,* 163–164, 168), as well as newspaper reports. (NB: The transcript put the fine at $150, but this was apparently a transcription error.) "did not seem to realize . . ." DAC of April 11, 1871.

136 **"Mrs. Fair's eyes blazed . . ."** *San Francisco Chronicle* (hereafter SFC) of April 12, 1871.

139 **an otherwise unremarkable fall evening** . . . The scene in the Occidental dining room was described by both Laura and Clara in their court testimony. See Marsh and Osbourne, *Official Report,* 34, 101, 115, 129–130, 163, 214; for a description of the dining room and the menu, see Haber, *Trials of Laura Fair,* 56, and Lamott, *Who Killed,* 32–34 (Lamott, 32, offers the information about the Martinez).

140 **staying right next door** . . . Marsh and Osbourne, *Official Report,* 101, 129–130, 163–164.

140 **"I sang one or two songs . . ."** Marsh and Osbourne, *Official Report,* 214.

141 **Laura decided to return** . . . Details on Laura's early retreat from San Francisco in Marsh and Osbourne, *Official Report,* 34, 101, 164.

141 **Mrs. Lane felt** . . . Marsh and Osbourne, *Official Report,* 101.

142 **the three of them came to an understanding** . . . Marsh and Osbourne, *Official Report,* 101.

142 **the entire proposed state constitution** . . . Green, *Nevada,* 91, calls it the second-longest telegram. (NB: One of the state's three electors was stranded by a snowstorm and could not cast his vote.)

143 **"When you have read these letters burn them . . ."** CFP, Box 9, Folder 26; "My own dear mother and father . . ." CFL, University of Washington Libraries, Civil War Letters, Item number CVW048.

143 **the first of three letters** . . . James gave three almost identical accounts of Churchill's ordeal in the three letters, CFL, University of Washington Libraries, Civil War Letters, dated November 2, 21, and 22, Item numbers CVW046, CVW047, and CVW048. (NB: James sometimes spells the name of Churchill's companion "Hartigan.")

144 **"My dear Uncle . . ."** CFL, Item number CVW024.

145 **Hardigan, "unworthy of the privilege . . ."** CFL, Item number CVW046.

145 **"Thus died the noblest . . ."** CFL, Item number CVW048.

145 **in early November** . . . APC traveled to San Francisco, CFP, Box 9, Folder 65; "bitterness & curses" per CFL, University of Washington Libraries, Item number CVW001; "I have never been so depressed . . ." CFP, Box 9, Folder 61.

146   **"I really think it best . . ."** CFP, Box 9, Folder 61; "Last night I did not close my eyes . . ." CFL, University of Washington Libraries, Item number CVW002.

146   **"Oh, this life is nothing but battle . . ."** CFP, Box 9, Folder 70; "In the midst of anything I may be doing . . ." CFP, Box 9, Folder 75.

146   **in enemy territory** . . . Complains of sitting among Yankees per CFP, Box 9, Folder 72; "Every day we live in this corrupt land . . ." CFP, Box 9, Folder 76.

147   **a devout Christian** . . . Clara's concerns about Churchill's and A.P.'s lack of faith per CFP, Box 9, Folder 87; "Should God call me hence . . ." CFP, Box 6, Folder 57; "I would be perfectly happy . . ." CFP, Box 7, Folder 85.

147   **claiming to look for some kind of religion** . . . All quotes in this paragraph from CFP, Box 9, Folder 71.

148   **"It is the [only] Christmas present . . ."** CFP, Box 9, Folder 86.

149   **the end of the Civil War** . . . Terms of surrender, DAC of April 11, 1865; "The batteries . . ." DAC of April 9, 1865; "Civilization has trampled medievalism . . ." DAC of April 8, 1865.

149   **a markedly different response** . . . Reaction to Lincoln's assassination per DAC of April 16, 1865.

150   **"The bells were ringing . . ."** CFP, Box 10, Folder 28.

150   **"The only reasons . . ."** CFP, Box 9, Folder 94.

150   **"So you came near to having an adventure . . ."** Frajola, *Crittenden Correspondence,* 6.

151   **"in charge of a Yankee"** . . . CFP, Box 9, Folder 100.

151   **"Come in, Madame"** . . . Marsh and Osbourne, *Official Report,* 164 (Clara's testimony).

151   **"It was worrying my life out . . ."** Marsh and Osbourne, *Official Report,* 214 (Laura's testimony); "It is me she wished to see . . ." Marsh and Osbourne, *Official Report,* 164 (Clara's testimony).

152   **he took out his derringer** . . . The gun flourishing in the doorway and "It frightened me . . ." Marsh and Osbourne, *Official Report,* 214 (Laura's testimony).

152   **"I talked with her . . ."** Marsh and Osbourne, *Official Report,* 164 (Clara's testimony).

152   **insisting that Clara return** . . . Marsh and Osbourne, *Official Report,* 164; "Pa thought that he had a good reason . . ." CFP, Box 10, Folder 6.

153   **his responses to them speak volumes** . . . All quoted material in these two paragraphs—from "My dear Clara" through "death is but a sleep"—are from CFP, Box 10, Folder 7.

154   **"Your letter . . ."** Frajola, *Crittenden Correspondence,* 9; "I am not dead . . ." CFP, Box 10, Folder 10.

154   **"asking me to write a love letter . . ."** CFP, Box 10, Folder 27; "I am going to write to Pa . . ." CFP, Box 10, Folders 32 and 33.

155   **come up to help Nannie** . . . Clara living with pregnant Nannie per Marsh and Osbourne, *Official Report,* 34 (Clara's testimony).

155   **she went to see Mrs. Fair** . . . Clara is the only one who discussed these visits, per Marsh and Osbourne, *Official Report,* 34.

156   **"He begged of me to allow it . . ."** Marsh and Osbourne, *Official Report,* 130.

156   **Reluctantly, Laura agreed** . . . The $600 Steinway, per Trial Exhibit #278 (letter of July 24, 1865), Marsh and Osbourne, *Official Report,* viii; "I didn't believe

it possible to live away from you . . ." Trial Exhibit, no number (letter of July 15, 1865), Marsh and Osbourne, *Official Report,* xi.

156   **"Darling, remember all your promises . . ."** Trial Exhibit #263 (letter of July 19, 1865), Marsh and Osbourne, *Official Report,* xiii; "I have never, since my arrival . . ." Trial Exhibit #268 (letter of July 22, 1865), Marsh and Osbourne, *Official Report,* ix.

157   **"I promised myself . . ."** Trial Exhibit #268 (letter of July 22, 1865), Marsh and Osbourne, *Official Report,* ix; "I think I am going to die . . ." Trial Exhibit #278 (letter of July 24, 1865), Marsh and Osbourne, *Official Report,* viii.

157   **"wretched city" . . .** Trial Exhibit #265 (letter of July 30, 1865), Marsh and Osbourne, *Official Report,* xi; Laura's provisos per Trial Exhibit #273 and #260 (letters of August 7 and 8, 1865), Marsh and Osbourne, *Official Report,* viii–ix; "I can't help dreading to see any of her goods . . ." Trial Exhibit (dated August 9, 1865) not in transcript but reprinted in the SFC of April 12, 1871; "This is the last letter I shall write to you . . ." Trial Exhibit #275 (letter of August 11, 1865), Marsh and Osbourne, *Official Report,* x. (NB: Judging from some of the letters, A.P. seems to have come to Warm Springs in person to ask her to return.)

158   **a panic in mining stocks . . .** Smith, *History of the Comstock Lode,* 58–60, 99; worries that Nevada would lose population to Idaho, see the SDU of April 12, 1865.

159   **"If my landlady was as young . . ."** CFP, Box 9, Folder 58; "[I] take my meals with Father . . ." CFP, Box 10, Folder 47.

159   **"As for that woman . . ."** CFP, Box 10, Folder 54.

159   **In December 1865 . . .** Clara would later testify that her husband returned to San Francisco in January 1866 (Marsh and Osbourne, *Official Report,* 165), but letters from Laura to A.P. used as evidence in the trial (cited in the next chapter) indicate that he left in early December 1865.

161   **"I read the signs of the times . . ."** Twain's lecture as quoted in the DAC of December 15, 1866.

163   **"In affairs of public morals . . ."** Bowles's reports were wired back for prompt publication in the *Springfield Republican,* and were later published as his book, *Across the Continent.* The quote is from that book, page 327.

164   **"with hunger and prayer and hope" . . .** Bowles, *Across,* 256; Bross's address ("The production of so vast an amount of the precious metals . . .") per Lavender, *Nothing Seemed Impossible,* 203.

164   **"full-armed in the elements of civilization . . ."** Bowles, *Across,* 161; "the most opulent edifice in the West" per Lavender, *Nothing Seemed Impossible,* 203; for Woodward's Gardens, see Berglund, *Making San Francisco American,* 70–72; "I would prefer that Paris . . ." from Sharon, "Ralston: Caesar of California," California Historical Society, unpaginated.

165   **"A trip to the dentist . . ."** Lotchin, *From Hamlet to City,* 257.

165   **"making the recently acquired . . ."** Berglund, *Making San Francisco American,* xii–xiii; "The best eating house . . ." Barker, *Memoirs, 1835–1851,* 172; "Nobody was so low . . ." Bowles, *Across,* 242–243; see also Berglund, *Making San Francisco American,* 116–117.

166   **race-based discrimination . . .** For the anti-Chinese legislation, see Heizer and Almquist, *Other Californians,* 163, and Jeong, "Ah Toy, Pioneering Prostitute,"

passim. For Ah Toy's arrest and the subsequent arrest of the Englishman "treating her as his wife," see the *Call* of March 27, 1866; see also Tong, *Unsubmissive Women,* 12.

166   **San Francisco's white press** . . . See Lotchin, *From Hamlet to City,* 132; "to spare the sensitive prejudices . . ." Harte, *San Francisco in 1866,* 24–25.

167   **in the wake of the 1863 Charlotte Brown suit** . . . For more on the judge's ruling in Charlotte Brown's case, see Hudson, *Making,* 50–51; "sudden fit of negrophobia" and "protecting white women . . ." Hudson, *Making,* 50.

167   **"proud and erect"** . . . Pleasant's usual bearing, according to an interview with Eduard Bergner (Holdredge Papers, Box 4, Folder 22); the scene on the NBMRR streetcar as depicted in Hudson, *Making,* 52–53.

167   **"willfully and purposely deprived . . ."** and "The damages were excessive . . ." *Pleasants v. North Beach & Mission Railroad,* 34 Cal., 586 (1868), https://cite.case.law /cal/34/586/. (NB: Apparently John James Pleasants was also a plaintiff in the case.)

168   **Lizette Woodworth had mentioned** . . . calling Pleasant "Mamma" Hudson, *Making,* 53.

169   **N. D. Anderson** . . . Trial Exhibit #11 (letter of March 19, 1866), Marsh and Osbourne, *Official Report,* ii–iii; "Oh, the desolation . . ." Trial Exhibit #287 (letter of December 5, 1865), *Official Report,* xii; "I do not feel secure . . ." Trial Exhibit #299 (letter of December 22, 1865), *Official Report,* xiv.

169   **"My God . . ."** Trial Exhibit #9 (letter of March 12, 1866), Marsh and Osbourne, *Official Report,* ii; "desecrating our happy home . . ." Trial Exhibit #8 (letter of March 10, 1866), *Official Report,* vi; "the charming Mrs. F" per CFP, Box 10, Folder 66; James's letter is printed in full in Fair, "Wolves," 43.

169   **"Why don't you let me come . . ."** Trial Exhibit #219 (letter of March 19, 1866), Marsh and Osbourne, *Official Report,* xi; "Oh, how I do want you . . ." Trial Exhibit #14 (letter of July 6, 1866), *Official Report,* vii.

170   **"We have long regarded this gentleman . . ."** Quoted in the Crittenden timeline, Russell McDonald Collection, Box 13 (Nevada Historical Society Library); for the partnership with Wilson, see Shuck, *History of the Bench and Bar,* 403; the move to South Park is in Lamott, *Who Killed,* 57–58; opposition to affair from Heydenfeldt, Tevis, etc., per Franklin, "Crittenden Correspondence Revisited," 21; see also Tevis trial testimony, Marsh and Osbourne, *Official Report,* 207.

171   **"Why, oh why . . ."** Trial Exhibit #15 (letter of August 16, 1866), Marsh and Osbourne, *Official Report,* vii.

171   **she was making arrangements** . . . Fair's move to San Francisco per Marsh and Osbourne, *Official Report,* 101–102, 114–115; see also letters reprinted in the SFC of April 11, 1871.

172   **The trouble began** . . . For details about Fair's return to San Francisco, and the trouble with Mr. Searles that led to her leaving Russ House, see her court testimony, Marsh and Osbourne, *Official Report,* 102, 114–115; see also Lamott, *Who Killed,* 63.

173   **a more discreet living arrangement** . . . Move to Rincon Hill, with servant, per Marsh and Osbourne, *Official Report,* 102; for Crittenden's paying Fair's expenses, see, for instance, Trial Exhibit #240 (letter of August 13, 1866). Marsh and Osbourne, *Official Report,* xi, and many of the letters from 1866—particularly

the one from August 13—reprinted in the SFC of April 11, 1871 (but not, for some reason, included in the trial transcript); William Jones's remark re: Crittenden's spending is found in CFP, Box 11, Folder 2.

174   **famously lenient divorce laws . . .** For divorce laws in the nineteenth century (and for Indiana's in particular) see especially Garber, "Divorce in Marion County," 1-6, and Goodheart, "Divorce, Antebellum Style."

174   **Crittenden insisted . . .** Crittenden's promise to take her to Indiana in December per Marsh and Osbourne, *Official Report,* 102.

174   **Once she became Mrs. Crittenden . . .** For the difference this would make for both Laura and Lillian, see especially Haber, *Trials of Laura Fair,* 37.

175   **Crittenden would renege . . .** His postponement of the December trip is per Marsh and Osbourne, *Official Report,* 102.

175   **Herculean amounts of work . . .** Twain's output and the quote ("If I do not get out of debt . . .") in Powers, *Mark Twain,* 157.

176   **"It appears that a 'Hasheesh' mania . . ."** As quoted in Komp, "Mark Twain's 'Hasheesh' Experience"; Twain's night in jail per Powers, *Mark Twain,* 159.

176   **his four-month stay in the islands . . .** For Twain's Hawaiian sojourn, see Powers, *Mark Twain,* 160–162. (NB: The San Francisco courts attached the receipts from Twain's local performances in order to pay off the old bail bond for Steve Gillis that he had skipped out on a few years earlier.)

177   **Bret Harte warned his friend . . .** Harte's advice not to lecture, and his subsequent review, are in Tarnoff, *Bohemians,* 130; quotes from the *Bulletin* and the *Examiner* as reprinted in the SDU of October 5, 1866; courts attaching Twain's receipts, see Powers, *Mark Twain,* 170.

177   **"My friends and fellow-citizens . . ."** For Twain's farewell address, see the DAC of December 15, 1866. (NB: Twain actually ended with the now-obscure ritual phrase of Freemasons, "So mote it be," but I have chosen to use a more modern and less potentially puzzling formulation of the sentiment.)

178   **Five days later . . .** For Twain's departure on the *America,* and the quote from the DAC, see Powers, *Mark Twain,* 170–171.

178   **investors were feeling gleeful . . .** Recovery in stock prices per Lamott, *Who Killed,* 75; reports and new strikes in Lavender, *Nothing Seemed Impossible,* 202; "Every man you met was a president . . ." Harte, *1866,* 57–58.

179   **"I have the mania upon me . . ."** Trial Exhibit #181, Marsh and Osbourne, *Official Report,* xvi; Fair's move to Mrs. Hammersmith's and Crittenden's multiple residences are in Lamott, *Who Killed,* 65–66; Fair's portfolio value per Fair, "Wolves," 31; buying stocks on margin in Marsh and Osbourne, *Official Report,* 139, and Trial Exhibit #181, *Official Report,* xvi; "I am still of the opinion . . ." Trial Exhibit #29, *Official Report,* iv; for more on the wave of speculation in mining stocks, see Smith, *History of the Comstock Lode,* 62–63.

179   **"As to Savage . . ."** and "In all of these matters, my darling . . ." Trial Exhibit #37, Marsh and Osbourne, *Official Report,* v.

179   **Tevis had sent him . . .** CFP, Box 11, Folder 4; "I am in the big arm chair . . ." Trial Exhibit #18, Marsh and Osbourne, *Official Report,* vii; "Man never loved woman as I do you . . ." Trial Exhibit #25, *Official Report,* iii–iv.

180   **a difficult few months . . .** For Laura and Lillian's sickness, O.D.'s troubles, and

Polly the parrot, see Trial Exhibits #195, 37, 181, 175, 176, and 177, Marsh and Osbourne, *Official Report,* v, ix, xiii, xvi–xvii.

181   **The current plan . . .** Laura's court testimony, Marsh and Osbourne, *Official Report,* 102.

181   **convinced of his sincerity . . .** Marsh and Osbourne, *Official Report,* 102.

181   **insisted that he could not get away . . .** Marsh and Osbourne, *Official Report,* 103; Crittenden as partner in Consolidated Virginia is in Smith, *History of the Comstock Lode,* 146.

182   **In July 1867 . . .** Departure on the *Sacramento* per Marsh and Osbourne, *Official Report,* 102, 116, and Lamott, *Who Killed,* 77.

183   **still couldn't join her . . .** Crittenden's reasons for not coming and for calling her back, Trial Exhibit #211, Marsh and Osbourne, *Official Report,* x; see also an exhibit letter from Crittenden to Fair dated October 29, 1867, which was absent from the published trial transcript but appeared in the SFC of April 9, 1871.

183   **popular at the time . . .** McCabe, *Lights and Shadows,* 307–308; "It is cruel to write as you do . . ." Trial Exhibit #211, Marsh and Osbourne, *Official Report,* x.

184   **"Am I free to ruin forever . . ."** Trial Exhibit #211, Marsh and Osbourne, *Official Report,* x.

184   **gender disparities in the moral code . . .** For a discussion of this issue focused on the era of the Comstock Lode, see Goldman, *Gold Diggers,* 139–141; "You have not said it . . ." Trial Exhibit #211, Marsh and Osbourne, *Official Report,* x.

185   **"Your two letters . . ."** Trial Exhibit #204, Marsh and Osbourne, *Official Report,* xiv; for the rumor about Mr. H, see the October 29, 1867, letter (SFC, April 9, 1871).

185   **"You will run me crazy . . ."** Trial Exhibit #328, Marsh and Osbourne, *Official Report,* ix.

186   **"It nearly killed me . . ."** Letter of October 29, 1867 (SFC, April 9, 1871).

186   **"I suffer so much more . . ."** Letter of December 20, 1865 (SFC, April 11, 1871).

187   **"a new era of great material prosperity" . . .** George, "What the Railroad Will Bring Us," 298; enriching the city's cultural life, "What the Railroad Will Bring Us," 304; "We shall have more home influences . . ." "What the Railroad Will Bring Us," 307.

188   **building a railroad with Chinese . . .** For the growth of Chinese labor and its predominance in the CP workforce, see Chang, *Ghosts of Gold Mountain,* 2, 16, 28.

188   **a new level of bitterness . . .** For the February 12 riot, see the DAC of February 13, 1867, and the SDU of February 14 (reprinting an earlier article from the *San Francisco Bulletin*).

189   **On June 25 . . .** For the Chinese rail strike, see especially Chang, *Ghosts of Gold Mountain,* 138–160; for Crocker's quote, see *Ghosts of Gold Mountain,* 141–142; "progressing rapidly" and "highly pleased . . ." *Ghosts of Gold Mountain,* 158.

190   **a steamer bound for Havana . . .** While her letter of October 11 (Trial Exhibit #204) says she would depart on October 17, her passport records (https://www .familysearch.org/ark:/61903/1:1:QGKJ-T8NY?cid=fs_copy) indicate that a New York notary signed her passport on October 22, suggesting that she was still

in the United States on that date; "give him up, if it was possible to forget him . . ." Marsh and Osbourne, *Official Report,* 103.

190 **quite a cosmopolitan metropolis** . . . For information about Havana at this time, see Tyng, *Stranger in the Tropics,* 13–16, 68–72, 95–101, 140–145; her alleged illness in Havana, Marsh and Osbourne, *Official Report,* 103; for Mr. Sauers and the quote ("the only gentleman . . .") *Official Report,* 103–104.

191 **"would return in two months . . ."** and "His letters and telegrams forced me back . . ." Marsh and Osbourne, *Official Report,* 104.

191 **January 2, 1868** . . . For the reunion scene with Crittenden, including all quotes ("for the sake of my little child" and "bear with all this talk . . ."), see Laura's court testimony, Marsh and Osbourne, *Official Report,* 104. (NB: The printed transcript has Fair saying that she returned on the "second of June," but this was certainly a transcription or typographical error; see, for instance, her own later testimony on 116 and Clara Crittenden's on 165.)

192 **chilly and businesslike** . . . See, for instance, Box 11, Folders 4 and 18; the end of the Sauers engagement is in Marsh and Osbourne, *Official Report,* 104.

193 **"The regular attendance . . ."** SFC of April 13, 1871.

193 **litany of witnesses** . . . Marsh and Osbourne, *Official Report,* 173–208; Cook citing authorities, *Official Report,* 170–173; "I have always understood . . ." *Official Report,* 174; the threat to kill Crittenden, *Official Report,* 185.

194 **Cook recalled the defendant** . . . Rebuttal of Abbott's testimony in Marsh and Osbourne, *Official Report,* 213–214.

194 **"I had reason to fear . . ."** and "to entreat her . . ." Marsh and Osbourne, *Official Report,* 164–165.

194 **"Do you remember the circumstances . . ."** Marsh and Osbourne, *Official Report,* 214.

197 **Sunday after Laura's return** . . . This entire scene and its dialogue are as reported in the combined court testimony of Clara Crittenden and Laura Fair (for once, there was very little disagreement between the two over what was said and done) in Marsh and Osbourne, *Official Report,* 164–165, 214–215.

197 **"as a woman, and as a mother . . ."** Clara's testimony, Marsh and Osbourne, *Official Report,* 165 (emphases mine).

198 **"I told her that he loved me . . ."** Laura's testimony, Marsh and Osbourne, *Official Report,* 214.

198 **"[This] of course startled me considerably . . ."** Clara's testimony, Marsh and Osbourne, *Official Report,* 165.

198 **Laura was just getting started** . . . All of the quotes are from Marsh and Osbourne, *Official Report,* 165 and 215.

199 **the last time the two women ever spoke** . . . Marsh and Osbourne, *Official Report,* 165.

199 **the wives of prominent movers and shakers** . . . For Mrs. Tevis and the society women of San Francisco, see Haber, *Trials of Laura Fair,* 36.

199 **hardly living an irreproachable life** . . . Ralston's scandal and Bierce's column per Lavender, *Nothing Seemed Impossible,* 262–264.

200 **"Anything that is calculated . . ."** Lavender, *Nothing Seemed Impossible,* 199.

200 **An immigrant Hungarian count** . . . For Havaszthy, see Lavender, *Nothing Seemed Impossible,* 172–173. (NB: Havaszthy and his company were soon

bankrupted, but others eventually moved in to pick up the vinicultural mantle.) For the popularity of Eclipse sparkling wine, see Conaway, *Napa,* 13.

201   **Ralston's latest project** . . . For the Belmont mansion, see Lavender, *Nothing Seemed Impossible,* 251–257.

201   **that aspirational San Francisco** . . . For Ralston's South of Market plans and the Grand Hotel, Lavender, *Nothing Seemed Impossible,* 246–252; California Theater and Bret Harte's commissioned play, *Nothing Seemed Impossible,* 261.

202   **"the material development of this Coast"** in Scharnhorst, *Bret Harte,* 35–37; "the center of the world" Tarnoff, *Bohemians,* 149–150.

202   **"lean too much . . ."** Tarnoff, *Bohemians,* 150; "I am trying to build up a literary taste . . ." Scharnhorst, *Bret Harte,* 38; "For years . . ." Tarnoff, *Bohemians,* 149–150.

203   **"is a pleasant land . . ."** *Overland Monthly* (July 1868), 18.

203   **"this picture of Californian society . . ."** Scharnhorst, *Bret Harte,* 39–40; "miners, gunslingers, golden-hearted prostitutes, and wanderers" in Powers, *Mark Twain,* 239.

203   **"Pacific freshness"** and "Far Western flavor" are in Tarnoff, *Bohemians,* 159; *Atlantic Monthly* and Dickens offers—are in Scharnhorst, *Bret Harte,* 41, 48.

204   **an extended stay of several months** . . . For Twain's 1868 return to San Francisco, see especially Powers, *Mark Twain,* 236–239.

205   **"Harte read all of the MS . . ."** As quoted in Powers, *Mark Twain,* 239.

205   **"sacrilegious allusions . . ."** and the other quotes in this paragraph are from Powers, *Mark Twain,* 237.

206   **"wit without vulgarity"** . . . is from the *Dramatic Chronicle* (precursor to the SFC), as quoted in Powers, *Mark Twain,* 239.

206   **"scorn and slander"** . . . Trial Exhibit #211, Marsh and Osbourne, *Official Report,* x; for the continuing scorn she faced, see also her undated letter from the SFC cache published on April 12, 1871; such "casual remarks" were alluded to by a former beat policeman named James Evrard, *Official Report,* 174; her dislike of San Francisco, *Official Report,* 105, 132.

206   **This latest delay** . . . Marsh and Osbourne, *Official Report,* 104; problems re: her divorce from Grayson, 132–135. (NB: In court, Fair claimed that she didn't know of a problem with the divorce until she physically returned to New Orleans in January or February 1869; however, she admits to receiving all kinds of correspondence from Grayson's lawyer—and from Grayson himself, begging her to return—ten years earlier. It seems doubtful that she could have been totally ignorant of the fact that her divorce decree had never been finalized. I suspect it was the prospect of marriage to Crittenden that led her to follow up on the matter at this late date.)

207   **A.P. accompanied Laura and Lillian** Crittenden taking her to the steamer in September 1868, promising to follow, are per Marsh and Osbourne, *Official Report,* 104, 116; see also Trial Exhibit #39, *Official Report,* v, for exact date of her departure (September 14).

208   **"I am making my arrangements . . ."** Trial Exhibit #2, Marsh and Osbourne, *Official Report,* i.

209   **late and sometimes out of order** . . . For a good example of their epistolary lack of sync, see Trial Exhibit 4, Marsh and Osbourne, *Official Report,* ii.

209   **"My own Darling . . ."** Letter of October 4, 1868 (SFC, April 9, 1871).

209   **"My darling: I have had the blues . . ."** Trial Exhibit #42, Marsh and Osbourne, *Official Report,* v.

210   **"If Pa continues to work . . ."** and "If he would only put what spare money he
has . . ." CFP, Box 11, Folders 42 and 43; "I find it hard to get any sleep . . ." Trial
Exhibit #42, Marsh and Osbourne, *Official Report,* v.

210   **Laura was taking care of business . . .** For the visit with the Mitchells and the
quote about Robert ("was not lawyer enough"), see Fair's court testimony in
Marsh and Osbourne, *Official Report,* 134–135.

211   **"All I had been able to accumulate . . ."** and the rest of the quotes in this paragraph are from his letter of April 8, 1869, Trial Exhibit #3, Marsh and Osbourne,
Official Report, i–ii.

211   **"Loss after loss has fallen on me . . ."** Trial Exhibit #2, Marsh and Osbourne,
Official Report, i.

212   **"I am sorry that Pa has lost again . . ."** CFP, Box 11, Folder 41; in Laura Sanchez's letter of April 23 (CFP, Box 11, Folder 43), she implies that Clara was
thinking of going.

212   **a festive entourage . . .** See Howard's letter to Clara, CFP, Box 11, Folder 53;
Howard's new job, CFP, Box 11, Folder 37; "ham and tongues and chicken and
oysters," CFP, Box 11, Folder 57.

213   **inevitable delays and discomforts . . .** For the description of the trip, see
CFP, Box 11, Folders 53, 55, and 57 ("There was much want of arrange-
ment . . ."), and the DAC of June 2, 1869; cost of transcontinental tickets as per
Ambrose, *Nothing Like It,* 372.

213   **"We lived high . . ."** CFP, Box 11, Folder 57; "Summing it up . . ."DAC, June 2,
1869.

214   **"No one recognized me . . ."** CFP, Box 11, Folder 57.

214   **heading to New Orleans . . .** For the reunion in New Orleans, see Marsh and
Osbourne, *Official Report,* 104 and 116 (Laura's account), 149 and 262 (Cook's
sum-up), and 225 (Prosecutor Campbell's reading of a letter from Laura professing horror at the thought of being known as "Mrs. Grayson"); for Crittenden's
taking care of the divorce decree, see *Official Report,* 135, 225.

214   **like any other happy and prosperous family . . .** For their summer travels, see
Marsh and Osbourne, *Official Report,* 116.

215   **the famous hot springs . . .** Crittenden's rheumatism ending when he crossed
Sierra Nevada is in CFP, Box 11, Folder 57; "there are some papers . . ."unnum-
bered Trial Exhibit (APC to LF, "Friday Night," 1869), Marsh and Osbourne,
Official Report, xv; "Mr. F.K." and "When I am with you . . ." unnumbered Trial
Exhibits, *Official Report,* xv.

216   **"I am getting tired of hotel life . . ."** CFP, Box 11, Folder 66.

216   **"Do you want me to come back . . ."** unnumbered Trial Exhibit (APC to LF,
July 16), Marsh and Osbourne, *Official Report,* xv.

216   **"I leave at 11 o'clock . . ."** Unnumbered Trial Exhibit (APC to LF, July 18),
Marsh and Osbourne, *Official Report,* xv; "I am going to leave this afternoon for
Baltimore . . ."unnumbered Trial Exhibit (APC to LF, July 19), *Official Report,* xv.

216   **"You can make the world all brightness or gloom . . ."** Trial Exhibit #53,
Marsh and Osbourne, *Official Report,* xiv; for the final week at White Sulphur

Springs, the visit from Howard, and the promise to return in a month, see defense attorney Cook's final summation for the jury, *Official Report,* 262.

217   **"A month! Think of it . . ."** Trial Exhibit #136, Marsh and Osbourne, *Official Report,* xiv.

217   **"A woman—curse her—wrote me . . ."** Trial Exhibit #136, Marsh and Osbourne, *Official Report,* xiv.

218   **tenth-largest metropolis . . .** Issel and Cherny, *San Francisco,* 14; "The prices they quoted . . ." Lavender, *Nothing Seemed Impossible,* 265.

219   **overbuilt dramatically . . .** For the non-appearance of the expected real estate boom, see Byington, *History of San Francisco,* 330, and Richardson, *Garnered Sheaves,* 299; Ralston's investments in Lavender, *Nothing Seemed Impossible,* 277–278; the U.S. mint maneuver, *Nothing Seemed Impossible,* 285.

219   **"all Asian females . . ."** Heizer and Almquist, *Other Californians,* 164–165.

220   **Moy Jin Mun . . .** Details are from Seligman, *Three Tough Chinamen,* 22, 28–29, and Hoy, "Moy Jin Mun," 11.

222   **continuing economic and social success . . .** For Pleasant's switch from domestic to proprietor, see Hudson, *Making,* 55; "fine food . . ." *Making,* 57; Newton Booth as tenant, *Making,* 58; Charlie Fairfax as tenant per Holdredge Papers, Box 4, Folder 26; assignations, see, for instance, the interviews with David Ruggles and others in the Holdredge Papers, Box 4, Folder 24; "Mammy had a way . . ." 1938 interview with Vena Dyer, Holdredge Papers, Box 4, Folder 25.

222   **"The officers of the Bank of California . . ."** Interview with George S. Lane, Holdredge Papers, Box 4, Folder 24. (NB: Pleasant's practice of listening in on her guests' conversations was mentioned by more than a few of Pleasant's associates interviewed for Holdredge's book.)

222   **"I have always noticed . . ."** From Davis, *Pandex,* 6; for her and Bell's arrival on the *Oregon,* and the lending of the shawl, see the December 30, 1950, interview with David W. Ruggles, Helen Holdredge Papers, Folder 24. (NB: This shawl is alleged to be the one in the Holdredge collection); for the partnership with Bell, see numerous interviews in the Holdredge collection, Folder 24; $100,000 Octavia Place mansion per Hudson, *Making,* 60.

222   **deemed highly inappropriate . . .** For San Franciscans' inability to accept Pleasant's success as anything but witchcraft, see especially Hudson, *Making,* 60–61 ("The Queen of the Voodoos" was the headline for an alleged exposé on Pleasant in the Sunday *Chronicle* of July 9, 1899.) NB: Susheel Bibbs has written a creditable book about Laveau and how she instructed a young Mary Ellen Pleasant on how to use Vodou to effect social change (*Heritage of Power;* see bibliography), but I remain skeptical.

223   **showed up unannounced one day . . .** Fair's arrival in September is per her testimony, Marsh and Osbourne, *Official Report,* 104–105, 116; "Why did you come? . . ." and Crittenden's explanation are in Defense's final argument, *Official Report,* 262, and Fair's testimony, 105.

224   **she would cede . . .** Her offer to give him up is in Lamott, *Who Killed,* 87.

224   **not even unpack . . .** and the debt run up by Parker per Fair's testimony, Marsh and Osbourne, *Official Report,* 105.

224   **various money problems . . .** For an example of Crittenden's sending her

money, see, for instance, his letter of October 1, 1868, as reprinted in the SFC of April 9, 1871; Fair's letter to him of August 13, 1866 (reprinted in the SFC of April 11, 1871) refers to her ruining herself and her child "for mere support, and not even that sometimes," indicating that he was sending her money regularly, at least at that point; for Fair's offer to give her entire fortune to Clara and family, see Marsh and Osbourne, *Official Report,* 132.

225 **resumed the affair** . . . Her rooms on Bush Street and Crittenden's daily visits per Marsh and Osbourne, *Official Report,* 104.

225 **late one night in November** . . . The scene in her rooms, with the quotes ("I am so fatigued . . ."), as per Fair's court testimony, Marsh and Osbourne, *Official Report,* 110–111.

225 **"in a good deal of distress . . ."** This and quotes in the following paragraphs through "My mother tried to stop me" are from Fair's testimony, Marsh and Osbourne, *Official Report,* 111.

226 **Accounts of what happened next** . . . The scene at the Ellis Street house is from the testimony of Fair herself (Marsh and Osbourne, *Official Report,* 110–112, 121, 123–124), Clara Crittenden (33–35), Laura Sanchez (30), and Parker Crittenden (18–19). (NB: Howard was living in Galveston, Texas, at the time of the trial and could not testify.) Where accounts differed—which they did mainly with respect to what exactly Laura Fair said—I have tried to use quotations from these witnesses as attributed in the notes.

227 **"Don't let her into the house"** . . . Clara's testimony, Marsh and Osbourne, *Official Report,* 33.

227 **"threatened to do some injury"** . . . Parker's testimony, Marsh and Osbourne, *Official Report,* 18; "there will be bloodshed . . ." Laura Sanchez's testimony, 31; see also Clara's testimony, 33.

227 **"I am disgusted with you women . . ."** Laura Fair's testimony, Marsh and Osbourne, *Official Report,* 111, Clara Crittenden's testimony, 33, Laura Sanchez's testimony, 30.

227 **When she finally left** . . . Her leaving as Parker and the police arrived is per Laura Fair's testimony, Marsh and Osbourne, *Official Report,* 111.

228 **In the days following the scene** . . . Her fury and refusing to see him per Marsh and Osbourne, *Official Report,*121, 123; "Last night I saw you and Baby at the window . . ." Trial Exhibit #59, *Official Report,* vi.

228 **On November 24** . . . Details about the night she shot at him ("about four or five feet from the floor") are in Marsh and Osbourne, *Official Report,* 121, 123.

229 **"I am coming to see you tonight . . ."** Trial Exhibit #59, Marsh and Osbourne, *Official Report,* vi.

229 **she wanted an apology** . . . Marsh and Osbourne, *Official Report,* 123; "I apologize . . ." exact quote as testified by Clara Crittenden, 36.

229 **Laura further stipulated** . . . For the promises before witnesses, see Marsh and Osbourne, *Official Report,* 123. (NB: Neither Ralston nor Mrs. Hammersmith were called as witnesses during the trial.)

230 **He assured her** . . . His claim that he had gone to Ellis Street only because a child was sick in Marsh and Osbourne, *Official Report,* 121; "It is too bad . . ." CFP, Box 12, Folder 37; "something the matter with his heart . . ." CFP, Box 12, Folder 51.

230   **"I gradually gave up trying . . ."** Marsh and Osbourne, *Official Report,* 124; Camilla Urso concert ("I ask this . . .") is from Trial Letter printed in the SFC of April 12, 1871 (undated, but Urso's series of San Francisco concerts took place in February 1870).

230   **one big promise . . .** The trip in July and $700 of wedding clothing per Marsh and Osbourne, *Official Report,* 105; Mrs. Lane's haranguing ("utterly ruined"), 108.

231   **Dr. Benjamin Lyford . . .** His various diagnoses as per his own testimony, Marsh and Osbourne, *Official Report,* 78; chloral hydrate, etc., *Official Report,* 87; the unspecified surgical procedure, and carrying away material in a basin, as described by Laura's servant at this time, Catherine McCormick, 161; "a speculation in gasoline . . ." and Clara's going east, 105.

232   **On Sunday, August 14 . . .** The Fair-Snyder wedding was reported in the next day's paper (DAC of August 15, 1870); Laura met him ten days earlier per Marsh and Osbourne, *Official Report,* 116.

232   **seeking in a suitor for her daughter . . .** Mary Lane encouraging courtship with Snyder, Marsh and Osbourne, *Official Report,* 108.

232   **as Snyder was visiting Laura . . .** The confrontation with Crittenden about Snyder, with all quotes ("Who is in there?," etc.) Marsh and Osbourne, *Official Report,* 116–117.

233   **Laura confessed to Jesse Snyder . . .** and the wedding, Marsh and Osbourne, *Official Report,* 117, 109.

233   **Crittenden nearly lost his mind . . .** Their conversation on California Street ("I must see you . . .") Marsh and Osbourne, *Official Report,* 108; "No—I can *not* . . ." note ruled out of testimony, but reproduced in *Official Report,* 57.

233   **"See you I must . . ."** Marsh and Osbourne, *Official Report,* 57; "I can not wait . . ." 49; her interpreting it as suicide threat, 108. (NB: In the trial, Fair is interrupted before she can report Mrs. Lane's reaction.)

234   **"Why have you done this thing"** and "swept away all the foundation" . . . Marsh and Osbourne, *Official Report,* 108.

234   **"I told him that I did love him . . ."** and "it was a simple matter . . ." and "never allow Mr. Snyder . . ." Marsh and Osbourne, *Official Report,* 109.

235   **what manner of persuasion . . .** For the arrangement by which the Snyder divorce was obtained, see Marsh and Osbourne, *Official Report,* 76, 110, and 210–211 (Snyder's own testimony); also the letters printed in the SFC of April 12, 1871. (NB: In his testimony, Snyder claimed—probably as part of their agreement—that Crittenden had nothing to do with preparing the divorce plot.) $10,000 bribe rumor is in Lamott, *Who Killed,* 106; the separation agreement, dated September 7, 1870, was produced in court per *Official Report,* 210.

235   **a breach between Laura and her mother . . .** Mrs. Lane's move per Lamott, *Who Killed,* 107.

235   **the newly reunited lovers . . .** Laura's insistence that they not live together per Marsh and Osbourne, *Official Report,* 241; several witnesses corroborated that the two were often seen together in public during this time: 100, 135–136; the move to Kearny Street, 63.

236   **one afternoon in late October . . .** Volberg and Fair had somewhat different recollections of how the information about Clara's return came out. See *Official*

Report, 25–27 (Volberg), 110 (Fair). (NB: It's possible that Mrs. Hammersmith had already hinted to Laura that Clara was returning, but it was only after the conversation with Volberg that Fair was worried enough to confront A.P. about it.)

236 **When she confronted A.P. about it . . .** Marsh and Osbourne, *Official Report,* 118.

236 **"When you return . . ."** and "I infer from your silence . . ." CFP, Box 13, Folder 31.

237 **"I lead a rather humdrum life . . ."** CFP, Box 13, Folder 39.

237 **"I feel unusually light-hearted . . ."** CFP, Box 13, Folder 46; "Pray, how long . . ." CFP, Box 13, Folder 49; "I suppose you will be surprised . . ." CFP, Box 13, Folder 53.

238 **"Don't come . . ."** CFP, Box 13, Folder 52; Clara's visits with family in Virginia and Kentucky are in CFP, Box 13, Folder 68.

238 **anxiety caused by Clara's mere presence . . .** Marsh and Osbourne, *Official Report,* 117–118.

238 **Laura would deny him her own bed . . .** The understanding about not sharing her bed was expressed in one of her letters to him after the Snyder divorce, not reprinted in full in the transcript but excerpted by her attorney Quint in his closing statement, per Marsh and Osbourne, *Official Report,* 241; Mrs. Marillier confirmed that Crittenden slept in his own bed the two nights he was there, 65; Crittenden's renting of the room at Mrs. Marillier's house and the reason, 64–65, 118.

239 **even after Crittenden engaged the room . . .** $40 rent, insomnia and head pains, "excited and weepy" are from Marsh and Osbourne, *Official Report,* 64–65; taking valerian and chloral hydrate, memory lapses, 79, 99–100.

239 **"the only wife he had on earth" . . .** Marsh and Osbourne, *Official Report,* 106.

239 *McCauley v. Fulton* . . . Marsh and Osbourne, *Official Report,* 183 (the witness here—an attorney named George R. Wells—claimed that it was the "Twelfth District Court," but this was a misstatement or a transcription error); "You have been crying . . ." and all other quotes in this paragraph are from *Official Report,* 106.

239 **he promised that he would return . . .** Marsh and Osbourne, *Official Report,* 106.

240 **Mrs. Marillier was surprised . . .** Details from Mrs. Marrillier's account of their departure and her return are per Marsh and Osbourne, *Official Report,* 65; "meet her without kissing her," 106, see also 65.

240 **She and her little traveling party . . .** The makeup of the traveling party and the boys' earlier ferry arrival comes from various bits of testimony from the people involved. See Marsh and Osbourne, *Official Report,* 15, 28–30, 32–33, as well as a letter from Parker to Nannie describing the shooting: CFP, Box 13, Folder 70.

241 **"was affectionately embraced . . ."** SFC of November 4, 1870; for the loving tone of the letters, see, for instance, CFP Box 13, Folder 51 (his to her) and Folder 68 (hers to him).

241 **"[Mrs. Fithian] is a very pretty and graceful woman . . ."** CFP, Box 13, Folder 68. (NB: Captain Fithian joined the train in Ogden, Utah.)

241 **When the horn . . .** All details in this paragraph, including the quote ("bright, sunshiny afternoon") are from Clara's court testimony: Marsh and Osbourne, *Official Report,* 32.

242   **Only then did Clara look up** . . . All details here are from Clara's testimony in
      Marsh and Osbourne, *Official Report,* 32–34, and her testimony at the coroner's
      inquest as reported in the SFC of November 11, 1870.

245   **November 7, 1870** . . . Rain as per DAC issues of November 7 and 8, 1870;
      "Mother Church of the Pacific Coast" is per "A Brief History of Trinity Church,"
      https://trinity-stpeters.org/about-the-church/ (accessed May 8, 2023); "The
      blow that struck him down . . ." and other details are per Haber, *Trials of Laura
      Fair,* 242.

245   **Spectators thronged the sidewalks** . . . All details are from the DAC and SFC
      issues of November 8, 1870.

246   **It had been four days** . . . The events after the shooting are compiled from the
      inquest and trial testimony of several witnesses, including Captain Kentzel, Cap-
      tain Bushnell, Dr. Nelson Bird, and Clara, Carrie, and Parker Crittenden, in
      Marsh and Osbourne, *Official Report,* 8, 11, 13, 15–17, 29–30, 32–33, 38, and the
      reports on the coroner's inquest as printed in the DAC and SFC of November 11,
      12, 15, and 17, 1870.

247   **having returned from his errand** . . . Details from the testimony of Parker
      Crittenden, Captain Kentzel, and Captain Bushnell are in Marsh and Osbourne,
      Official Report, 8, 13, 15.

247   **"This is the woman . . ."** and "Yes, I did it . . ." as per Parker Crittenden's testi-
      mony, Marsh and Osbourne, *Official Report,* 15. (NB: Parker claimed that Fair
      also said "and I meant to kill him," but since this was not corroborated by Captain
      Kentzel, who certainly would have mentioned such a crucial detail in his testi-
      mony, I suspect it is the young man's invention.)

247   **"took hold of her"** . . . and escorted her aft, request to see Crittenden, etc., are
      per Marsh and Osbourne, *Official Report,* 8–9.

248   **The wounded Crittenden** . . . mattress, half dozen men, people in the wagon,
      etc., are per Marsh and Osbourne, *Official Report,* 13, 15, 38 (NB: Dr. Bird's name
      is sometimes rendered as "Burd" in the transcript); chloroform and morphine,
      unidentified doctor's notes, CFP, Box 1; time of death is from a telegram of
      November 5, 1870, from R. B. Sanchez to Nannie Van Wyck, CFP, Box 1; for
      other details about the shooting and Crittenden's suffering and death, see also a
      letter from Parker Crittenden to his sister Nannie, dated November 4, 1870, in
      CFP, Box 13, Folder 70.

248   **Murder was common enough** . . . Murder statistics as per the studies of scholar
      and former San Francisco police chief Kevin Mullen, who used newspaper re-
      ports on homicides to supplement crime statistics lost in the 1906 earthquake
      and fire (see his database at the website of Ohio State University's Criminal
      Justice Research Center: https://cjrc.osu.edu/research/interdisciplinary/hvd
      /united-states/san-francisco). Articles about "The Crittenden Tragedy" were re-
      printed, for instance, in the NYT of November 13, the *Chicago Tribune* of No-
      vember 11, and the *Memphis Public Ledger* of November 16 (all 1870).

249   **"It is reckoned a very slight offense . . ."** SFC of November 5, 1870; "A Bold,
      Bad Woman" is a headline from the same newspaper's November 4 edition.

249   **a living symbol of lawlessness** . . . For the wild stories printed in the newspa-
      pers about Fair's past, see Haber, *Trials of Laura Fair,* 38, 41–43; also see the SFC
      of November 4, 1870. (NB: According to Haber, the paper also claimed that

Laura was naked at the time, but I failed to see that detail in the version of the article I read.)

249   **incarcerated at City Prison . . .** Sheet-iron cell painted pink is from SFC, November 8, 1870; Fair's behavior in the cell as per the trial testimony of the nurse and Dr. Trask, Marsh and Osbourne, *Official Report,* 57–63, 91–99; "unladylike" per DAC of November 4, 1870 (NB: There was some disagreement over exactly how thick the glass was that Fair bit a chunk out of). See also *Official Report,* 57, 66, 70, 81; brain fever, see Lamott, *Who Killed,* 128.

250   **the newly completed Crittenden home . . .** The splendor of the Crittenden mansion as per the SFC, November 11, 1870; Coroner's jury verdict per SFC, November 16, 1870.

251   **"No! I have nothing to say . . ."** SFC of November 11, 1870.

251   **being unable to find a lawyer . . .** Mrs. Lane's difficulty in engaging a lawyer per DAC of November 14, 1870 (NB: The DAC and the SFC differed on the amount of money offered, refused, and finally accepted by various attorneys); $15,000 for Cook and Quint, see Haber, *Trials of Laura Fair,* 45; for information on Cook, see Shuck, *History of the Bench and Bar,* 442; on Quint, see Lang, *History of Tuolumne County,* 377.

251   **still reeling from the death . . .** Clara falling down the stairs per CFP, Box 13, Folder 74; on H. H. Byrne, see Shuck, *History of the Bench and Bar,* 442–445; on Campbell, *Bench and Bar,* 517–518.

252   **In early February 1871 . . .** For the surveyor's determination on the location of the shooting and the Alameda County indictment, see SFC, January 7 and 8, 1871; see also Marsh and Osbourne, *Official Report,* 2.

252   **The prisoner was transported . . .** Fair's indictment is in DAC, February 6, 1871; Arraignment ("She looked very pale and worn . . .") is in SFC, February 26, 1871.

252   **the general line of defense . . .** For the defense's intentions, see, for instance, Cook's opening statement in Marsh and Osbourne, *Official Report,* 50–52.

253   **much higher ambitions . . .** For the prosecution's intentions, see, for instance, Byrne's closing statement in Marsh and Osbourne, *Official Report,* 295–296, 305; "The lines of class and caste . . . ," "a distinctive San Francisco product," and "a screw loose somewhere in our social mechanism . . . Hoodlumism . . ." are in Williams, "City of the Golden Gate," 279, 276–277.

253   **it was critical to show the world . . .** That the reputation of the city was at stake was made explicit in Byrne's closing statement in Marsh and Osbourne, *Official Report,* 321; "punishment of lawbreakers . . ." as quoted in SFGate of May 2, 2015.

255   **"Yesterday, in the Fifteenth District Court . . ."** SFC of March 28, 1871.

255   **The suffragists were there for Laura . . .** For Emily Pitts Stevens (often misspelled as "Pitt Stevens"), see Haber, *Trials of Laura Fair,* 45, Lamott, *Who Killed,* 142, and Willard, *Woman of the Century,* 686 ("a woman's paper . . ."); "Strange as it may seem . . ." is from the DAC of April 8, 1871.

256   **"We defend the rights of women fearlessly . . ."** As quoted in Bennion, *Equal to the Occasion,* 58. (NB: The newspaper was called the *Sunday Mercury* when Pitts Stevens first bought it, but she quickly changed the name to *The Pioneer.*)

256   **"Bold, Bad Woman" . . .** SFC of November 4, 1870.

256   **The first few days of the trial** . . . Most of the details about the court proceed-
       ings come from Marsh and Osbourne, *Official Report*; "the reputation of the
       Court" and "prevent scandal" from DAC of March 29, 1871; sequestering a jury
       as unprecedented in California is in Haber, *Trials of Laura Fair*, 48.

257   **proceeded with inexorable logic** . . . Early witnesses per Marsh and Osbourne,
       Official Report, 7–14, 23–25, 28–30.

257   **Campbell also called** . . . Charles Volberg, Parker Crittenden, and Laura San-
       chez per Marsh and Osbourne, *Official Report*, 15–22, 25–27, 30–32; the wit-
       nesses who testified to her admission were Captain Kentzel (8), Parker Crittenden
       (15), J. A. Woodson (23), and J. W. Wilbur (24).

258   **did what they could on cross-examination** . . . Volberg's lawsuit per Marsh
       and Osbourne, *Official Report*, 26; Tommy and Carrie Crittenden's inconsistent
       testimony, 28–30.

259   **"I turned from her . . ."** Marsh and Osbourne, *Official Report*, 32.

259   **"Did you go to her house . . ."** Marsh and Osbourne, *Official Report*, 34.

260   **adjectives that Campbell used frequently** . . . ("bold, bad," "manly," and "un-
       feminine"), see, for instance, Marsh and Osbourne, *Official Report*, 233–234.

260   **Having thus established** . . . Marsh and Osbourne, *Official Report*, 48.

260   **a very different narrative** . . . For the "unwritten law," see especially Ireland,
       "The Libertine Must Die," 27–44 ("that an outraged husband . . ." 27); see also
       Haber, *Trials of Laura Fair*, 5–8, on the relevance of these cases to the Fair trial.

261   **"Gentlemen of the jury . . ."** Marsh and Osbourne, *Official Report*, 48.

261   **"No two living beings . . ."** Marsh and Osbourne, *Official Report*, 48.

262   **a greedy, kept woman** . . . Marsh and Osbourne, *Official Report*, 52.

262   **". . . Mrs. Fair was insane"** . . . and all other quotes in this paragraph per Marsh
       and Osbourne, *Official Report*, 49–50.

263   **"I was so much afraid . . ."** Marsh and Osbourne, *Official Report*, 57; for the
       other testimony about her insane behavior, see, 57–63, 65–67, 70–72.

263   **"She was not well for five weeks . . ."** and other testimony per Marsh and Os-
       bourne, *Official Report*, 64–65.

264   **Benjamin Lyford** . . . Lyford's testimony ("It is to be expected . . ." etc.) per
       Marsh and Osbourne, *Official Report*, 78.

265   **"most positive, absolute mania . . ."** and "induce her to commit almost any
       insane act," and "The suddenness of an outbreak . . ." See Marsh and Osbourne,
       Official Report, 79–81.

265   **On cross-examination** . . . Campbell refers to Lyford as a "professional moun-
       tebank" in his closing statement, per Marsh and Osbourne, *Official Report*, 222;
       the Q&A about Lyford's training and qualifications on 86–88.

268   **Dr. John Trask** . . . Trask's testimony ("hysterical mania," etc.) per Marsh and
       Osbourne, *Official Report*, 90–99.

269   **"the majority of the insanity . . ."** Testimony of Joseph Tucker per Marsh and
       Osbourne, *Official Report*, 148.

269   **contrary to California law** . . . Defendants were first allowed to give evidence
       in California courtrooms in 1866; see Cal. Stat. 1865, ch. 644, §§ 1–2, at 865
       (1866).

270   **providing illustrations of all three images** . . . Fair's various antics in the court-
       room were described in the daily newspaper reports and by Byrne in his closing

statement ("sighs and tears and groans," etc.) in Marsh and Osbourne, *Official Report,* 308.

271   **"the chief topic of conversation . . ."** SFC of April 2, 1871; "but unfortunately she ventured . . ." from the *New York World* of April 10, 1871, as reprinted in the DAC of April 19, 1871; "We would call attention . . ." NYT of April 15, 1871. (NB: For the *Times'* reactions to the Sickles and McFarland verdicts, see the issues of April 28, 1859, and May 11, 1870; in the Cole case, the paper's editors disagreed with the acquittal since the outraged husband had known about the adultery long before shooting the perpetrator, NYT of December 11, 1868.)

272   **"May not a woman . . ."** From *The Pioneer,* as quoted in Lamott, *Who Killed,* 183; "There are grievous sins . . ." *The Revolution,* April 27, 1871. (NB: The other major suffragist journal of the day, Julia Ward Howe's *Woman's Journal,* was somewhat less sympathetic to Laura Fair, but ultimately took the same line re: equal treatment of the sexes.)

272   **"strong-minded"** . . . and "loud and determined tone of voice" from DAC of April 5, 1871; "I know I reached my hand out . . ." Marsh and Osbourne, *Official Report,* 106.

273   **"he would kill any man . . ."** Marsh and Osbourne, *Official Report,* 104.

273   **"he would have made Mr. Campbell . . ."** Marsh and Osbourne, *Official Report,* 107.

273   **burst into applause . . .** The reaction of the suffragists, and "You will have to draw heavily . . ." Marsh and Osbourne, *Official Report,* 107.

274   **"I beg your pardon . . ."** Marsh and Osbourne, *Official Report,* 118.

275   **"Then your idea is . . ."** Marsh and Osbourne, *Official Report,* 118.

275   **an extended bout of legal wrangling . . .** The haggling over admission of the letters is found in Marsh and Osbourne, *Official Report,* 137–139.

276   **the letters might actually help their case . . .** The SFC reprinted dozens of the letters in their issues of April 9, 11, and 12, 1871; they were described as "a rich feast of gushing sentimentality" in a headline of the April 9 edition.

276   **On Tuesday, April 11 . . .** Prosecution rebuttal per Marsh and Osbourne, *Official Report,* 162; "That's a lie!" on 164; "Mrs Fair's eyes blazed in fury," SFC of April 12, 1871; "gross insult" and "contempt of Court," *Official Report,* 168.

277   **a big mistake in their case . . .** Witnesses to Fair's "bad reputation" per Marsh and Osbourne, *Official Report,* 170–182, 193, 199–208.

277   **On Saturday, April 15 . . .** Discussion of order of final arguments, see Marsh and Osbourne, *Official Report,* 252.

278   **making explicit the prosecution's main theme . . .** Marsh and Osbourne, *Official Report,* 221–234; "doctrines and principles . . ." 221; "a new system of morality . . ." 229; "woman who takes a fancy . . ." and "That your verdict . . ." 234.

278   **over the course of the next six days . . .** Marsh and Osbourne, *Official Report,* 234–252; Sickles, McFarland, and Cole cases on 249–250.

279   **logical inconsistencies in the narrative . . .** Cook's argument, Marsh and Osbourne, *Official Report,* 252–295; "as her protector . . ." on 292.

279   **had the last word . . .** Byrne's argument per Marsh and Osbourne, *Official Report,* 295–322; "the most important trial . . ." and "strikes at the very foundation . . ." 295.

280   **"the greatest man . . ."** Marsh and Osbourne, *Official Report,* 301; "a female

Hercules" and "a regiment of Crittendens," 312; "Why, gentlemen . . ." 313; "The demands . . ." 321.

280 **the culmination of four exhausting weeks . . .** Church and *Othello* excursions for the jury are in Lamott, *Who Killed,* 171; "in a fit of temporary insanity" is per the SFC of April 4, 1871; for details of the scene surrounding the verdict, see Marsh and Osbourne, *Official Report,* 324–325, and the SFC of April 27, 1871.

282 **"It may not be improper to say . . ."** NYT of April 27, 1871.

282 **"was a triumph . . ."** DAC of June 4, 1871; "Upon the streets, in saloons . . ." SFC of April 27, 1871.

283 **"I will never buy another lump of coal . . ."** From the SFC of May 7, 1871; "My sympathies are all with the defendant . . ." Letter from Goodwin to his sister Mary, June 4, 1871, James V. Medler Crime Collection, Clements Library, University of Michigan (for more on Goodwin, see the *Atlanta Constitution* of February 6, 1869).

283 **"These six months of sorrows . . ."** and other details of Clara's ordeal ("totally prostrated"), CFP, Box 13, Folder 86.

284 **"one error during a lifetime . . ."** and "His name shall always be sacred . . ." CFP, Box 13, Folder 86.

284 **A.P.'s will . . .** CFP, Box 1; see also A. P. Crittenden's Estate Papers I and II— Box 16, Folders 3 and 4 (*Bank of California and William C. Ralston v. Clara Crittenden, Executrix*); James's taking of the law library and Heydenfeldt's letter is per A. P. Crittenden's Estate Papers III—Box 16, Folder 5.

284 **adding to the family's heartache . . .** Howard details are in CFP, Box 13, Folders 14, 82, and 85 ("You all need not expect to hear from me . . .").

285 **Cook and Quint filed a motion . . .** For the denial of a new trial, and the quotes, see the DAC of June 4, 1871.

285 **"You have got what you want now, haven't you . . ."** DAC of June 4, 1871.

285 **"the only correct likeness of Mrs. Laura D. Fair . . ."** DAC of May 9, 1871; Lyford's embalming ads ("FIRM AS STONE . . .") as reproduced in Haber, *Trials of Laura Fair,* 128; the NYC coroner's office incident is per DAC of June 30, 1871 (reprinting a story from the *New York Herald* of June 17).

286 **many civil cases generated . . .** For the Trask and Lane lawsuits, see the DAC of January 18 and the DAC and *San Francisco Examiner* of April 2, 1872.

286 **On July 10 . . .** Stay of execution as reprinted in the DAC of July 13, 1871.

286 **busily writing a four-act dramatization . . .** DAC of November 4, 1871; "Those fantastic theories . . ." *New York Tribune* of April 28, 1871.

287 **Greeley was still talking . . .** Greeley's letter ("The Advanced Female of the Laura Fair type . . .") as quoted in Haber, *Trials of Laura Fair,* 139; see also the DAC of August 10, 1871; Stanton's response ("What has that to do with our movement . . .") as quoted in *Trials of Laura Fair,* 139.

287 **the two insisted on being taken . . .** Visit to the jail, per DAC of July 14, 1871; "Mrs. Fair may not have been a saint . . ." as quoted in Lamott, *Who Killed,* 286– 287; "It was A. P. Crittenden . . ." as quoted in Haber, *Trials of Laura Fair,* 134.

288 **The night after this visit . . .** For Anthony's speech in Platt's Hall ("Woman must not depend . . ." and "Never in all my hard experience . . ."), see Lutz, *Susan B. Anthony,* 188–189 (NB: Anthony's speech at Platt's Hall was reported in slightly different words in Sherr, *Failure Is Impossible,* 215–216); for the presence

of Mrs. Lane and Lillian in the audience, see Haber, *Trials of Laura Fair,* 135; see also the DAC of July 13, 1871.

288   **overturned the results . . .** The state supreme court decision is in "The People of the State of California v. Laura D. Fair." *Reports of Cases Determined in the Supreme Court of the State of California,* Vol. 43 (San Francisco: Bancroft-Whitney Company, January 1906); "Judgment reversed . . ." per Marsh and Osbourne, *Official Report,* 157. (NB: Because of scheduling issues and illness, only two out of five supreme court justices ruled in the case: Associate Justices William Wallace and Joseph Crockett. See Cole, "The Laura Fair Affair," 18.)

289   **The second trial of Laura Fair . . .** Cook's death, DAC of January 2, 1872; Byrne's death, DAC of March 2, 1872; Byrne's marital history, Cole, "The Laura Fair Affair," 19, and Shuck, *History of the Bench and Bar,* 442–445; for Campbell's hypocritical arguments, see Haber, *Trials of Laura Fair,* 144.

289   **As for the defendant . . .** Fair's alleged death, DAC of April 6, 1872; "pale and emaciated," DAC of September 10, 1872; N. Greene Curtis, see Shuck, *History of the Bench and Bar,* 464–465; defense and prosecution teams and Judge Reardon, DAC of September 10, 1872. (NB: Since no transcript of the retrial seems to exist, I have relied mainly on daily newspaper accounts for details.)

290   **potential jurors . . .** Initial pool of four hundred is per DAC of September 10, 1872; further calls for jurors and $200 fine for no-shows per DAC of September 14, 1872.

290   **Finally, on September 17 . . .** Final juror chosen, DAC of September 18, 1872; "willing to confess that they are idiots," SFC of September 10, 1872; "I take the paper but don't read it . . ." DAC of September 14, 1872; "The humorist who invented trial by jury . . ." in a letter to Whitelaw Reid dated March 7, 1873, via the Mark Twain Project (https://www.marktwainproject.org/xtf/view?docId =letters/UCCL00883.xml&brand=mtp&style=letter#X).

291   **watching from the defense table . . .** Fair's weeping, court adjourned, DAC and SFC of September 18, 1872.

291   **"There was a general feeling . . ."** DAC of September 19, 1872; Lyford's testimony as reported in the DAC and SFC of September 20, 1872.

292   **other differences besides the speed of the proceedings . . .** Medical experts for the prosecution, DAC and SFC of September 25, 26, and 27, 1872; $250 payment; Mrs. Lane's testimony about family madness and spells, DAC and SFC of September 24, 1872.

292   **Curtis's presentation . . .** Opening statement as per the SFC and DAC ("poor, frail, unfortunate humanity" and "the God-Man of Nazareth . . .") of September 20, 1872; contrary to her own wishes . . . Curtis apparently had to forcefully talk Fair out of testifying on her own behalf, see the SFC of October 1, 1872.

293   **the whole matter looked a little different . . .** Curtis's summations as per the DACs of September 20 ("There are other and more vital interests . . .") and September 28, 1872 ("crazed by the man who had her in her grasp").

294   **"Threats were made . . ."** DAC of September 29, 1872.

294   **more than sixty-four hours after . . .** The verdict and Fair's reaction per SFC and DAC of October 1, 1872.

295   **"Murder Licensed . . ."** DAC of October 1, 1872.

295   **"By the first trial and its result . . ."** DAC of October 1, 1872.

296 **"The result is nothing less . . ."** NYT of October 1, 1872; "The jury in her case . . ." as quoted in Haber, *Trials of Laura Fair,* 179.

296 **"marvelously ignorant San Francisco jury"** . . . NYT of October 1, 1872; "a revolt . . ." Young, *San Francisco,* 452.

297 **"Fair Lunatic"** . . . SFC of October 2, 1872; "the most infernal din . . ." and the rumors of James's threat, SFC of October 1, 1872.

297 **Contrary to her lawyers' promises** . . . "return to her native land," see summary of Curtis's final argument in the DAC of September 28, 1872; suing the cartoonist, see Haber, *Trials of Laura Fair,* 197–198; demanding return of the pistol, SDU of November 5, 1872; "looking defiance," etc., per NYT of January 19, 1874; the incident with the streetcar conductor ("I suppose nowadays to stop the car . . ."), see SFC of November 19, 1872.

298 **her bold return to the stage** . . . All quotes and references in this paragraph are from Fair, "Wolves," 3, 11–12, 23–28.

298 **the night of November 21** . . . For the account of the canceled lecture at Platt's and the quote ("not of the class . . ."), see the DAC of November 22, 1872; see also Haber, *Trials of Laura Fair,* 189–191; for her later successful suit against the Platt's owners, see *Trials of Laura Fair,* 191, and the NYT of May 25, 1873. (She won $96—the rental cost of the hall, plus the printing costs for posters.)

299 **tried to reschedule the event** . . . Beer hall lecture, see DAC of January 26, 1873; Hansel Hall lecture, see *Stockton Independent* of February 5, 1853; Hamilton Hall lecture, SDU of February 6, 1873; blaming the press, see Fair, "Wolves," 10; failure of "Wolves" per Haber, *Trials of Laura Fair,* 200.

299 **still had money** . . . $75,000 gain in Ophir per NYT of January 19, 1874; "[Mrs. Fair] lives in style . . ." Dixon, *White Conquest,* 169.

300 **Twain was prospering** . . . For the story behind *The Gilded Age,* see French, *Mark Twain,* Franklin Walker ("An Influence"), and Powers, *Mark Twain,* 327–342; "a thoroughgoing exposé of its times" per French, 141.

300 **"The jury system . . . puts a ban . . ."** As quoted in French, *Mark Twain,* 549–550; for the reviews, see Powers, *Mark Twain,* 341–342; for the pirated stage version, see Powers, 352; for Twain's own *Colonel Sellers* and the quote ("I have killed the only man I ever loved"), see French, 557–561.

301 **slipping in the public's esteem** . . . For Ralston's shenanigans, financial collapse, and death, see Brechin, *Imperial San Francisco,* 86–90, and Lavender, *Nothing Seemed Impossible,* 356–382; "No matter what he has done . . ." as quoted in the DAC of September 17, 1876.

302 **A final irony** . . . The Palace Hotel opened on October 14, 1875 per Lavender, *Nothing Seemed Impossible,* 384; Sherman's visit, as reported in the DAC of September 17, 1876.

302 **became destitute again** . . . Adams suit per DAC and SFC editions of April 6, 1877; bankruptcy, DAC of April 12, 1877; "We have, all of us, immense desires . . ." Fair, "Wolves," 44.

305 **"Marvelous has been the growth of San Francisco . . ."** Williams, "City of the Golden Gate," 266.

305 **"the most imposing pageant . . ."** DAC of July 5, 1876.

305 **marking the centennial** . . . June 29, 1776, establishing of Mission Dolores,

Richards, *Historic*, 31. (NB: Byington, *History of San Francisco*, 30, says that the date was September 17.)

305 **come a long way** . . . "the commercial metropolis" and 60 percent of manufactures, see Godfrey, *Neighborhoods in Transition*, 62; "The stranger . . ." as quoted in Lewis, *This Was San Francisco*, 184; complaints about lack of parks and gardens, see MacGregor, *San Francisco*, 15; "I don't know that in all my travels . . ." Barker, *More*, 224.

306 **ahead of its time** . . . For Hallidie and the Clay Street cable-car line, see Lavender, *Nothing Seemed Impossible*, 357; Godfrey, *Neighborhoods in Transition*, 63; Brechin, *Imperial San Francisco*, 65; and Richards, *Historic*, 135–136.

307 **"It is New York . . ."** As quoted in Lewis, *This Was San Francisco*, 175–176.

307 **certain civic improvements** . . . Father Neri's three arc lights, see Coleman, *P.G. and E.*, 51–52; first city to have a central generating station, Coleman, 51, and Brechin, *Imperial San Francisco*, 255.

307 **"startling white radiance"** . . . Coleman, *P.G. and E.*, 52; details about the groups marching in the parade come principally from the DAC of July 5, 1876, and the SFC of July 6, 1876.

308 **total absence of Chinese marchers** . . . Unemployment and the Chinese, see Cherney, "Patterns of Toleration," 133.

308 **"Pacific Coast's conscience"** . . . Tarnoff, *Bohemians*, 60; details about "The Heathen Chinee," see Scharnhorst, *Bret Harte*, 51–58.

309 **"Like a transplanted piñon tree"** . . . As quoted in Scharnhorst, *Bret Harte*, 63; "Society [here], as it has gained in respectability . . ." as quoted in *Bret Harte*, 58.

310 **apparently retired** . . . Siler, *White Devil's Daughters*, 34; move to San Jose, marriage, and the Page Act, see Jeong, "Ah Toy, Pioneering Prostitute"; later life and death, see *Oakland Tribune* of February 2, 1928.

310 **less insulated from the rising tide** . . . For Moy's escape from the Irish mob, see Seligman, *Three Tough Chinamen*, 30–31; brings wife back and opens shop on Dupont per Chung, *In Pursuit of Gold*, 180–181, and Seligman, *Three Tough Chinamen*, 71; Six Companies leader and triad war mediator, *Three Tough Chinamen*, 216–217; co-owner of Shanghai Low, 221; "unofficially the 'mayor' of Chinatown," 222.

311 **she continued to promote the local Black community** . . . For the partnership with Bell and the comment resulting from their cohabitation of the Octavia Street mansion, see Hudson, *Making*, 61–62; "As Voodoo Queen . . ." from an interview with William Tomlinson as recorded in the Holdredge Papers, Box 4, Folder 24.

311 **often playing into stereotypes** . . . see Hudson, *Making*, 115–116; "I am a whole theater in myself," as quoted in Bennett, "Mystery," Part 2, 71.

312 **Pleasant did lose much of her fortune** . . . Bell's death, see Hudson, *Making*, 79–80 (NB: Regarding these "eyewitness" accounts of Bell's death, one frustrated Pleasant biographer comically lamented: "Mammy has been placed at the foot of the stairs, the second floor, third floor, and on each step in between, as well as in bed alone, with a man, with a woman, awake, asleep, nude, fully clothed, in a trance staring into a hypnotized snake's eyes, and what not." [Conrich, "Mammy Pleasant Legend," 122]); "Listen . . ." as quoted in Bennett, "Mystery," Part 1, 90;

Mary Ellen Pleasant Memorial Park and the "Mother of Civil Rights in California," see the photo in Hudson, *Making,* just before page 63; "A Friend of John Brown," Chambers, NYT Interactive Overlooked obituary.

312 **As for Laura D. Fair** . . . Clara Crittenden death, *Oakland Tribune* of December 30, 1881; few blocks away as per Crocker-Langley city directories of late 1870s; state supreme courts limiting insanity defense, see Ireland, "The Libertine Must Die," 38; rarity of insanity defense, Covey, "Temporary Insanity," 1668; lecturing in New York and elsewhere, Haber, *Trials of Laura Fair,* 202–204; "sharp, sarcastic, and bitter," DAC of September 17, 1876; "The woman in San Francisco who has not some scandal . . ." as quoted in the DAC of September 25, 1879.

313 **her doings after this lecture tour** . . . Baby carriage story, *Reno Weekly Gazette* of June 26, 1879, and the DAC of August 3, 1879; thrown down stairs, *Santa Cruz Weekly Sentinel* of January 28, 1882 (see also the *Truckee Republican* of February 1, 1882, which has a more complete report); how she had aged, see, for instance, the SDU of December 12, 1885; shooting James Crittenden, *San Francisco Call* of March 16, 1895.

314 **"ingenuous charm"** . . . and "new cosmopolitanism . . ." Neville, *Fantastic City,* 251. (NB: There is some controversy over the true story behind some of these inventions—chop suey in particular—but some support for all of them as San Francisco creations); Mrs. Lane apparently died in 1895, when the *San Francisco Call* of March 16, 1895, reported her as "dying"; Lillian died in poverty in 1913, see Haber, *Trials of Laura Fair,* 214–215, and the *San Francisco Call* of February 7, 1913; Fair's death and estate value as per the SFC, the *San Francisco Call,* and the *Oakland Tribune* issues of October 15, 1919.

Bibliography

HISTORICAL NEWSPAPERS

Daily Alta California (DAC)
San Francisco Chronicle (SFC)
New York Times (NYT)
Sacramento Daily Union (SDU)
The Pioneer
The Revolution

The Liberator
Oakland Tribune
San Francisco Bulletin
San Francisco Call
San Francisco Examiner

COURT AND GOVERNMENT RECORDS

Charlotte L. Brown v. the Omnibus Rail Road Company. California Historical Society (accessed at https://digitallibrary.californiahistoricalsociety.org/object/ms-228a).

California State Assembly Journals for 1849–50, 1852 (accessed at https://clerk.assembly.ca.gov).

Alexander Parker Crittenden, Edmund Randolph, and William Walker depositions from *McDonald v. Garrison and Morgan.* Isaiah Thornton Williams Papers, Manuscripts and Archives Division, New York Public Library.

"The People of the State of California v. Laura D. Fair." *Reports of Cases Determined in the Supreme Court of the State of California*, Vol. 43, 137–158. San Francisco: Bancroft-Whitney Company, January 1906.

Marsh, Andrew J., and Samuel Osbourne. *Official report of the trial of Laura D. Fair, for the murder of Alex. P. Crittenden: including the testimony, the arguments of counsel, and the charge of the court, reported verbatim, and the entire correspondence of the parties, with portraits of the defendant and the deceased.* San Francisco: San Francisco Co-operative Print Co., 1871. (NB: Some letters that were apparently admitted into evidence but were somehow not reprinted in this publication did appear in the *San Francisco Chronicle* of April 9, 11, and 12, 1871.)

PAPERS, ARCHIVAL COLLECTIONS, AND OTHER UNPUBLISHED MATERIAL

Crittenden Family Papers (CFP), Clements Library, University of Michigan

Crittenden Family Letters (CFL), University of Washington Digital Collections, Civil War Letters, Accession No. 256-1

Crittenden Family Miscellany, 1862–1874 (Society of California Pioneers)

Albert Sidney Johnston Papers (Tulane University)

Henry H. Ellis Letters (California Historical Society Library)

Helen Holdredge Papers (San Francisco Public Library History Center)

Edward Byram Scrapbooks (California Historical Society Library)

Russell McDonald Collection (Nevada Historical Society Library)

Allan Bérubé and Eric Garber Collections (GLBT Historical Society, San Francisco)

Sharon, William F. "Ralston: Caesar of California," unpublished address (California Historical Society Library)

Conrich, J. Lloyd. "The Mammy Pleasant Legend," unpublished typescript (California Historical Society Library)

Isaiah Thornton Williams Papers (Manuscripts and Archives Division, New York Public Library)

James V. Medler Crime Collection (Clements Library, University of Michigan)

John H. Parcell Journal 1876 (Clements Library, University of Michigan)

James V. Mansfield Papers (Clements Library, University of Michigan)

Shine, Gregory Paynter. "A Study of Public Memory: Juana Briones and Mary Ellen Pleasant" (M.A. Thesis, San Francisco State University, May 2000)

Streeter, Holly. "The Sordid Trial of Laura D. Fair: Victorian Family Values." Gender and Legal History in American Papers, Georgetown University Law Library Special Collections

BOOKS AND ARTICLES

Adkins, Jan Batiste. *African Americans of San Francisco.* Charleston, SC: Arcade Publishing, 2012.

Alexander, Thomas. "The Crittenden Correspondence." *The Chronicle of the U.S. Classic Postal Issues* 33, no. 3 (August 1981): Chronicle 111.

Almagauer, Tomás. *Racial Faultlines: The Historical Origins of White Supremacy in California.* Berkeley: University of California Press, 1994.

Ambrose, Stephen. *Nothing Like It in the World: The Men Who Built the Transcontinental Railroad, 1863–1869.* New York: Simon & Schuster, 2000.

Asbury, Herbert. *The Barbary Coast: An Informal History of the San Francisco Underworld.* New York: Alfred A. Knopf, 1933.

Bakken, Morris, and Brenda Farrington. *Women Who Kill Men: California Courts, Gender, and the Press.* Lincoln: University of Nebraska Press, 2009.

Bancroft, Hubert Howe. *Literary Industries.* San Francisco: The History Company Publishers, 1890.

———. *Popular Tribunals.* Vol. 1. San Francisco: The History Company, 1887.

Barker, Malcolm E., ed. *San Francisco Memoirs, 1835–1851: Eyewitness Accounts of the Birth of a City.* San Francisco: Londonborn Publications, 1994.

———. *More San Francisco Memoirs, 1852–1899: The Ripening Years.* San Francisco: Londonborn Publications, 1996.

Barnhart, Jacqueline Baker. *The Fair but Frail: Prostitution in San Francisco, 1849–1900.* Reno: University of Nevada Press, 1986.

Barry, T. A., and B. A. Patten. *Men and Memories of San Francisco in the "Spring of '50."* San Francisco: A. L. Bancroft and Co., 1873.

Bartlett, W. C. "Overland Reminiscences." *Overland Monthly* 32, no. 187 (July 1898): 41–46.

Beasley, Delilah L. *The Negro Trail Blazers of California: A Compilation of Records,* etc. Los Angeles: Privately published, 1919.

———. "Slavery in California." *The Journal of Negro History* 3, no. 1 (January 1918): 33–44.

Bennett, Lerone, Jr. "The Mystery of Mary Ellen Pleasant: A Historical Detective Story," Parts 1 and 2. *Ebony,* April–May 1979.

Bennion, Sherilyn Cox. *Equal to the Occasion: Women Editors of the Nineteenth-Century West.* Reno: University of Nevada Press, 1990.

Berglund, Barbara. *Making San Francisco American: Cultural Frontiers in the Urban West, 1846–1906.* Lawrence: University Press of Kansas, 2007.

Bérubé, Allan. *My Desire for History: Essays in Gay, Community, and Labor History,* edited by John D'Emilio and Estelle B Freedman. University of North Carolina Press, 2011.

Bibbs, Susheel. *Heritage of Power: Marie LaVeaux to Mary Ellen Pleasant.* Sacramento: MEP Productions, 2012 (Enhanced Edition).

———. *The Legacies of Mary Ellen Pleasant—Mother of Civil Rights in California.* San Francisco: MEP Productions, 1998.

Borthwick, John David. *Three Years in California.* London: Blackwood and Sons, 1857.

Bowles, Samuel. *Across the Continent: A Stage Ride over the Plains.* Springfield, MA: Samuel Bowles and Company, 1865 (New Edition 1869).

———. *Our New West.* Hartford, CT: Hartford Publishing Company, 1869.

Boyd, Nan Alamilla. *Wide Open Town: A History of Queer San Francisco to 1965.* Berkeley: University of California Press, 2003.

Branch, Edgar M., ed. *Clemens of the "Call": Mark Twain in San Francisco.* Berkeley: University of California Press, 1969.

Brechin, Gray. *Imperial San Francisco: Urban Power, Earthly Ruin.* Berkeley: University of California Press, 1999.

Brooks, Noah. "Early Days of 'The Overland Monthly.'" *Overland Monthly* 32, no. 187 (July 1898): 3–11.

Brown, John H. *Reminiscences and Incidents of "The Early Days" of San Francisco, Actual Experience of an Eye-Witness from 1845–1850.* San Francisco: Mission Journal, 1886.

Browning, Peter, ed. *San Francisco Yerba Buena: From the Beginning to the Gold Rush, 1769–1849.* Lafayette CA: Great West Books, 1998.

Byington, Lewis Francis, ed. *A History of San Francisco.* Vol. 1. San Francisco: The S. J. Clarke Publishing Company, 1931.

Callejo-Pérez, David M. "Chapter Three: Holly Springs: Introduction to a North Mississippi City." *Counterpoints* 153 (2001): 20–32. http://www.jstor.org/stable /42976499. Accessed February 9, 2024.

Carr, Albert Z. *The World and William Walker.* New York: Harper & Row, 1963.

Castañeda, Laura, and Shannon Campbell, eds. *News and Sexuality: Media Portraits of Diversity*. Thousand Oaks, CA: Sage Publications, 2006.

Chambers, Veronica. "Overlooked: Mary Ellen Pleasant." *New York Times* (https://www.nytimes.com/interactive/2019/obituaries/mary-ellen-pleasant-overlooked.html).

Chandler, Robert J. "California's 1863 Loyalty Oaths—Another Look." *Arizona and the West* 21, no. 3 (Autumn 1979): 215–234.

———. "In the Van: Spiritualists as Catalysts for the California Women's Suffrage Movement." *California History* 73, no. 3 (Fall 1994): 188–201.

———. "The Mythical Johnston Conspiracy Revisited: An Educated Guess." *The Californians* 4 (November–December 1986): 36–41.

Chang, Gordon. *Ghosts of Gold Mountain: The Epic Story of the Chinese Who Built the Transcontinental Railroad*. Boston: Houghton Mifflin Harcourt, 2019.

Chen, Yong. *Chinese San Francisco, 1850–1943: A Trans-Pacific Community*. Stanford: Stanford University Press, 2000.

Cherney, Robert W. "Patterns of Toleration and Discrimination in San Francisco: The Civil War to World War I." *California History* 73, no. 2 (Summer 1994): 130–141.

Chung, Sue Fawn. *In Pursuit of Gold: Chinese American Miners and Merchants in the American West*. Champaign: University of Illinois Press, 2011.

Cilker, Noel C. "A Little China Leader, a Brothel Owner, and Their Clashing American Dreams in Gold Rush San Francisco." *Chinese America: History & Perspectives* (January 1, 2018). Chinese Historical Society of America.

Cole, Holly. "The Laura Fair Affair: Women & the Death Penalty in Victorian San Francisco." *California Supreme Court Historical Society Newsletter* (Spring–Summer 2006).

Coleman, Charles M. *P.G. and E. of California: The Centennial Story of Pacific Gas and Electric Company, 1852–1952*. New York: McGraw Hill Book Company, 1952.

Conaway, James. *Napa*. New York: Houghton Mifflin Company, 1990.

Covey, Russell D. "Temporary Insanity: The Strange Life and Times of the Perfect Defense." *Boston University Law Review* 91 (2011).

Cowan, Robert Ernest. "The Leidesdorff-Folsom Estate: A Forgotten Chapter in the Romantic History of Early San Francisco." *California Historical Society Quarterly* 7, no. 2 (June 1928): 105–111.

Dana, Richard Henry, Jr. *Two Years Before the Mast*. New York: Harper & Brothers, 1840 (Paperback Edition: New York: Penguin Books, 1981).

Dando-Collins, Stephen. *Tycoon's War: How Cornelius Vanderbilt Invaded a Country to Overthrow America's Most Famous Military Adventurer*. Cambridge, MA: Da Capo Press, 2008.

Daniels, Douglas Henry. *Pioneer Urbanites: A Social and Cultural History of Black San Francisco*. Berkeley: University of California Press, 1990.

Davis, Sam. "How a Colored Woman Aided John Brown." Reprint: *People's Press*, January 5, 1904.

Davis, Sam, ed. "'Mammy' Pleasant, Memoirs and Autobiography." *The Pandex of the Press* 1, no. 1 (January 1902).

Davis, Winfield J. *History of Political Conventions in California, 1849–1892*. Sacramento: California State Library, 1893.

de Graaf, Lawrence B., Kevin Mulroy, and Quintard Taylor, eds. *Seeking El Dorado: African Americans in California*. Seattle: University of Washington Press, 2001.

Delmatier, Royce D., Clarence F. McIntosh, and Earl G. Waters. *The Rumble of California Politics, 1848–1970.* New York: John Wiley & Sons, 1970.

Dixon, William Hepworth. *White Conquest.* London: Chatto and Windus, 1876.

Donoghue, Emma. *Frog Music.* New York: Little, Brown and Company, 2014.

———. "The San Miguel Mystery: The Documents" (a PDF bibliography located on Donoghue's website—https://emmadonoghue/images/pdf/the-san-miguel-mystery -the-documents.pdf).

Duckett, Margaret. *Mark Twain and Bret Harte.* Norman: University of Oklahoma Press, 1964.

Duberman, Martin Bauml, Martha Vicinus, and George Chauncey Jr., eds. *Hidden from History: Reclaiming the Gay and Lesbian Past.* New York: New American Library, 1989.

Ellison, William Henry. *A Self-Governing Dominion: California, 1849–1860.* Berkeley: University of California Press, 1950.

Eubank, Damon. *In the Shadow of the Patriarch: The John J. Crittenden Family in War and Peace.* Macon, GA: Mercer University Press, 2009.

Fair, Laura D. "Wolves in the Fold: A Lecture by Laura D. Fair, also, A Statement of Facts and Defense of Her Cause." San Francisco: privately published, 1873.

Fisher, James A. "The Struggle for Negro Testimony in California, 1851–1863." *Southern California Quarterly* (January 1969): 313–324.

Fracchia, Charles A. *When the Water Came Up to Montgomery Street: San Francisco During the Gold Rush.* Virginia Beach: The Donning Company Publishers, 2009.

Frajola, Richard C., Inc. *The Crittenden Correspondence* (auction catalog for collection of letters auctioned October 13, 1981). Danbury, CT: Frajola, 1981.

Franklin, Paul. "Crittenden Correspondence Revisited—Lawyer, Adventurer, Confederate Partisan and Philanderer." *Western Express: Research Journal of Early Western Mails* 66, no. 1 (March 2016): 5–25.

French, Bryant Morey. *Mark Twain and the Gilded Age: The Book That Named an Era.* Dallas: Southern Methodist University Press, 1965.

———. "Mark Twain, Laura D. Fair and the New York Criminal Courts." *American Quarterly* 16, no. 4 (Winter 1964): 545–561.

Garber, William S. "Divorce in Marion County." *The Indiana Magazine of History* 6, no. 1 (March 1910).

George, Henry. "What the Railroad Will Bring Us." *Overland Monthly* 1, no. 4 (October 1868): 297–306.

Gibbs, Mifflin Wistar. *Shadow and Light: An Autobiography with Reminiscences of the Last and Present Century.* Washington, DC: n.p., 1902.

Godfrey, Brian J. *Neighborhoods in Transition: The Making of San Francisco's Ethnic and Nonconformist Communities.* Berkeley: University of California Press, 1988.

Goldman, Marion S. *Gold Diggers & Silver Miners: Prostitution and Social Life on the Comstock Lode.* Ann Arbor: University of Michigan Press, 1981.

Goodheart, Adam. "Divorce, Antebellum Style." *New York Times,* Opinionator, March 8, 2011.

Graves, Donna J., and Shayne E. Watson. *Citywide Historic Context Statement for LGBTQ History in San Francisco.* San Francisco: San Francisco Planning Department.

Green, Michael S. *Nevada: A History of the Silver State.* Reno: University of Nevada Press, 2015.

Grenier, Judson A. " 'Officialdom': California State Government, 1849–1879." *California History* 81, no. 3–4 (January 2003).

Haber, Carole. *The Trials of Laura Fair: Sex, Murder, and Insanity in the Victorian West.* Chapel Hill: University of North Carolina Press, 2013.

Hardaway, Roger D. "African-American Women on the Western Frontier." *Negro History Bulletin* 60, no. 1 (1997): 8–13.

Harpending, Asbury. *The Great Diamond Hoax: and Other Stirring Incidents in the Life of Asbury Harpending.* San Francisco: James H. Barry Company, 1913.

Harte, Bret. *San Francisco in 1866: Being Letters to the Springfield Republican.* George R. Stewart and Edwin S Fussell, editors. San Francisco: The Book Club of California, 1951.

Harte, Bret, and Mark Twain. *Sketches of the Sixties.* San Francisco: John Howell, 1926.

Hay, Melba Porter, et al. *The Papers of Henry Clay: The Whig Leader, January 1, 1837–December 31, 1843.* Lexington: The University Press of Kentucky, 2015.

Heizer, Robert F., and Alan J. Almquist. *The Other Californians: Prejudice and Discrimination under Spain, Mexico, and the United States to 1920.* 2nd ed. Berkeley: University of California Press, 1977.

Hickle, Warren, and Frederic Hobbs. *The Richest Place on Earth: The Story of Virginia City, Nevada, and the Heyday of the Comstock Lode.* Boston: Houghton Mifflin, 1978.

Hittell, Theodore Henry. *History of California.* Vol. 4. San Francisco: Pacific Press Publishing House, 1885.

Hom, Montgomery. "Discovering My Great-Grandfather Moy Jin Mun." In *Voices from the Railroad: Stories by Descendants of Chinese Railroad Workers,* edited by Sue Lee et al. San Francisco: Chinese Historical Society of America, 2019.

Howe, Daniel Walker. "American Victorianism as a Culture." *American Quarterly* 27, no. 5 (December 1975): 507–532.

Hoy, William. "Moy Jin Mun: Chinese Pioneer." *Pony Express Courier,* August 1936, 11, 16; September 1936, 16.

Hudson, Lynn. *The Making of "Mammy Pleasant": A Black Entrepreneur in Nineteenth-Century San Francisco.* Urbana and Chicago: University of Illinois Press, 2003.

————. *West of Jim Crow: The Fight Against California's Color Line.* Urbana: University of Illinois Press, 2020.

Hurtado, Albert. *Intimate Frontiers: Sex, Gender, and Culture in Old California.* Albuquerque: University of New Mexico Press, 1999.

Hussey, John Adam. "New Light upon Talbot H. Green: As Revealed by His Own Letters and Other Sources." *California Historical Society Quarterly* 18, no. 1 (1939): 32–63. https://doi.org/10.2307/25160810.

Ireland, Robert M. "The Libertine Must Die: Sexual Dishonor and the Unwritten Law in the Nineteenth-Century United States." *Journal of Social History* 23, no. 1 (Autumn 1989): 27–44.

Issel, William, and Robern Cherny. *San Francisco, 1865–1932: Politics, Power, and Urban Development.* Berkeley: University of California Press, 1986.

James, Ronald M. *The Roar and the Silence: A History of Virginia City and the Comstock Lode.* Reno: University of Nevada Press, 1998.

Jeong, May. "Ah Toy, Pioneering Prostitute of Gold Rush California." *The New York Review of Books,* June 19, 2020.

Kamiya, Gary. *Cool Gray City of Love: 49 Views of San Francisco.* New York: Bloomsbury, 2013.

Kibby, Leo P. "California, the Civil War, and the Indian Problem: An Account of California's Participation in the Great Conflict." *Journal of the West* 4, no. 2 (April 1965): 183–209.

Komp, Ellen. "Mark Twain's 'Hasheesh' Experience in SF." *SFGate,* https://www.sfgate.com/opinion/article/Mark-Twain-s-hasheesh-experience-in-S-F-2328992.php.

Lamott, Kenneth. *Who Killed Mr. Crittenden?: Being a True Account of the Notorious Murder Trial That Stunned San Francisco.* New York: David McKay Company, 1963.

Lang, Herbert O. *History of Tuolumne County, compiled from the most Authentic Records.* San Francisco: B. F. Alley, 1882.

Lapp, Rudolph M. *Blacks in Gold Rush California.* New Haven and London: Yale University Press, 1977.

Lavender, David. *Nothing Seemed Impossible: William C. Ralston and Early San Francisco.* Palo Alto: American West Publishing, 1975.

Lewis, Oscar, ed. *This Was San Francisco: Being First-hand Accounts of the Evolution of One of America's Favorite Cities.* New York: David McKay, 1962.

Limerick, Patricia Nelson. *The Legacy of Conquest: The Unbroken Past of the American West.* New York: W. W. Norton, 1987.

Lotchin, Roger W. *San Francisco, 1846–1856: From Hamlet to City.* Lincoln: University of Nebraska Press, 1979.

Lutz, Alma. *Susan B. Anthony: Rebel, Crusader, Humanitarian.* Washington, DC: Zenger Publishing, 1959.

Lyman, George. *Ralston's Ring: The Plundering of the Comstock Lode.* New York: Charles Scribner's Sons, 1937 (Paperback Reprint: New York: Ballantine Books, 1971).

MacGregor, William Laird. *San Francisco, California, in 1876*: For Private Circulation Only. Edinburgh: Thomas Laurie, 1876.

Madley, Benjamin. *An American Genocide: The United States and the California Indian Catastrophe, 1846–1873.* New Haven: Yale University Press, 2016.

Martelle, Scott. *William Walker's Wars: How One Man's Private American Army Tried to Conquer Mexico, Nicaragua, and Honduras.* Chicago: Chicago Review Press, 2018.

Marvin, Betty. "Special Delivery: A 2000-Mile Journey by Land and Sea in 1849 [. . .]." *Arizona Highways* 77, no. 1 (January 2001): 36–37.

Matthews, Glenna. *The Golden State in the Civil War: Thomas Starr King, the Republican Party, and the Birth of Modern California.* New York: Cambridge University Press, 2012.

McCabe, James Dabney. *Lights and Shadows of New York Life; or, The Sights and Sensations of New York in All Its Various Phases.* Philadelphia: National Publishing Company, 1872.

McClain, Charles J. *In Search of Equality: The Chinese Struggle Against Discrimination in Nineteenth-Century America.* Berkeley: University of California Press, 1996.

McDonough, James Lee. *William Tecumseh Sherman: In the Service of My Country: A Life.* New York: W. W. Norton, 2016.

McGrath, Roger D. "A Violent Birth: Disorder, Crime, and Law Enforcement, 1848–1890." *California History* 81, no. 3–4, as reprinted in *Taming the Elephant: Politics, Government, and Law in Pioneer California,* edited by John F. Burns et al. Oakland: University of California Press, 2003, 27–73.

Merwin, Henry Childs. *The Life of Bret Harte, with some account of the California Pioneers.* Boston: Houghton Mifflin, 1911.

Monzingo, Robert. *Thomas Starr King: Eminent Californian, Civil War Statesman, Unitarian Minister.* Pacific Grove, CA: Boxwood Press, 1991.

Morse, John T., Jr. *Famous Trials: The Tichborne Claimant. Troppmann. Prince Pierre Bonaparte. Mrs. Wharton. The Meteor. Mrs. Fair.* Boston: Little, Brown and Company, 1874.

Mullen, Kevin J. *Dangerous Strangers: Minority Newcomers and Criminal Violence in the Urban West, 1850–2000.* New York: Palgrave Macmillan, 2005.

———. *Let Justice Be Done: Crime and Politics in Early San Francisco.* Reno: University of Nevada Press, 1989.

———. *The Toughest Gang in Town: Police Stories from Old San Francisco.* Novato, CA: Noir Publications, 2005.

Neville, Amelia Ransome. *The Fantastic City: Memoirs of the Social and Romantic Life of Old San Francisco.* Boston: Houghton Mifflin, 1932.

Nunis Jr., Doyce B., ed. *The San Francisco Vigilance Committee of 1856: Three Views* [i.e., by W. T. Coleman, W. T. Sherman, and James O'Meara]. Los Angeles: Los Angeles Westerners, 1971.

O'Brien, Robert. "Wolves in the Fold: The Case of Laura D. Fair." In *San Francisco Murders,* edited by Joseph Henry Jackson. New York: Duell, Sloan and Pearce, 1947.

O'Meara, James. *Broderick and Gwin: The Most Extraordinary Contest for a Seat in the Senate of the United States Ever Known; A Brief History of Early Politics in California.* San Francisco: Bacon and Co., 1881.

———. "The Chinese in Early Days." *Overland Monthly* 3, no. 5 (May 1884): 477–481.

———. "San Francisco in Early Days." *Overland Monthly* 1, no. 2 (February 1883): 129–136.

Palgon, Gary Mitchell. *William Alexander Leidesdorff: First Black Millionaire, American Consul and California Pioneer.* Atlanta: Gary Palgon, 2005.

Palmer, Louise. "How We Live in Nevada." *Overland Monthly* 2, no. 5 (May 1869): 457–462.

Pfaelzer, Jean. *California, a Slave State.* New Haven: Yale University Press, 2023.

Powers, Ron. *Mark Twain: A Life.* New York: Free Press, 2005.

Prieto, Guillermo. *San Francisco in the Seventies: The City as Viewed by a Mexican Political Exile.* Translated and edited by Edwin S. Morby. San Francisco: John Henry Nash, 1938.

Quert (pseudonym). "Chinese Letters." (Translation of letters written by Luchong.) *The Pioneer* (March 1855): 161–166. (NB: I have my doubts about whether these letters are genuine or an invention of the "translator" Quert.)

Rhodehamel, Josephine Dewitt, and Raymond Francis Wood. *Ina Coolbrith: Librarian and Laureate of California.* Provo: Brigham Young University Press, 1973.

Richards, Leonard L. *The California Gold Rush and the Coming of the Civil War.* New York: Knopf, 2007.

Richards, Rand. *Historic San Francisco: A Concise History and Guide.* San Francisco: Heritage House, 2007.

———. *Mud, Blood, and Gold: San Francisco in 1849.* San Francisco, Heritage House, 2009.

Richardson, Albert D. *Beyond the Mississippi*. Hartford, CT: American Publishing Company, 1867. New expanded edition, 1869.

———. *Garnered Sheaves from the Writings of Albert D. Richardson: Collected and Arranged by His Wife*. Hartford, CT: Columbian Book Company, 1871.

Rouse, Wendy. "People v. Hall." In *Defining Documents: Manifest Destiny and the New Nation (1803–1860)*. Ipswich, MA: Salem Press/EBSCO Publishing, 2013.

San Francisco Lesbian and Gay History Project. *"She Even Chewed Tobacco": A Pictorial Narrative of Passing Women in America*. (Reprinted in Duberman et al., *Hidden from History: Reclaiming the Gay and Lesbian Past*.)

Sears, Clare. *Arresting Dress: Cross-Dressing, Law, and Fascination in Nineteenth-Century San Francisco*. Durham, NC: Duke University Press, 2015.

Scharnhorst, Gary. *Bret Harte: Opening the American Literary West*. Norman: University of Oklahoma Press, 2000.

Scharnhorst, Gary, ed. *Selected Letters of Bret Harte*. Norman: University of Oklahoma Press, 1997.

———. *Twain in His Own Time: A Biographical Chronicle of His Life, Drawn from Recollections, Interviews, and Memoirs by Family, Friends, and Associates*. Iowa City: University of Iowa Press, 2010.

Schuele, Donna C. "'None Could Deny the Eloquence of This Lady': Women, Law, and Government in California, 1850–1890." *California History* 81, no. ¾ (2003): 169–198.

Seligman, Scott. *Three Tough Chinamen*. Hong Kong: Earnshaw Books, 2012.

Sherman, William T. *Personal Memoirs of Gen. W. T. Sherman*. Vol. 1. New York: Charles L. Webster & Co, 1890.

Sherr, Lynn. *Failure Is Impossible: Susan B. Anthony in Her Own Words*. New York: Crown Publishers, 1995.

Shuck, Oscar T. *History of the Bench and Bar of California*. Los Angeles: The Commercial Printing House, 1901.

Sides, Josh. *Erotic City: Sexual Revolutions and the Making of Modern San Francisco*. New York: Oxford University Press, 2009.

Siler, Julia Flynn. *The White Devil's Daughters: The Women Who Fought Slavery in San Francisco's Chinatown*. New York: Knopf, 2019.

Smith, Grant. *The History of the Comstock Lode, 1850–1920*. University of Nevada Bulletin, Geology and Mining Series 37, no. 3 (July 1, 1943).

Smith, Stacey L. "Remaking Slavery in a Free State: Masters and Slaves in Gold Rush California." *Pacific Historical Review* 80, no. 1 (February 2011): 28–63.

Solnit, Rebecca, ed. *Infinite City: A San Francisco Atlas*. Berkeley: University of California Press, 2010.

Soulé, Frank, John H. Gibson, and James Nesbit. *The Annals of San Francisco*. New York: D. Appleton & Company, 1855.

Sparks, Edith. *Capital Intentions: Female Proprietors in San Francisco, 1850–1920*. Chapel Hill: University of North Carolina Press, 2006.

Starr, Kevin. *Americans and the California Dream: 1850–1915*. Santa Barbara: Peregrine-Smith, paperback edition 1981.

Stewart, George R. *The California Trail: An Epic with Many Heroes*. University of Nebraska Press, 1983.

Stewart, Robert E. *Aurora: Nevada's Ghost City of the Dawn*. Las Vegas: Nevada Publications, 2004.

Stiles, T. J. *The First Tycoon: The Epic Life of Cornelius Vanderbilt*. New York: Knopf, 2009.

Stryker, Susan, and Jim Van Buskirk. *Gay by the Bay: A History of Queer Culture in the San Francisco Bay Area*. San Francisco: Chronicle Books, 1996.

Summers Sandoval Jr., Tomas F. *Latinos at the Golden Gate: Creating Community and Identity in San Francisco*. Chapel Hill: University of North Carolina Press, 2013.

Swasey, William F. *The Early Days and Men of California*. Oakland: Pacific Press, 1891.

Tarnoff, Ben. *The Bohemians: Mark Twain and the San Francisco Writers Who Reinvented American Literature*. New York: Penguin Press, 2014.

Taylor, Bayard. *El Dorado: or, Adventures in the Path of Empire* (1850). Reprint. New York: Alfred A. Knopf, 1949.

Tennis, George. "California's First State Election, November 13, 1849." *Southern California Quarterly* 50, no. 4 (1968): 357–394.

Tong, Benson: *Unsubmissive Women: Chinese Prostitutes in Nineteenth-Century San Francisco*. Norman: University of Oklahoma Press, 1994.

Tyng, C. D. *The Stranger in the Tropics: Being a Handbook for Havana and Guide Book for Travelers*. New York: American News Company, 1868.

Walker, Franklin. "An Influence from San Francisco on Mark Twain's *The Gilded Age*." *American Literature* 8, no. 1 (March 1936): 63–66.

Walker, William. *The War in Nicaragua*. Mobile and New York: S. H. Goetzel & Company, 1860.

Watson, Douglas S., and Washington A. Bartlett. "An Hour's Walk Through Yerba Buena, Which Later Became San Francisco." *California Historical Society Quarterly* 17, no. 4 (1938): 291–302.

Willard, Frances Elizabeth. *A Woman of the Century: Fourteen Hundred Seventy Biographical Sketches Accompanied by Portraits of Leading American Women in All Walks of Life*. Buffalo, NY: Moulton, 1893.

Willett, Donald E., and Margaret Swett Henson, eds. *The Texas That Might Have Been: Sam Houston's Foes Write to Albert Sidney Johnston*. College Station, TX: Texas A&M Press, 2009.

Williams, George III. *Mark Twain: His Life in Virginia City, Nevada*. Riverside, CA: Tree by the River Publishing, 1986.

Williams, Samuel. "City of the Golden Gate." *Scribner's Monthly*, July 1875, 266–285.

Wills, Shomari. *Black Fortunes: The Story of the First Six African Americans Who Escaped Slavery and Became Millionaires*. New York: Amistad, 2018.

Woodbridge, Sally B. *San Francisco in Maps and Views*. New York: Rizzoli International Publications, 2006.

Wright, Les. "San Francisco." In *Queer Sites: Gay Urban Histories Since 1600*, edited by David Higgs. London: Taylor & Francis Group, 1999.

Young, John P. *San Francisco: A History of the Pacific Coast Metropolis*. Vol. 1. San Francisco: S. J. Clarke Publishing, 1912.

Acknowledgments

Trespassers at the Golden Gate is my fourth city-based narrative history book, and it has taken me to more places for library and archival research than any of the others—from San Francisco proper (along with numerous institutions around the Bay Area) to New Orleans, New York City, Washington, D.C., Ann Arbor, and various places in Nevada (Reno, Carson City, Virginia City). As you can imagine, I owe a debt of gratitude to people in all of those places for their help and support, often rendered under the difficult circumstances of an ongoing pandemic.

Thanks, first of all, to the National Endowment for the Humanities for making all of that travel possible with a generous Public Scholar grant. My fellowship period technically started mid-lockdown, and thus much of the travel had to be postponed until the COVID pandemic subsided. But the grant helped keep me afloat even while waiting for libraries and archives to reopen. Meanwhile, even as the virus raged on, internet resources like archive.org allowed my research to continue, as did the labors of many of the people listed below who were willing to digitize key documents and send them to me via email.

Once travel became possible again, my first destination was the William L. Clements Library at the University of Michigan, which houses the Crittenden family papers. Never in my career as a researcher have I dealt with a richer source of primary material. It's rare for a relatively little-known figure like A. P. Crittenden to be so well-documented, and I suspect the gratitude must go to his daughter Nannie for collecting and preserving the hundreds of letters contained in this archive (and to the library's curators for reassembling them in latter days). Many thanks to Terese Murphy (head of reader services), Cheney Schopieray (curator of manuscripts), Clayton Lewis (curator of graphic materials, now retired), and the staff of the Clements Library's impeccably managed reading room. Special thanks go to two others associated with this rich collection of Crittendeniana: Richard Frajola, the rare manuscript dealer who handled the auction sale of the bulk of the correspondence many years ago, after it was unearthed in a Brooklyn warehouse, and Paul Franklin, a writer who preceded me into the Crittenden archives and who gave me much excellent advice on navigating the collection.

In San Francisco, where I fortunately had done a good bit of research before the pandemic set in, I owe thanks to Lynda Letona and Francis Kaplan of the California Historical Society Library; Katherine Ets-Hokin, Tim Wilson, Tom Carey, and the staff at the San Francisco History Center of the San Francisco Public Library; Isaac Feldman at the GLBT Historical Society; and Patricia Keats and Lauren Menzies at the Alice Phelan Sullivan Library of the Society of California Pioneers. Across the bay, my gratitude goes out to the staffs of the Bancroft Library at Berkeley, the Oakland Public Library, and the African American Museum and Library at Oakland. And in Nevada, hats off to Robert Nylen of the Nevada State Museum in Carson City; Sheryln L. Hayes-Zorn, curator of manuscripts at the Nevada Historical Society in Reno; and Paul Hoyle, owner-operator of the Tahoe House Hotel and Bar in Virginia City, where my wife and I stayed for a couple of nights in a room that just possibly could have been A. P. Crittenden's.

Heading east, I also owe thanks to the staff at the Louisiana Research Collection at Tulane University in New Orleans (where I also spent a lot of time a decade ago when researching my book *Empire of Sin*); Netisha Currie, archives specialist at the National Archives in College Park, Maryland; Lara Szypszak and Patrick Kerwin, reference librarians in the Manuscript Division at the Library of Congress; and Hannah Miller-Kim, special collections librarian at the Georgetown University Law Library in Washington, D.C. Closer to home, I'd like to thank Meredith Mann and the staff of the Brooke Russell Astor Reading Room for Rare Books and Manuscripts at the New York Public Library and the ever-helpful staff of the same institution's Milstein Division and Rose Main Reading Room. And a special tip of the hat to Deborah Bull for so ably taking on the task of photo research for this book, as she did for my last book, *The Mirage Factory*.

More personal thanks go out to a bevy of friends and colleagues who helped out in various ways, large and small: Michael Kazin, Kriste Lindenmeyer, Lisa Zeidner, Meghan Houser, Meredith Hindley, T. J. Stiles, and Jonathan White.

And much appreciation to Calliope Nicholas, Monika Burczyk, and Millay Arts for providing a wonderful month at Edna St. Vincent Millay's old farm in Austerlitz, New York, at a late stage in the revision of this book. This was actually my second residency at Millay—the first was in 1985—and I was delighted to be in the same bedroom and studio in Vincent's barn where I spent a month thirty-eight years earlier. (No, the rooms have not been renovated in the meantime, but that was just as I would have wished it.)

At Crown, where I have had a happy publishing home now for four books, I owe tremendous thanks to Paul Whitlatch and Katie Berry, a matchless editorial team who each contributed keen editorial guidance and numerous suggestions and comments that ultimately made this a richer and better book. My gratitude also goes out to the rest of the team at Crown, including Chantelle Walker, Julie Cepler, Abby Oladipo, Aubrey Khan, Philip Leung, Rachelle Mandik, and Rabiya Gupta (who designed a truly stunning hardcover jacket). Many thanks for their support to the people upstairs too: David Drake, Gillian Blake, and Annsley Rosner. And the one constant over my four books at Crown has been publicist extraordinaire Dyana Messina, who now runs the whole department but did me the distinct honor of assigning herself to handle the publicity for this book.

Speaking of constants, I am still lucky enough to have the best literary agent in the business as my representative and friend—Eric Simonoff at William Morris Endeavor. An extra thanks to Eric's assistant, Criss Moon, whose emails always made my day a little brighter. And at WME in Beverly Hills, my gratitude goes to Hilary Zaitz-Michaels and Elizabeth Wachtel.

Finally, as ever, my biggest and best thanks go out to the bedrock of my existence—my wife, Elizabeth Cheng Krist, and our child, Anna, to whom this book is lovingly dedicated.

Art Credits

Page 1, top: Clements Library, University of Michigan.

Page 1, bottom: Clements Library, University of Michigan.

Page 2, top: Library of Congress, Prints and Photographs Division.

Page 2, bottom: Library of Congress, Prints and Photographs Division.

Page 3, top left: Portrait file of the Bancroft Library. BANC PIC 1905.0002—POR Sherman.

Page 3, top right: Courtesy of the California History Room, California State Library, Sacramento, California.

Page 3, bottom: Fire in San Francisco (California) in the night from 3–4 May, 1851, Robert B. Honeyman, Jr., Collection of Early Californian and Western American Pictorial Material, BANC PIC 1963.002:0037 (variant)—A. The Bancroft Library, University of California, Berkeley.

Page 4, top left: From the San Francisco History Center, San Francisco Public Library (digitalsf.org).

Page 4, bottom: Library of Congress, Prints and Photographs Division.

Page 5, top left: African American Museum & Library at Oakland, Oakland Public Library.

Page 5, bottom: Library of Congress, Prints and Photographs Division.

Page 6, top left: National Portrait Gallery, Smithsonian Institution.

Page 6, top right: Library of Congress, Prints and Photographs Division.

Page 6, bottom: Library of Congress, Prints and Photographs Division.

Page 7, bottom: Society of California Pioneers. The Lawrence & Houseworth Photography 1860–1870. California Views. SCP 1295 L&H1566 Railroad Ferry Steamer *El Capitan*.

Page 8, bottom: Library of Congress, Prints and Photographs Division.

Index

About the Author

GARY KRIST is the author of four previous narrative nonfiction books: *The White Cascade, City of Scoundrels, Empire of Sin,* and *The Mirage Factory.* He has also written three novels and two short story collections. A widely published journalist and book reviewer, Krist has been the recipient of the Stephen Crane Award, the Sue Kaufman Prize from the American Academy of Arts and Letters, a Lowell Thomas Gold Medal for Travel Journalism, a fiction fellowship from the National Endowment for the Arts, and a Public Scholar grant from the National Endowment for the Humanities.